Present Laughter

*P*resent *L*aughter

AN ANTHOLOGY OF MODERN COMIC FICTION

Edited by

MALCOLM BRADBURY

Weidenfeld & Nicolson, London

First published in Great Britain in 1994 by
Weidenfeld & Nicolson

The Orion Publishing Group Ltd
Orion House
5 Upper Saint Martin's Lane
London WC2H 9EA

A catalogue record for this book is
available from the British Library

ISBN 0 297 81485 0

Typeset by Deltatype Ltd, Ellesmere Port, Wirral
Printed in Great Britain by Clays Ltd, St Ives plc

CONTENTS

Acknowledgements: The editor and publishers wish to thank the following for permission to use copyright material:

Bloomsbury Publishing plc for 'A Short History of the English Novel' from *Grey Area* by Will Self, to be published in November 1994;

Jonathan Clowes Ltd, London, on behalf of Kingsley Amis, for 'Interesting Things' from *My Enemy's Enemy*. Copyright 1956, © 1962 Kingsley Amis;

Gerald Duckworth & Co Ltd for Beryl Bainbridge, 'The Longstop' from *Mum and Mr Armitage: Selected Stories of Beryl Bainbridge*, 1985; and with Viking Penguin, a division of Penguin Books USA Inc., for Dorothy Parker, 'The Waltz' from *The Portable Dorothy Parker*, introduction by Brendan Gill. Copyright 1933, renewed © 1961 by Dorothy Parker;

Faber and Faber Ltd for Adam Mars-Jones, 'Lantern Lecture' from *Lantern Lecture and Other Stories*, 1981; and Garrison Keillor, 'The Royal Family' from *Leaving Home*, 1988;

Hamish Hamilton Ltd with Alfred A. Knopf, Inc. for John Updike, 'The Bulgarian Poetess' from *Bech: A Book* (Penguin Books 1972, first published in UK by André Deutsch). Copyright © John Updike, 1965, 1966, 1968, 1970;

David Higham Associates Ltd on behalf of the author for Muriel Spark, 'A Member of the Family' from *The Collected Stories of Muriel Spark*, Penguin Books, 1994;

Alfred A. Knopf, Inc. for Milan Kundera, 'Nobody Will Laugh' from *Laughable Loves*, trans. S. Rappaport. Copyright © 1974 by Alfred A. Knopf, Inc.;

Penguin Books Ltd for T. Coraghessan Boyle, 'Modern Love' from *If the River Was Whiskey* (Granta, 1993). Copyright © T. Coraghessan Boyle 1989, 1993; and Jorge Luis Borges, 'Pierre Menard, Author of Don Quixote' from *Ficciones*, first published in 1944, first translated into English in 1962 by A. Kerrigan, Viking Penguin. Copyright © The Estate of Jorge Luis Borges;

Peters Fraser & Dunlop Group Ltd on behalf of the authors for Martin Amis, 'Career Move', *The New Yorker*, 29th June 1992; and Evelyn Waugh, 'Excursion in Reality' from *Work Suspended and Other Stories*, 1951;

Murray Pollinger on behalf of the author's Estate, for Roald Dahl, 'The Champion of the World' from *Kiss Kiss*, Michael Joseph and Penguin Books, 1970;

Random House, Inc. for Woody Allen, 'The Kugelmass Episode' from *Side Effects*. Copyright © 1977 by Woody Allen;

Random House UK Ltd with McClelland and Stewart, Toronto for Margaret Atwood, 'Lives of the Poets' from *Dancing Girls and Other Stories*, Jonathan Cape, 1977; Aldous Huxley, 'The Tillotson Banquet' from *Mortal Coils: Five Stories*, 1955; and with Viking Penguin, a division of Penguin Books USA Inc. for Isaac Bashevis Singer, 'Gimpel the Fool' from *Isaac Bashevis Singer, The Collected Stories*, 1982, Random Century, and *A Treasury of Yiddish Stories*, translated by Saul Bellow, by Irving Howe and Eliezer Greenberg. Copyright 1953 by The Partisan Review, renewed © 1981 by Isaac Bashevis Singer;

Reed Consumer Books Ltd for Angus Wilson, 'The Wrong Set' from *The Wrong Set and Other Stories*, Martin Secker & Warburg, 1949; Andrew Davies, 'The New Baboon' from *Dirty Faxes*, Methuen London, 1990; and with Viking Penguin, a division of Penguin Books USA Inc. for Jonathan Wilson, 'Schoom' from *Schoom*, Lime Tree, 1993. Copyright © 1993 by Jonathan Wilson;

Rogers, Coleridge & White Ltd on behalf of the authors for Clare Boylan, 'The Stolen Child' from *Writing on the Wall*, in association with Weidenfeld & Nicolson, 1993; Clive Sinclair, 'Uncle Vlad' from *Hearts of Gold*, King Penguin, 1979; Angela Carter, 'The Kitchen Child,' from *Black Venus*, Chatto & Windus, 1985; and Peter Carey, 'American Dreams' from *The Fat Man in History*, Faber and Faber, 1980;

Sheil Land Associates Ltd on behalf of the author's Estate, for Mary Lavin, 'My Vocation' from *Stories of Mary Lavin, Vol. I*, 1964;

A. P. Watt Ltd on behalf of the author, for Suzannah Dunn, 'An Outer London Childhood' from *Darker Days Than Usual*, Serpent's Tail Publishing, 1990;

George Weidenfeld & Nicolson Ltd for Vladimir Nabokov, 'The Assistant Producer' from *Nabokov's Dozen*, 1938;

Wylie, Aitken & Stone, Inc. on behalf of the author and Little, Brown and Company, for Donald Barthelme, 'To London & Rome' from *Come Back, Dr. Caligari*, 1964. Copyright © 1964 by Donald Barthelme.

Every effort has been made to trace all the copyright holders but if any have been inadvertently overlooked the publishers will be pleased to make the necessary arrangement at the first opportunity.

INTRODUCTION

Aristodemus was only half awake and did not hear the beginning of the discourse. The main thing he remembered was Socrates compelling the others to admit the genius of comedy was as great as that of tragedy, and the true artist in tragedy was an artist in comedy too. To this they were inclined to assent – being drowsy and not following the argument.

Plato, *The Symposium*

And it has to be said at once that there is something slightly absurd about writing solemnly and seriously about the comic, a highly complicated form of human expression designed to provoke just the opposite set of emotions. As the great American cartoonist Saul Steinberg once said, 'Trying to define humour is one of the definitions of humour.' The fact remains that, both as a reader and as a writer, I have always taken comedy with a good deal of (ever delighted) seriousness. Indeed it is hard to think about the art of fiction without thinking about the art of comedy, for the two have always gone together, hand in hand. When Chaucer's pilgrims set out to relieve the solemn piety of their travels to the holy shrine at Canterbury, or Boccaccio's talkative Florentines sought escape from the perils of the plague, they did so by telling stories. And a good many of those stories were comic tales, part of the great carnival of the human comedy and the eternal need to arrest life's tragedies with comic relief.

Likewise, when at the start of the seventeenth century the novel began to develop as a major modern form – we generally reckon its beginning came with the appearance of Miguel de Cervantes' *History and Adventures of the Renowned Don Quixote* (volume I 1605, volume II 1615) – it was born in the delighted spirit of comedy. The skinny old knight from La Mancha has been book-maddened by reading the chivalric romances, of which the adventures that follow form a parody. He sets out on his travels accompanied by his down-to-earth companion and servant, Sancho Panza, one of the world's great philosophical realists, who tolerates his master's heroic delusions while knowing they are quite ridiculous. The Don and his servant, the bookish dreamer and the simple realist, the chaser of high illusions and the lover of simple bodily comforts, eternally bonded together, are one of the great odd couples of literature, and two distinct parts of an eternally divided (and so comic) human condition. The birth of the long prose tale was, then, the birth of a new vision of the human comedy, and from that time it seems prose stories and comedy have never been far apart. We have no shortage of heroic and romantic, sentimental and tragic tales, sober philosophical fictions and tales of the suffering human spirit. But no sooner does solemnity arise in art than it seems to find its opposite, a Panza to go with its Quixote, and one way the novel came to prosper was through its development of the comic vision.

And so it has been ever since; comedy and fiction have been constant companions. A century after Cervantes, the novel became a dominant popular form in Britain – perhaps somehow especially suiting a very empirical people who had little taste for abstract philosophy, and were intensely obsessed by ordinary social life and manners. In a short span of fifty years close to the beginning of the eighteenth century, the novel became a central expression of English experience; it has been so ever since. Of the six great innovators of this new species, four identified the novel with the comic spirit (the two who did not were Daniel Defoe, an extraordinary realist, and Samuel Richardson, a romantic sentimentalist). In *Gulliver's Travels* (1726) Jonathan Swift not only parodied one of the day's most popular genres, travel-writing, but bitterly and savagely mocked the political, philosophical and religious ideas of his time – and, for good measure, the absurd unpleasantness and ridiculousness of human nature itself. Amazingly, he somehow succeeded in writing one of the most successful children's books ever. Henry Fielding, angered by the sentimentalism of Richardson's novels, set out to parody them in *Joseph Andrews* (1742), and also to create something he called 'the comic epic in prose' (this was the closest he could come to giving a sensible neo-classical description to this new form which nobody had yet managed to define as the novel). Starting off in wicked parody, Fielding ended up writing benign comedy – and produced, in *Tom Jones* (1749), one of the most shapely and good-hearted of all our comic fictions. Tobias Smollett was an eighteenth-century translator of Cervantes, and as a novelist he not surprisingly set out to follow his master. So he gave British readers, and British fiction, their own version of the picaresque – the tale of roguery, travel and adventures – in works like *Roderick Random* (1748). And now the novel was born, it clearly needed its adversary, the anti-novel. Laurence Sterne, an obscure Yorkshire parson, set out to tease and upturn the form in *The Life and Opinions of Tristram Shandy* (1759–67), where he included blank pages, put the preface in the middle, started not with the birth of the hero but with his botched conception, and conceived of no end to the story other than the actual death of its author. Savage satire; benign social comedy; picaresque adventure; black humour and the anti-novel – all these were given to British fiction over a few brief decades.

It has sometimes been argued – mostly, in fact, by the British – that the British uniquely possess a sense of humour and an original tradition of comic writing; perhaps this is what they have instead of ideas, or sex. '*O Humour*, Thou whose Name is known / To *Britain's* favor'd Isle alone . . .' wrote William Collins in his patriotic ode 'The Manners', and various other commentators, including Thackeray, took a similar view. But even if disregarded, comic fiction was flourishing elsewhere: Cervantes, of course, and Rabelais, Voltaire and Diderot, and then, in the nineteenth century, Gogol and Dostoevsky were all adding to the complex variety of the comic tradition. As George Meredith granted, rather more generously, in his stout and respectful study of this ever-interesting topic, *On Comedy and the Uses of the Comic Spirit* (1877), 'The stroke of the great humorist is world-wide, with lights of Tragedy in his laughter.' Even so, it remains true that the comic tradition has been remarkably central to the development of British fiction – through Jane Austen and Peacock, Dickens and Thackeray, Meredith and Samuel Butler, and so on to many of the most interesting writers of the present day, as I hope the following pages will show. It has also, and increasingly, played a part in an American tradition once better noted, through most of the nineteenth century, for its commitment to romance, gothic and western fiction. Mark Twain made all the difference, bringing the tradition of vernacular humour into the mainstream of the American story. Since then American story-telling has been invested with a strong tradition of humour, burlesque and satire, as well as the smart sophisticated wit of the *New Yorker*.

What this means is that it has been possible to put this anthology of comic stories together in the faith that the old connection stays firm. Comedy and fiction still, in modern culture, have a peculiar and intricate relation to one another, and some of our finest writers to this day go on practising and extending the comic form. As a writer myself, I have always believed in this crucial connection, and found that one of the essential impulses of my writing and my world-view is the need to see human life and society in the comic or ironic gaze. I write humour or comedy not just because it gives pleasure (and, I hope, to others as well as myself) but because it is an illumination – a central perspective on our changing human experience, a way of looking on the world through the revealing lenses of irony, satire, absurdity and laughter. Writers over time have given us many different accounts of their comic impulse. For Fielding, the subject of comedy was always the sense of the ridiculous, which turned human characters into caricatures and stories into comic epics. For Swift, the task was one of ridicule itself, since the world and humankind evidently deserved no better. For Pirandello, the comic is based on the sentiment of contrariness. For Beckett, writing is comic because it displays the absurd nature of the human mind itself. For the Czech writer Milan Kundera, growing up in a totalitarian society, laughter is what disputes an ideological view of the world, renders light the unbearable heaviness of being, and gives to life something deceptive and unfamiliar that might almost be called love. Comedy can be a relief, a stay against life's misfortunes: '. . . I live in a constant endeavour to fence against the infirmities of ill health, and other evils of life, by Mirth,' Laurence Sterne wrote in his unsolemn dedication of *Tristram Shandy* to the Prime Minister Mr Pitt, 'being firmly persuaded that every time a man smiles, – but much more so when he laughs, – it adds something to this Fragment of Life.' But it can also be a form of extremity and despair. As Samuel Beckett wisely tells us in his play *Endgame*, 'Nothing is funnier than unhappiness.'

In short, as psychologists ever since Sigmund Freud (who was much concerned with humour) have told us, comedy is a complex human phenomenon. It has to do with pain as well as pleasure, anxiety as well as delight, cruelty, victimization and chaos as well as what Umberto Eco calls the attempt 'to heal the broken frame' and restore the sense of wholeness, levity or happiness. The comic is a medley of visions and voices, tones and techniques, yet still has the power to give us a sense of happiness. In his essay 'Wit and Its Relation to the Unconscious' (1905), Freud tells us that the comic is, like dream-work itself, a form of 'unintentional discovery'. It upsets the social rule and the code of reality; it is one of the mechanisms of release, and part of the carnival of irreverence. There are certain things which human beings commonly laugh at, wherever in the world they are or whatever age they live in; it is an aspect of the psyche that has been with us as long as human nature. But comedy is also a social form – and so it has a history which keeps on changing, along with our human history itself. In fact the comic is often a way of observing that history and how we live in and by it. In the twentieth century comedy has actually become ever more central and urgent in our writing, and that may have to do with the fact that other forms that once seemed fundamental to art and literature – the heroic, the romantic, the sentimental, even the purely tragic – have lost much of their certainty and moved towards a kind of general irony. We have lived through what mostly seems a uniquely bleak and disaster-ridden century; it is no surprise that comedy itself has darkened and grown blacker. 'Ours is a tragic age, but we refuse to take it tragically'; this is the opening life of

D. H. Lawrence's *Lady Chatterley's Lover* (1928), a work that does try to take the age tragically, if not apocalyptically (though it also has its own leaven of comedy). But more commonly our writers have chosen to take the tragic age tragi-comically; hence that sense of darkened laughter running through a good deal of the literature of our troubled era. Even some of what seem our grimmest books have their own dimension of humour. Kafka's novels dismay us with their vision of human isolation and meaningless-ness; they also have a strong comic quality. Evelyn Waugh writes of a time of decline and fall, vile bodies, wasteland corruption, sexual betrayal, but he emerges in retrospect as one of the great British writers of modern black comedy. Samuel Beckett deals with the writer (and writing) at the end of his tether, in an age of minimalism and absurdity – but there is still the support of the comic instinct, the grim but necessary clowning granted to those abandoned in a godless world. As Thomas Mann once said, we live in an age of the death of the sublime, when the one common style is irony, the spirit of bitter comedy.

Capturing something of this distinctive note in the comic writing of our time had to be one of my aims in selecting the very varied stories of this anthology. But it has certainly not been the only one. For it is the whole point of comedy that it eludes our definitions and critical certainties, and takes us off in many directions, most hopefully into the realm of pleasure itself. Comedy is a riot of forms, a multiplication and upsetting of the species and the genres. And it springs from an enormous spectrum of methods and means: farce, burlesque and comic fantasy, satire and irony, parody and pastiche. As Umberto Eco – himself an important and playful comedian in fiction – once put it: 'From antiquity to Freud or Bergson, every attempt to define "comic" seems to be jeopardized by the fact that this is an umbrella term . . . that gathers together a disturbing ensemble of diverse and not completely homogeneous phenomena, such as humor, comedy, grotesque, parody, satire, wit, and so on.' This wonderful mixture of 'not completely homogeneous phenomena' is another thing I have tried to bring into this book. I have included both literary parody (Borges, Allen) and broad farce (Bainbridge). I have taken in realistic social observation of human manners (Amis) and strange fantasy (Carter), as well as stories that oddly mix the two (Carey). There is dense metaphysical humour (Singer) and sharp and distanced irony (Spark). There is political humour from a totalitarian time (Kundera), and playful metafictional experiment at the expense of writing itself (Barthelme). There is the gentle humour of confusion and imperfect human understanding (Updike), biting black humour (Atwood) and modern folk humour (Keillor). When categories fail – as they so often have a way of doing with comedy, thank goodness – I have applied to the stories the oldest and fairest test of all: did it make me smile; better still, did it make me laugh?

Most of the stories here come from British and American writers, but Irish, Canadian, Australian, Polish and Czech writing also claimed the right to make an appearance. I have interpreted 'modern' as mainly post-World War II, although definitions are rarely that tidy and some pre-war modern originators demanded inclusion. Perhaps a few – extremely imperfect – generalizations on the results may be in order. Comedy is, of course, an international phenomenon, but there are also certain signs that it still falls into distinct national traditions. Yiddish humour tends to the metaphysical, Irish to the religious, German humour to the grotesque and unusual, and so on. British comedy, like British life itself, seems – right up to our own uneasy day – often highly preoccupied with matters of social class, custom and nuance. W. H. Auden once said that comedy tended to develop in societies 'to the degree that its members are simultaneously conscious of being each a unique individual and of being all in common subjection to unalterable laws'. British comic fiction has certainly often reflected the weighty mass of the British social order, and the obscure and labyrinthine complexities of social codes and manners. Quite a few of the British stories that follow – Angus Wilson, Roald Dahl, Muriel Spark, for instance – are about social contrasts and ironies. American humour has a way of being more concerned with the human condition or metaphysical absurdity. It also reflects the powerful impact on post-war American writing of the largely European tradition of Jewish humour ('I am the son in the Jewish joke,' complains Philip Roth's Alexander Portnoy, '– *only it ain't no joke!*'). The 'black humour' of the sixties – Kurt Vonnegut, Joseph Heller, James Purdy, Thomas Pynchon – was itself a response to 'the madness in our midst', an expression of the climate of horror and absurdity that marked the Cold War; it was also part of the revival of the long tradition of absurdist satire (or gallows humour) that has become part of modern style. This in turn crossed with the 'metafictional' humour of Borges and Nabokov, with its unstable registers and playful acknowledgment of the writing process itself, giving a new importance to parody and pastiche. So Donald Barthelme, Woody Allen and T. Coraghessan Boyle seem to hit a different note.

Yet the power of nationality in comedy may now be growing weaker – as the work of distinctly mid-Atlantic writers like Jonathan Wilson or Martin Amis suggests. In our age of literary internationalism, all forms and styles freely cross borders; and that is as true of the spirit of comedy as it is of other aspects of our late modern cultural mosaic. The notes of American humour sound in British comedy; so do those of Indian or African tale-telling, coming from powerful migrant writers like Salman Rushdie or Hanif Kureishi; as a result the mixture is changing again. A few years ago publishers began reporting the decline of fictional comedy, and its replacement by a tone of wall-to-wall grimness. Happily, as I read along the shelves to draw together this anthology, I am left with the opposite impression. My own regrets are not about shortage, but about the many comic pleasures I was not able to include: no Bellow or Roth, no Calvino or Bernhardt, no Beckett or Márquez, no Ishmael Read or Don DeLillo, no Ian McEwan or Howard Jacobson, no Rushdie or Kureishi. Exploring my way through what seemed to me a rich contemporary tradition, I decided to follow the rule of hunting variety, range of form, difference of generations, mixture of mood. The largest aim of comedy is to give pleasure, and so I have tried to multiply the pleasures as much as I can.

There are few books that could be more of a joy to compile; I simply hope there is just as much joy in the reading. But comedy, I am afraid, remains a serious matter, or we would not need it so much. There is a firm purpose behind the volume; I hope it will display to readers and writers alike the rich and invaluable role that comedy plays in the present and, surely, the future of fiction. After all, comedy is the great leaven of writing. It relieves stories of the drab dull weight of realism and reportage, the endless dependence on autobiography, reminiscence or travel-record, that we so often think the first business of fiction. It casts new and strange light, adds distance, invigorates, makes our world unusual and yet comprehensible to our imaginations. It gives us a vision of ourselves that does not come from the usual positions and certainties, direct ideological convictions or categorical imperatives (that is why, historically, comedy has often been thought subversive, from Aristotle on). It comes from the sense of the extreme, the ridiculous, the absurd, our awareness of hypocrisy and self-delusion, ultimately from a recognition of our ironic, vulnerable status as human animals. It teases our values, upsets our lovemakings, touches our terrors, lays bare our pretensions, imperfections, and insecurities. It tells us that the world is not as we usually see it, but a stranger, more disturbing, but also funnier place. It rejects our hierarchies, upturns our statues, defaces our monuments. It tests the very nature of writing itself, and sees the act of creation as a strange and obscure comic intuition. If it often resists criticism, and leaves us adrift in the sheer strangeness of stories, that is all to the good. And if, as it sometimes seems to us, we live in uniquely difficult and sombre times, it can display to us what is difficult about them, and also provide the release of laughter. Graham Greene observed in his novel *The Comedians* (1966) that the modern world is a bitter comedy, which is why it always needs its comedians: 'We mustn't complain too much of being comedians – it's an honourable profession. If only we could be good ones the world might gain at least a sense of style. We have failed, that's all. We are bad comedians, we aren't bad men.' Here, I hope and believe, are some of the good comedians of our age, who help give us a sense of style.

I must acknowledge several debts. One is to Elsbeth Lindner of Weidenfeld & Nicolson; another is to my colleague Professor John Fletcher, with whom I taught a course on comic fiction at the University of East Anglia, and to the various students who took it in all solemnity. The last and most important is to my wife Elizabeth Bradbury, whose avid reading played a big part in helping me pick up some of the threads that make up the untired spirit of modern comic fiction.

Malcolm Bradbury
Norwich, 1994

ALDOUS HUXLEY

The Tillotson Banquet

Aldous Huxley (1894–1963) was born into an influential family. His grandfather, T. H. Huxley, was a noted scientist and supporter of Darwin, his mother was a niece of Matthew Arnold. Unfit for service during the Great War because of near-blindness, he soon established himself as a poet and then, after the war, as one of the chief satirists of the twenties, a time when comic fiction prospered in the climate of bitter disillusionment that followed the conflict. His satirical early novels – *Crome Yellow* (1921), *Antic Hay* (1923), *Those Barren Leaves* (1925) and *Point Counter Point* (1928) – showed the influence of Peacock, Anatole France and Max Beerbohm, but they dealt decisively with the sexual, emotional and philosophical crises of his generation and remain among Huxley's most powerful work. There were also notable collections of short stories – *Limbo* (1920), *Mortal Coils* (1922), *The Little Mexican* (1924) – that extended his comic reputation and showed the economy of his wit. In later life, after he moved to California in 1937, Huxley increasingly became a critic of modern social organization, and a meditative mystic.

'The Tillotson Banquet', from *Mortal Coils: Five Stories*, shows Aldous Huxley's humanity as well as his satirical and ironic energy. Like many of his stories it deals with writers and artists, their dependence on society and aristocratic patronage, and the problems of the young man on the make. It also displays the bitter wit and powerful intelligence of this still youthful author, whose first novel had only just appeared. Tillotson himself is a sad figure, a haunting of art from the Victorian past; but what makes the story work so well is its engaging intellectual humour and its sense of absurdity. It remains a classic piece of Huxley – a writer who was, in his way, to go on to have a stronger influence on modern fiction (writers like Waugh, Anthony Powell, and Angus Wilson) than any of the now more famed figures of modernism, and who greatly shaped our sense of modern comedy.

1

Young Spode was not a snob; he was too intelligent for that, too fundamentally decent. Not a snob; but all the same he could not help feeling very well pleased at the thought that he was dining, alone and intimately, with Lord Badgery. It was a definite event in his life, a step forward, he felt, towards that final success, social, material, and literary, which he had come to London with the fixed intention of making. The conquest and capture of Badgery was an almost essential strategical move in the campaign.

Edmund, forty-seventh Baron Badgery, was a lineal descendant of that Edmund, surnamed Le Blayreau, who landed on English soil in the train of William the Conqueror. Ennobled by William Rufus, the Badgerys had been one of the very few baronial families to survive the Wars of the Roses and all the other changes and chances of English history. They were a sensible and philoprogenitive race. No Badgery had ever fought in any war, no Badgery had ever engaged in any kind of politics. They had been content to live and quietly to propagate their species in a huge machicolated Norman castle, surrounded by a triple moat, only sallying forth to cultivate their property and to collect their rents. In the eighteenth century, when life had become relatively secure, the Badgerys began to venture forth into civilized society. From boorish squires they blossomed into *grands seigneurs*, patrons of the arts, virtuosi. Their property was large, they were rich; and with the growth of industrialism their riches also grew. Villages on their estate turned into manufacturing towns, unsuspected coal was discovered beneath the surface of their barren moorlands. By the middle of the nineteenth century the Badgerys were among the richest of English noble families. The forty-seventh baron disposed of an income of at least two hundred thousand pounds a year. Following the great Badgery tradition, he had refused to have anything to do with politics or war. He occupied himself by collecting pictures; he took an interest in theatrical productions; he was the friend and patron of men of letters, of painters, and musicians. A personage, in a word, of considerable consequence in that particular world in which young Spode had elected to make his success.

Spode had only recently left the university. Simon Gollamy, the editor of the *World's Review* (the 'Best of all possible Worlds'), had got to know him – he was always on the lookout for youthful talent – had seen possibilities in the young man, and appointed him art critic of his paper. Gollamy liked to have young and teachable people about him. The possession of disciples flattered his vanity, and he found it easier, moreover, to run his paper with docile collaborators than with men grown obstinate and case-hardened with age. Spode had not done badly at his new job. At any rate, his articles had been intelligent enough to arouse the interest of Lord Badgery. It was, ultimately, to them that he owed the honour of sitting tonight in the dining room of Badgery House.

Fortified by several varieties of wine and a glass of aged brandy, Spode felt more confident and at ease than he had done the whole evening. Badgery was rather a disquieting host. He had an alarming habit of changing the subject of any conversation that had lasted for more than two minutes. Spode had found it, for example, horribly mortifying when his host, cutting across what was, he prided himself, a particularly subtle and illuminating disquisition on baroque art, had turned a wandering eye about the room and asked him abruptly whether he liked parrots. He had flushed and glanced suspiciously towards him, fancying that the man was trying to be offensive. But no; Badgery's white, fleshy, Hanoverian face wore an expression of perfect good faith. There was no malice in his small greenish eyes. He evidently did genuinely want to know if Spode liked parrots. The young man swallowed his irritation and replied that he did. Badgery then told a good story about parrots. Spode was on the point of capping it with a better story, when his host began to talk about Beethoven. And so the game went on. Spode cut his conversation to suit his host's requirements. In the course of ten minutes he had made a more or less witty epigram on Benvenuto Cellini, Queen Victoria, sport, God, Stephen Phillips, and Moorish architecture. Lord Badgery thought him the most charming young man, and so intelligent.

'If you've quite finished your coffee,' he said, rising to his feet as he spoke, 'we'll go and look at the pictures.'

Spode jumped up with alacrity, and only then realized that he had drunk just ever so little too much. He would have to be careful, talk deliberately, plant his feet consciously, one after the other.

'This house is quite cluttered up with pictures,' Lord Badgery complained. 'I had a whole wagon-load taken away to the country last week; but there are still far too many. My ancestors would have their portraits painted by Romney. Such a shocking artist, don't you think? Why couldn't they have chosen Gainsborough, or even Reynolds? I've had all the Romneys hung in the servants' hall now. It's such a comfort to know that one can never possibly see them again. I suppose you know all about the ancient Hittites?'

'Well . . .' the young man replied, with befitting modesty.

'Look at that, then.' He indicated a large stone head which stood in a case near the dining-room door. 'It's not Greek, or Egyptian, or Persian, or anything else; so if it isn't ancient Hittite, I don't know what it is. And that reminds me of that story about Lord George Sanger, the Circus King . . .' and, without giving Spode time to examine the Hittite relic, he led the way up the huge staircase, pausing every now and then in his anecdote to point out some new object of curiosity or beauty.

'I suppose you know Deburau's pantomimes?' Spode rapped out as soon as the story was over. He was in an itch to let out his information about Deburau. Badgery had given him a perfect opening with his ridiculous Sanger. 'What a perfect man, isn't he? He used to . . .'

'This is my main gallery,' said Lord Badgery, throwing open one leaf of a tall folding door. 'I must apologize for it. It looks like a roller-skating rink.' He fumbled with the electric switches and there was suddenly light – light that revealed an enormous gallery, duly receding into distance according to all the laws of perspective. 'I dare say you've heard of my poor father,' Lord Badgery continued. 'A little insane, you know; sort of mechanical genius with a screw loose. He used to have a toy railway in this room. No end of fun he had, crawling about the floor after his trains. And all the pictures were stacked in the cellars. I can't tell you what they were like when I found them: mushrooms growing out of the Botticellis. Now I'm rather proud of this Poussin; he painted it for Scarron.'

'Exquisite!' Spode exclaimed, making with his hand a gesture as though he were modelling a pure form in the air. 'How splendid the onrush of those trees and leaning figures is! And the way they're caught up, as it were, and stemmed by that single godlike form opposing them with his contrary movement! And the draperies . . .'

But Lord Badgery had moved on, and was standing in front of a little fifteenth-century Virgin of carved wood.

'School of Rheims,' he explained.

They 'did' the gallery at high speed. Badgery never permitted his guest to halt for more than forty seconds before any work of art. Spode would have liked to spend a few moments of recollection and tranquillity in front of some of these lovely things. But it was not permitted.

The gallery done, they passed into a little room leading out of it. At the sight of what the lights revealed, Spode gasped.

'It's like something out of Balzac,' he exclaimed. 'Un de ces salons dorés où se déploie un luxe insolent. You know.'

'My nineteenth-century chamber,' Badgery explained. 'The best thing of its kind, I flatter myself, outside the State Apartments at Windsor.'

Spode tiptoed round the room, peering with astonishment at all the objects in glass, in gilded bronze, in china, in feathers, in embroidered and painted silk, in beads, in wax, objects of the most fantastic shapes and colours, all the queer products of a decadent tradition, with which the room was crowded. There were paintings on the walls – a Martin, a Wilkie, an early Landseer, several Ettys, a big Haydon, a slight pretty water-colour of a girl by Wainewright, the pupil of Blake and arsenic poisoner, and a score of others. But the picture which arrested Spode's attention was a medium-sized canvas representing Troilus riding into Troy among the flowers and plaudits of an admiring crowd, and oblivious (you could see from his expression) of everything but the eyes of Cressida, who looked down at him from a window, with Pandarus smiling over her shoulder.

'What an absurd and enchanting picture!' Spode exclaimed.

'Ah, you've spotted my Troilus.' Lord Badgery was pleased.

'What bright harmonious colours! Like Etty's, only stronger, not so obviously pretty. And there's an energy about it that reminds one of Haydon. Only Haydon could never have done anything so impeccable in taste. Who is it by?' Spode turned to his host inquiringly.

'You were right in detecting Haydon,' Lord Badgery answered. 'It's by his pupil, Tillotson. I wish I could get hold of more of his work. But nobody seems to know anything about him. And he seems to have done so little.'

This time it was the younger man who interrupted.

'Tillotson, Tillotson . . .' He put his hand to his forehead. A frown incongruously distorted his round, floridly curved face. 'No . . . yes, I have it.' He looked up triumphantly with serene and childish brows. 'Tillotson, Walter Tillotson – the man's still alive.'

Badgery smiled. 'This picture was painted in 1846, you know.'

'Well, that's all right. Say he was born in 1820, painted his masterpiece when he was twenty-six, and it's 1913 now; that's to say he's only ninety-three. Not as old as Titian yet.'

'But he's not been heard of since 1860,' Lord Badgery protested.

'Precisely. Your mention of his name reminded me of the discovery I made the other day when I was looking through the obituary notices in the archives of the *World's Review*. (One has to bring them up to date every year or so for fear of being caught napping if one of these old birds chooses to shuffle off suddenly.) Well there, among them – I remember my astonishment at the time – there I found Walter Tillotson's biography. Pretty full to 1860, and then a blank, except for a pencil note in the early nineteen hundreds to the effect that he had returned from the East. The obituary has never been used or added to. I draw the obvious conclusion: the old chap isn't dead yet. He's just been overlooked somehow.'

'But this is extraordinary,' Lord Badgery exclaimed. 'You must find him, Spode – you must find him. I'll commission him to paint frescoes round this room. It's just what I've always vainly longed for – a real nineteenth-century artist to decorate this place for me. Oh, we must find him at once – at once.'

Lord Badgery strode up and down in a state of great excitement.

'I can see how this room could be made quite perfect,' he went on. 'We'd clear away all these cases and have the whole of that wall filled by a heroic fresco of Hector and Andromache, or "Distraining for Rent", or Fanny Kemble as Belvidera in "Venice Preserved" – anything like that, provided it's in the grand manner of the thirties and forties. And here I'd have a

landscape with lovely receding perspectives, or else something architec-
tural and grand in the style of Belshazzar's feast. Then we'll have this
Adam fireplace taken down and replaced by something Mauro-Gothic.
And on these walls I'll have mirrors, or no! let me see . . .'

He sank into meditative silence, from which he finally roused himself to
shout:

'The old man, the old man! Spode, we must find this astonishing old
creature. And don't breathe a word to anybody. Tillotson shall be our
secret. Oh, it's too perfect, it's incredible! Think of the frescoes.'

Lord Badgery's face had become positively animated. He had talked of a
single subject for nearly a quarter of an hour.

2

Three weeks later Lord Badgery was aroused from his usual after-
luncheon somnolence by the arrival of a telegram. The message was a
short one. 'Found. – SPODE.' A look of pleasure and intelligence made
human Lord Badgery's clayey face of surfeit. 'No answer,' he said. The
footman padded away on noiseless feet.

Lord Badgery closed his eyes and began to contemplate. Found! What a
room he would have! There would be nothing like it in the world. The
frescoes, the fireplace, the mirrors, the ceiling . . . And a small, shrivelled
old man clambering about the scaffolding, agile and quick like one of those
whiskered little monkeys at the Zoo, painting away, painting away . . .
Fanny Kemble at Belvidera, Hector and Andromache, or why not the
Duke of Clarence in the Butt, the Duke of Malmsey, the Butt of Clarence
. . . Lord Badgery was asleep.

Spode did not lag long behind his telegram. He was at Badgery House
by six o'clock. His lordship was in the nineteenth-century chamber,
engaged in clearing away with his own hands the bric-à-brac. Spode found
him looking hot and out of breath.

'Ah, there you are,' said Lord Badgery. 'You see me already preparing
for the great man's coming. Now you must tell me all about him.'

'He's older even than I thought,' said Spode. 'He's ninety-seven this
year. Born in 1816. Incredible, isn't it! There, I'm beginning at the wrong
end.'

'Begin where you like,' said Badgery genially.

'I won't tell you all the incidents of the hunt. You've no idea what a job I
had to run him to earth. It was like a Sherlock Holmes story, immensely
elaborate, too elaborate. I shall write a book about it some day. At any
rate, I found him at last.'

'Where?'

'In a sort of respectable slum in Holloway, older and poorer and lonelier than you could have believed possible. I found out how it was he came to be forgotten, how he came to drop out of life in the way he did. He took it into his head, somewhere about the sixties, to go to Palestine to get local colour for his religious pictures – scapegoats and things, you know. Well, he went to Jerusalem and then on to Mount Lebanon and on and on, and then, somewhere in the middle of Asia Minor, he got stuck. He got stuck for about forty years.'

'But what did he do all that time?'

'Oh, he painted, and started a mission, and converted three Turks, and taught the local Pashas the rudiments of English, Latin, and perspective, and God knows what else. Then, in about 1904, it seems to have occurred to him that he was getting rather old and had been away from home for rather a long time. So he made his way back to England, only to find that everyone he had known was dead, that the dealers had never heard of him and wouldn't buy his pictures, that he was simply a ridiculous old figure of fun. So he got a job as a drawing-master in a girls' school in Holloway, and there he's been ever since, growing older and older, and feebler and feebler, and blinder and deafer, and generally more gaga, until finally the school has given him the sack. He had about ten pounds in the world when I found him. He lives in a kind of black hole in a basement full of beetles. When his ten pounds are spent, I suppose he'll just quietly die there.'

Badgery held up a white hand. 'No more, no more. I find literature quite depressing enough. I insist that life at least shall be a little gayer. Did you tell him I wanted him to paint my room?'

'But he can't paint. He's too blind and palsied.'

'Can't paint?' Badgery exclaimed in horror. 'Then what's the good of the old creature?'

'Well, if you put it like that . . .' Spode began.

'I shall never have my frescoes. Ring the bell, will you?'

Spode rang.

'What right has Tillotson to go on existing if he can't paint?' went on Lord Badgery petulantly. 'After all, that was his only justification for occupying a place in the sun.'

'He doesn't have much sun in his basement.'

The footman appeared at the door.

'Get someone to put all these things back in their places,' Lord Badgery commanded, indicating with a wave of the hand the ravaged cases, the confusion of glass and china with which he had littered the floor, the pictures unhooked. 'We'll go to the library, Spode; it's more comfortable there.'

He led the way through the long gallery and down the stairs.

'I'm sorry old Tillotson has been such a disappointment,' said Spode sympathetically.

'Let us talk about something else; he ceases to interest me.'

'But don't you think we ought to do something about him? He's only got ten pounds between him and the workhouse. And if you'd seen the blackbeetles in his basement!'

'Enough – enough. I'll do everything you think fitting.'

'I thought we might get up a subscription amongst lovers of the arts.'

'There aren't any,' said Badgery.

'No; but there are plenty of people who will subscribe out of snobbism.'

'Not unless you give them something for their money.'

'That's true. I hadn't thought of that.' Spode was silent for a moment. 'We might have a dinner in his honour. The Great Tillotson Banquet. Doyen of British Art. A Link with the Past. Can't you see it in the papers? I'd make a stunt of it in the *World's Review*. That ought to bring in the snobs.'

'And we'll invite a lot of artists and critics – all the ones who can't stand one another. It will be fun to see them squabbling.' Badgery laughed. Then his face darkened once again. 'Still,' he added, 'it'll be a very poor second best to my frescoes. You'll stay to dinner, of course.'

'Well, since you suggest it. Thanks very much.'

3

The Tillotson Banquet was fixed to take place about three weeks later. Spode, who had charge of the arrangements, proved himself an excellent organizer. He secured the big banqueting room at the Café Bomba, and was successful in bullying and cajoling the manager into giving fifty persons dinner at twelve shillings a head, including wine. He sent out invitations and collected subscriptions. He wrote an article on Tillotson in the *World's Review* – one of those charming, witty articles, couched in the tone of amused patronage and contempt with which one speaks of the great men of 1840. Nor did he neglect Tillotson himself. He used to go to Holloway almost every day to listen to the old man's endless stories about Asia Minor and the Great Exhibition of '51 and Benjamin Robert Haydon. He was sincerely sorry for this relic of another age.

Mr Tillotson's room was about ten feet below the level of the soil of South Holloway. A little grey light percolated through the area bars, forced a difficult passage through panes opaque with dirt, and spent itself, like a drop of milk that falls into an inkpot, among the inveterate shadows of the dungeon. The place was haunted by the sour smell of damp plaster and of woodwork that has begun to moulder secretly at the heart. A little miscellaneous furniture, including a bed, a washstand and chest of drawers, a table and one or two chairs, lurked in the obscure corners of the den or ventured furtively out into the open. Hither Spode now came almost every day, bringing the old man news of the progress of the banquet scheme. Every day he found Mr Tillotson sitting in the same place under the window, bathing, as it were, in his tiny puddle of light. 'The oldest man that ever wore grey hairs,' Spode reflected as he looked at him. Only there were very few hairs left on that bald, unpolished head. At the sound of the visitor's knock Mr Tillotson would turn in his chair, stare in the direction of the door with blinking, uncertain eyes. He was always full of apologies for being so slow in recognizing who was there.

'No discourtesy meant,' he would say, after asking. 'It's not as if I had forgotten who you were. Only it's so dark and my sight isn't what it was.'

After that he never failed to give a little laugh, and, pointing out of the window at the area railings, would say:

'Ah, this is the place for somebody with good sight. It's the place for looking at ankles. It's the grandstand.'

It was the day before the great event. Spode came as usual, and Mr Tillotson punctually made his little joke about the ankles, and Spode as punctually laughed.

'Well, Mr Tillotson,' he said, after the reverberation of the joke had died away, 'tomorrow you make your re-entry into the world of art and fashion. You'll find some changes.'

'I've always had such extraordinary luck,' said Mr Tillotson, and Spode could see by his expression that he genuinely believed it, that he had forgotten the black hole and the blackbeetles and the almost exhausted ten pounds that stood between him and the workhouse. 'What an amazing piece of good fortune, for instance, that you should have found me just when you did. Now, this dinner will bring me back to my place in the world. I shall have money, and in a little while – who knows? – I shall be able to see well enough to paint again. I believe my eyes are getting better, you know. Ah, the future is very rosy.'

Mr Tillotson looked up, his face puckered into a smile, and nodded his head in affirmation of his words.

'You believe in the life to come?' said Spode, and immediately flushed for shame at the cruelty of the words.

But Mr Tillotson was in far too cheerful a mood to have caught their significance.

'Life to come,' he repeated. 'No, I don't believe in any of that stuff – not since 1859. The *Origin of Species* changed my views, you know. No life to come for me, thank you! You don't remember the excitement, of course. You're very young, Mr Spode.'

'Well, I'm not so old as I was,' Spode replied. 'You know how middle-aged one is as a schoolboy and undergraduate. Now I'm old enough to know I'm young.'

Spode was about to develop this little paradox further, but he noticed that Mr Tillotson had not been listening. He made a note of the gambit for use in companies that were more appreciative of the subtleties.

'You were talking about the *Origin of Species*,' he said.

'Was I?' said Mr Tillotson, waking from reverie.

'About its effect on your faith, Mr Tillotson.'

'To be sure, yes. It shattered my faith. But I remember a fine thing by the Poet Laureate, something about there being more faith in honest doubt, believe me, than in all the . . . all the . . . I forget exactly what; but you see the train of thought. Oh, it was a bad time for religion. I am glad my master Haydon never lived to see it. He was a man of fervour. I remember him pacing up and down his studio in Lisson Grove, singing and shouting and praying all at once. It used almost to frighten me. Oh, but he was a wonderful man, a great man. Take him for all in all, we shall not look upon his like again. As usual, the Bard is right. But it was all very long ago, before your time, Mr Spode.'

'Well, I'm not as old as I was,' said Spode, in the hope of having his paradox appreciated this time. But Mr Tillotson went on without noticing the interruption.

'It's a very, very long time. And yet, when I look back on it, it all seems but a day or two ago. Strange that each day should seem so long and that many days added together should be less than an hour. How clearly I can see old Haydon pacing up and down! Much more clearly, indeed, than I see you, Mr Spode. The eyes of memory don't grow dim. But my sight is improving, I assure you; it's improving daily. I shall soon be able to see those ankles.' He laughed, like a cracked bell – one of those little old bells, Spode fancied, that ring, with much rattling of wires, in the far-off servants' quarters of ancient houses. 'And very soon,' Mr Tillotson went on, 'I shall be painting again. Ah, Mr Spode, my luck is extraordinary. I believe in it, I trust it. And after all, what is luck? Simply another name for Providence, in spite of the *Origin of Species* and the rest of it. How right the Laureate was when he said that there was more faith in honest doubt, believe me, than in all the . . . er, the . . . er . . . well, you know. I regard you, Mr Spode, as the emissary of Providence. Your coming marked a turning-point in my life, and the beginning, for me, of happier days. Do you know, one of the first things I shall do when my fortunes are restored will be to buy a hedgehog.'

'A hedgehog, Mr Tillotson?'

'For the blackbeetles. There's nothing like a hedgehog for beetles. It will eat blackbeetles till it's sick, till it dies of surfeit. That reminds me of the time when I told my poor great master Haydon – in joke, of course – that he ought to send in a cartoon of King John dying of a surfeit of lampreys for the frescoes in the new Houses of Parliament. As I told him, it's a most notable event in the annals of British liberty – the providential and exemplary removal of a tyrant.'

Mr Tillotson laughed again – the little bell in the deserted house; a ghostly hand pulling the cord in the drawing room, and phantom footmen responding to the thin, flawed note.

'I remember he laughed, laughed like a bull in his old grand manner. But oh, it was a terrible blow when they rejected his designs, a terrible blow! It was the first and fundamental cause of his suicide.'

Mr Tillotson paused. There was a long silence. Spode felt strangely moved, he hardly knew why, in the presence of this man, so frail, so ancient, in body three parts dead, in the spirit so full of life and hopeful patience. He felt ashamed. What was the use of his own youth and cleverness? He saw himself suddenly as a boy with a rattle scaring birds – rattling his noisy cleverness, waving his arms in ceaseless and futile activity, never resting in his efforts to scare away the birds that were always trying to settle in his mind. And what birds! wide-winged and beautiful, all those serene thoughts and faiths and emotions that only visit minds that have humbled themselves to quiet. Those gracious visitants he was for ever using all his energies to drive away. But this old man, with his hedgehogs and his honest doubts and all the rest of it – his mind was like a field made beautiful by the free coming and going, the unafraid alightings of a multitude of white, bright-winged creatures. He felt ashamed. But then, was it possible to alter one's life? Wasn't it a little absurd to risk a conversion? Spode shrugged his shoulders.

'I'll get you a hedgehog at once,' he said. 'They're sure to have some at Whiteley's.'

Before he left that evening Spode made an alarming discovery. Mr Tillotson did not possess a dress-suit. It was hopeless to think of getting one made at this short notice, and, besides, what an unnecessary expense!

'We shall have to borrow a suit, Mr Tillotson. I ought to have thought of that before.'

'Dear me, dear me.' Mr Tillotson was a little chagrined by this unlucky discovery. 'Borrow a suit?'

Spode hurried away for counsel to Badgery House. Lord Badgery surprisingly rose to the occasion. 'Ask Boreham to come and see me,' he told the footman who answered his ring. Boreham was one of those immemorial butlers who linger on, generation after generation, in the houses of the great. He was over eighty now, bent, dried up, shrivelled with age.

'All old men are about the same size,' said Lord Badgery. It was a comforting theory. 'Ah, here he is. Have you got a spare suit of evening clothes, Boreham?'

'I have an old suit, my lord, that I stopped wearing in – let me see – was it nineteen seven or eight?'

'That's the very thing. I should be most grateful, Boreham, if you could lend it to me for Mr Spode here for a day.'

The old man went out, and soon reappeared carrying over his arm a very old black suit. He held up the coat and trousers for inspection. In the light of day they were deplorable.

'You've no idea, sir,' said Boreham deprecatingly to Spode – 'you've no idea how easy things get stained with grease and gravy and what not. However careful you are, sir – however careful.'

'I should imagine so.' Spode was sympathetic.

'However careful, sir.'

'But in artificial light they'll look all right.'

'Perfectly all right,' Lord Badgery repeated. 'Thank you, Boreham; you shall have them back on Thursday.'

'You're welcome, my lord, I'm sure.' And the old man bowed and disappeared.

On the afternoon of the great day Spode carried up to Holloway a parcel containing Boreham's retired evening-suit and all the necessary appurtenances in the way of shirts and collars. Owing to the darkness and his own feeble sight Mr Tillotson was happily unaware of the defects in the suit. He was in a state of extreme nervous agitation. It was with some difficulty that Spode could prevent him, although it was only three o'clock, from starting his toilet on the spot.

'Take it easy, Mr Tillotson, take it easy. We needn't start till half past seven, you know.'

Spode left an hour later, and as soon as he was safely out of the room Mr Tillotson began to prepare himself for the banquet. He lighted the gas and a couple of candles, and, blinking myopically at the image that fronted him in the tiny looking-glass that stood on his chest of drawers, he set to work, with all the ardour of a young girl preparing for her first ball. At six o'clock, when the last touches had been given, he was not unsatisfied.

He marched up and down his cellar, humming to himself the gay song which had been so popular in his middle years:

> '*Oh, oh, Anna Maria Jones!*
> *Queen of the tambourine, the cymbals, and the bones!*'

Spode arrived an hour later in Lord Badgery's second Rolls-Royce. Opening the door of the old man's dungeon, he stood for a moment, wide-eyed with astonishment, on the threshold. Mr Tillotson was standing by the empty grate, one elbow resting on the mantelpiece, one leg crossed over the other in a jaunty and gentlemanly attitude. The effect of the candlelight shining on his face was to deepen every line and wrinkle with intense black shadow; he looked immeasurably old. It was a noble and pathetic head. On the other hand, Boreham's outworn evening-suit was simply buffoonish. The coat was too long in the sleeves and the tail; the trousers bagged in elephantine creases about his ankles. Some of the grease-spots were visible even in candlelight. The white tie, over which Mr Tillotson had taken infinite pains and which he believed in his purblindness to be perfect, was fantastically lopsided. He had buttoned up his waistcoat in such a fashion that one button was widowed of its hole and one hole of its button. Across his shirt-front lay the broad green ribbon of some unknown Order.

'Queen of the tambourine, the cymbals, and the bones,' Mr Tillotson concluded in a gnat-like voice before welcoming his visitor.

'Well, Spode, here you are. I'm dressed already, you see. The suit, I flatter myself, fits very well, almost as though it had been made for me. I am all gratitude to the gentleman who was kind enough to lend it to me; I shall take the greatest care of it. It's a dangerous thing to lend clothes. For loan oft loseth both itself and friend. The Bard is always right.'

'Just one thing,' said Spode. 'A touch to your waistcoat.' He unbuttoned the dissipated garment and did it up again more symmetrically.

Mr Tillotson was a little piqued at being found so absurdly in the wrong. 'Thanks, thanks,' he said protestingly, trying to edge away from his valet. 'It's all right, you know; I can do it myself. Foolish oversight. I flatter myself the suit fits very well.'

'And perhaps the tie might . . .' Spode began tentatively. But the old man would not hear of it.

'No, no. The tie's all right. I can tie a tie, Mr Spode. The tie's all right. Leave it as it is, I beg.'

'I like your Order.'

Mr Tillotson looked down complacently at his shirt-front. 'Ah, you've noticed my Order. It's a long time since I wore that. It was given me by the Grand Porte, you know, for services rendered in the Russo-Turkish War. It's the Order of Chastity, the second class. They only give the first class to crowned heads, you know – crowned heads and ambassadors. And only Pashas of the highest rank get the second. Mine's the second. They only give the first class to crowned heads . . .'

'Of course, of course,' said Spode.

'Do you think I look all right, Mr Spode?' Mr Tillotson asked, a little anxiously.

'Splendid, Mr Tillotson – splendid. The Order's magnificent.'

The old man's face brightened once more. 'I flatter myself,' he said, 'that this borrowed suit fits me very well. But I don't like borrowing clothes. For loan oft loseth both itself and friend, you know. And the Bard is always right.'

'Ugh, there's one of those horrible beetles!' Spode exclaimed.

Mr Tillotson bent down and stared at the floor. 'I see it,' he said, and stamped on a small piece of coal, which crunched to powder under his foot. 'I shall certainly buy a hedgehog.'

It was time for them to start. A crowd of little boys and girls had collected round Lord Badgery's enormous car. The chauffeur, who felt that honour and dignity were at stake, pretended not to notice the children, but sat gazing, like a statue, into eternity. At the sight of Spode and Mr Tillotson emerging from the house a yell of mingled awe and derision went up. It subsided to an astonished silence as they climbed into the car. 'Bomba's,' Spode directed. The Rolls-Royce gave a faintly stertorous sigh and began to move. The children yelled again, and ran along beside the car, waving their arms in a frenzy of excitement. It was then that Mr Tillotson, with an incomparably noble gesture, leaned forward and tossed among the seething crowd of urchins his three last coppers.

4

In Bomba's big room the company was assembling. The long gilt-edged mirrors reflected a singular collection of people. Middle-aged Academicians shot suspicious glances at youths whom they suspected, only too correctly, of being iconoclasts, organizers of Post-Impressionist Exhibitions. Rival art critics, brought suddenly face to face, quivered with restrained hatred. Mrs Nobes, Mrs Cayman, and Mrs Mandragore, those indefatigable hunters of artistic big game, came on one another all unawares in this well-stored menagerie, where each had expected to hunt alone, and were filled with rage. Through this crowd of mutually repellent vanities Lord Badgery moved with a suavity that seemed unconscious of all the feuds and hatreds. He was enjoying himself immensely. Behind the heavy waxen mask of his face, ambushed behind the Hanoverian nose, the little lustreless pig's eyes, the pale thick lips, there lurked a small devil of happy malice that rocked with laughter.

'So nice of you to have come, Mrs Mandragore, to do honour to England's artistic past. And I'm so glad to see you've brought dear Mrs Cayman. And is that Mrs Nobes, too? So it is! I hadn't noticed her before. How delightful! I knew we could depend on your love of art.'

And he hurried away to seize the opportunity of introducing that eminent sculptor, Sir Herbert Herne, to the bright young critic who had called him, in the public prints, a monumental mason.

A moment later the maître d'hôtel came to the door of the gilded saloon and announced, loudly and impressively, 'Mr Walter Tillotson.' Guided from behind by young Spode, Mr Tillotson came into the room slowly and hesitatingly. In the glare of the lights his eyelids beat heavily, painfully,

23

like the wings of an imprisoned moth, over his filmy eyes. Once inside the door he halted and drew himself up with a conscious assumption of dignity. Lord Badgery hurried forward and seized his hand.

'Welcome, Mr Tillotson – welcome in the name of English art!'

Mr Tillotson inclined his head in silence. He was too full of emotion to be able to reply.

'I should like to introduce you to a few of your younger colleagues, who have assembled here to do you honour.'

Lord Badgery presented everyone in the room to the old painter, who bowed, shook hands, made little noises in his throat, but still found himself unable to speak. Mrs Nobes, Mrs Cayman, and Mrs Mandragore all said charming things.

Dinner was served; the party took their places. Lord Badgery sat at the head of the table, with Mr Tillotson on his right hand and Sir Herbert Herne on his left. Confronted with Bomba's succulent cooking and Bomba's wines, Mr Tillotson ate and drank a good deal. He had the appetite of one who has lived on greens and potatoes for ten years among the blackbeetles. After the second glass of wine he began to talk, suddenly and in a flood, as though a sluice had been pulled up.

'In Asia Minor,' he began, 'it is the custom, when one goes to dinner, to hiccough as a sign of appreciative fullness. *Eructavit cor meum*, as the Psalmist has it; he was an Oriental himself.'

Spode had arranged to sit next to Mrs Cayman; he had designs upon her. She was an impossible woman, of course, but rich and useful; he wanted to bamboozle her into buying some of his young friends' pictures.

'In a cellar?' Mrs Cayman was saying, 'with blackbeetles? Oh, how dreadful! Poor old man! And he's ninety-seven, didn't you say? Isn't that shocking! I only hope the subscription will be a large one. Of course, one wishes one could have given more oneself. But then, you know, one has so many expenses, and things are so difficult now.'

'I know, I know,' said Spode, with feeling.

'It's all because of Labour,' Mrs Cayman explained. 'Of course, I should simply love to have him in to dinner sometimes. But, then, I feel he's really too old, too *farouche* and *gâteux*; it would not be doing a kindness to him, would it? And so you are working with Mr Gollamy now? What a charming man, so talented, such conversation . . .'

'*Eructavit cor meum*,' said Mr Tillotson for the third time. Lord Badgery tried to head him off the subject of Turkish etiquette, but in vain.

By half past nine a kinder vinolent atmosphere had put to sleep the hatreds and suspicions of before dinner. Sir Herbert Herne had discovered that the young Cubist sitting next him was not insane and actually knew a surprising amount about the Old Masters. For their part these young men had realized that their elders were not at all malignant; they were just very stupid and pathetic. It was only in the bosoms of Mrs Nobes, Mrs Cayman, and Mrs Mandragore that hatred still reigned undiminished. Being ladies and old-fashioned, they had drunk almost no wine.

The moment for speech-making arrived. Lord Badgery rose to his feet, said what was expected of him, and called upon Sir Herbert to propose the toast of the evening. Sir Herbert coughed, smiled, and began. In the course of a speech that lasted twenty minutes he told anecdotes of Mr Gladstone, Lord Leighton, Sir Alma-Tadema, and the late Bishop of Bombay; he made three puns, he quoted Shakespeare and Whittier, he was playful, he was eloquent, he was grave . . . At the end of his harangue Sir Herbert handed to Mr Tillotson a silk purse containing fifty-eight pounds ten shillings, the total amount of the subscription. The old man's health was drunk with acclamation.

Mr Tillotson rose with difficulty to his feet. The dry, snake-like skin of his face was flushed; his tie was more crooked than ever; the green ribbon of the Order of Chastity of the second class had somehow climbed up his crumpled and maculate shirt-front.

'My lords, ladies, and gentlemen,' he began in a choking voice, and then broke down completely. It was a very painful and pathetic spectacle. A feeling of intense discomfort afflicted the minds of all who looked upon that trembling relic of a man, as he stood there weeping and stammering. It was as though a breath of the wind of death had blown suddenly through the room, lifting the vapours of wine and tobacco-smoke, quenching the laughter and the candle flames. Eyes floated uneasily, not knowing where to look. Lord Badgery, with great presence of mind, offered the old man a glass of wine. Mr Tillotson began to recover. The guests heard him murmur a few disconnected words.

'This great honour . . . overwhelmed with kindness . . . this magnificent banquet . . . not used to it . . . in Asia Minor . . . *eructavit cor meum.*'

At this point Lord Badgery plucked sharply at one of his long coat-tails. Mr Tillotson paused, took another sip of wine, and then went on with a newly won coherence and energy.

'The life of the artist is a hard one. His work is unlike other men's work, which may be done mechanically, by rote and almost, as it were, in sleep. It demands from him a constant expense of spirit. He gives continually of his best life, and in return he receives much joy, it is true – much fame, it may be – but of material blessings, very few. It is eighty years since first I devoted my life to the service of art; eighty years, and almost every one of those years has brought me fresh and painful proof of what I have been saying: the artist's life is a hard one.'

This unexpected deviation into sense increased the general feeling of discomfort. It became necessary to take the old man seriously, to regard him as a human being. Up till then he had been no more than an object of curiosity, a mummy in an absurd suit of evening clothes with a green ribbon across the shirt-front. People could not help wishing that they had subscribed a little more. Fifty-eight pounds ten – it wasn't enormous. But happily for the peace of mind of the company, Mr Tillotson paused again, took another sip of wine, and began to live up to his proper character by talking absurdly.

'When I consider the life of that great man Benjamin Robert Haydon, one of the greatest men England has ever produced . . .' The audience heaved a sigh of relief; this was all as it should be. There was a burst of loud bravoing and clapping. Mr Tillotson turned his dim eyes round the room, and smiled gratefully at the misty figures he beheld. 'That great man, Benjamin Robert Haydon,' he continued, 'whom I am proud to call my master and who, it rejoices my heart to see, still lives in your memory and esteem – that great man, one of the greatest that England has ever produced, led a life so deplorable that I cannot think of it without a tear.'

And with infinite repetitions and divagations, Mr Tillotson related the history of B. R. Haydon, his imprisonments for debt, his battle with the Academy, his triumphs, his failures, his despair, his suicide. Half past ten struck. Mr Tillotson was declaiming against the stupid and prejudiced judges who had rejected Haydon's designs for the decoration of the new Houses of Parliament in favour of the paltriest German scribblings.

'That great man, one of the greatest England has ever produced, that great Benjamin Robert Haydon, whom I am proud to call my master and who, it rejoices me to see, still lives on in your memory and esteem – at that affront his great heart burst; it was the unkindest cut of all. He who had worked all his life for the recognition of the artist by the State, he who had petitioned every Prime Minister, including the Duke of Wellington, for thirty years, begging them to employ artists to decorate public buildings, he to whom the scheme for decorating the Houses of Parliament was undeniably due . . .' Mr Tillotson lost a grip on his syntax and began a new sentence. 'It was the unkindest cut of all, it was the last straw. The artist's life is a hard one.'

At eleven Mr Tillotson was talking about the pre-Raphaelites. At a quarter past he had begun to tell the story of B. R. Haydon all over again. At twenty-five minutes to twelve he collapsed quite speechless into his chair. Most of the guests had already gone away; the few who remained made haste to depart. Lord Badgery led the old man to the door and packed him into the second Rolls-Royce. The Tillotson Banquet was over; it had been a pleasant evening, but a little too long.

Spode walked back to his rooms in Bloomsbury, whistling as he went. The arc lamps of Oxford Street reflected in the polished surface of the road: canals of dark bronze. He would have to bring that into an article some time. The Cayman woman had been very successfully nobbled. 'Voi che sapete,' he whistled – somewhat out of tune, but he could not hear that.

When Mr Tillotson's landlady came in to call him on the following morning, she found the old man lying fully dressed on his bed. He looked very ill and very, very old; Boreham's dress-suit was in a terrible state, and the green ribbon of the Order of Chastity was ruined. Mr Tillotson lay very still, but he was not asleep. Hearing the sound of footsteps, he opened his eyes a little and faintly groaned. His landlady looked down at him menacingly.

'Disgusting!' she said; 'disgusting, I call it. At your age.'

Mr Tillotson groaned again. Making a great effort, he drew out of his trouser pocket a large silk purse, opened it, and extracted a sovereign.

'The artist's life is a hard one, Mrs Green,' he said, handing her the coin. 'Would you mind sending for the doctor? I don't feel very well. And oh, what shall I do about these clothes? What shall I say to the gentleman who was kind enough to lend them to me? Loan oft loseth both itself and friend. The Bard is always right.'

DOROTHY PARKER

The Waltz

Dorothy Parker (1893–1967), née Rothschild, was born in West End, New Jersey, and worked as a columnist for *Vogue* and *Vanity Fair*, writing also for the *New Yorker* and *Esquire*; later she wrote screenplays in Hollywood. She was one of a group of New York writers who met regularly at the Algonquin Hotel, and became famous for her outspoken wit and, in her columns, her trenchant commentary, indeed her cynicism. It was Dorothy Parker who said, 'If all the young ladies who attended the Yale prom were laid end to end, no one would be in the least bit surprised,' and described Katharine Hepburn's acting as 'running the whole gamut of emotion from A to B'. She published a number of volumes of witty poems – including *Enough Rope* (1926) and *Death and Taxes* (1931) – and two of short stories, collected together in the volume *Here Lies* (1939). *The Viking Portable Dorothy Parker* (1944) made available most of her major work.

'The Waltz', from her second story collection, *Laments for the Living* (1930), is one of her classic pieces, or sketches (another is the story 'Big Blonde'). Much of her writing is a commentary on the imperfect relations between the sexes ('Woman wants monogamy; / Man delights in novelty . . .'), and the word 'sardonic' might have been confected to describe her tone. 'The Waltz' plays smartly in the space between the spoken and the unspoken, and is a wonderfully pointed observation of social and sexual hypocrisy, if not our eternal self-deceit. But above all it is an example of concentrated modern wit, line after line offering a distilled verbal gag or a wonderful social or sexual observation.

W *hy, thank you so much. I'd adore to.*

I don't want to dance with him. I don't want to dance with anybody. And even if I did, it wouldn't be him. He'd be well down among the last ten. I've seen the way he dances; it looks like something you do on Saint Walpurgis Night. Just think, not a quarter of an hour ago, here I was sitting, feeling so sorry for the poor girl he was dancing with. And now *I'm* going to be the poor girl. Well, well. Isn't it a small world?

And a peach of a world, too. A true little corker. Its events are so fascinatingly unpredictable, are not they? Here I was, minding my own business, not doing a stitch of harm to any living soul. And then he comes into my life, all smiles and city manners, to sue me for the favor of one memorable mazurka. Why, he scarcely knows my name, let alone what it stands for. It stands for Despair, Bewilderment, Futility, Degradation, and Premeditated Murder, but little does he wot. I don't wot his name, either; I haven't any idea what it is. Jukes, would be my guess from the look in his eyes. How do you do, Mr Jukes? And how is that dear little brother of yours, with the two heads?

Ah, now why did he have to come around me, with his low requests? Why can't he let me lead my own life? I ask so little – just to be left alone in my quiet corner of the table, to do my evening brooding over all my sorrows. And he must come, with his bows and his scrapes and his may-I-have-this ones. And I had to go and tell him that I'd adore to dance with him. I cannot understand why I wasn't struck right down dead. Yes, and being struck dead would look like a day in the country, compared to struggling out a dance with this boy. But what could I do? Everyone else at the table had got up to dance, except him and me. There was I, trapped. Trapped like a trap in a trap.

What can you say, when a man asks you to dance with him? I most certainly will *not* dance with you, I'll see you in hell first. Why, thank you, I'd like to awfully, but I'm having labor pains. Oh, yes, *do* let's dance together – it's so nice to meet a man who isn't a scaredy-cat about catching my beri-beri. No. There was nothing for me to do, but say I'd adore to. Well, we might as well get it over with. All right, Cannonball, let's run out on the field. You won the toss; you can lead.

Why, I think it's more of a waltz, really. Isn't it? We might just listen to the music a second. Shall we? Oh, yes, it's a waltz. Mind? Why, I'm simply thrilled. I'd love to waltz with you.

I'd love to waltz with you. I'd love to waltz with you. I'd love to have my tonsils out, I'd love to be in a midnight fire at sea. Well, it's too late now. We're getting under way. *Oh.* Oh, dear. Oh, dear, dear, dear. Oh, this is even worse than I thought it would be. I suppose that's the one dependable law of life – everything is always worse than you thought it was going to be. Oh, if I had any real grasp of what this dance would be like, I'd have held out for sitting it out. Well, it will probably amount to the same thing in the end. We'll be sitting it out on the floor in a minute, if he keeps this up.

I'm so glad I brought it to his attention that this is a waltz they're playing. Heaven knows what might have happened, if he had thought it was something fast; we'd have blown the sides right out of the building. Why does he always want to be somewhere that he isn't? Why can't we stay in one place just long enough to get acclimated? It's this constant rush, rush, rush, that's the curse of American life. That's the reason that we're all of us so – Ow! For God's sake, don't *kick*, you idiot; this is only second down. Oh, my shin. My poor, poor shin, that I've had ever since I was a little girl!

Oh, no, no, no. Goodness, no. It didn't hurt the least little bit. And anyway it was my fault. Really it was. Truly. Well, you're just being sweet, to say that. It really was all my fault.

I wonder what I'd better do – kill him this instant, with my naked hands, or wait and let him drop in his traces. Maybe it's best not to make a scene. I guess I'll just lie low, and watch the pace get him. He can't keep this up indefinitely – he's only flesh and blood. Die he must, and die he shall, for what he did to me. I don't want to be of the oversensitive type, but you can't tell me that kick was unpremeditated. Freud says there are no accidents. I've led no cloistered life, I've known dancing partners who have spoiled my slippers and torn my dress; but when it comes to kicking, I am Outraged Womanhood. When you kick me in the shin, *smile*.

Maybe he didn't do it maliciously. Maybe it's just his way of showing his high spirits. I suppose I ought to be glad that one of us is having such a good time. I suppose I ought to think myself lucky if he brings me back alive. Maybe it's captious to demand of a practically strange man that he leave your shins as he found them. After all, the poor boy's doing the best he can. Probably he grew up in the hill country, and never had no larnin'. I bet they had to throw him on his back to get shoes on him.

Yes, it's lovely, isn't it? It's simply lovely. It's the loveliest waltz. Isn't it? Oh, I think it's lovely, too.

Why, I'm getting positively drawn to the Triple Threat here. He's my hero. He has the heart of a lion, and the sinews of a buffalo. Look at him – never a thought of the consequences, never afraid of his face, hurling himself into every scrimmage, eyes shining, cheeks ablaze. And shall it be said that I hung back? No, a thousand times no. What's it to me if I have to spend the next couple of years in a plaster cast? Come on, Butch, right through them! Who wants to live for ever?

Oh. Oh, dear. Oh, he's all right, thank goodness. For a while I thought they'd have to carry him off the field. Ah, I couldn't bear to have anything happen to him. I love him. I love him better than anybody in the world.

Look at the spirit he gets into a dreary, commonplace waltz; how effete the other dancers seem, beside him. He is youth and vigor and courage, he is strength and gaiety and – *Ow!* Get off my instep, you hulking peasant! What do you think I am, anyway – a gangplank? *Ow!*

No, of course it didn't hurt. Why, it didn't a bit. Honestly. And it was all my fault. You see, that little step of yours – well, it's perfectly lovely, but it's just a tiny bit tricky to follow at first. Oh, did you work it up yourself? You really did? Well, aren't you amazing! Oh, now I think I've got it. Oh, I think it's lovely. I was watching you do it when you were dancing before. It's awfully effective when you look at it.

It's awfully effective when you look at it. I bet I'm awfully effective when you look at me. My hair is hanging along my cheeks, my skirt is swaddled about me, I can feel the cold damp of my brow. I must look like something out of the 'Fall of the House of Usher.' This sort of thing takes a fearful toll of a woman my age. And he worked up his little step himself, he with his degenerate cunning. And it was just a tiny bit tricky at first, but now I think I've got it. Two stumbles, slip, and a twenty-yard dash; yes. I've got it. I've got several other things, too, including a split shin and a bitter heart. I hate this creature I'm chained to. I hated him the moment I saw his leering, bestial face. And here I've been locked in his noxious embrace for the thirty-five years this waltz has lasted. Is that orchestra never going to stop playing? Or must this obscene travesty of a dance go on until hell burns out?

Oh, they're going to play another encore. Oh, goody. Oh, that's lovely. Tired? I should say I'm not tired. I'd like to go on like this for ever.

I should say I'm not tired. I'm dead, that's all I am. Dead, and in what a cause! And the music is never going to stop playing, and we're going on like this, Double-Time Charlie and I, throughout eternity. I suppose I won't care any more, after the first hundred thousand years. I suppose nothing will matter then, not heat nor pain nor broken heart nor cruel, aching weariness. Well. It can't come too soon for me.

I wonder why I didn't tell him I was tired. I wonder why I didn't suggest going back to the table. I could have said let's just listen to the music. Yes, and if he would, that would be the first bit of attention he has given it all evening. George Jean Nathan said that the lovely rhythms of the waltz should be listened to in stillness and not be accompanied by strange gyrations of the human body. I think that's what he said. I think it was George Jean Nathan. Anyhow, whatever he said whoever he was and whatever he's doing now, he's better off than I am. That's safe. Anybody who isn't waltzing with this Mrs O'Leary's cow I've got here is having a good time.

Still if we were back at the table, I'd probably have to talk to him. Look at him – what could you say to a thing like that! Did you go to the circus this year, what's your favorite kind of ice-cream, how do you spell cat? I guess I'm as well off here. As well off as if I were in a cement mixer in full action.

I'm past all feeling now. The only way I can tell when he steps on me is that I can hear the splintering of bones. And all the events of my life are passing before my eyes. There was the time I was in a hurricane in the West Indies, there was the day I got my head cut open in the taxi smash, there was the night the drunken lady threw a bronze ash-tray at her own true love and got me instead, there was that summer that the sailboat kept capsizing. Ah, what an easy, peaceful time was mine, until I fell in with Swifty, here. I didn't know what trouble was, before I got drawn into this *danse macabre*. I think my mind is beginning to wander. It almost seems to me as if the orchestra were stopping. It couldn't be, of course; it could never, never be. And yet in my ears there is a silence like the sound of angel voices . . .

Oh, they've stopped, the mean things. They're not going to play any more. Oh darn. Oh, do you think they would? Do you really think so, if you gave them twenty dollars? Oh, that would be lovely. And look, do tell them to play this same thing. I'd simply adore to go on waltzing.

EVELYN WAUGH

Excursion in Reality

Evelyn Waugh (1903–66) was born in Hampstead, London, and first hoped to be an artist. He turned to fiction with his 'illustrated novelette' *Decline and Fall* (1928), one of the most significant novels to come from the bright, bitter 1920s, and about its moral chaos, the world of its Bright Young Things, and the spinning rush of modern absurdities in which they find themselves. Waugh ranks among the finest of modern British writers, though sometimes undervalued because he used comedy as the way into his intensely serious (and increasingly religious) vision of modern life. He is one of the makers of a true modern humour, fast-paced, absurdist, often extreme and 'black'. Waugh followed the story of his generation through works of increasing complexity and seriousness, including the comic tragedy *A Handful of Dust* (1934), the brilliant satire of the press *Scoop* (1938), and the powerful if sentimental evocation of emotional tragedy, political mis-management and troubled Catholicism in the interwar years, *Brideshead Revisited* (1945). His novel about Californian burial rites, *The Loved One* (1948), showcases his supreme skill at international 'black humour'.

'Excursion in Reality', from *Mr Loveday's Little Outing and Other Sad Stories* (1936), is one of the regrettably few short stories he wrote. It shows his ironic view of a time when daily reality has acquired just the same fantastic surreality as the world of movie-making, which the story's small hero, the writer Simon Lent, perhaps unwisely enters, having 'modernly' decided that the age of the printed word is finished and the writer has to become a member of the working proletariat. The story shows something that is always at the heart of Waugh's tragicomic vision: there is a fundamental disorder in the world that can only be met with the grim comic awareness that nothing in modern life is 'normal' or 'real' – that unreality is the one reality. Waugh remains central to modern comic writing because beyond his sense of farce and absurdity is one of pain and dismay, as well as because his fast, hard, filmic method of story-telling has a pervasive quality of modernity.

The commissionaire at Espinoza's restaurant seems to maintain under his particular authority all the most decrepit taxicabs in London. He is a commanding man; across his great chest the student of military medals may construe a tale of heroism and experience; Boer farms sink to ashes, fanatical Fuzzi-wuzzies hurl themselves to paradise, supercilious mandarins survey the smashing of their porcelain and rending of fine silk, in that triple row of decorations. He has only to run from the steps of Espinoza's to call to your service a vehicle as crazy as all the enemies of the King-Emperor.

Half a crown into the white cotton glove, because Simon Lent was too tired to ask for change. He and Sylvia huddled into the darkness on broken springs, between draughty windows. It had been an unsatisfactory evening. They had sat over their table until two because it was an extension night. Sylvia would not drink anything because Simon had said he was broke. So they sat for five or six hours, sometimes silent, sometimes bickering, sometimes exchanging listless greetings with the passing couples. Simon dropped Sylvia at her door; a kiss, clumsily offered, coldly accepted; then back to the attic flat, over a sleepless garage, for which Simon paid six guineas a week.

Outside his door they were sluicing a limousine. He squeezed round it and climbed the narrow stairs that had once echoed to the whistling of ostlers, stamping down to the stables before dawn. (Woe to young men in Mewses! Oh woe to bachelors half in love, living on £800 a year!) There was a small heap of letters on his dressing-table, which had arrived that evening while he was dressing. He lit his gas fire and began to open them. Tailor's bill £56, hosier £43; a reminder that his club subscription for that year had not yet been paid; his account from Espinoza's with a note informing him that the terms were strict, net cash monthly, and that no further credit would be extended to him; 'it appeared from the books' of his bank that his last cheque overdrew his account £10 16s. beyond the limit of his guaranteed overdraft; a demand from the income-tax collector for particulars of his employees and their wages (Mrs Shaw, who came in to make his bed and orange juice for 4s 6d a day); small bills for books, spectacles, cigars, hair lotion and Sylvia's last four birthday presents. (Woe to shops that serve young men in Mewses!).

The other part of his mail was in marked contrast to this. There was a box of preserved figs from an admirer in Fresno, California; two letters from young ladies who said they were composing papers about his work for their college literary societies, and would he send a photograph; press cuttings describing him as a 'popular', 'brilliant', 'meteorically success-ful', and 'enviable' young novelist; a request for the loan of two hundred pounds from a paralysed journalist; an invitation to luncheon from Lady Metroland; six pages of closely reasoned abuse from a lunatic asylum in the North of England. For the truth, which no one who saw into Simon Lent's heart could possibly have suspected, was that he was in his way and within his limits quite a famous young man.

There was a last letter with a typewritten address which Simon opened with little expectation of pleasure. The page was headed with the name of a Film Studio in one of the suburbs of London. The letter was brief and businesslike:

> Dear Simon Lent [a form of address, he had noted before, largely favoured by the theatrical profession],
>
> I wonder whether you have ever considered writing for the Films. We should value your angle on a picture we are now making. Perhaps you would meet me for luncheon tomorrow at the Garrick Club and let me know your reactions to this. Will you leave a message with my night secretary some time before 8 a.m. tomorrow morning or with my day secretary after that hour?
>
> Cordially yours,

Below this were two words written in pen and ink which seemed to be *Jewee Mecceee* with below them the explanatory typescript (*Sir James Macrae*).

Simon read this through twice. Then he rang up Sir James Macrae and informed his night secretary that he would keep the luncheon appointment next day. He had barely put down the telephone before the bell rang.

'This is Sir James Macrae's night secretary speaking. Sir James would be very pleased if Mr Lent would come round and see him this evening at his house in Hampstead.'

Simon looked at his watch. It was nearly three. 'Well . . . it's rather late to go so far tonight . . .'

'Sir James is sending a car for you.'

Simon was no longer tired. As he waited for the car the telephone rang again. 'Simon,' said Sylvia's voice, 'are you asleep?' . . .

'No; in fact I'm just going out.'

'Simon . . . I say, was I beastly tonight?'

'Lousy.'

'Well, I thought you were lousy, too.'

'Never mind. See you some time.'

'Aren't you going to go on talking?'

'Can't, I'm afraid. I've got to do some work.'

'*Simon*, what *can* you mean?'

'Can't explain now. There's a car waiting.'

'When am I seeing you – tomorrow?'

'Well, I don't really know. Ring me up in the morning. Good night.'

A quarter of a mile away, Sylvia put down the telephone, rose from the hearthrug, where she had settled herself in the expectation of twenty minutes' intimate explanation and crept disconsolately into bed.

Simon bowled off to Hampstead through deserted streets. He sat back in the car in a state of pleasant excitement. Presently they began to climb the steep little hill and emergéd into an open space with a pond and the tops of trees, black and deep as a jungle in the darkness. The night butler admitted him to the low Georgian house and led him to the library, where Sir James Macrae was standing before the fire, dressed in ginger-coloured plus-fours. A table was laid with supper.

'Evening, Lent. Nice of you to come. Have to fit in business when I can. Cocoa or whisky? Have some rabbit pie; it's rather good. First chance of a meal I've had since breakfast. Ring for some more cocoa, there's a good chap. Now what was it you wanted to see me about?'

'Well, I thought *you* wanted to see *me*.'

'Did I? Very likely. Miss Bentham'll know. She arranged the appointment. You might ring the bell on the desk, will you?'

Simon rang and there instantly appeared the neat night secretary.

'Miss Bentham, what did I want to see Mr Lent about?'

'I'm afraid I couldn't say, Sir James. Miss Harper is responsible for Mr Lent. When I came on duty this evening I merely found a note from her asking me to fix an appointment as soon as possible.'

'Pity,' said Sir James. 'We'll have to wait until Miss Harper comes on tomorrow.'

'I think it was something about writing for films.'

'Very likely,' said Sir James. 'Sure to be something of the kind. I'll let you know without delay. Thanks for dropping in.' He put down his cup of cocoa and held out his hand with unaffected cordiality. 'Good-night, my dear boy.' He rang the bell for the night butler. 'Sanders, I want Benson to run Mr Lent back.'

'I'm sorry, sir. Benson has just gone down to the studio to fetch Miss Grits.'

'Pity,' said Sir James. 'Still, I expect you'll be able to pick up a taxi or something.'

2

Simon got to bed at half past four. At ten minutes past eight the telephone by his bed was ringing.

'Mr Lent? This is Sir James Macrae's secretary speaking. Sir James's car will call for you at half past eight to take you to the studio.'

'I shan't be ready as soon as that, I'm afraid.'

There was a shocked pause; then the day secretary said:

'Very well, Mr Lent. I will see if some alternative arrangement is possible and ring you in a few minutes.'

In the intervening time Simon fell asleep again. Then the bell woke him once more and the same impersonal voice addressed him.

'Mr Lent? I have spoken to Sir James. His car will call for you at eight forty-five.'

Simon dressed hastily. Mrs Shaw had not yet arrived, so there was no breakfast for him. He found some stale cake in the kitchen cupboard and was eating it when Sir James's car arrived. He took a slice down with him, still munching.

'You needn't have brought that,' said a severe voice from inside the car. 'Sir James has sent you some breakfast. Get in quickly; we're late.'

In the corner, huddled in rugs, sat a young woman in a jaunty red hat; she had bright eyes and a very firm mouth.

'I expect that you are Miss Harper.'

'No, I'm Elfreda Grits. We're working together on this film, I believe. I've been up all night with Sir James. If you don't mind I'll go to sleep for twenty minutes. You'll find a thermos of cocoa and some rabbit pie in the basket on the floor.'

'Does Sir James live on cocoa and rabbit pie?'

'No; those are the remains of his supper. Please don't talk. I want to sleep.'

Simon disregarded the pie, but poured some steaming cocoa into the metal cap of the thermos flask. In the corner Miss Grits composed herself for sleep. She took off the jaunty red hat and laid it between them on the seat, veiled her eyes with two blue-pigmented lids and allowed the firm lips to relax and gape a little. Her platinum-blonde windswept head bobbed and swayed with the motion of the car as they swept out of London through converging and diverging tramlines. Stucco gave place to brick and the façades of the tube stations changed from tile to concrete; unoccupied building plots appeared and newly-planted trees along unnamed avenues. Five minutes exactly before their arrival at the studio Miss Grits opened her eyes, powdered her nose, touched her lips with red, and pulling her hat on to the side of her scalp, sat bolt upright, ready for another day.

Sir James was at work on the lot when they arrived. In a white-hot incandescent hell two young people were carrying on an infinitely tedious conversation at what was presumably the table of a restaurant. A dozen emaciated couples in evening dress danced listlessly behind them. At the other end of the huge shed some carpenters were at work building the façade of a Tudor manor house. Men in eyeshades scuttled in and out.

Notices stood everywhere. 'Do not Smoke.' 'Do not Speak.' 'Keep away from the high-power cable.'

Miss Grits, in defiance of these regulations, lit a cigarette, kicked some electric apparatus out of her path, said, 'He's busy. I expect he'll see us when he's through with this scene,' and disappeared through a door marked 'No admittance'.

Shortly after eleven o'clock Sir James caught sight of Simon. 'Nice of you to come. Shan't be long now,' he called out to him. 'Mr Briggs, get a chair for Mr Lent.'

At two o'clock he noticed him again. 'Had any lunch?'

'No,' said Simon.

'No more have I. Just coming.'

At half past three Miss Grits joined him and said: 'Well, it's been an easy day so far. You mustn't think we're always as slack as this. There's a canteen across the yard. Come and have something to eat.'

An enormous buffet was full of people in a variety of costumes and make-up. Disappointed actresses in languorous attitudes served cups of tea and hard-boiled eggs. Simon and Miss Grits ordered sandwiches and were about to eat them when a loudspeaker above their heads suddenly announced with alarming distinctness, 'Sir James Macrae calling Mr Lent and Miss Grits in the Conference Room.'

'Come on, quick,' said Miss Grits. She bustled him through the swing doors, across the yard, into the office buildings and up a flight of stairs to a solid oak door marked 'Conference. Keep out'.

Too late.

'Sir James has been called away,' said the secretary. 'Will you meet him at the West End office at five thirty.'

Back to London, this time by tube. At five thirty they were at the Piccadilly office ready for the next clue in their treasure hunt. This took them to Hampstead. Finally at eight they were back at the studio. Miss Grits showed no sign of exhaustion.

'Decent of the old boy to give us a day off,' she remarked. 'He's easy to work with in that way – after Hollywood. Let's get some supper.'

But as they opened the canteen doors and felt the warm breath of light refreshments, the loudspeaker again announced: 'Sir James Macrae calling Mr Lent and Miss Grits in the Conference Room.'

This time they were not too late. Sir James was there at the head of an oval table; round him were grouped the chiefs of his staff. He sat in a greatcoat with his head hung forward, elbows on the table and his hands clasped behind his neck. The staff sat in respectful sympathy. Presently he looked up, shook himself and smiled pleasantly.

'Nice of you to come,' he said. 'Sorry I couldn't see you before. Lots of small things to see to on a job like this. Had dinner?'

41

'Not yet.'

'Pity. Have to eat, you know. Can't work at full pressure unless you eat plenty.'

Then Simon and Miss Grits sat down and Sir James explained his plan. 'I want, ladies and gentlemen, to introduce Mr Lent to you. I'm sure you all know his name already and I daresay some of you know his work. Well, I've called him in to help us and I hope that when he's heard the plan he'll consent to join us. I want to produce a film of *Hamlet*. I daresay you don't think that's a very original idea – but it's Angle that counts in the film world. I'm going to do it from an entirely new angle. That's why I've called in Mr Lent. I want him to write dialogue for us.'

'But surely,' said Simon, 'there's quite a lot of dialogue there already?'

'Ah, you don't see my angle. There have been plenty of productions of Shakespeare in modern dress. We are going to produce him in modern speech. How can you expect the public to enjoy Shakespeare when they can't make head or tail of the dialogue. D'you know I began reading a copy the other day and blessed if *I* could understand it. At once I said, "What the public wants is Shakespeare with all his beauty of thought and character translated into the language of every day life." Now Mr Lent here was the man whose name naturally suggested itself. Many of the most high-class critics have commended Mr Lent's dialogue. Now my idea is that Miss Grits here shall act in an advisory capacity, helping with the continuity and the technical side, and that Mr Lent shall be given a free hand with the scenario . . .'

The discourse lasted for a quarter of an hour; then the chiefs of staff nodded sagely; Simon was taken into another room and given a contract to sign by which he received £50 a week retaining fee and £250 advance.

'You had better fix up with Miss Grits the times of work most suitable to you. I shall expect your first treatment by the end of the week. I should go and get some dinner if I were you. Must eat.'

Slightly dizzy, Simon hurried to the canteen where two languorous blondes were packing up for the night.

'We've been on since four o'clock this morning,' they said, 'and the supers have eaten everything except the nougat. Sorry.'

Sucking a bar of nougat Simon emerged into the now deserted studio. On three sides of him, to the height of twelve feet, rose in appalling completeness the marble walls of the scene-restaurant; at his elbow a bottle of imitation champagne still stood in its pail of melted ice; above and beyond extended the vast gloom of rafters and ceiling.

'*Fact*,' said Simon to himself, 'the world of action . . . the pulse of life . . . Money, hunger . . . *Reality*.'

*

Next morning he was called with the words, 'Two young ladies waiting to see you.'

'Two?'

Simon put on his dressing-gown and, orange juice in hand, entered his sitting room. Miss Grits nodded pleasantly.

'We arranged to start at ten,' she said. 'But it doesn't really matter. I shall not require you very much in the early stages. This is Miss Dawkins. She is one of the staff stenographers. Sir James thought you would need one. Miss Dawkins will be attached to you until further notice. He also sent two copies of *Hamlet*. When you've had your bath, I'll read you my notes for our first treatment.'

But this was not to be; before Simon was dressed Miss Grits had been recalled to the studio on urgent business.

'I'll ring up and tell you when I am free,' she said.

Simon spent the morning dictating letters to everyone he could think of; they began – *Please forgive me for dictating this, but I am so busy just now that I have little time for personal correspondence* . . . Miss Dawkins sat deferentially over her pad. He gave her Sylvia's number.

'Will you get on to this number and present my compliments to Miss Lennox and ask her to luncheon at Espinoza's . . . And book a table for two there at one forty-five.'

'Darling,' said Sylvia, when they met, 'why were you out all yesterday, and *who* was that voice this morning?'

'Oh, that was Miss Dawkins, my stenographer.'

'Simon, what *can* you mean?'

'You see, I've joined the film industry.'

'*Darling*. Do give me a job.'

'Well, I'm not paying much attention to casting at the moment – but I'll bear you in mind.'

'Goodness. How you've changed in two days!'

'Yes!' said Simon, with great complacency. 'Yes, I think I have. You see, for the first time in my life I have come into contact with Real Life. I'm going to give up writing novels. It was a mug's game anyway. The written word is dead – first the papyrus, then the printed book, now the film. The artist must no longer work alone. He is part of the age in which he lives; he must share (only of course, my dear Sylvia, in very different proportions) the weekly wage envelope of the proletarian. Vital art implies a corresponding set of social relationships. Co-operation . . . co-ordination . . . the hive endeavour of the community directed to a single end . . .'

Simon continued in this strain at some length, eating meantime a luncheon of Dickensian dimensions, until, in a small miserable voice, Sylvia said: 'It seems to me that you've fallen for some ghastly film star.'

'Oh God,' said Simon, 'only a virgin could be as vulgar as that.'

They were about to start one of their old, interminable quarrels when the telephone boy brought a message that Miss Grits wished to resume work instantly.

'So that's her name,' said Sylvia.

'If you only knew how funny that was,' said Simon, scribbling his initials on the bill and leaving the table while Sylvia was still groping with gloves and bag.

As things turned out, however, he became Miss Grits' lover before the week was out. The idea was hers. She suggested it to him one evening at his flat as they corrected the typescript of the final version of their first treatment.

'No, really,' Simon said aghast. 'No, really. It would be quite impossible. I'm sorry, but . . .'

'Why? Don't you like women?'

'Yes, but . . .'

'Oh, come along,' Miss Grits said briskly. 'We don't get much time for amusement . . .' And later, as she packed their manuscripts into her attaché case she said, 'We must do it again if we have time. Besides I find it's so much easier to work with a man if you're having an *affaire* with him.'

3

For three weeks Simon and Miss Grits (he always thought of her by this name in spite of all subsequent intimacies) worked together in complete harmony. His life was redirected and transfigured. No longer did he lie in bed, glumly preparing himself for the coming day; no longer did he say every morning 'I *must* get down to the country and finish that book,' and every evening find himself slinking back to the same urban flat; no longer did he sit over supper tables with Sylvia, idly bickering; no more listless explanations over the telephone. Instead he pursued a routine of incalculable variety, summoned by telephone at all hours to conferences which rarely assembled; sometimes to Hampstead, sometimes to the studios, once to Brighton. He spent long periods of work pacing up and down his sitting room, with Miss Grits pacing backwards and forwards along the other wall and Miss Dawkins obediently perched between them, as the two dictated, corrected and redrafted their scenario. There were meals at improbable times and vivid, unsentimental passages of love with Miss Grits. He ate irregular and improbable meals, bowling through the suburbs in Sir James's car, pacing the carpet dictating to Miss Dawkins, perched in deserted lots upon scenery which seemed made to survive the collapse of civilization. He lapsed, like Miss Grits, into brief spells of death-like unconsciousness, often awakening, startled, to find that a street or desert or factory had come into being about him while he slept.

The film meanwhile grew rapidly, daily putting out new shoots and changing under their eyes in a hundred unexpected ways. Each conference produced some radical change in the story. Miss Grits in her precise, invariable voice would read out the fruits of their work. Sir James would sit with his head in his hand, rocking slightly from side to side and giving vent to occasional low moans and whimpers: round him sat the experts – production, direction, casting, continuity, cutting and costing managers, bright eyes, eager to attract the great man's attention with some apt intrusion.

'Well,' Sir James would say, 'I think we can OK that. Any suggestions, gentlemen?'

There would be a pause, until one by one the experts began to deliver their contributions . . . 'I've been thinking, sir, that it won't do to have the scene laid in Denmark. The public won't stand for travel stuff. How about setting it in Scotland – then we could have some kilts and clan-gathering scenes?'

'Yes, that's a very sensible suggestion. Make a note of that, Lent . . .'

'I was thinking we'd better drop this character of the Queen. She'd much better be dead before the action starts. She hangs up the action. The public won't stand for him abusing his mother.'

'Yes, make a note of that, Lent.'

'How would it be, sir, to make the ghost the Queen instead of the King . . .'

'Yes, make a note of that, Lent . . .'

'Don't you think, sir, it would be better if Ophelia were Horatio's sister. More poignant, if you see what I mean.'

'Yes, make a note of that . . .'

'I think we are losing sight of the essence of the story in the last sequence. After all, it is first and foremost a Ghost Story, isn't it . . .'

And so from simple beginnings the story spread majestically. It was in the second week that Sir James, after, it must be admitted, considerable debate, adopted the idea of incorporating with it the story of *Macbeth*. Simon was opposed to the proposition at first, but the appeal of the three witches proved too strong. The title was then changed to *The White Lady of Dunsinane*, and he and Miss Grits settled down to a prodigious week's work in rewriting their entire scenarios.

4

The end came as suddenly as everything else in this remarkable episode.

The third conference was being held at an hotel in the New Forest where Sir James happened to be staying; the experts had assembled by train, car and motor-bicycle at a moment's notice and were tired and unresponsive. Miss Grits read the latest scenario; it took some time, for it had now reached the stage when it could be taken as 'white script' ready for shooting. Sir James sat sunk in reflection longer than usual. When he raised his head, it was to utter the single word:

'No.'

'No?'

'No, it won't do. We must scrap the whole thing. We've got much too far from the original story. I can't think why you need introduce Julius Caesar and King Arthur at all.'

'But, sir, they were your own suggestions at the last conference.'

'Were they? Well, I can't help it. I must have been tired and not paying full attention . . . Besides, I don't like the dialogue. It misses all the poetry of the original. What the public wants is Shakespeare, the whole of Shakespeare and nothing but Shakespeare. Now this scenario you've written is all very well in its way – but it's not Shakespeare. I'll tell you what we'll do. We'll use the play exactly as he wrote it and record from that. Make a note of it, Miss Grits.'

'Then you'll hardly require my services any more?' said Simon.

'No, I don't think I shall. Still, nice of you to have come.'

Next morning Simon woke bright and cheerful as usual and was about to leap from his bed when he suddenly remembered the events of last night. There was nothing for him to do. An empty day lay before him. No Miss Grits, no Miss Dawkins, no scampering off to conferences or dictating of dialogue. He rang up Miss Grits and asked her to lunch with him.

'No, quite impossible, I'm afraid. I have to do the continuity for a scenario of St John's Gospel before the end of the week. Pretty tough job. We're setting it in Algeria so as to get the atmosphere. Off to Hollywood next month. Don't suppose I shall see you again. Goodbye.'

Simon lay in bed with all his energy slowly slipping away. Nothing to do. Well, he supposed, now was the time to go away to the country and get on with his novel. Or should he go abroad? Some quiet café-restaurant in the sun where he could work out those intractable last chapters. That was what he would do . . . some time . . . the end of the week perhaps.

Meanwhile he leaned over on his elbow, lifted the telephone and, asking for Sylvia's number, prepared himself for twenty-five minutes' acrimonious reconciliation.

JORGE LUIS BORGES

Pierre Menard, Author of Don Quixote

Jorge Luis Borges (1899–1986) was born in Buenos Aires, Argentina. His family were of polyglot background, and were in Europe when the Great War broke out. Borges spent most of the wartime years in Switzerland and then went for a time to Spain where, a bookish young man, he began to write under the influence of Spanish modernism. Back in Argentina in the 1920s, he became well known as an avant-garde poet. Towards the end of the 1930s he began writing short fiction, producing the volume *Ficciones* in 1944. Though his output remained modest (less than fifty stories), he became one of the best-known and most influential of late modernist writers when his international fame grew in the 1950s and 1960s.

'Pierre Menard, Author of Don Quixote' is one of the earliest (written in 1939) and the most famous of his stories. Like many of his works, it turns on a fundamental literary joke: would a work written under the name of another man with a different mental history, and published at another time, still be the great work we believe it to be under its present credentials? (Cervantes – author of what is generally called the first novel, a major comic work – was himself aware of just these same ambiguities, and played with them in his magnificent work.) The joke is about an absurd task, but it is fundamentally serious. We read many things into books – their supposed author, the time they were written – and detached from those things they become what essentially they are: texts. Borges returned writing to being writing, and then explored its ambiguities. He did it with the profound intellectual wit that made him a major twentieth-century figure. 'Pierre Menard', alongside Borges' other teasing stories and parodies (and the work of fellow authors like Beckett, Queneau, and Nabokov), connected fiction to its own comic beginnings and the huge, confusing library of all past literature – to which, after all, every new piece of writing must be a footnote.

The *visible* works left by this novelist are easily and briefly enumerated. It is therefore impossible to forgive the omissions and additions perpetrated by Madame Henri Bachelier in a fallacious catalogue that a certain newspaper, whose Protestant tendencies are no secret, was inconsiderate enough to inflict on its wretched readers – even though they are few and Calvinist, if not Masonic and circumcised. Menard's true friends regarded this catalogue with alarm, and even with a certain sadness. It is as if yesterday we were gathered together before the final marble and the fateful cypresses, and already Error is trying to tarnish his Memory . . . Decidedly, a brief rectification is inevitable.

I am certain that it would be very easy to challenge my meagre authority. I hope, nevertheless, that I will not be prevented from mentioning two important testimonials. The Baroness de Bacourt (at whose unforgettable *vendredis* I had the honour of becoming acquainted with the late lamented poet) has seen fit to approve these lines. The Countess de Bagnoregio, one of the most refined minds in the Principality of Monaco (and now of Pittsburgh, Pennsylvania, since her recent marriage to the international philanthropist Simon Kautsch who, alas, has been so slandered by the victims of his disinterested handiwork), has sacrificed to 'truth and death' (those are her words) that majestic reserve which distinguishes her, and in an open letter published in the magazine *Luxe* also grants me her consent. These authorizations, I believe, are not insufficient.

I have said that Menard's *visible* lifework is easily enumerated. Having carefully examined his private archives, I have been able to verify that it consists of the following:

(a) A symbolist sonnet which appeared twice (with variations) in the magazine *La Conque* (the March and October issues of 1899).

(b) A monograph on the possibility of constructing a poetic vocabulary of concepts that would not be synonyms or periphrases of those which make up ordinary language, 'but ideal objects created by means of common agreement and destined essentially to fill poetic needs' (Nîmes, 1901).

(c) A monograph on 'certain connections or affinities' among the ideas of Descartes, Leibnitz and John Wilkins (Nîmes, 1903).

(d) A monograph on the *Characteristica Universalis* of Leibnitz (Nîmes, 1904).

(e) A technical article on the possibility of enriching the game of chess by means of eliminating one of the rooks' pawns. Menard proposes, recommends, disputes, and ends by rejecting this innovation.

(f) A monograph on the *Ars Magna Generalis* of Ramón Lull (Nîmes, 1906).

(g) A translation with prologue and notes of the *Libro de la invención y arte del juego del axedrez* by Ruy López de Segura (Paris, 1907).

(h) The rough draft of a monograph on the symbolic logic of George Boole.

(i) An examination of the metric laws essential to French prose, illustrated with examples from Saint-Simon (*Revue des langues romanes*, Montpellier, October, 1909).

(j) An answer to Luc Durtain (who had denied the existence of such laws) illustrated with examples from Luc Durtain (*Revue des langues romanes*, Montpellier, December, 1909).

(k) A manuscript translation of the *Aguja de navegar cultos* of Quevedo, entitled *La boussole des précieux*.

(l) A preface to the catalogue of the exposition of lithographs by Carolus Hourcade (Nîmes, 1914).

(m) His work, *Les problèmes d'un problème* (Paris, 1917), which takes up in chronological order the various solutions of the famous problem of Achilles and the tortoise. Two editions of this book have appeared so far; the second has as an epigraph Leibnitz' advice 'Ne craignez point, monsieur, la tortue', and contains revisions of the chapters dedicated to Russell and Descartes.

(n) An obstinate analysis of the 'syntactic habits' of Toulet (*N.R.F.*, March, 1921). I remember that Menard used to declare that censuring and praising were sentimental operations which had nothing to do with criticism.

(o) A transposition into Alexandrines of *Le Cimetière marin* of Paul Valéry (*N.R.F.*, January, 1928).

(p) An invective against Paul Valéry in the *Journal for the Suppression of Reality* of Jacques Reboul. (This invective, it should be stated parenthetically, is the exact reverse of his true opinion of Valéry. The latter understood it as such, and the old friendship between the two was never endangered.)

(q) A 'definition' of the Countess of Bagnoregio in the 'victorious volume' – the phrase is that of another collaborator, Gabriele d'Annunzio – which this lady publishes yearly to rectify the inevitable falsifications of journalism and to present 'to the world and to Italy' an authentic effigy of her person, which is so exposed (by reason of her beauty and her activities) to erroneous or hasty interpretations.

(r) A cycle of admirable sonnets for the Baroness de Bacourt (1934).

(s) A manuscript list of verses which owe their effectiveness to punctuation.*

Up to this point (with no other omission than that of some vague,

* Madame Henri Bachelier also lists a literal translation of a literal translation done by Quevedo of the *Introduction à la vie dévote* of St Francis of Sales. In Pierre Menard's library there are no traces of such a work. She must have misunderstood a remark of his which he had intended as a joke.

circumstantial sonnets for the hospitable, or greedy, album of Madame Henri Bachelier) we have the *visible* part of Menard's works in chronological order. Now I will pass over to that other part, which is subterranean, interminably heroic, and unequalled, and which is also – oh, the possibilities inherent in the man! – inconclusive. This work, possibly the most significant of our time, consists of the ninth and thirty-eighth chapters of Part One of *Don Quixote* and a fragment of the twenty-second chapter. I realize that such an affirmation seems absurd; but the justification of this 'absurdity' is the primary object of this note.*

Two texts of unequal value inspired the undertaking. One was that philological fragment of Novalis – No. 2005 of the Dresden edition – which outlines the theme of *total* identification with a specific author. The other was one of those parasitic books which places Christ on a boulevard, Hamlet on the Cannebière and Don Quixote on Wall Street. Like any man of good taste, Menard detested these useless carnivals, only suitable – he used to say – for evoking plebeian delight in anachronism, or (what is worse) charming us with the primary idea that all epochs are the same, or that they are different. He considered more interesting, even though it had been carried out in a contradictory and superficial way, Daudet's famous plan: to unite, in *one* figure, Tartarin, the Ingenious Gentleman and his squire . . . Any insinuation that Menard dedicated his life to the writing of a contemporary *Don Quixote* is a calumny of his illustrious memory.

He did not want to compose another *Don Quixote* – which would be so easy – but *the Don Quixote*. It is unnecessary to add that his aim was never to produce a mechanical transcription of the original; he did not propose to copy it. His admirable ambition was to produce pages which would coincide – word for word and line for line – with those of Miguel de Cervantes.

'My intent is merely astonishing,' he wrote me from Bayonne on 30 December, 1934. 'The ultimate goal of a theological or metaphysical demonstration – the external world, God, chance, universal forms – is no less anterior or common than this novel which I am now developing. The only difference is that philosophers publish in pleasant volumes the intermediary stages of their work and that I have decided to lose them.' And, in fact, not one page of a rough draft remains to bear witness to this work of years.

The initial method he conceived was relatively simple: to know Spanish well, to re-embrace the Catholic faith, to fight against Moors and Turks, to forget European history between 1602 and 1918, and to *be* Miguel de

---

* I also had another, secondary intent – that of sketching a portrait of Pierre Menard. But how would I dare to compete with the golden pages the Baroness de Bacourt tells me she is preparing, or with the delicate and precise pencil of Carolus Hourcade?

Cervantes. Pierre Menard studied this procedure (I know that he arrived at a rather faithful handling of seventeenth-century Spanish) but rejected it as too easy. Rather because it was impossible, the reader will say! I agree, but the undertaking was impossible from the start, and of all the possible means of carrying it out, this one was the least interesting. To be, in the twentieth century, a popular novelist of the seventeenth seemed to him a diminution. To be, in some way, Cervantes and to arrive at *Don Quixote* seemed to him less arduous – and consequently less interesting – than to continue being Pierre Menard and to arrive at *Don Quixote* through the experiences of Pierre Menard. (This conviction, let it be said in passing, forced him to exclude the autobiographical prologue of the second part of *Don Quixote*. To include this prologue would have meant creating another personage – Cervantes – but it would also have meant presenting *Don Quixote* as the work of this personage and not of Menard. He naturally denied himself such an easy solution.) 'My undertaking is not essentially difficult,' I read in another part of the same letter. 'I would only have to be immortal in order to carry it out.' Shall I confess that I often imagine that he finished it and that I am reading *Don Quixote* – the entire work – as if Menard had conceived it? Several nights ago, while leafing through Chapter XXVI – which he had never attempted – I recognized our friend's style and, as it were, his voice in this exceptional phrase: *the nymphs of the rivers, mournful and humid Echo*. This effective combination of two adjectives, one moral and the other physical, reminded me of a line from Shakespeare which we discussed one afternoon:

Where a malignant and turbaned Turk . . .

Why precisely *Don Quixote*, our reader will ask. Such a preference would not have been inexplicable in a Spaniard; but it undoubtedly was in a symbolist from Nîmes, essentially devoted to Poe, who engendered Baudelaire, who engendered Mallarmé, who engendered Valéry, who engendered Edmond Teste. The letter quoted above clarifies this point. '*Don Quixote*,' Menard explains, 'interests me profoundly, but it does not seem to me to have been – how shall I say it – inevitable. I cannot imagine the universe without the interjection of Edgar Allan Poe

Ah, bear in mind this garden was enchanted!

or without the *Bateau ivre* or the *Ancient Mariner*, but I know that I am capable of imagining it without *Don Quixote*. (I speak, naturally, of my personal capacity, not of the historical repercussions of these works.) *Don Quixote* is an accidental book, *Don Quixote* is unnecessary. I can premeditate writing, I can write it, without incurring a tautology. When I was twelve or thirteen years old I read it, perhaps in its entirety. Since then I have reread several chapters attentively, but not the ones I am going to undertake. I have likewise studied the *entremeses*, the comedies, the *Galatea*, the exemplary novels, and the undoubtedly laborious efforts of *Pésiles y Sigismunda* and the *Viaje al Parnaso* . . . My general memory of *Don Quixote*, simplified by forgetfulness and indifference, is much the same as the imprecise, anterior image of a book not yet written. Once this image (which no one can deny me in good faith) has been postulated, my problems are undeniably considerably more difficult than those which Cervantes faced. My affable precursor did not refuse the collaboration of fate; he went along composing his immortal work a little *à la diable*, swept along by inertias of language and invention. I have contracted the mysterious duty of reconstructing literally his spontaneous work. My solitary game is governed by two polar laws. The first permits me to attempt variants of a formal and psychological nature; the second obliges me to sacrifice them to the "original" text and irrefutably to rationalize this annihilation . . . To these artificial obstacles one must add another congenital one. To compose *Don Quixote* at the beginning of the seventeenth century was a reasonable, necessary and perhaps inevitable undertaking; at the beginning of the twentieth century it is almost impossible. It is not in vain that three hundred years have passed, charged with the most complex happenings – among them, to mention only one, that same *Don Quixote*.'

In spite of these three obstacles, the fragmentary *Don Quixote* of Menard is more subtle than that of Cervantes. The latter indulges in a rather coarse opposition between tales of knighthood and the meagre, provincial reality of his country; Menard chooses as 'reality' the land of Carmen during the century of Lepanto and Lope. What Hispanophile would not have advised Maurice Barrès or Dr Rodríguez Larreta to make such a choice! Menard, as if it were the most natural thing in the world, eludes them. In his work there are neither bands of gypsies, conquistadors, mystics, Philip the Seconds, nor autos-da-fé. He disregards or proscribes local colour. This disdain indicates a new approach to the historical novel. This disdain condemns *Salammbô* without appeal.

It is no less astonishing to consider isolated chapters. Let us examine, for instance, Chapter XXXVIII of Part One 'which treats of the curious discourse that Don Quixote delivered on the subject of arms and letters'. As is known, Don Quixote (like Quevedo in a later, analogous passage of *La hora de todos*) passes judgment against letters and in favour of arms. Cervantes was an old soldier, which explains such a judgment. But that the *Don Quixote* of Pierre Menard – a contemporary of *La trahison des clercs* and Bertrand Russell – should relapse into these nebulous sophistries! Madame Bachelier has seen in them an admirable and typical subordination of the author to the psychology of the hero; others (by no means perspicaciously) a *transcription* of *Don Quixote*; the Baroness de Bacourt, the influence of Nietzsche. To this third interpretation (which seems to me irrefutable) I do not know if I would dare to add a fourth, which coincides very well with the divine modesty of Pierre Menard: his resigned or ironic habit of propounding ideas which were the strict reverse of those he preferred. (One will remember his diatribe against Paul Valéry in the ephemeral journal of the superrealist Jacques Reboul.) The text of Cervantes and that of Menard are verbally identical, but the second is almost infinitely richer. (More ambiguous, his detractors will say; but ambiguity is a richness.) It is a revelation to compare the *Don Quixote* of Menard with that of Cervantes. The latter, for instance, wrote (*Don Quixote*, Part One, Chapter Nine):

> . . . *la verdad, cuya madre es la historia, émula del tiempo, depósito de las acciones, testigo de lo pasado, ejemplo y aviso de lo presente, advertencia de lo por venir.*
> [. . . truth, whose mother is history, who is the rival of time, depository of deeds, witness of the past, example and lesson to the present, and warning to the future.]

Written in the seventeenth century, written by the 'ingenious layman' Cervantes, this enumeration is a mere rhetorical eulogy of history. Menard, on the other hand, writes:

> . . . *la verdad, cuya madre es la historia, émula del tiempo, depósito de las acciones, testigo de lo pasado, ejemplo y aviso de lo presente, advertencia de lo por venir.*
> [. . . truth, whose mother is history, who is the rival of time, depository of deeds, witness of the past, example and lesson to the present, and warning to the future.]

History, *mother* of truth; the idea is astounding. Menard, a contemporary of William James, does not define history as an investigation of reality, but as its origin. Historical truth, for him, is not what took place; it is what we think took place. The final clauses – *example and lesson to the present, and warning to the future* – are shamelessly pragmatic.

Equally vivid is the contrast in styles. The archaic style of Menard – in the last analysis, a foreigner – suffers from a certain affectation. Not so that of his precursor, who handles easily the ordinary Spanish of his time.

There is no intellectual exercise which is not ultimately useless. A philosophical doctrine is in the beginning a seemingly true description of the universe; as the years pass it becomes a mere chapter – if not a paragraph or a noun – in the history of philosophy. In literature, this ultimate decay is even more notorious. '*Don Quixote*,' Menard once told me, 'was above all an agreeable book; now it is an occasion for patriotic toasts, grammatical arrogance and obscene de-luxe editions. Glory is an incomprehension, and perhaps the worst.'

The nihilist arguments contain nothing new; what is unusual is the

54

decision Pierre Menard derived from them. He resolved to outstrip that vanity which awaits all the woes of mankind; he undertook a task that was complex in the extreme and futile from the outset. He dedicated his conscience and nightly studies to the repetition of a pre-existing book in a foreign tongue. The number of rough drafts kept on increasing; he tenaciously made corrections and tore up thousands of manuscript pages.* He did not permit them to be examined, and he took great care that they would not survive him. It is in vain that I have tried to reconstruct them.

I have thought that it is legitimate to consider the 'final' *Don Quixote* as a kind of palimpsest, in which should appear traces – tenuous but not undecipherable – of the 'previous' handwriting of our friend. Unfortunately, only a second Pierre Menard, inverting the work of the former, could exhume and resuscitate these Troys . . .

'To think, analyse and invent,' he also wrote me, 'are not anomalous acts, but the normal respiration of the intelligence. To glorify the occasional fulfilment of this function, to treasure ancient thoughts of others, to remember with incredulous amazement what the *doctor universalis* thought, is to confess our languor or barbarism. Every man should be capable of all ideas, and I believe that in the future he will be.'

Menard (perhaps without wishing to) has enriched, by means of a new technique, the hesitant and rudimentary art of reading: the technique is one of deliberate anachronism and erroneous attributions. This technique, with its infinite applications, urges us to run through the *Odyssey* as if it were written after the *Aeneid*, and to read *Le jardin du Centaure* by Madame Henri Bachelier as if it were by Madame Henri Bachelier. This technique would fill the dullest books with adventure. Would not the attributing of *The Imitation of Christ* to Louis Ferdinand Céline or James Joyce be a sufficient renovation of its tenuous spiritual counsels?

(Translated by Anthony Bonner)

---

* I remember his square-ruled notebooks, the black streaks where he had crossed out words, his peculiar typographical symbols and his insect-like handwriting. In the late afternoon he liked to go for walks on the outskirts of Nîmes; he would take a notebook with him and make a gay bonfire.

VLADIMIR NABOKOV

The Assistant Producer

Vladimir Nabokov (1899–1977) was born in St Petersburg, Russia, to a wealthy and famous family which was forced into exile by the Bolshevik Revolution. He became himself an *émigré*, studying at Cambridge, writing in Berlin, and then, in 1940, moving to the USA, where he began to write in English. His many novels include *The Real Life of Sebastian Knight* (1941), *Bend Sinister* (1948), the wonderfully comic *Pnin* (1957) and his famous satire on sex and America, *Lolita* (1955, Paris; 1958, USA). Later came the game- like poem-and-novel *Pale Fire* (1962) and the complex *Ada or Ardour: A Family Chronicle* (1969).

'The Assistant Producer', from his collection *Nabokov's Dozen: Thirteen Stories* (1958), and written in Boston in 1943, is typical of his work. It deals with a no doubt true and decidedly gloomy subject, the deceptions and murders to which Russian exiles were subjected by the Russian regime. (It is part of the tragic background to this tale that his own father was assassinated in Berlin.) But, if the theme is one of sadness and loss, the spirit is comic, and the prose style superb, showing Nabokov's inheritance from Gogol, Pushkin and the Russian symbolists, as well as his own very distinct voice ('I want all your attention now, for it would be a pity to miss the subtleties of the situation'). Nabokov creates a devious and disappointing world, but one that is redeemed by style, language and pure comic wit. He was to become one of the greatest of late-twentieth-century stylists, and a maker of some of its most complex comedy.

Meaning? Well, because sometimes life is merely that – an Assistant Producer. Tonight we shall go to the movies. Back to the thirties, and down the twenties, and round the corner to the old Europe Picture Palace. She was a celebrated singer. Not opera, not even *Cavalleria Rusticana*, not anything like that. 'La Slavska' – that is what the French called her. Style: one-tenth *tzigane*, one-seventh Russian peasant girl (she had been that herself originally), and five-ninths popular – and by popular I mean a hodge-podge of artificial folklore, military melodrama, and official patriotism. The fraction left unfilled seems sufficient to represent the physical splendour of her prodigious voice.

Coming from what was, geographically at least, the very heart of Russia, it eventually reached the big cities, Moscow, St Petersburg, and the Tsar's milieu where that sort of style was greatly appreciated. In Feodor Chaliapin's dressing room there hung a photograph of her; Russian headgear with pearls, hand propping cheek, dazzling teeth between fleshy lips, and a great clumsy scrawl right across: 'For you, Fedyusha.' Stars of snow, each revealing, before the edges melted, its complex symmetry, would gently come to rest on the shoulders and sleeves and moustaches and caps – all waiting in a queue for the box office to open. Up to her very death she treasured above all – or pretended to do so – a fancy medal and a huge brooch that had been given her by the Tsarina. They came from the firm of jewellers which used to do such profitable business by presenting the Imperial couple on every festive occasion with this or that emblem (each year increasing in worth) of massive Tsardom: some great lump of amethyst with a ruby-studded bronze troika stranded on top like a Noah's Ark on Mount Ararat, or a sphere of crystal the size of a water melon surmounted by a gold eagle with square diamond eyes very much like those of Rasputin (many years later some of the less symbolic ones were exhibited at a World's Fair by the Soviets as samples of their own thriving Art).

Had things gone on as they were seeming to go, she might have been still singing tonight in a central-heated Hall of Nobility or at Tsanskoye, and I should be turning off her broadcast voice in some remote corner of steppe-mother Siberia. But destiny took the wrong turning; and when the Revolution happened, followed by the War of the Reds and the Whites, her wily peasant soul chose the more practical party.

Ghostly multitudes of ghostly Cossacks on ghost-horseback are seen charging through the fading name of the assistant producer. Then dapper General Golubkov is disclosed idly scanning the battlefield through a pair of opera glasses. When movies and we were young, we used to be shown what the sights divulged neatly framed in two connected circles. Not now.

What we do see next is General Golubkov, all indolence suddenly gone, leaping into the saddle, looming sky-high for an instant on his rearing steed and then rocketing into a crazy attack.

But the unexpected is the infra-red in the spectrum of Art: instead of the conditional *ra-ta-ta* reflex of machine gunnery, a woman's voice is heard singing afar. Nearer, still nearer, and finally all-pervading. A gorgeous contralto voice expanding into whatever the musical director found in his files in the way of Russian lilt. Who is this leading the infra-Reds? A woman. The singing spirit of that particular, especially well-trained battalion. Marching in front, trampling the alfalfa and pouring her Volga-Volga song. Dapper and daring *djighit* Golubkov (now we know what he had descried), although wounded in several spots, manages to snatch her up on the gallop, and, lusciously struggling, she is borne away.

Strangely enough, that vile script was enacted in reality. I myself have known at least two reliable witnesses of the event; and the sentries of history have let it pass unchallenged. Very soon we find her maddening the officers' mess with her buxom beauty and wild, wild songs. She was a Belle Dame with a good deal of Merci, and there was a punch about her that Louise von Lenz or the Green Lady lacked. She it was who sweetened the general retreat of the Whites, which began shortly after her magic appearance at General Golubkov's camp. We get a gloomy glimpse of ravens, or crows, or whatever birds proved available, wheeling in the dusk and slowly descending upon a plain littered with bodies somewhere in Ventura County. A White soldier's dead hand is still clutching a medallion with his mother's face. A Red soldier nearby has on his shattered breast a letter from home with the same old woman blinking through the dissolving lines.

And then, in traditional contrast, pat comes a mighty burst of music and song with a rhythmic clapping of hands and stamping of booted feet and we see General Golubkov's staff in full revelry – a lithe Georgian dancing with a dagger, the self-conscious samovar reflecting distorted faces, the Slavska throwing her head back with a throaty laugh, and the fat man of the corps, horribly drunk, braided collar undone, greasy lips pursed for a bestial kiss, leaning across the table (close-up of an overturned glass) to hug – nothingness, for wiry and perfectly sober General Golubkov had deftly removed her and now, as they both stand facing the gang, says in a cold, clear voice: 'Gentlemen, I want to present you my bride' – and in the stunned silence that follows, a stray bullet from outside chances to shatter the dawn-blue window-pane, after which a roar of applause greets the glamorous couple.

There is little doubt that her capture had not been wholly a fortuitous occurrence. Indeterminism is banned from the studio. It is even less doubtful that when the great exodus began and they, as many others, meandered via Sirkedji to Motzstrasse and Rue Vaugirard, the General and his wife already formed one team, one song, one cipher. Quite naturally he became an efficient member of the WW (White Warriors Union), travelling about, organizing military courses for Russian boys, arranging relief concerts, unearthing barracks for the destitute, settling local disputes, and doing all this in a most unobtrusive manner. I suppose it was useful in some ways, that WW. Unfortunately for its spiritual welfare, it was quite incapable of cutting itself off from monarchist groups abroad and did not feel, as the *émigré* intelligentsia felt, the dreadful vulgarity, the Ur-Hitlerism of those ludicrous but vicious organizations. When well-meaning Americans ask me whether I knew charming Colonel So-and-So or grand old Count de Kickoffsky, I have not the heart to tell them the dismal truth.

But there was also another type of person connected with the WW. I am thinking of those adventurous souls who helped the cause by crossing the frontier through some snow-muffled fir forest, to potter about their native land in the various disguises worked out, oddly enough, by the social revolutionaries of yore, and quietly bring back to the little café in Paris called 'Esh-Bubliki', or to the little *Kneipe* in Berlin that had no special name, the kind of useful trifles which spies are supposed to bring back to their employers. Some of those men had become abstrusely entangled with the spying departments of other nations and would give an amusing jump if you came from behind and tapped them on the shoulder. A few went a-scouting for the fun of the thing. One or two perhaps really believed that in some mystical way they were preparing the resurrection of a sacred, if somewhat musty, past.

2

We are now going to witness a most weirdly monotonous series of events. The first president of the WW to die was the leader of the whole White movement and by far the best man of the lot; and certain dark symptoms attending his sudden illness suggested a poisoner's shadow. The next president, a huge, strong fellow with a voice of thunder and a head like a cannon ball, was kidnapped by persons unknown; and there are reasons to believe that he died from an overdose of chloroform. The third president – but my reel is going too fast. Actually it took seven years to remove the first two – not because this sort of thing cannot be done more briskly, but because there were particular circumstances that necessitated some very precise timing, so as to coordinate one's steady ascent with the spacing of sudden vacancies. Let us explain.

Golubkov was not only a very versatile spy (a triple agent to be exact);

he was also an exceedingly ambitious little fellow. Why the vision of presiding over an organization that was but a sunset behind a cemetery happened to be so dear to him is a conundrum only for those who have no hobbies or passions. He wanted it very badly – that is all. What is less intelligible is the faith he had in being able to safeguard his puny existence in the crush between the formidable parties whose dangerous money and dangerous help he received. I want all your attention now, for it would be a pity to miss the subtleties of the situation.

The Soviets could not be much disturbed by the highly improbable prospect of a phantom White Army ever being able to resume war operations against their consolidated bulk; but they could be very much irritated by the fact that scraps of information about forts and factories, gathered by elusive WW meddlers, were automatically falling into grateful German hands. The Germans were little interested in the recondite colour variations of *émigré* politics, but what did annoy them was the blunt patriotism of a WW president every now and then obstructing on ethical grounds the smooth flow of friendly collaboration.

Thus, General Golubkov was a godsend. The Soviet firmly expected that under his rule all WW spies would be well known to them – and shrewdly supplied with false information for eager German consumption. The Germans were equally sure that through him they would be guaranteed a good cropping of their own absolutely trustworthy agents distributed among the usual WW ones. Neither side had any illusions concerning Golubkov's loyalty, but each assumed that it would turn to its own profit the fluctuations of double-crossing. The dreams of simple Russian folk, hard-working families in remote parts of the Russian diaspora, plying their humble but honest trades, as they would in Saratov or Tver, bearing fragile children and naïvely believing that the WW was a kind of King Arthur's Round Table that stood for all that had been, and would be, sweet and decent and strong in fairy-tale Russia – these dreams may well strike the film pruners as an excrescence upon the main theme.

When the WW was founded, General Golubkov's candidacy (purely theoretical, of course, for nobody expected the leader to die) was very far down the list – not because his legendary gallantry was insufficiently appreciated by his fellow officers, but because he happened to be the youngest general in the army. Towards the time of the next president's election Golubkov had already disclosed such tremendous capacities as an organizer that he felt he could safely cross out quite a few intermediate names in the list, incidentally sparing the lives of their bearers. After the second general had been removed, many of the WW members were convinced that General Fedchenko, the next candidate, would surrender in favour of the younger and more efficient man the rights that his age, reputation, and academic distinction entitled him to enjoy. The old gentleman, however, though doubtful of the enjoyment, thought it cowardly to avoid a job that had cost two men their lives. So Golubkov set his teeth and started to dig again.

Physically he lacked attraction. There was nothing of your popular Russian general about him, nothing of that good, burly, pop-eyed, thick-necked sort. He was lean, frail, with sharp features, a clipped moustache, and the kind of haircut that is called by Russians 'hedgehog'; short, wiry, upright, and compact. There was a thin silver bracelet round his hairy wrist, and he offered you neat home-made Russian cigarettes or English 'Kapstens', as he pronounced it, snugly arranged in an old roomy cigarette case of black leather that had accompanied him through the presumable smoke of numberless battles. He was extremely polite and extremely inconspicuous.

Whenever the Slavska 'received', which she would do at the homes of her various Maecenases (a Baltic baron of sorts, a Dr Bachrach whose first wife had been a famous Carmen, or a Russian merchant of the old school who, in inflation-mad Berlin, was having a wonderful time buying up blocks of houses for ten pounds sterling apiece), her silent husband would unobtrusively thread his way among the visitors, bringing you a sausage-and-cucumber sandwich or a tiny frosty-pale glass of vodka; and while the Slavska sang (on these informal occasions she used to sing seated with her fist at her cheek and her elbow cupped in the palm of her other hand) he would stand apart, leaning against something, or would tiptoe towards a distant ash-tray which he would gently place on the fat arm of your chair.

I consider that, artistically, he overstressed his effacement, unwittingly introducing a hired-lackey note – which now seems singularly appropriate; but he of course was trying to base his existence upon the principle of contrast and would get a marvellous thrill from exactly knowing by certain sweet signs – a bent head, a rolling eye – that So-and-So at the far end of the room was drawing a newcomer's attention to the fascinating fact that such a dim, modest man was the hero of incredible exploits in a legendary war (taking towns single-handed and that sort of thing).

3

German film companies, which kept sprouting like poisonous mushrooms in those days (just before the child of light learned to talk), found cheap labour in hiring those among the Russian *émigrés* whose only hope and profession was their past – that is, a set of totally unreal people – to represent 'real' audiences in pictures. The dovetailing of one phantasm into another produced upon a sensitive person the impression of living in a Hall of Mirrors, or rather a prison of mirrors, and not even knowing which was the glass and which was yourself.

Indeed, when I recall the halls where the Slavska sang, both in Berlin and in Paris, and the type of people one saw there, I feel as if I were Technicoloring and sonorizing some very ancient motion picture where life had been a grey vibration and funerals a scamper, and where only the sea had been tinted (a sickly blue), while some hand machine imitated offstage the hiss of asynchronous surf. A certain shady character, the terror of relief organizations, a bald-headed man with mad eyes, slowly floats across my vision with his legs bent in a sitting position, like an elderly foetus, and then miraculously fits into a back-row seat. Our friend the Count is also here, complete with high collar and dingy spats. A venerable but worldly priest, with his cross gently heaving on his ample chest, sits in the front row and looks straight ahead.

The items of these Right Wing festivals that the Slavska's name evokes in my mind were of the same unreal nature as was her audience. A variety artist with a fake Slav name, one of those guitar virtuosos that come as a cheap first in music-hall programmes, would be most welcome here; and the flashy ornaments on his glass-panelled instrument, and his sky-blue silk pants, would go well with the rest of the show. Then some bearded old rascal in a shabby cut-away coat, former member of the Holy Russ First, would take the chair and vividly describe what the Israel-sons and the Phreemasons (two secret Semitic tribes) were doing to the Russian people.

And now, ladies and gentlemen, we have the great pleasure and honour – There she would stand against a dreadful background of palms and national flags, and moisten her rich painted lips with her pale tongue, and leisurely clasp her kid-gloved hands on her corseted stomach, while her constant accompanist, marble-faced Joseph Levinsky, who had followed her, in the shadow of her song, to the Tsar's private concert hall and to Comrade Lunacharsky's salon, and to nondescript places in Constantinople, produced his brief introductory series of stepping-stone notes.

Sometimes, if the house was of the right sort, she would sing the national anthem before launching upon her limited but ever welcome repertoire. Inevitably there would be that 'Old Road to Kaluga' (with a thunder-struck pine tree at the forty-ninth verse), and the one that begins, in the German translation printed beneath the Russian text, '*Du bist im Schnee begraben, mein Russland*', and the ancient folk-ballad (written by a private person in the eighties) about the robber chieftain and his lovely Persian Princess, whom he threw into the Volga when his crew accused him of going soft.

Her artistic taste was nowhere, her technique haphazard, her general style atrocious; but the kind of people for whom music and sentiment are one, or who like songs to be mediums for the spirits of circumstances under which they had been first apprehended in an individual past, gratefully found in the tremendous sonorities of her voice both a nostalgic solace and a patriotic kick. She was considered especially effective when a strain of wild recklessness rang through her song. Had this abandon been less blatantly shammed it might still have saved her from utter vulgarity. The small, hard thing, that was her soul stuck out of her song, and the most her temperament could attain was but an eddy, not a free torrent. When nowadays in some Russian household the gramophone is put on, and I hear her canned contralto, it is with something of a shudder that I recall the meretricious imitation she gave of reaching her vocal climax, the anatomy of her mouth fully displayed in a last passionate cry, her blue-black hair beautifully waved, her crossed hands pressed to the beribboned medal on her bosom as she acknowledged the orgy of applause, her broad dusky body rigid even when she bowed, crammed as it was into strong silver satin which made her look like a matron of snow or a mermaid of honour.

4

You will see her next (if the censor does not find what follows offensive to piety) kneeling in the honey-coloured haze of a crowded Russian church, lustily sobbing side by side with the wife or widow (she knew exactly which) of the General whose kidnapping had been so nicely arranged by her husband and so deftly performed by those big, efficient, anonymous men that the boss had sent down to Paris.

You will see her also on another day, two or three years later, while she is singing in a certain *appartement*, Rue George-Sand, surrounded by admiring friends – and look, her eyes narrow slightly, her singing smile fades, as her husband, who had been detained by the final details of the business in hand, now quietly slips in and with a soft gesture rebukes a grizzled colonel's attempt to offer him his own seat; and through the unconscious flow of a song delivered for the ten-thousandth time she peers at him (she is slightly near-sighted like Anna Karenin) trying to discern some definite sign, and then, as she drowns and his painted boats sail away, and the last tell-tale circular ripple on the Volga River, Samara County, dissolves into dull eternity (for this is the very last song that she will ever sing), her husband comes up to her and says in a voice that no clapping of human hands can muffle: 'Masha, the tree will be felled tomorrow!'

That bit about the tree was the only dramatic treat that Golubkov allowed himself during his dove-grey career. We shall condone the outburst if we remember that this was the ultimate General blocking his way and that next day's event would automatically bring on his own election. There had been lately some mild jesting among their friends (Russian humour being a wee bird satisfied with a crumb) about the amusing little quarrel that those two big children were having, she petulantly demanding the removal of the huge old poplar that darkened her studio window at their suburban summer house, and he contending that the sturdy old fellow was her greenest admirer (side-splitting, this) and so ought to be spared. Note too the good-natured roguishness of the fat lady in the ermine cape as she taunts the gallant General for giving in so soon, and the Slavska's radiant smile and outstretched jelly-cold arms.

Next day, late in the afternoon, General Golubkov escorted his wife to her dressmaker, sat there for a while reading the *Paris-Soir*, and then was sent back to fetch one of the dresses she wanted loosened and had forgotten to bring. At suitable intervals she gave a passable imitation of telephoning home and volubly directing his search. The dressmaker, an Armenian lady, and a seamstress, little Princess Tumanov, were much entertained in the adjacent room by the variety of her rustic oaths (which helped her not to dry up in a part that her imagination alone could not improvise). This threadbare alibi was not intended for the patching up of past tenses in case anything went wrong – for nothing could go wrong; it was merely meant to provide a man whom none would ever dream of suspecting with a routine account of his movements when people would want to know who had seen General Fedchenko last. After enough imaginary wardrobes had been ransacked Golubkov was seen to return with the dress (which long ago, of course, had been placed in the car). He went on reading his paper while his wife kept trying things on.

5

The thirty-five minutes or so during which he was gone proved quite a comfortable margin. About the time she started fooling with that dead telephone, he had already picked up the General at an unfrequented corner and was driving him to an imaginary appointment the circumstances of which had been so framed in advance as to make its secrecy natural and its attendance a duty. A few minutes later he pulled up and they both got out. 'This is not the right street,' said General Fedchenko. 'No,' said General Golubkov, 'but it is a convenient one to park my car on. I should not like to leave it right in front of the café. We shall take a short cut through that lane. It is only two minutes' walk.' 'Good, let us walk,' said the old man and cleared his throat.

In that particular quarter of Paris the streets are called after various philosophers, and the lane they were following had been named by some well-read city father Rue Pierre Labime. It gently steered you past a dark church and some scaffolding into a vague region of shuttered private houses standing somewhat aloof within their own grounds behind iron railings on which moribund maple leaves would pause in their flight between bare branch and wet pavement. Along the left side of that lane there was a long wall with crossword puzzles of brick showing here and there through its rough greyness; and in that wall there was at one spot a little green door.

As they approached it, General Golubkov produced his battle-scarred cigarette case and presently stopped to light up. General Fedchenko, a courteous non-smoker, stopped too. There was a gusty wind ruffling the dusk, and the first match went out. 'I still think –' said General Fedchenko in reference to some petty business they had been discussing lately, 'I still think,' he said (to say something as he stood near that little green door), 'that if Father Fedor insists on paying for all those lodgings out of his own funds, the least we can do is to supply the fuel.' The second match went out too. The back of a passer-by hazily receding in the distance at last disappeared. General Golubkov cursed the wind at the top of his voice, and as this was the all-clear signal the green door opened and three pairs of hands with incredible speed and skill whisked the old man out of sight. The door slammed. General Golubkov lighted his cigarette and briskly walked back the way he had come.

The old man was never seen again. The quiet foreigners who had rented a certain quiet house for one quiet month had been innocent Dutchmen or Danes. It was but an optical trick. There is no green door, but only a grey one, which no human strength can burst open. I have vainly searched through admirable encyclopaedias: there is no philosopher called Pierre Labime.

But I have seen the toad in her eyes. We have a saying in Russian: *vsevo dvoe i est; smert' da sovest'* – which may be rendered thus: 'There are only two things that really exist – one's death and one's conscience.' The lovely thing about humanity is that at times one may be unaware of doing right, but one is always aware of doing wrong. A very horrible criminal, whose wife had been even a worse one, once told me in the days when I was a priest that what had troubled him all through was the inner shame of being stopped by a still deeper shame from discussing with her the puzzle: whether perhaps in her heart of hearts she despised him or whether she secretly wondered if perhaps in his heart of hearts he despised her. And that is why I knew perfectly well the kind of face General Golubkov and his wife had when the two were at last alone.

6

Not for very long, however. About 10 p.m. General L., the WW Secretary, was informed by General R. that Mrs Fedchenko was extremely worried by her husband's unaccountable absence. Only then did General L. remember that about lunch time the President had told him in a rather casual way (but that was the old gentleman's manner) that he had some business in town in the late afternoon and that if he was not back by 8 p.m. would General L. please read a note left in the middle drawer of the President's desk. The two generals now rushed to the office, stopped short, rushed back for the keys General L. had forgotten, rushed again, and finally found the note. It read: 'An odd feeling obsesses me of which later I may be ashamed. I have an appointment at 5.30 p.m. in a café 45 Rue Descartes. I am to meet an informer from the other side. I suspect a trap. The whole thing has been arranged by General Golubkov, who is taking me there in his car.'

We shall skip what General L. said and what General R. replied – but apparently they were slow thinkers and proceeded to lose some more time in a muddled telephone talk with an indignant café owner. It was almost midnight when the Slavska, clad in a flowery dressing-gown and trying to look very sleepy, let them in. She was unwilling to disturb her husband, who, she said, was already asleep. She wanted to know what it was all about and had perhaps something happened to General Fedchenko. 'He has vanished,' said honest General L. The Slavska said, 'Akh!' and crashed in a dead swoon, almost wrecking the parlour in the process. The stage had not lost quite so much as most of her admirers thought.

Somehow or other the two generals managed not to impart to General Golubkov anything about the little note, so that when he accompanied them to the WW headquarters he was under the impression that they really wanted to discuss with him whether to ring up the police at once or first go for advice to eighty-eight-year-old Admiral Gromoboyev, who for some obscure reason was considered the Solomon of the WW.

'What does this mean?' said General L. handing the fatal note to Golubkov. 'Peruse it, please.'

Golubkov perused – and knew at once that all was lost. We shall not bend over the abyss of his feelings. He handed the note back with a shrug of his thin shoulders.

'If this has been really written by the General,' he said, 'and I must admit it looks very similar to his hand, then all I can say is that somebody has been impersonating me. However, I have grounds to believe that Admiral Gromoboyev will be able to exonerate me. I suggest we go there at once.'

'Yes,' said General L., 'we had better go now, although it is very late.'

General Golubkov swished himself into his raincoat and went out first. General R. helped General L. to retrieve his muffler. It had half slipped down from one of those vestibule chairs which are doomed to accommodate things, not people. General L. sighed and put on his old felt hat, using both hands for this gentle action. He moved to the door. 'One moment, General,' said General R. in a low voice. 'I want to ask you something. As one officer to another, are you absolutely sure that . . . well, that General Golubkov is speaking the truth?'

'That's what we shall find out,' answered General L., who was one of those people who believe that so long as a sentence is a sentence it is bound to mean something.

They delicately touched each other's elbows in the doorway. Finally the slightly older man accepted the privilege and made a jaunty exit. Then they both paused on the landing, for the staircase struck them as being very still. 'General!' cried General L. in a downward direction. Then they looked at each other. Then hurriedly, clumsily, they stomped down the ugly steps, and emerged, and stopped under a black drizzle, and looked this way and that, and then at each other again.

She was arrested early on the following morning. Never once during the inquest did she depart from her attitude of grief-stricken innocence. The French police displayed a queer listlessness in dealing with possible clues as if it assumed that the disappearance of Russian generals was a kind of curious local custom, an Oriental phenomenon, a dissolving process which perhaps ought not to occur but which could not be prevented. One had, however, the impression that the Sûreté knew more about the workings of that vanishing trick than diplomatic wisdom found fit to discuss. Newspapers abroad treated the whole matter in a good-natured but bantering and slightly bored manner. On the whole, 'L'affaire Slavska' did not make good headlines – Russian *émigrés* were decidedly out of focus. By an amusing coincidence both a German press agency and a Soviet one laconically stated that a pair of White Russian generals in Paris had absconded with the White Army funds.

7

The trial was strangely inconclusive and muddled, witnesses did not shine, and the final conviction of the Slavska on a charge of kidnapping was debatable on legal grounds. Irrelevant trifles kept obscuring the main issue. The wrong people remembered the right things and vice versa. There was a bill signed by a certain Gaston Coulot, farmer, '*pour un arbre abattu.*' General L. and General R. had a dreadful time at the hands of a sadistic barrister. A Parisian *clochard*, one of those colourful ripe-nosed unshaven beings (an easy part, that) who keep all their earthly belongings in their voluminous pockets and wrap their feet in layers of bursting newspapers when the last sock is gone and are seen comfortably seated, with wide-spread legs and a bottle of wine against the crumbling wall of some building that has never been completed, gave a lurid account of having observed from a certain vantage point an old man being roughly handled. Two Russian women, one of whom had been treated some time before for acute hysteria, said they saw on the day of the crime General Golubkov and General Fedchenko driving in the former's car. A Russian violinist while sitting in the diner of a German train – but it is useless to retell all those lame rumours.

We get a few last glimpses of the Slavska in prison. Meekly knitting in a corner. Writing to Mrs Fedchenko tear-stained letters in which she said that they were sisters now, because both their husbands had been captured by the Bolsheviks. Begging to be allowed the use of a lipstick. Sobbing and praying in the arms of a pale young Russian nun who had come to tell her of a vision she had had which disclosed the innocence of General Golubkov. Clamouring for the New Testament which the police were keeping – keeping mainly from the experts who had so nicely begun deciphering certain notes scribbled in the margin of St John's Gospel. Some time after the outbreak of World War II, she developed an obscure internal trouble and when, one summer morning, three German officers arrived at the prison hospital and desired to see her, at once, they were told she was dead – which possibly was the truth.

ISAAC BASHEVIS SINGER

Gimpel the Fool

Isaac Bashevis Singer (1904–91), winner of the Nobel Prize for Literature in 1978, wrote 'Gimpel the Fool' in Yiddish, the initial language of most of his work. The famous tale was translated in 1953 by another Nobel prize-winner, Saul Bellow. Singer was born in Poland, the son of generations of rabbis, and though he became sceptical of the orthodox faith he retained its spirit. He lived in various parts of Poland, especially Warsaw, until he moved permanently to the USA in 1935, becoming a journalist on Jewish newspapers. The largest part of his substantial body of fiction – which includes many notable novels (*The Magician of Lublin*, 1957; *The Manor*, 1967; *The King of the Fields*, 1988) – is set in Poland, in Warsaw or the *stetl* villages, and draws on Yiddish and Polish folklore as much as it does on Singer's American and twentieth-century experience.

'Gimpel the Fool' remains a classic work of Yiddish comedy. Though it displays the seeming simplicity of the European Jewish folk tradition, it is a sophisticated tale with a complex form and effect. In this story of a holy innocent, caught in the ambiguous relation of the spiritual and the real worlds, the figure of Gimpel suggests to us that it is better to be foolish than evil; from foolishness there comes a true awareness of the world's strangeness that leads to innocent wisdom, and to comedy. Singer's writing, and this story particularly, has influenced both the post-war Jewish-American tradition of comedy as well as that of other explorers of fantastic modern humour. Saul Bellow explains that in such works of profound Jewish humour 'laughter and trembling are so curiously mingled that it is not easy to determine the relations of the two. At times the laughter seems simply to restore the equilibrium of sanity; at times the figures of the story, or parable, appear to invite or encourage trembling with the secret aim of overcoming it by laughter.'

1

I am Gimpel the fool. I don't think myself a fool. On the contrary. But that's what folks call me. They gave me the name while I was still in school. I had seven names in all: imbecile, donkey, flax-head, dope, glump, ninny, and fool. The last name stuck. What did my foolishness consist of? I was easy to take in. They said, 'Gimpel, you know the rabbi's wife has been brought to childbed?' So I skipped school. Well, it turned out to be a lie. How was I supposed to know? She hadn't had a big belly. But I never looked at her belly. Was that really so foolish? The gang laughed and hee-hawed, stomped and danced and chanted a good-night prayer. And instead of the raisins they give when a woman's lying in, they stuffed my hand full of goat turds. I was no weakling. If I slapped someone he'd see all the way to Cracow. But I'm really not a slugger by nature. I think to myself: Let it pass. So they take advantage of me.

I was coming home from school and heard a dog barking. I'm not afraid of dogs, but of course I never want to start up with them. One of them may be mad, and if he bites there's not a Tartar in the world who can help you. So I made tracks. Then I looked around and saw the whole market-place wild with laughter. It was no dog at all but Wolf-Leib the thief. How was I supposed to know it was he? It sounded like a howling bitch.

When the pranksters and leg-pullers found that I was easy to fool, every one of them tried his luck with me. 'Gimpel, the czar is coming to Frampol; Gimpel, the moon fell down in Turbeen; Gimpel, little Hodel Furpiece found a treasure behind the bathhouse.' And I like a golem believed everyone. In the first place, everything is possible, as it is written in *The Wisdom of the Fathers*, I've forgotten just how. Second, I had to believe when the whole town came down on me! If I ever dared to say, 'Ah, you're kidding!' there was trouble. People got angry. 'What do you mean! You want to call everyone a liar?' What was I to do? I believed them, and I hope at least that did them some good.

I was an orphan. My grandfather who brought me up was already bent toward the grave. So they turned me over to a baker, and what a time they gave me there! Every woman or girl who came to bake a batch of noodles had to fool me at least once. 'Gimpel, there's a fair in Heaven; Gimpel, the rabbi gave birth to a calf in the seventh month; Gimpel, a cow flew over the roof and laid brass eggs.' A student from the yeshiva came once to buy a roll, and he said, 'You, Gimpel, while you stand here scraping with your baker's shovel the Messiah has come. The dead have arisen.' 'What do you mean?' I said. 'I heard no one blowing the ram's horn!' He said, 'Are you deaf?' And all began to cry, 'We heard it, we heard!' Then in came Rietze the candle-dipper and called out in her hoarse voice, 'Gimpel, your father and mother have stood up from the grave. They're looking for you.'

To tell the truth, I knew very well that nothing of the sort had happened, but all the same, as folks were talking, I threw on my wool vest and went out. Maybe something had happened. What did I stand to lose by looking? Well, what a cat music went up! And then I took a vow to believe nothing more. But that was no go either. They confused me so that I didn't know the big end from the small.

I went to the rabbi to get some advice. He said, 'It is written, better to be a fool all your days than for one hour to be evil. You are not a fool. They are the fools. For he who causes his neighbor to feel shame loses Paradise himself.' Nevertheless, the rabbi's daughter took me in. As I left the rabbinical court she said, 'Have you kissed the wall yet?' I said, 'No; what for?' She answered, 'It's the law; you've got to do it after every visit.' Well, there didn't seem to be any harm in it. And she burst out laughing. It was a fine trick. She put one over on me, all right.

I wanted to go off to another town, but then everyone got busy matchmaking, and they were after me so they nearly tore my coat tails off. They talked at me and talked until I got water on the ear. She was no chaste maiden, but they told me she was virgin pure. She had a limp, and they said it was deliberate, from coyness. She had a bastard, and they told me the child was her little brother. I cried, 'You're wasting your time. I'll never marry that whore.' But they said indignantly, 'What a way to talk! Aren't you ashamed of yourself? We can take you to the rabbi and have you fined for giving her a bad name.' I saw then that I wouldn't escape them so easily and I thought: They're set on making me their butt. But when you're married the husband's the master, and if that's all right with her it's agreeable to me too. Besides, you can't pass through life unscathed, nor expect to.

I went to her clay house, which was built on the sand, and the whole gang, hollering and chorusing, came after me. They acted like bear-baiters. When we came to the well they stopped all the same. They were afraid to start anything with Elka. Her mouth would open as if it were on a hinge, and she had a fierce tongue. I entered the house. Lines were strung from wall to wall and clothes were drying. Barefoot she stood by the tub, doing the wash. She was dressed in a worn hand-me-down gown of plush. She had her hair put up in braids and pinned across her head. It took my breath away, almost, the reek of it all.

Evidently she knew who I was. She took a look at me and said, 'Look who's here! He's come, the drip. Grab a seat.'

I told her all; I denied nothing. 'Tell me the truth,' I said, 'are you really a virgin, and is that mischievous Yechiel actually your little brother? Don't be deceitful with me, for I'm an orphan.'

'I'm an orphan myself,' she answered, 'and whoever tries to twist you up, may the end of his nose take a twist. But don't let them think they can take advantage of me. I want a dowry of fifty guilders, and let them take up a collection besides. Otherwise they can kiss my you-know-what.' She was very plain-spoken. I said, 'It's the bride and not the groom who gives a dowry.' Then she said, 'Don't bargain with me. Either a flat yes or a flat no. Go back where you came from.'

I thought: No bread will ever be baked from *this* dough. But ours is not a poor town. They consented to everything and proceeded with the wedding. It so happened that there was a dysentery epidemic at the time. The ceremony was held at the cemetery gates, near the little corpse-washing hut. The fellows got drunk. While the marriage contract was being drawn up I heard the most pious high rabbi ask, 'Is the bride a widow or a divorced woman?' And the sexton's wife answered for her, 'Both a widow and divorced.' It was a black moment for me. But what was I to do, run away from under the marriage canopy?

There was singing and dancing. An old granny danced opposite me, hugging a braided white hallah. The master of revels made a 'God 'a mercy' in memory of the bride's parents. The schoolboys threw burrs, as on Tishe b'Av fast day. There were a lot of gifts after the sermon: a noodle board, a kneading trough, a bucket, brooms, ladles, household articles galore. Then I took a look and saw two strapping young men carrying a crib. 'What do we need this for?' I asked. So they said, 'Don't rack your brains about it. It's all right, it'll come in handy.' I realized I was going to be rooked. Take it another way though, what did I stand to lose? I reflected: I'll see what comes of it. A whole town can't go altogether crazy.

2

At night I came where my wife lay, but she wouldn't let me in. 'Say, look here, is this what they married us for?' I said. And she said, 'My monthly has come.' 'But yesterday they took you to the ritual bath, and that's afterwards, isn't it supposed to be?' 'Today isn't yesterday,' said she, 'and yesterday's not today. You can beat it if you don't like it.' In short, I waited.

Not four months later, she was in childbed. The townsfolk hid their laughter with their knuckles. But what could I do? She suffered intolerable pains and clawed at the walls. 'Gimpel,' she cried, 'I'm going. Forgive me!' The house filled with women. They were boiling pans of water. The screams rose to the welkin.

The thing to do was to go to the house of prayer to repeat psalms, and that was what I did.

The townsfolk liked that, all right. I stood in a corner saying psalms and prayers, and they shook their heads at me. 'Pray, pray!' they told me.

'Prayer never made any woman pregnant.' One of the congregation put a straw to my mouth and said, 'Hay for the cows.' There was something to that too, by God!

She gave birth to a boy. Friday at the synagogue the sexton stood up before the Ark, pounded on the reading table, and announced, 'The wealthy Reb Gimpel invites the congregation to a feast in honor of the birth of a son.' The whole house of prayer rang with laughter. My face was flaming. But there was nothing I could do. After all, I *was* the one responsible for the circumcision honors and rituals.

Half the town came running. You couldn't wedge another soul in. Women brought peppered chickpeas, and there was a keg of beer from the tavern. I ate and drank as much as anyone, and they all congratulated me. Then there was a circumcision, and I named the boy after my father, may he rest in peace. When all were gone and I was left with my wife alone, she thrust her head through the bed-curtain and called me to her.

'Gimpel,' said she, 'why are you silent? Has your ship gone and sunk?'

'What shall I say?' I answered. 'A fine thing you've done to me! If my mother had known of it she'd have died a second time.'

She said, 'Are you crazy, or what?'

'How can you make such a fool,' I said, 'of one who should be the lord and master?'

'What's the matter with you?' she said. 'What have you taken it into your head to imagine?'

I saw that I must speak bluntly and openly. 'Do you think this is the way to use an orphan?' I said. 'You have borne a bastard.'

She answered, 'Drive this foolishness out of your head. The child is yours.'

'How can he be mine?' I argued. 'He was born seventeen weeks after the wedding.'

She told me then that he was premature. I said, 'Isn't he a little too premature?' She said, she had had a grandmother who carried just as short a time and she resembled this grandmother of hers as one drop of water does another. She swore to it with such oaths that you would have believed a peasant at the fair if he had used them. To tell the plain truth, I didn't believe her; but when I talked it over next day with the schoolmaster, he told me that the very same thing had happened to Adam and Eve. Two they went up to bed, and four they descended.

'There isn't a woman in the world who is not the granddaughter of Eve,' he said.

That was how it was; they argued me dumb. But then, who really knows how such things are?

I began to forget my sorrow. I loved the child madly, and he loved me too. As soon as he saw me he'd wave his little hands and want me to pick

76

him up, and when he was colicky I was the only one who could pacify him. I bought him a little bone teething ring and a little gilded cap. He was forever catching the evil eye from someone, and then I had to run to get one of those abracadabras for him that would get him out of it. I worked like an ox. You know how expenses go up when there's an infant in the house. I don't want to lie about it; I didn't dislike Elka either, for that matter. She swore at me and cursed, and I couldn't get enough of her. What strength she had! One of her looks could rob you of the power of speech. And her orations! Pitch and sulphur, that's what they were full of, and yet somehow also full of charm. I adored her every word. She gave me bloody wounds though.

In the evening I brought her a white loaf as well as a dark one, and also poppyseed rolls I baked myself. I thieved because of her and swiped everything I could lay hands on: macaroons, raisins, almonds, cakes. I hope I may be forgiven for stealing from the Saturday pots the women left to warm in the baker's oven. I would take out scraps of meat, a chunk of pudding, a chicken leg or head, a piece of tripe, whatever I could nip quickly. She ate and became fat and handsome.

I had to sleep away from home all during the week, at the bakery. On Friday nights when I got home she always made an excuse of some sort. Either she had heartburn, or a stitch in the side, or hiccups, or headaches. You know what women's excuses are. I had a bitter time of it. It was rough. To add to it, this little brother of hers, the bastard, was growing bigger. He'd put lumps on me, and when I wanted to hit back she'd open her mouth and curse so powerfully I saw a green haze floating before my eyes. Ten times a day she threatened to divorce me. Another man in my place would have taken French leave and disappeared. But I'm the type that bears it and says nothing. What's one to do? Shoulders are from God, and burdens too.

One night there was a calamity in the bakery; the oven burst, and we almost had a fire. There was nothing to do but go home, so I went home. Let me, I thought, also taste the joy of sleeping in bed in midweek. I didn't want to wake the sleeping mite and tiptoed into the house. Coming in, it seemed to me that I heard not the snoring of one but, as it were, a double snore, one a thin enough snore and the other like the snoring of a slaughtered ox. Oh, I didn't like that! I didn't like it at all. I went up to the bed, and things suddenly turned black. Next to Elka lay a man's form. Another in my place would have made an uproar, and enough noise to rouse the whole town, but the thought occurred to me that I might wake the child. A little thing like that – why frighten a little swallow, I thought. All right then, I went back to the bakery and stretched out on a sack of flour and till morning I never shut an eye. I shivered as if I had had malaria. 'Enough of being a donkey,' I said to myself. 'Gimpel isn't going to be a sucker all his life. There's a limit even to the foolishness of a fool like Gimpel.'

In the morning I went to the rabbi to get advice, and it made a great commotion in the town. They sent the beadle for Elka right away. She came, carrying the child. And what do you think she did? She denied it, denied everything, bone and stone! 'He's out of his head,' she said. 'I know nothing of dreams or divinations.' They yelled at her, warned her, hammered on the table, but she stuck to her guns: it was a false accusation, she said.

The butchers and the horse-traders took her part. One of the lads from the slaughterhouse came by and said to me, 'We've got our eye on you, you're a marked man.' Meanwhile, the child started to bear down and soiled itself. In the rabbinical court there was an Ark of the Covenant, and they couldn't allow that, so they sent Elka away.

I said to the rabbi. 'What shall I do?'

'You must divorce her at once,' said he.

'And what if she refuses?' I asked.

He said, 'You must serve the divorce. That's all you'll have to do.'

I said, 'Well, all right, Rabbi. Let me think about it.'

'There's nothing to think about,' said he. 'You mustn't remain under the same roof with her.'

'And if I want to see the child?' I asked.

'Let her go, the harlot,' said he, 'and her brood of bastards with her.'

The verdict he gave was that I mustn't even cross her threshold – never again, as long as I should live.

During the day it didn't bother me so much. I thought: It was bound to happen, the abscess had to burst. But at night when I stretched out upon the sacks I felt it all very bitterly. A longing took me, for her and for the child. I wanted to be angry, but that's my misfortune exactly, I don't have it in me to be really angry. In the first place – this was how my thoughts went – there's bound to be a slip sometimes. You can't live without errors. Probably that lad who was with her led her on and gave her presents and what not, and women are often long on hair and short on sense, and so he got around her. And then since she denies it so, maybe I was only seeing things? Hallucinations do happen. You see a figure or a mannikin or something, but when you come up closer it's nothing, there's not a thing there. And if that's so, I'm doing her an injustice. And when I got so far in my thoughts I started to weep. I sobbed so that I wet the flour where I lay. In the morning I went to the rabbi and told him that I had made a mistake. The rabbi wrote on with his quill, and he said that if that were so he would have to reconsider the whole case. Until he had finished I wasn't to go near my wife, but I might send her bread and money by messenger.

3

Nine months passed before all the rabbis could come to an agreement. Letters went back and forth. I hadn't realized that there could be so much erudition about a matter like this.

Meanwhile, Elka gave birth to still another child, a girl this time. On the Sabbath I went to the synagogue and invoked a blessing on her. They called me up to the Torah, and I named the child for my mother-in-law – may she rest in peace. The louts and loudmouths of the town who came into the bakery gave me a going over. All Frampol refreshed its spirits because of my trouble and grief. However, I resolved that I would always believe what I was told. What's the good of *not* believing? Today it's your wife you don't believe; tomorrow it's God Himself you won't take stock in.

By an apprentice who was her neighbor I sent her daily a corn or a wheat loaf, or a piece of pastry, rolls or bagels, or, when I got the chance, a slab of pudding, a slice of honey cake, or wedding strudel – whatever came my way. The apprentice was a good-hearted lad, and more than once he added something on his own. He had formerly annoyed me a lot, plucking my nose and digging me in the ribs, but when he started to be a visitor to my house he became kind and friendly. 'Hey, you, Gimpel,' he said to me, 'you have a very decent little wife and two fine kids. You don't deserve them.'

'But the things people say about her,' I said.

'Well, they have long tongues,' he said, 'and nothing to do with them but babble. Ignore it as you ignore the cold of last winter.'

One day the rabbi sent for me and said, 'Are you certain, Gimpel, that you were wrong about your wife?'

I said, 'I'm certain.'

'Why, but look here! You yourself saw it.'

'It must have been a shadow,' I said.

'The shadow of what?'

'Just of one of the beams, I think.'

'You can go home then. You owe thanks to the Yanover rabbi. He found an obscure reference in Maimonides that favored you.'

I seized the rabbi's hand and kissed it.

I wanted to run home immediately. It's no small thing to be separated for so long a time from wife and child. Then I reflected: I'd better go back to work now, and go home in the evening. I said nothing to anyone, although as far as my heart was concerned it was like one of the Holy Days. The women teased and twitted me as they did every day, but my thought was: Go on, with your loose talk. The truth is out, like the oil upon the water. Maimonides says it's right, and therefore it is right!

At night, when I had covered the dough to let it rise, I took my share of bread and a little sack of flour and started homeward. The moon was full and the stars were glistening, something to terrify the soul. I hurried onward, and before me darted a long shadow. It was winter, and a fresh snow had fallen. I had a mind to sing, but it was growing late and I didn't want to wake the householders. Then I felt like whistling, but I remembered that you don't whistle at night because it brings the demons out. So I was silent and walked as fast as I could.

Dogs in the Christian yards barked at me when I passed, but I thought: Bark your teeth out! What are you but mere dogs? Whereas I am a man, the husband of a fine wife, the father of promising children.

As I approached the house my heart started to pound as though it were the heart of a criminal. I felt no fear, but my heart went thump! thump! Well, no drawing back. I quietly lifted the latch and went in. Elka was asleep. I looked at the infant's cradle. The shutter was closed, but the moon forced its way through the cracks. I saw the newborn child's face and loved it as soon as I saw it – immediately – each tiny bone.

Then I came nearer to the bed. And what did I see but the apprentice lying there beside Elka. The moon went out all at once. It was utterly black, and I trembled. My teeth chattered. The bread fell from my hands, and my wife waked and said, 'Who is that, ah?'

I muttered, 'It's me.'

'Gimpel?' she asked. 'How come you're here? I thought it was forbidden.'

'The rabbi said,' I answered and shook as with a fever.

'Listen to me, Gimpel,' she said, 'go out to the shed and see if the goat's all right. It seems she's been sick.' I have forgotten to say that we had a goat. When I heard she was unwell I went into the yard. The nanny goat was a good little creature. I had a nearly human feeling for her.

With hesitant steps I went up to the shed and opened the door. The goat stood there on her four feet. I felt her everywhere, drew her by the horns, examined her udders, and found nothing wrong. She had probably eaten too much bark. 'Good-night, little goat,' I said. 'Keep well.' And the little beast answered with a 'Maa' as though to thank me for the good will.

I went back. The apprentice had vanished.

'Where,' I asked, 'is the lad?'

'What lad?' my wife answered.

'What do you mean?' I said. 'The apprentice. You were sleeping with him.'

'The things I have dreamed this night and the night before,' she said, 'may they come true and lay you low, body and soul! An evil spirit has taken root in you and dazzles your sight.' She screamed out, 'You hateful creature! You moon calf! You spook! You uncouth man! Get out, or I'll scream all Frampol out of bed!'

Before I could move, her brother sprang out from behind the oven and struck me a blow on the back of the head. I thought he had broken my neck. I felt that something about me was deeply wrong, and I said, 'Don't make a scandal. All that's needed now is that people should accuse me of raising spooks and dybbuks.' For that was what she had meant. 'No one will touch bread of my baking.'

In short, I somehow calmed her.

'Well,' she said, 'that's enough. Lie down, and be shattered by wheels.'

Next morning I called the apprentice aside. 'Listen here, brother!' I said. And so on and so forth. 'What do you say?' He stared at me as though I had dropped from the roof or something.

'I swear,' he said, 'you'd better go to an herb doctor or some healer. I'm afraid you have a screw loose, but I'll hush it up for you.' And that's how the thing stood.

To make a long story short, I lived twenty years with my wife. She bore me six children, four daughters and two sons. All kinds of things happened, but I neither saw nor heard. I believed, and that's all. The rabbi recently said to me, 'Belief in itself is beneficial. It is written that a good man lives by his faith.'

Suddenly my wife took sick. It began with a trifle, a little growth upon the breast. But she evidently was not destined to live long; she had no years. I spent a fortune on her. I have forgotten to say that by this time I had a bakery of my own and in Frampol was considered to be something of a rich man. Daily the healer came, and every witch doctor in the neighborhood was brought. They decided to use leeches, and after that to try cupping. They even called a doctor from Lublin, but it was too late. Before she died she called me to her bed and said, 'Forgive me, Gimpel.'

I said, 'What is there to forgive? You have been a good and faithful wife.'

'Woe, Gimpel!' she said. 'It was ugly how I deceived you all these years. I want to go clean to my Maker, and so I have to tell you that the children are not yours.'

If I had been clouted on the head with a piece of wood it couldn't have bewildered me more.

'Whose are they?' I asked.

'I don't know,' she said. 'There were a lot . . . but they're not yours.' And as she spoke she tossed her head to the side, her eyes turned glassy, and it was all up with Elka. On her whitened lips there remained a smile.

I imagined that, dead as she was, she was saying, 'I deceived Gimpel. That was the meaning of my brief life.'

4

One night, when the period of mourning was done, as I lay dreaming on the flour sacks, there came the Spirit of Evil himself and said to me, 'Gimpel, why do you sleep?'

I said, 'What should I be doing? Eating kreplech?'

'The whole world deceives you,' he said, 'and you ought to deceive the world in your turn.'

'How can I deceive all the world?' I asked him.

He answered, 'You might accumulate a bucket of urine every day and at night pour it into the dough. Let the sages of Frampol eat filth.'

'What about the judgment in the world to come?' I said.

'There is no world to come,' he said. 'They've sold you a bill of goods and talked you into believing you carried a cat in your belly. What nonsense!'

'Well then,' I said, 'and is there a God?'

He answered, 'There is no God either.'

'What,' I said, '*is* there, then?'

'A thick mire.'

He stood before my eyes with a goatish beard and horn, long-toothed, and with a tail. Hearing such words, I wanted to snatch him by the tail, but I tumbled from the flour sacks and nearly broke a rib. Then it happened that I had to answer the call of nature, and, passing, I saw the risen dough, which seemed to say to me, 'Do it!' In brief, I let myself be persuaded.

At dawn the apprentice came. We kneaded the bread, scattered caraway seeds on it, and set it to bake. Then the apprentice went away, and I was left sitting in the little trench by the oven, on a pile of rags. Well, Gimpel, I thought, you've revenged yourself on them for all the shame they've put on you. Outside the frost glittered, but it was warm beside the oven. The flames heated my face. I bent my head and fell into a doze.

I saw in a dream, at once, Elka in her shroud. She called to me, 'What have you done, Gimpel?'

I said to her, 'It's all your fault,' and started to cry.

'You fool!' she said. 'You fool! Because I was false is everything false too? I never deceived anyone but myself. I'm paying for it all, Gimpel. They spare you nothing here.'

I looked at her face. It was black; I was startled and waked, and remained sitting dumb. I sensed that everything hung in the balance. A false step now and I'd lose eternal life. But God gave me His help. I seized the long shovel and took out the loaves, carried them into the yard, and started to dig a hole in the frozen earth.

My apprentice came back as I was doing it. 'What are you doing, boss?' he said, and grew pale as a corpse.

'I know what I'm doing,' I said, and I buried it all before his very eyes.

Then I went home, took my hoard from its hiding place, and divided it among the children. 'I saw your mother tonight,' I said. 'She's turning black, poor thing.'

They were so astounded they couldn't speak a word.

'Be well,' I said, 'and forget that such a one as Gimpel ever existed.' I put on my short coat, a pair of boots, took the bag that held my prayer shawl in one hand, my stock in the other, and kissed the mezuzah. When people saw me in the street they were greatly surprised.

'Where are you going?' they said.

I answered, 'Into the world.' And so I departed from Frampol.

I wandered over the land, and good people did not neglect me. After many years I became old and white; I heard a great deal, many lies and falsehoods, but the longer I lived the more I understood that there were really no lies. Whatever doesn't really happen is dreamed at night. It happens to one if it doesn't happen to another, tomorrow if not today, or a century hence if not next year. What difference can it make? Often I heard tales of which I said, 'Now this is a thing that cannot happen.' But before a year had elapsed I heard that it actually had come to pass somewhere.

Going from place to place, eating at strange tables, it often happens that I spin yarns – improbable things that could never have happened – about devils, magicians, windmills, and the like. The children run after me, calling, 'Grandfather, tell us a story.' Sometimes they ask for particular stories, and I try to please them. A fat young boy once said to me, 'Grandfather, it's the same story you told us before.' The little rogue, he was right.

So it is with dreams too. It is many years since I left Frampol, but as soon as I shut my eyes I am there again. And whom do you think I see? Elka. She is standing by the washtub, as at our first encounter, but her face is shining and her eyes are as radiant as the eyes of a saint, and she speaks outlandish words to me, strange things. When I wake I have forgotten it all. But while the dream lasts I am comforted. She answers all my queries, and what comes out is that all is right. I weep and implore, 'Let me be with you.' And she consoles me and tells me to be patient. The time is nearer than it is far. Sometimes she strokes and kisses me and weeps upon my face. When I awaken I feel her lips and taste the salt of her tears.

No doubt the world is entirely an imaginary world, but it is only once removed from the true world. At the door of the hovel where I lie, there stands the plank on which the dead are taken away. The grave-digger Jew has his spade ready. The grave waits and the worms are hungry; the shrouds are prepared – I carry them in my beggar's sack. Another *shnorrer* is waiting to inherit my bed of straw. When the time comes I will go joyfully. Whatever may be there, it will be real, without complication, without ridicule, without deception. God be praised: there even Gimpel cannot be deceived.

(translated by Saul Bellow)

ANGUS WILSON

The Wrong Set

Angus Wilson (1913–92) was surely Britain's finest post-war satirist in fiction. He started writing just as the Second World War finished, and first came to notice with two remarkable volumes of biting short stories exploring the early post-war climate, *The Wrong Set* (1949) and *Such Darling Dodos* (1950). He was then to become famous as a major and ambitious novelist (*Anglo-Saxon Attitudes*, 1956; *The Middle Age of Mrs Eliot*, 1958; *No Laughing Matter*, 1967), a story-teller who, in the Dickensian spirit, chronicled, tested and satirized the social, political and moral climate of Britain from the fifties to the eighties.

Like most of Wilson's early stories, 'The Wrong Set' is a work of sharp and bitter satire, written in Wilson's very distinctive camp manner, which owes something to Evelyn Waugh and Ronald Firbank. It is about a Britain where a quiet social revolution is occurring, as a product of the war, the fading of Empire, and the coming of a new egalitarianism as a result of Clement Attlee's post-war Labour Government and its Welfare State policies. Two generations exist: the old bourgeoisie, Wilson's 'darling dodos', certainly have not given up their attitudes and snobberies, while younger people reflect the more egalitarian mood. 'The Wrong Set' is one of a good many stories Wilson wrote about these social ironies: it does not take us long to realize that the 'wrong set' is probably the right one, and vice versa. This was a conflict of ages and values Wilson would explore at greater length and in greater moral depth in his early novels, about the dilemmas of modern liberalism and 'Anglo-Saxon attitudes'. That last phrase, which became one of his best known titles, was borrowed from Lewis Carroll's *Through the Looking Glass*: 'He's an Anglo-Saxon messenger – and those are Anglo-Saxon attitudes. He only does them when he's happy.' And 'Anglo-Saxon attitudes' have been one of the key themes of British comedy.

Just before the club closed, Mrs Lippiatt asked very specially for a medley of old numbers. Mr Pontresoli himself came over and told Terry. 'It's for your bundle of charms,' he said, 'so don't blame me.' Vi wanted to refuse when Terry asked her – she had a filthy headache and anyway she was sick of being kept late. 'Tell the old cow to go and . . .' she was saying, when Terry put a finger on her lips. 'Do it for me, dear,' he said. 'Remember without her I don't eat.' Poor kid! thought Vi, having to do it with an old trout like that, old enough to be his grandmother – still, she stank of money, he was on to a good thing if he could keep it. So she put on a special sweet smile and waved at Mrs Lippiatt. 'Here's wishing you all you wish yourself, dear,' she called. Then she smiled at Mr Pontresoli, just to show him how hard she worked for his lousy club – might as well kill two birds with one stone. 'Let it go, Terry,' she called and the two pianos jazzed out the old duet routine – 'Souvenirs', 'Paper Doll', 'Some of these Days', 'Blue Again', everything nice and corny. It was while they were playing 'The Sheik of Araby' that she noticed Mrs Lippiatt's face – all lit up with memories. Christ! she must be old if she goes back to that, thought Vi, and then she said to herself, 'Poor old bitch, she must have been pretty once, but, there you are, that's life, makes you hard.' At least she'd got a nice bit of stuff in Terry, best-looking boy in the place; not that she didn't prefer something a bit nearer her own age herself, and she gazed proudly over at Trevor, with his wavy grey hair and soldier's moustache, talking to Mr Pontresoli. Funny how class told. Old Pontresoli could have bought Trevor up any day, but there he was, respectful as anything, listening to what Trevor had to say. She could hear Trevor's voice above the music, 'My dear old Ponto, you'll never change that sort of thing in this country till you clear out the Yids.' If Mr Pontresoli knew what Trevor really thought of him! 'Filthy wop,' he'd said, but he'd agreed to be nice, because of Vi's piano act and until he got a job they needed all the money she could earn.

After closing time she had a drink with Terry and Mrs Lippiatt. Mrs Lippiatt said what was the good of having money, there was nothing to spend it on. Vi thought to herself what she would like was to have some money to spend, but aloud she said in her smart voice, 'Yes, isn't it awful? With this government you have to be grateful for the air you breathe. Look at the things we can't have – food, clothes, foreign travel.' 'Ah, yes, foreign travel,' said Mrs Lippiatt, though she knew damned well Vi had never been abroad. 'It's bad enough for you and me, Mrs Cawston, but think of this poor boy,' and she put her fat, beringed hand on Terry's knee, '*he*'s never been out of England. Never mind, darling, you shall have your trip to Nice the day we get a proper government back.' Mr Pontresoli and Trevor joined them. Trevor was the real public schoolboy with his monocle and calling Mrs Lippiatt 'my dear lady', Vi could see that Terry was worried – he was frightened that Trevor was muscling in; but that was just Trevor's natural way with women – he had perfect manners. Later in the evening he asked Vi who the hell the old trout was.

'The Major's got a good one about Attlee,' said Mr Pontresoli in his thick, adenoidal Italian cockney, his series of blue stubbled chins wobbling as he spoke.

'It's impossible to be as funny about this government as they are themselves,' said Trevor. He had *such* a quiet sense of humour. 'They're a regular Fred Karno show.' But they all begged to hear the story, so he gave it to them. 'An empty taxi drove up to No. 10,' he said, 'and Mr Attlee got out.' Beautifully told it was, with his monocle taken out of his eye and polished just at the right moment.

'Well Sir Stafford gives me the creeps,' said Terry. No one thought that very funny except Mrs Lippiatt and she roared.

'Are you ready, young woman?' Trevor said to Vi with mock severity, 'because I'm not waiting all night.' As she was coming out of the ladies', Vi met Mona and her girlfriend. She stopped and talked to them for a minute although she knew Trevor would disapprove. It was true, of course, that that sort of thing was on the increase and Trevor said it was the ruin of England, but then he said that about so many things – Jews and foreigners, the Labour Government and the Ballet. Anyhow Mona's crowd had been very kind to her in the old days when she was down to her last sausage, and when they'd found she wasn't their sort there'd never been so much as a word to upset her.

'For Christ's sake, kiddie,' said Trevor, 'I wish you wouldn't talk to those Lizzies.'

On the stairs they met young Mr Solomons. Vi *had* to talk to him, whatever Trevor said. First of all he was important at the club, and then his smile always got her – nice and warm somehow like a cat purring, but that was what she felt about a lot of Jews. 'She's stood me up, Vi,' he said, his eyes round with pretended dismay, 'left me in the lurch. Ah! I ought to have stuck to nice girls like you.' Vi couldn't help laughing, but Trevor was wild with anger. He stood quite still for a moment in Denman Street under the electric sign which read 'Passion Fruit Club'. 'If I catch that lousy Yid hanging around you again, girlie,' he said, 'I'll knock his ruddy block off.' All the way in the tube to Earls Court he was in a rage. Vi wanted to tell him that she was going to visit her nephew Norman tomorrow, but she feared his reception of the news. Trevor had talked big about helping Norman, when she told him the boy had won a scholarship at London University and was coming to live with them. But somehow her sister Ivy had got word that she wasn't really married to Trevor and they'd sent the boy elsewhere. She and Trevor had taken him out to dinner once in the West End – a funny boy with tousled black hair and thick spectacles who never said a word, though he'd eaten a hearty enough meal and laughed fit to split at the Palladium. Trevor said he wasn't all there and the less they saw of him the better, but Vi thought of him as her only relative in London and after all Ivy *was* her sister, even if she was so narrow.

'I'm going to see Norman tomorrow,' Vi said timidly, as they crossed the Earls Court Road.

'Good God,' cried Trevor. 'What on earth for, girlie?'

'I've written once or twice to that Hampstead address and had no reply.'

'Well, let the little swine stew in his own juice if he hasn't the decency to answer,' said Trevor.

'Blood's blood after all,' countered Vi, and so they argued until they were back in their bed-sitting-room. Vi put on a kimono and feathered mules, washed off her make-up and covered her face in cream until it shone with highlights. Then she sat plucking her eyebrows. Trevor put his trousers to press under the mattress, gave himself a whisky in the toothglass, refilled it with Milton and water and put in his dentures. Then he sat in his pants, suspenders and socks squeezing blackheads from his nose in front of a mirror. All this time they kept on rowing. At last Vi cried out, 'All right, all right, Trevor Cawston, but I'm *still* going.' 'OK,' said Trevor, 'how's about a little loving?' So then they broke into the old routine.

When the time came to visit Norman, Vi was in quite a quandary about what to wear. She didn't want the people he lived with to put her down as tarty – there'd probably been quite enough of that sort of talk already – on the other hand she wasn't going to look a frump for anyone. She compromised with her black suit, white lace jabot and gold pocket seal, with coral nail varnish instead of scarlet.

The house when she got there wasn't in Hampstead at all, but in Kilburn. Respectable, she decided, but a bit poor-looking.

'Norman's out at the demo,' said Mrs Thursby, 'but he should be back any time now. You'll come in and have a cup of tea, won't you?' Vi said she thought she would. She hadn't quite understood where her nephew was, but if he was coming back soon, she might as well wait. The parlour into which she was ushered brought her home in Leicester back to her – all that plush, and the tassels and the china with crests on it got her down properly now. One thing they wouldn't have had at home though and that was all those books, cases full of them, and stacks of newspapers and magazines piled on the floor, and then there was a typewriter – probably a studious home, she decided. She did wish the little dowdy, bright-eyed woman with the bobbed hair would sit down instead of hopping about like a bird. But Mrs Thursby had heard something about Vi, and she was at once nervous and hostile; she stood making little plucking gestures at her necklace and her sleeve-ends and shooting staccato inquiries at Vi in a chirping voice that had an undertone of sarcasm.

'Mrs . . . Mrs Cawston, is it?'

'That's right,' said Vi.

'Oh yes. I wasn't quite sure. It's so difficult to know sometimes these days, isn't it? with . . .' and Mrs Thursby's voice trailed away.

Vi felt she was being got at. But Mrs Thursby went on talking.

'Oh! The man *will* be sorry you came when he was out.' By calling Norman, 'The man', she seemed to be claiming a greater relationship to him than that of a mere aunt. 'He's talked of you,' and she paused, then added drily, 'a certain amount. I won't say a great deal, but then he's not a great talker.'

'Where did you say he was?' asked Vi.

'At Trafalgar Square,' said Mrs Thursby. 'They're rallying there to hear Pollitt or one of those people. My two went, they're both CP, and Norman's gone with them. Though I'm glad to say he's had the good sense not to join up completely, he's just a fellow traveller as they call them.'

Vi was too bemused to say much, but she managed to ask for what purpose they were rallying.

'To make trouble for the government they put into power,' said Mrs Thursby drily. 'It makes me very angry sometimes. It's taken us forty years to get a real Labour Government and then just because they don't move fast enough for these young people, it's criticism, criticism all the time. But, there it is, I've always said the same, there's no fool like a young fool,' and she closed her tight, little mouth with relish, 'they'll come round in time. Hilda, that's my girl, was just the same about the chapel, but now it seems they've agreed to the worship of God. Very kind of them I'm sure. I expect you feel the same as I do, Mrs Cawston.'

Vi wasn't quite sure exactly what Mrs Thursby did feel, but she *was* sure that she didn't agree, so she said defiantly, 'I'm Conservative.'

'Lena,' said Mrs Thursby in a dry, abrupt voice to a tall, middle-aged woman who was bringing in the tea-tray, 'we've got a Tory in the house. The first for many a day.'

'Oh no!' said Lena, and everything about her was charming and gemütlich from her foreign accent to her smile of welcome. 'I am so pleased to meet you but it is terrible that you are a Tory.'

'Miss Untermayer teaches the man German,' said Mrs Thursby. 'Mrs Cawston is Norman's aunt.'

'Oh!' cried Miss Untermayer, her gaunt features lit up with almost girlish pleasure. 'Then I congratulate you. You have a very clever nephew.'

Vi said she was sure she was pleased to hear that, but she didn't quite like the sound of these rallies.

'Oh! that,' said Miss Untermayer. 'He will grow out of that. All this processions and violence, it is for children. But Norman is a very spiritual boy, I am sure that he is a true pacifist.'

'I'm sure I hope not,' said Vi who was getting really angry. 'I've never had anything to do with conchies.'

'Then you've missed contact with a very fine body of men,' said Mrs Thursby, 'Mr Thursby was an objector.'

'I'm sorry, I'm sure,' said Vi. 'Major Cawston was right through the war.'

'The important thing is that he came out the other side,' remarked Mrs Thursby drily.

'There are so many kinds of bravery, so many kinds of courage. I think we must respect them all.' Miss Untermayer's years as a refugee had made her an adept at glossing over divisions of opinion. All the same she gave a sigh of relief when Norman's voice was heard in the hall, at least the responsibility would not be on *her* any more.

'Hilda and Jack have gone on to a meeting,' he shouted, 'I'd have gone too but I've got to get on with this essay.'

'Your aunt's come to see you,' shouted back Mrs Thursby.

Norman came into the room sideways like a crab, he was overcome with confusion at the sight of Vi and he stood, running his hands through his hair and blinking behind his spectacles.

'You were such a long time answering my letters that I thought I'd better come down and see what sort of mischief you'd got into,' said Vi, 'and I have,' she added bitterly. 'Demonstrations indeed. I'd like to know what your mother would say, Norman Hackett?'

Norman's face was scarlet as he looked up, but he answered firmly. 'I don't think Mum would disapprove, not if she understood. And even if she did, it couldn't make any difference.'

'Not make any difference what your mother said? I'm ashamed of you, Norman, mixing up with a lot of reds and Jews.'

'That's enough of that,' cried Mrs Thursby. 'We'll not have any talk against Jews in this house. No, not even from Rahab herself.'

Vi's face flushed purple underneath her make-up. 'You ought to be ashamed,' she cried, 'an old woman like you to let a boy of Norman's age mix up with all this trash.'

'You've no right to say that . . .' began Norman, but Mrs Thursby interrupted him. 'Oh let the woman say her say, Norman. I've had a windful of Tory talk before now and it hasn't killed me. If Father and I have taught the man to stand up for his own class, we're proud of it. And now, Mrs Cawston, if you've nothing more to say to Norman, I think you'd better go.'

*

Vi arrived at the Unicorn sharp at opening-time that evening. She'd got over most of her indignation, after all Ivy didn't think much about *her*, and if the boy wanted to go to pot, good riddance. She had a couple of gins and lime as she waited for Trevor.

Mr Pontresoli came across the saloon bar. 'Hello, Vi,' he said in his thick voice. 'Have you heard the news about Solomons? Dreadful, isn't it?'

It really gave Vi quite a shock to hear that they'd charged young Mr Solomons – something to do with clothing coupons. She had felt quite guilty towards him after speaking out like that against the Jews, and now to hear of this, it made you wonder what sort of government we *had* got. As Mr Pontresoli said, 'It's getting to be the end of liberty, you mark my words.'

'Trevor'll have something to say about this, Mr Pontresoli,' Vi said, and then she remembered what Trevor said about the Jews, it was all too difficult, one could never tell. Mr Pontresoli offered her another gin, so she said yes. 'I'll tell you what,' said Mr Pontresoli, 'it's going to make a difference to me financially. Solomons was one of my best backers at the club. It may mean cutting down a bit. We shan't be needing two pianos.'

What with the gin – will you have another? said Mr Pontresoli, and yes said Vi – and the tiring day she'd had, Vi felt quite cast down as she thought of Terry out of a job. A nice boy like that. But then he'd got Mrs Lippiatt.

'Poor Terry, Mr Pontresoli,' she said, her eyes filling with tears. 'We *shall* miss him at the club. Here's wishing him more Mrs Lippiatts,' and she drained her glass. 'This one's on me, Mr Pontresoli,' she said, and Mr Pontresoli agreed.

'We couldn't afford to let Terry go,' said Mr Pontresoli, 'that's certain. Mrs Lippiatt says he draws all the women, and she ought to know, she spends so much money.'

Vi worked all this out and it seemed to come round to her. This made her angry. 'Why that's nonsense, Mr Pontresoli,' she said, and she smiled broad-mindedly, 'surely you know Terry's a pansy.'

Mr Pontresoli's fat, cheerful face only winked. 'That gets 'em all ways,' he said and walked out of the saloon bar.

Vi felt quite desperate. She couldn't think where Trevor had got to. 'Have you seen my husband Major Cawston, Gertie?' she asked the barmaid. No one could say I haven't got dignity when I want it, she thought. Gertie hadn't seen Trevor, but Mona's girlfriend said she had, twenty minutes ago at the George *and* stinking. No job and Trevor stinking. It all made Vi feel very low. Life was hell anyhow, and with all those Reds, she'd go after Trevor and fetch Norman back. She was about to get down from the high stool, when she noticed that Mona's girlfriend's eyes were red. 'What's the matter, dear?' she asked.

'Mona's gone off with that Bretonne bitch,' said the girl. 'Oh dear,' said Vi solemnly. 'That's very bad.' So they both had another drink to help them on. Vi was in battling mood. 'Go out and fetch Mona back,' she cried. 'You won't get anywhere sitting still.' 'You do talk silly sometimes,' said the girl. 'What can I do against a Bretonne, they're so passionate.'

The sadness of it all overcame Vi, it was all so true and so sad and so true – all those Bretonnes and Reds and passionates, and Trevor going off to demos, no, Norman going off to demos, and Mr Solomons in the hands of the Government, and her nephew in the hands of the Reds. Yes, that was the chief thing.

'I must let my sister know that her son's in trouble,' she said. 'How can I tell her?'

'Ring her up,' suggested Mona's friend, but Vi told her Ivy had no phone. 'Send a telegram, dear, that's what I should do,' said Gertie. 'You can use the phone at the back of the bar. Just dial TEL.'

It took Vi some time to get through to Telegrams, the telephone at the Unicorn seemed to be such a difficult one. I mustn't let Ivy know that I'm in this condition, she thought, she was always the grand lady with Ivy, so holding herself erect and drawling slightly, she said, 'I want to send a telegram to my sister, please. The name is Hackett – 44 Guybourne Road, Leicester. Terribly worried.' It sounded very Mayfair and she repeated it. 'Terribly worried. Norman in the Wrong Set. Vi.' 'I feel much better now, Gertie,' she said as she stumbled back to the bar. 'I've done my duty.'

ROALD DAHL

The Champion of the World

Roald Dahl (1916–90) was born in Glamorgan, Wales, of part-Norwegian parentage. He served in the air force and in the British Embassy in Washington, and lived in both Britain and the USA. He became one of the most successful writers of children's fiction of his generation (*Charlie and the Chocolate Factory*, 1964; *The Enormous Crocodile*, 1978; *The Witches*, 1983, Whitbread Prize; and many others). He was also a noted short-story writer, with a great many collections, including *Kiss, Kiss* (1960), *The Best of Dahl* (1978) and *Tales of the Unexpected* (1979), which established him, both in print and on television, as the 'master of the unexpected twist in the tale'.

'The Champion of the World', from the volume *Kiss, Kiss*, was originally published in the *New Yorker*, and is a classic and highly amusing example of Roald Dahl's methods. It employs a conventional enough technique of story-telling but turns on an unexpected basic situation. A somewhat exoticized rural England is pervaded with an air of the macabre or the fantastic – leading to the famous Dahl twist in the tale. The simple and direct approach suggests his skill in writing plainly and directly for young people (this story was itself later reworked into a children's tale) and it is also the basis of his humour, which is always founded on a strong sense of the bizarre and the grotesque.

All day, in between serving customers, we had been crouching over the table in the office of the filling-station, preparing the raisins. They were plump and soft and swollen from being soaked in water, and when you nicked them with a razor-blade the skin sprang open and the jelly stuff inside squeezed out as easily as you could wish.

But we had a hundred and ninety-six of them to do altogether and the evening was nearly upon us before we had finished.

'Don't they look marvellous!' Claud cried, rubbing his hands together hard. 'What time is it, Gordon?'

'Just after five.'

Through the window we could see a station-waggon pulling up at the pumps with a woman at the wheel and about eight children in the back eating ice-creams.

'We ought to be moving soon,' Claud said. 'The whole thing'll be a washout if we don't arrive before sunset, you realize that.' He was getting twitchy now. His face had the same flushed and pop-eyed look it got before a dog-race or when there was a date with Clarice in the evening.

We both went outside and Claud gave the woman the number of gallons she wanted. When she had gone, he remained standing in the middle of the driveway squinting anxiously up at the sun which was now only the width of a man's hand above the line of trees along the crest of the ridge on the far side of the valley.

'All right,' I said. 'Lock up.'

He went quickly from pump to pump, securing each nozzle in its holder with a small padlock.

'You'd better take off that yellow pullover,' he said.

'Why should I?'

'You'll be shining like a bloody beacon out there in the moonlight.'

'I'll be all right.'

'You will not,' he said. 'Take it off, Gordon, please. I'll see you in three minutes.' He disappeared into his caravan behind the filling-station, and I went indoors and changed my yellow pullover for a blue one.

When we met again outside, Claud was dressed in a pair of black trousers and a dark-green turtleneck sweater. On his head he wore a brown cloth cap with the peak pulled down low over his eyes, and he looked like an apache actor out of a nightclub.

'What's under there?' I asked, seeing the bulge at his waistline.

He pulled up his sweater and showed me two thin but very large white cotton sacks which were bound neat and tight around his belly. 'To carry the stuff,' he said darkly.

'I see.'

'Let's go,' he said,

'I still think we ought to take the car.'

'It's too risky. They'll see it parked.'

'But it's over three miles up to that wood.'

'Yes,' he said. 'And I suppose you realize we can get six months in the clink if they catch us.'

'You never told me that.'

'Didn't I?'

'I'm not coming,' I said. 'It's not worth it.'

'The walk will do you good, Gordon. Come on.'

It was a calm sunny evening with little wisps of brilliant white cloud hanging motionless in the sky, and the valley was cool and very quiet as the two of us began walking together along the grass verge on the side of the road that ran between the hills towards Oxford.

'You got the raisins?' Claud asked.

'They're in my pocket.'

'Good,' he said. 'Marvellous.'

Ten minutes later we turned left off the main road into a narrow lane with high hedges on either side and from now on it was all uphill.

'How many keepers are there?' I asked.

'Three.'

Claud threw away a half-finished cigarette. A minute later he lit another.

'I don't usually approve of new methods,' he said. 'Not on this sort of a job.'

'Of course.'

'But by God, Gordon, I think we're on to a hot one this time.'

'You do?'

'There's no question about it.'

'I hope you're right.'

'It'll be a milestone in the history of poaching,' he said. 'But don't you go telling a single soul how we've done it, you understand. Because if this ever leaked out we'd have every bloody fool in the district doing the same thing and there wouldn't be a pheasant left.'

'I won't say a word.'

'You ought to be very proud of yourself,' he went on. 'There's been men with brains studying this problem for hundreds of years and not one of them's ever come up with anything even a quarter as artful as you have. Why didn't you tell me about it before?'

'You never invited my opinion,' I said.

And that was the truth. In fact, up until the day before, Claud had never even offered to discuss with me the sacred subject of poaching. Often enough, on a summer's evening when work was finished, I had seen him with cap on head sliding quietly out of his caravan and disappearing up the road towards the woods; and sometimes, watching him through the window of the filling-station, I would find myself wondering exactly what he was going to do, what wily tricks he was going to practise all alone up there under the trees in the dead of night. He seldom came back until very late, and never, absolutely never did he bring any of the spoils with him personally on his return. But the following afternoon – and I couldn't imagine how he did it – there would always be a pheasant or a hare or a brace of partridges hanging up in the shed behind the filling-station for us to eat.

This summer he had been particularly active, and during the last couple of months he had stepped up the tempo to a point where he was going out four and sometimes five nights a week. But that was not all. It seemed to me that recently his whole attitude towards poaching had undergone a subtle and mysterious change. He was more purposeful about it now, more tight-lipped and intense than before, and I had the impression that this was not so much a game any longer as a crusade, a sort of private war that Claud was waging single-handed against an invisible and hated enemy.

But who?

I wasn't sure about this, but I had a suspicion that it was none other than the famous Mr Victor Hazel himself, the owner of the land and the pheasants. Mr Hazel was a pie and sausage manufacturer with an unbelievably arrogant manner. He was rich beyond words, and his property stretched for miles along either side of the valley. He was a self-made man with no charm at all and precious few virtues. He loathed all persons of humble station, having once been one of them himself, and he strove desperately to mingle with what he believed were the right kind of folk. He hunted with the hounds and gave shooting-parties and wore fancy waistcoats, and every weekday he drove an enormous black Rolls-Royce past the filling-station on his way to the factory. As he flashed by, we would sometimes catch a glimpse of the great glistening butcher's face above the wheel, pink as a ham, all soft and inflamed from eating too much meat.

Anyway, yesterday afternoon, right out of the blue, Claud had suddenly said to me, 'I'll be going on up to Hazel's woods again tonight. Why don't you come along?'

'Who, me?'

'It's about the last chance this year for pheasants,' he had said. 'The shooting season opens Saturday and the birds'll be scattered all over the place after that – if there's any left.'

'Why the sudden invitation?' I had asked, greatly suspicious.

'No special reason, Gordon. No reason at all.'

'Is it risky?'

He hadn't answered this.

'I suppose you keep a gun or something hidden away up there?'

'A gun!' he cried, disgusted. 'Nobody ever *shoots* pheasants, didn't you know that? You've only got to fire a *cap-pistol* in Hazel's woods and the keepers'll be on you.'

'Then how do you do it?'

'Ah,' he said, and the eyelids drooped over the eyes, veiled and secretive.

There was a long pause. Then he said, 'Do you think you could keep your mouth shut if I was to tell you a thing or two?'

'Definitely.'

'I've never told this to anyone else in my whole life, Gordon.'

'I am greatly honoured,' I said. 'You can trust me completely.'

He turned his head, fixing me with pale eyes. The eyes were large and wet and ox-like, and they were so near to me that I could see my own face reflected upside down in the centre of each.

'I am now about to let you in on the three best ways in the world of poaching a pheasant,' he said. 'And seeing that you're the guest on this little trip, I am going to give you the choice of which one you'd like us to use tonight. How's that?'

'There's a catch in this.'

'There's no catch, Gordon. I swear it.'

'All right, go on.'

'Now, here's the thing,' he said. 'Here's the first big secret.' He paused and took a long suck at his cigarette. 'Pheasants,' he whispered softly, 'is *crazy* about raisins.'

'Raisins?'

'Just ordinary raisins. It's like a mania with them. My dad discovered that more than forty years ago just like he discovered all three of these methods I'm about to describe to you now.'

'I thought you said your dad was a drunk.'

'Maybe he was. But he was also a great poacher, Gordon. Possibly the greatest there's ever been in the history of England. My dad studied poaching like a scientist.'

'Is that so?'

'I mean it. I really mean it.'

'I believe you.'

'Do you know,' he said, 'my dad used to keep a whole flock of prime cockerels in the back yard purely for experimental purposes.'

'Cockerels?'

'That's right. And whenever he thought up some new stunt for catching a pheasant, he'd try it out on a cockerel first to see how it worked. That's how he discovered about raisins. It's also how he invented the horsehair method.'

Claud paused and glanced over his shoulder as though to make sure that there was nobody listening. 'Here's how it's done,' he said. 'First you take a few raisins and you soak them overnight in water to make them nice and plump and juicy. Then you get a bit of good stiff horsehair and you cut it up into half-inch lengths. Then you push one of these lengths of horsehair through the middle of each raisin so that there's about an eighth of an inch of it sticking out on either side. You follow?'

'Yes.'

'Now – the old pheasant comes along and eats one of these raisins. Right? And you're watching him from behind a tree. So what then?'

'I imagine it sticks in his throat.'

'That's obvious, Gordon. But here's the amazing thing. Here's what my dad discovered. The moment this happens, the bird *never moves his feet again!* He becomes absolutely rooted to the spot, and there he stands pumping his silly neck up and down just like it was a piston, and all you've got to do is walk calmly out from the place where you're hiding and pick him up in your hands.'

'I don't believe that.'

'I swear it,' he said. 'Once a pheasant's had the horsehair you can fire a rifle in his ear and he won't even jump. It's just one of those unexplainable little things. But it takes a genius to discover it.'

He paused, and there was a gleam of pride in his eye now as he dwelt for a moment or two upon the memory of his father, the great inventor.

'So that's Method Number One,' he said. 'Method Number Two is even more simple still. All you do is you have a fishing-line. Then you bait the hook with a raisin and you fish for the pheasant just like you fish for a fish. You pay out the line about fifty yards and you lie there on your stomach in the bushes waiting till you get a bite. Then you haul him in.'

'I don't think your father invented that one.'

'It's very popular with fishermen,' he said, choosing not to hear me. 'Keen fishermen who can't get down to the seaside as often as they want. It gives them a bit of the old thrill. The only trouble is it's rather noisy. The pheasant squawks like hell as you haul him in, and then every keeper in the wood comes running.'

'What is Method Number Three?' I asked.

'Ah,' he said. 'Number Three's a real beauty. It was the last one my dad ever invented before he passed away.'

'His final great work?'

'Exactly, Gordon. And I can even remember the very day it happened, a Sunday morning it was, and suddenly my dad comes into the kitchen holding a huge white cockerel in his hands and he says, "I think I've got it." There's a little smile on his face and a shine of glory in his eyes and he comes in very soft and quiet and he puts the bird down right in the middle of the kitchen table and he says, "By God, I think I've got a good one this time." "A good what?" Mum says, looking up from the sink. "Horace, take that filthy bird off my table." The cockerel has a funny little paper hat over its head, like an ice-cream cone upside down, and my dad is pointing to it proudly. "Stroke him," he says. "He won't move an inch." The cockerel starts scratching away at the paper hat with one of its feet, but the hat seems to be stuck on with glue and it won't come off. "No bird in the world is going to run away once you cover up his eyes," my dad says, and he starts poking the cockerel with his finger and pushing it around on the table, but it doesn't take the slightest bit of notice. "You can have this one," he says, talking to Mum. "You can kill it and dish it up for dinner as a celebration of what I have just invented." And then straight away he takes me by the arm and marches me quickly out the door and off we go over the fields and up into the big forest the other side of Haddenham which used to belong to the Duke of Buckingham, and in less than two hours we get five lovely fat pheasants with no more trouble than it takes to go out and buy them in a shop.'

Claud paused for breath. His eyes were huge and moist and dreamy as they gazed back into the wonderful world of his youth.

'I don't quite follow this,' I said. 'How did he get the paper hats over the pheasants' heads up in the woods?'

'You'd never guess it.'

'I'm sure I wouldn't.'

'Then here it is. First of all you dig a little hole in the ground. Then you twist a piece of paper into the shape of a cone and you fit this into the hole, hollow end upward, like a cup. Then you smear the paper cup all around the inside with bird-lime and drop in a few raisins. At the same time you lay a trail of raisins along the ground leading up to it. Now – the old pheasant comes pecking along the trail, and when he gets to the hole he pops his head inside to gobble the raisins and the next thing he knows he's got a paper hat stuck over his eyes and he can't see a thing. Isn't it marvellous what some people think of, Gordon? Don't you agree?'

'Your dad was a genius,' I said.

'Then take your pick. Choose whichever one of the three methods you fancy and we'll use it tonight.'

'You don't think they're all just a trifle on the crude side, do you?'

'Crude!' he cried, aghast. 'Oh my God! And who's been having roasted pheasant in the house nearly every single day for the last six months and not a penny to pay?'

He turned and walked away towards the door of the workshop. I could see that he was deeply pained by my remark.

'Wait a minute,' I said. 'Don't go.'

'You want to come or don't you?'

'Yes, but let me ask you something first. I've just had a bit of an idea.'

'Keep it,' he said. 'You are talking about a subject you don't know the first thing about.'

'Do you remember that bottle of sleeping pills the doc gave me last month when I had a bad back?'

'What about them?'

'Is there any reason why those wouldn't work on a pheasant?'

Claud closed his eyes and shook his head pityingly from side to side.

'Wait,' I said.

'It's not worth discussing,' he said. 'No pheasant in the world is going to swallow those lousy red capsules. Don't you know any better than that?'

'You are forgetting the raisins,' I said. 'Now listen to this. We take a raisin. Then we soak it till it swells. Then we make a tiny slit in one side of it with a razor-blade. Then we hollow it out a little. Then we open up one of my red capsules and pour all the powder into the raisin. Then we get a needle and cotton and very carefully we sew up the slit. Now . . .'

Out of the corner of my eye, I saw Claud's mouth slowly beginning to open.

'Now,' I said. 'We have a nice clean-looking raisin with two and a half grains of seconal inside it, and let me tell *you* something now. That's enough dope to knock the average *man* unconscious, never mind about *birds!*'

I paused for ten seconds to allow the full impact of this to strike home.

'What's more, with this method we could operate on a really grand scale. We could prepare *twenty* raisins if we felt like it, and all we'd have to do is scatter them around the feeding-grounds at sunset and then walk away. Half an hour later we'd come back, and the pills would be beginning to work, and the pheasants would be up in the trees by then, roosting, and they'd be starting to feel groggy, and they'd be wobbling and trying to keep their balance, and soon every pheasant that had eaten *one single raisin* would keel over unconscious and fall to the ground. My dear boy, they'd be dropping out of the trees like apples, and all we'd have to do is walk around picking them up!'

Claud was staring at me, rapt.

'Oh Christ,' he said softly.

'And they'd never catch us either. We'd simply stroll through the woods dropping a few raisins here and there as we went, and even if they were *watching* us they wouldn't notice anything.'

'Gordon,' he said, laying a hand on my knee and gazing at me with eyes large and bright as two stars. 'If this thing works, it will *revolutionize* poaching.'

'I'm glad to hear it.'

'How many pills have you got left?' he asked.

'Forty-nine. There were fifty in the bottle and I've only used one.'

'Forty-nine's not enough. We want at least two hundred.'

'Are you mad!' I cried.

103

He walked slowly away and stood by the door with his back to me, gazing at the sky.

'Two hundred's the bare minimum,' he said quietly. 'There's really not much point in doing it unless we have two hundred.'

What is it now, I wondered. What the hell's he trying to do?

'This is the last chance we'll have before the season opens,' he said.

'I couldn't possibly get any more.'

'You wouldn't want us to come back empty-handed, would you?'

'But why so *many*?'

Claud turned his head and looked at me with large innocent eyes. 'Why not?' he said gently. 'Do you have any objection?'

My God, I thought suddenly. The crazy bastard is out to wreck Mr Victor Hazel's opening-day shooting party.

'You get us two hundred of those pills,' he said, 'and then it'll be worth doing.'

'I can't.'

'You could try, couldn't you?'

Mr Hazel's party took place on the first of October every year and it was a very famous event. Debilitated gentlemen in tweed suits, some with titles and some who were merely rich, motored in from miles around with their gun-bearers and dogs and wives, and all day long the noise of shooting rolled across the valley. There were always enough pheasants to go round, for each summer the woods were methodically restocked with dozens and dozens of young birds at incredible expense. I had heard it said that the cost of rearing and keeping each pheasant up to the time when it was ready to be shot was well over five pounds (which is approximately the price of two hundred loaves of bread). But to Mr Hazel it was worth every penny of it. He became, if only for a few hours, a big cheese in a little world and even the Lord Lieutenant of the County slapped him on the back and tried to remember his first name when he said goodbye.

'How would it be if we just reduced the dose?' Claud asked. 'Why couldn't we divide the contents of one capsule among four raisins?'

'I suppose you could if you wanted to.'

'But would a quarter of a capsule be strong enough for each bird?'

One simply had to admire the man's nerve. It was dangerous enough to poach a single pheasant up in those woods at this time of year and here he was planning to knock off the bloody lot.

'A quarter would be plenty,' I said.

'You're sure of that?'

'Work it out for yourself. It's all done by body-weight. You'd still be giving about twenty times more than is necessary.'

'Then we'll quarter the dose,' he said, rubbing his hands. He paused and calculated for a moment. 'We'll have one hundred and ninety-six raisins!'

'Do you realize what that involves?' I said. 'They'll take hours to prepare.'

'What of it!' he cried. 'We'll go tomorrow instead. We'll soak the raisins overnight and then we'll have all morning and afternoon to get them ready.'

And that was precisely what we did.

Now, twenty-four hours later, we were on our way. We had been walking steadily for about forty minutes and we were nearing the point where the lane curved round to the right and ran along the crest of the hill towards the big wood where the pheasants lived. There was about a mile to go.

'I don't suppose by any chance these keepers might be carrying guns?' I asked.

'All keepers carry guns,' Claud said.

I had been afraid of that.

'It's for the vermin mostly.'

'Ah.'

'Of course there's no guarantee they won't take a pot at a poacher now and again.'

'You're joking.'

'Not at all. But they only do it from behind. Only when you're running away. They like to pepper you in the legs at about fifty yards.'

'They can't do that!' I cried. 'It's a criminal offence!'

'So is poaching,' Claud said.

We walked on awhile in silence. The sun was below the high hedge on our right now and the lane was in shadow.

'You can consider yourself lucky this isn't thirty years ago,' he went on. 'They used to shoot you on sight in those days.'

'Do you believe that?'

'I know it,' he said. 'Many's the night when I was a nipper I've gone into the kitchen and seen my old dad lying face downward on the table and Mum standing over him digging the grapeshot out of his buttocks with a potato knife.'

'Stop,' I said. 'It makes me nervous.'

'You believe me, don't you?'

'Yes, I believe you.'

'Towards the end he was so covered in tiny little white scars he looked exactly like it was snowing.'

'Yes,' I said. 'All right.'

'Poacher's arse, they used to call it,' Claud said. 'And there wasn't a man in the whole village who didn't have a bit of it one way or another. But my dad was the champion.'

'Good luck to him,' I said.

'I wish to hell he was here now,' Claud said, wistful. 'He'd have given anything in the world to be coming with us on this job tonight.'

'He could take my place,' I said. 'Gladly.'

We had reached the crest of the hill and now we could see the wood ahead of us, huge and dark with the sun going down behind the trees and little sparks of gold shining through.

'You'd better let me have those raisins,' Claud said.

I gave him the bag and he slid it gently into his trouser pocket.

'No talking once we're inside,' he said. 'Just follow me and try not to go snapping any branches.'

Five minutes later we were there. The lane ran right up to the wood itself and then skirted the edge of it for about three hundred yards with only a little hedge between. Claud slipped through the hedge on all fours and I followed.

It was cool and dark inside the wood. No sunlight came in at all.

'This is spooky,' I said.

'Ssshh!'

Claud was very tense. He was walking just ahead of me, picking his feet up high and putting them down gently on the moist ground. He kept his head moving all the time, the eyes sweeping slowly from side to side, searching for danger. I tried doing the same, but soon I began to see a keeper behind every tree, so I gave it up.

Then a large patch of sky appeared ahead of us in the roof of the forest and I knew that this must be the clearing. Claud had told me that the clearing was the place where the young birds were introduced into the woods in early July, where they were fed and watered and guarded by the keepers, and where many of them stayed from force of habit until the shooting began.

'There's always plenty of pheasants in the clearing,' he had said.

'Keepers too, I suppose.'

'Yes, but there's thick bushes all around and that helps.'

We were now advancing in a series of quick crouching spurts, running from tree to tree and stopping and waiting and listening and running on again, and then at last we were kneeling safely behind a big clump of alder right on the edge of the clearing and Claud was grinning and nudging me in the ribs and pointing through the branches at the pheasants.

The place was absolutely stiff with birds. There must have been two hundred of them at least strutting around among the tree-stumps.

'You see what I mean?' Claud whispered.

It was an astonishing sight, a sort of poacher's dream come true. And how close they were! Some of them were not more than ten paces from where we knelt. The hens were plump and creamy-brown and they were so fat their breast-feathers almost brushed the ground as they walked. The cocks were slim and beautiful, with long tails and brilliant red patches around the eyes, like scarlet spectacles. I glanced at Claud. His big ox-like face was transfixed in ecstasy. The mouth was slightly open and the eyes had a kind of glazy look about them as they stared at the pheasants.

I believe that all poachers react in roughly the same way as this on sighting game. They are like women who sight large emeralds in a jeweller's window, the only difference being that the women are less dignified in the methods they employ later on to acquire the loot. Poacher's arse is nothing to the punishment that a female is willing to endure.

'Ah-ha,' Claud said softly. 'You see the keeper?'

'Where?'

'Over the other side, by that big tree. Look carefully.'

'My God!'

'It's all right. He can't see *us*.'

We crouched close to the ground, watching the keeper. He was a smallish man with a cap on his head and a gun under his arm. He never moved. He was like a little post standing there.

'Let's go,' I whispered.

The keeper's face was shadowed by the peak of his cap, but it seemed to me that he was looking directly at us.

'I'm not staying here,' I said.

'Hush,' Claud said.

Slowly, never taking his eyes from the keeper, he reached into his pocket and brought out a single raisin. He placed it in the palm of his right hand, and then quickly, with a little flick of the wrist, he threw the raisin high into the air. I watched it as it went sailing over the bushes and I saw it land within a yard or so of two henbirds standing together beside an old tree-stump. Both birds turned their heads sharply at the drop of the raisin. Then one of them hopped over and made a quick peck at the ground and that must have been it.

I glanced up at the keeper. He hadn't moved.

Claud threw a second raisin into the clearing; then a third, and a fourth, and a fifth.

At this point, I saw the keeper turn away his head in order to survey the wood behind him.

Quick as a flash, Claud pulled the paper bag out of his pocket and tipped a huge pile of raisins into the cup of his right hand.

'Stop,' I said.

But with a great sweep of the arm he flung the whole handful high over the bushes into the clearing.

They fell with a soft little patter, like raindrops on dry leaves, and every single pheasant in the place must either have seen them coming or heard them fall. There was a flurry of wings and a rush to find the treasure.

The keeper's head flicked round as though there were a spring inside his neck. The birds were all pecking away madly at the raisins. The keeper took two quick paces forward and for a moment I thought he was going in to investigate. But then he stopped, and his face came up and his eyes began travelling slowly around the perimeter of the clearing.

'Follow me,' Claud whispered. 'And *keep down*.' He started crawling away swiftly on all fours, like some kind of a monkey.

I went after him. He had his nose close to the ground and his huge tight buttocks were winking at the sky and it was easy to see now how poacher's arse had come to be an occupational disease among the fraternity.

We went along like this for about a hundred yards.

'Now run,' Claud said.

We got to our feet and ran, and a few minutes later we emerged through the hedge into the lovely open safety of the lane.

'It went marvellous,' Claud said, breathing heavily. 'Didn't it go absolutely marvellous?' The big face was scarlet and glowing with triumph.

'It was a mess,' I said.

'What!' he cried.

'Of course it was. We can't possibly go back now. That keeper knows there was someone there.'

'He knows nothing,' Claud said. 'In another five minutes it'll be pitch dark inside the wood and he'll be sloping off home to his supper.'

'I think I'll join him.'

'You're a great poacher,' Claud said. He sat down on the grassy bank under the hedge and lit a cigarette.

The sun had set now and the sky was a pale smoke blue, faintly glazed with yellow. In the wood behind us the shadows and the spaces in between the trees were turning from grey to black.

'How long does a sleeping pill take to work?' Claud asked.

'Look out,' I said. 'There's someone coming.'

The man had appeared suddenly and silently out of the dusk and he was only thirty yards away when I saw him.

'Another bloody keeper,' Claud said.

We both looked at the keeper as he came down the lane towards us. He had a shotgun under his arm and there was a black Labrador walking at his heels. He stopped when he was a few paces away and the dog stopped with him and stayed behind him, watching us through the keeper's legs.

'Good evening,' Claud said, nice and friendly.

This one was a tall bony man about forty with a swift eye and a hard cheek and hard dangerous hands.

'I know you,' he said softly, coming closer. 'I know the both of you.'

Claud didn't answer this.

'You're from the fillin'-station. Right?'

His lips were thin and dry, with some sort of a brownish crust over them.

'You're Cubbage and Hawes and you're from the fillin'-station on the main road. Right?'

'What are we playing?' Claud said. 'Twenty Questions?'

The keeper spat out a big gob of spit and I saw it go floating through the air and land with a plop on a patch of dry dust six inches from Claud's feet. It looked like a little baby oyster lying there.

'Beat it,' the man said. 'Go on. Get out.'

Claud sat on the bank smoking his cigarette and looking at the gob of spit.

'Go on,' the man said. 'Get out.'

When he spoke, the upper lip lifted above the gum and I could see a row of small discoloured teeth, one of them black, the others quince and ochre.

'This happens to be a public highway,' Claud said. 'Kindly do not molest us.'

The keeper shifted the gun from his left arm to his right.

'You're loiterin',' he said, 'with intent to commit a felony. I could run you in for that.'

'No you couldn't,' Claud said.

All this made me rather nervous.

'I've had my eye on you for some time,' the keeper said, looking at Claud.

'It's getting late,' I said. 'Shall we stroll on?'

Claud flipped away his cigarette and got slowly to his feet. 'All right,' he said. 'Let's go.'

We wandered off down the lane the way we had come, leaving the keeper standing there, and soon the man was out of sight in the half-darkness behind us.

'That's the head keeper,' Claud said. 'His name is Rabbetts.'

'Let's get the hell out,' I said.

'Come in here,' Claud said.

There was a gate on our left leading into a field and we climbed over it and sat down behind the hedge.

'Mr Rabbetts is also due for his supper,' Claud said. 'You mustn't worry about him.'

We sat quietly behind the hedge waiting for the keeper to walk past us on his way home. A few stars were showing and a bright three-quarter moon was coming up over the hills behind us in the east.

'Here he is,' Claud whispered. 'Don't move.'

The keeper came loping softly up the lane with the dog padding quick

109

and soft-footed at his heels, and we watched them through the hedge as they went by.

'He won't be coming back tonight,' Claud said.

'How do you know that?'

'A keeper never waits for you in the wood if he knows where you live. He goes to your house and hides outside and watches for you to come back.'

'That's worse.'

'No, it isn't, not if you dump the loot somewhere else before you go home. He can't touch you then.'

'What about the other one, the one in the clearing?'

'He's gone too.'

'You can't be sure of that.'

'I've been studying these bastards for months, Gordon, honest I have. I know all their habits. There's no danger.'

Reluctantly I followed him back into the wood. It was pitch dark in there now and very silent, and as we moved cautiously forward the noise of our footsteps seemed to go echoing around the walls of the forest as though we were walking in a cathedral.

'Here's where we threw the raisins,' Claud said.

I peered through the bushes.

The clearing lay dim and milky in the moonlight.

'You're quite sure the keeper's gone?'

'I *know* he's gone.'

I could just see Claud's face under the peak of his cap, the pale lips, the soft pale cheeks, and the large eyes with a little spark of excitement dancing slowly in each.

'Are they roosting?'

'Yes.'

'Whereabouts?'

'All around. They don't go far.'

'What do we do next?'

'We stay here and wait. I brought you a light,' he added, and he handed me one of those small pocket flashlights shaped like a fountain-pen. 'You may need it.'

I was beginning to feel better. 'Shall we see if we can spot some of them sitting in the trees?' I said.

'No.'

'I should like to see how they look when they're roosting.'

'This isn't a nature-study,' Claud said. 'Please be quiet.'

We stood there for a long time waiting for something to happen.

'I've just had a nasty thought,' I said. 'If a bird can keep its balance on a branch when it's asleep, then surely there isn't any reason why the pills should make it fall down.'

Claud looked at me quick.

'After all,' I said, 'it's not dead. It's still only sleeping.'

'It's doped,' Claud said.

'But that's just a *deeper* sort of sleep. Why should we expect it to fall down just because it's in a *deeper* sleep?'

There was a gloomy silence.

'We should've tried it with chickens,' Claud said. 'My dad would've done that.'

'Your dad was a genius,' I said.

At that moment there came a soft thump from the wood behind us.

'Hey!'

'Ssshh!'

We stood listening.

Thump.

'There's another!'

It was a deep muffled sound as though a bag of sand had been dropped from about shoulder height.

Thump!

'They're pheasants!' I cried.

'Wait!'

'I'm sure they're pheasants!'

Thump! Thump!

'You're right!'

We ran back into the wood.

'Where were they?'

'Over here! Two of them were over here!'

'I thought they were this way.'

'Keep looking!' Claud shouted. 'They can't be far.'

We searched for about a minute.

'Here's one!' he called.

When I got to him he was holding a magnificent cockbird in both hands. We examined it closely with our flashlights.

'It's doped to the gills,' Claud said. 'It's still alive, I can feel its heart, but it's doped to the bloody gills.'

Thump!

'There's another!'

Thump! Thump!

'Two more!'

Thump!

Thump! Thump! Thump!

'Jesus Christ!'

Thump! Thump! Thump! Thump!

Thump! Thump!

All around us the pheasants were starting to rain down out of the trees. We began rushing around madly in the dark, sweeping the ground with our flashlights.

Thump! Thump! Thump! This lot fell almost on top of me. I was right under the tree as they came down and I found all three of them immediately – two cocks and a hen. They were limp and warm, the feathers wonderfully soft in the hand.

'Where shall I put them?' I called out. I was holding them by the legs.

'Lay them here, Gordon! Just pile them up here where it's light!'

Claud was standing on the edge of the clearing with the moonlight streaming down all over him and a great bunch of pheasants in each hand. His face was bright, his eyes big and bright and wonderful, and he was staring around him like a child who has just discovered that the whole world is made of chocolate.

Thump!

Thump! Thump!

'I don't like it,' I said. 'It's too many.'

'It's beautiful!' he cried and he dumped the birds he was carrying and ran off to look for more.

Thump! Thump! Thump! Thump!

Thump!

It was easy to find them now. There were one or two lying under every tree. I quickly collected six more, three in each hand, and ran back and dumped them with the others. Then six more. Then six more after that.

And still they kept falling.

Claud was in a whirl of ecstasy now, dashing about like a mad ghost under the trees. I could see the beam of his flashlight waving around in the dark and each time he found a bird he gave a little yelp of triumph.

Thump! Thump! Thump!

'That bugger Hazel ought to hear this!' he called out.

'Don't shout,' I said. 'It frightens me.'

'What's that?'

'Don't *shout*. There might be keepers.'

'Screw the keepers!' he cried. 'They're all eating!'

For three or four minutes, the pheasants kept on falling. Then suddenly they stopped.

'Keep searching!' Claud shouted. 'There's plenty more on the ground!'

'Don't you think we ought to get out while the going's good?'

'No,' he said.

We went on searching. Between us we looked under every tree within a hundred yards of the clearing, north, south, east, and west, and I think we found most of them in the end. At the collecting-point there was a pile of pheasants as big as a bonfire.

'It's a miracle,' Claud was saying. 'It's a bloody miracle.' He was staring at them in a kind of trance.

'We'd better just take half a dozen each and get out quick,' I said.

'I would like to count them, Gordon.'

'There's no time for that.'

'I must count them.'

'No,' I said. 'Come on.'

'One . . .

'Two . . .

'Three . . .

'Four . . .'

He began counting them very carefully, picking up each bird in turn and laying it carefully to one side. The moon was directly overhead now and the whole clearing was brilliantly illuminated.

'I'm not standing around here like this,' I said. I walked back a few paces and hid myself in the shadows, waiting for him to finish.

'A hundred and seventeen . . . a hundred and eighteen . . . a hundred and nineteen . . . *a hundred and twenty*!' he cried. '*One hundred and twenty birds!* It's an all-time record!'

I didn't doubt it for a moment.

'The most my dad ever got in one night was fifteen and he was drunk for a week afterwards!'

'You're the champion of the world,' I said. 'Are you ready now?'

'One minute,' he answered and he pulled up his sweater and proceeded to unwind the two big white cotton sacks from around his belly. 'Here's yours,' he said, handing one of them to me. 'Fill it up quick.'

The light of the moon was so strong I could read the small print along the base of the sack. J. W. CRUMP, it said. KESTON FLOUR MILLS, LONDON SW17.

'You don't think that bastard with the brown teeth is watching us this very moment from behind a tree?'

'There's no chance of that,' Claud said. 'He's down at the filling-station like I told you, waiting for us to come home.'

We started loading the pheasants into the sacks. They were soft and floppy-necked and the skin underneath the feathers was still warm.

'There'll be a taxi waiting for us in the lane,' Claud said.

'What?'

'I always go back in a taxi, Gordon, didn't you know that?'

I told him I didn't.

'A taxi is anonymous,' Claud said. 'Nobody knows who's inside a taxi except the driver. My dad taught me that.'

'Which driver?'

'Charlie Kinch. He's only too glad to oblige.'

We finished loading the pheasants and then we humped the sacks on to our shoulders and started staggering through the pitch-black wood towards the lane.

'I'm not walking all the way back to the village with this,' I said. My sack had sixty birds inside it and it must have weighed a hundredweight and a half at least.

'Charlie's never let me down yet,' Claud said.

We came to the margin of the wood and peered through the hedge into the lane. Claud said, 'Charlie boy' very softly and the old man behind the wheel of the taxi not five yards away poked his head out into the moonlight and gave us a sly toothless grin. We slid through the hedge, dragging the sacks after us along the ground.

'Hello!' Charlie said. 'What's this?'

'It's cabbages,' Claud told him. 'Open the door.'

Two minutes later we were safely inside the taxi, cruising slowly down the hill towards the village.

It was all over now bar the shouting. Claud was triumphant, bursting with pride and excitement, and he kept leaning forward and tapping Charlie Kinch on the shoulder and saying, 'How about it, Charlie? How about this for a haul?' and Charlie kept glancing back popeyed at the huge bulging sacks lying on the floor between us and saying, 'Jesus Christ, man, how did you do it?'

'There's six brace of them for you, Charlie,' Claud said. And Charlie said, 'I reckon pheasants is going to be a bit scarce up at Mr Victor Hazel's opening-day shoot this year,' and Claud said, 'I imagine they are, Charlie, I imagine they are.'

'What in God's name are you going to do with a hundred and twenty pheasants?' I asked.

'Put them in cold storage for the winter,' Claud said. 'Put them in with the dogmeat in the deepfreeze at the filling-station.'

'Not tonight, I trust?'

'No, Gordon, not tonight. We leave them at Bessie's house tonight.'

'Bessie who?'

'Bessie Organ.'

'Bessie *Organ*!'

'Bessie always delivers my game, didn't you know that?'

'I don't know anything,' I said. I was completely stunned. Mrs Organ was the wife of the Reverend Jack Organ, the local vicar.

'Always choose a respectable woman to deliver your game,' Claud announced. 'That's correct, Charlie, isn't it?'

'Bessie's a right smart girl,' Charlie said.

We were driving through the village now and the street-lamps were still on and the men were wandering home from the pubs. I saw Will Prattley letting himself in quietly by the side door of his fishmonger's shop and Mrs Prattley's head was sticking out of the window just above him, but he didn't know it.

'The vicar is very partial to roasted pheasant,' Claud said.

'He hangs it eighteen days,' Charlie said, 'then he gives it a couple of good shakes and all the feathers drop off.'

The taxi turned left and swung in through the gates of the vicarage. There were no lights on in the house and nobody met us. Claud and I dumped the pheasants in the coalshed at the rear, and then we said goodbye to Charlie Kinch and walked back in the moonlight to the filling-station, empty-handed. Whether or not Mr Rabbetts was watching us as we went in, I do not know. We saw no sign of him.

'Here she comes,' Claud said to me the next morning.

'Who?'

'Bessie – Bessie Organ.' He spoke the name proudly and with a slight proprietary air, as though he were a general referring to his bravest officer.

I followed him outside.

'Down there,' he said, pointing.

Far away down the road I could see a small female figure advancing towards us.

'What's she pushing?' I asked.

Claud gave me a sly look.

'There's only one safe way of delivering game,' he announced, 'and that's under a baby.'

'Yes,' I murmured, 'yes, of course.'

'That'll be young Christopher Organ in there, aged one and a half. He's a lovely child, Gordon.'

I could just make out the small dot of a baby sitting high up in the pram, which had its hood folded down.

'There's sixty or seventy pheasants at least under that little nipper,' Claud said happily. 'You just imagine that.'

'You can't put sixty or seventy pheasants in a pram.'

'You can if it's got a good deep well underneath it, and if you take out the mattress and pack them in tight, right up to the top. All you need then is a sheet. You'll be surprised how little room a pheasant takes up when it's limp.'

We stood beside the pumps waiting for Bessie Organ to arrive. It was one of those warm windless September mornings with a darkening sky and a smell of thunder in the air.

'Right through the village bold as brass,' Claud said. 'Good old Bessie.'

'She seems in rather a hurry to me.'

Claud lit a new cigarette from the stub of the old one. 'Bessie is never in a hurry,' he said.

'She certainly isn't walking normal,' I told him. 'You look.'

He squinted at her through the smoke of his cigarette. Then he took the cigarette out of his mouth and looked again.

'Well?' I said.

'She does seem to be going a tiny bit quick, doesn't she?' he said carefully.

'She's going damn quick.'

There was a pause. Claud was beginning to stare very hard at the approaching woman.

'Perhaps she doesn't want to be caught in the rain, Gordon. I'll bet that's exactly what it is, she thinks it's going to rain and she don't want the baby to get wet.'

'Why doesn't she put the hood up?'

He didn't answer this.

'She's *running*!' I cried. 'Look!' Bessie had suddenly broken into a full sprint.

Claud stood very still, watching the woman; and in the silence that followed I fancied I could hear a baby screaming.

'What's up?'

He didn't answer.

'There's something wrong with that baby,' I said. 'Listen.'

At this point, Bessie was about two hundred yards away from us but closing fast.

'Can you hear him now?' I said.

'Yes.'

'He's yelling his head off.'

The small shrill voice in the distance was growing louder every second, frantic, piercing, nonstop, almost hysterical.

'He's having a fit,' Claud announced.

'I think he must be.'

'That's why she's running, Gordon. She wants to get him in here quick and put him under a cold tap.'

'I'm sure you're right,' I said. 'In fact I know you're right. Just listen to that noise.'

'If it isn't a fit, you can bet your life it's something like it.'

'I quite agree.'

Claud shifted his feet uneasily on the gravel of the driveway. 'There's a thousand and one different things keep happening every day to little babies like that,' he said.

'Of course.'

'I knew a baby once who caught his fingers in the spokes of the pram wheel. He lost the lot. It cut them clean off.'

'Yes.'

'Whatever it is,' Claud said, 'I wish to Christ she'd stop running.'

A long truck loaded with bricks came up behind Bessie and the driver slowed down and poked his head out of the window to stare. Bessie ignored him and flew on, and she was so close now I could see her big red face with the mouth wide open, panting for breath. I noticed she was wearing white gloves on her hands, very prim and dainty, and there was a funny little white hat to match perched right on the top of her head, like a mushroom.

Suddenly, out of the pram, straight up into the air, flew an enormous pheasant!

Claud let out a cry of horror.

The fool in the truck going along beside Bessie started roaring with laughter.

The pheasant flapped around drunkenly for a few seconds, then it lost height and landed in the grass by the side of the road.

A grocer's van came up behind the truck and began hooting to get by. Bessie kept on running.

Then – *whoosh!* – a second pheasant flew up out of the pram.

Then a third, and a fourth. Then a fifth.

'My God!' I said. 'It's the pills! They're wearing off!'

Claud didn't say anything.

Bessie covered the last fifty yards at a tremendous pace, and she came swinging into the driveway of the filling-station with birds flying up out of the pram in all directions.

'What the hell's going on?' she cried.

'Go round the back!' I shouted. 'Go round the back!' But she pulled up sharp against the first pump in the line and before we could reach her she had seized the screaming infant in her arms and dragged him clear.

'No! No!' Claud cried, racing towards her. 'Don't lift the baby! Put him back! Hold down the sheet!' But she wasn't even listening, and with the weight of the child suddenly lifted away, a great cloud of pheasants rose up out of the pram, fifty or sixty of them, at least, and the whole sky above us was filled with huge brown birds clapping their wings furiously to gain height.

Claud and I started running up and down the driveway waving our arms to frighten them off the premises. 'Go away!' we shouted. 'Shoo! Go away!' But they were too dopey still to take any notice of us and within half a minute down they came again and settled themselves like a swarm of locusts all over the front of my filling-station. The place was covered with them. They sat wing to wing along the edges of the roof and on the concrete canopy that came out over the pumps, and a dozen at least were clinging to the sill of the office window. Some had flown down on to the rack that held the bottles of lubricating-oil, and others were sliding about on the bonnets of my second-hand cars. One cockbird with a fine tail was perched superbly on top of a petrol pump, and quite a number, those that were too drunk to stay aloft, simply squatted in the driveway at our feet, fluffing their feathers and blinking their small eyes.

Across the road, a line of cars had already started forming behind the brick-lorry and the grocery van, and people were opening their doors and getting out and beginning to cross over to have a closer look. I glanced at my watch. It was twenty to nine. Any moment now, I thought, a large black car is going to come streaking along the road from the direction of the village, and the car will be a Rolls, and the face behind the wheel will be the great glistening butcher's face of Mr Victor Hazel, maker of sausages and pies.

'They near pecked him to pieces!' Bessie was shouting, clasping the screaming baby to her bosom.

'You go on home, Bessie,' Claud said, white in the face.

'Lock up,' I said. 'Put out the sign. We've gone for the day.'

KINGSLEY AMIS

Interesting Things

Kingsley Amis (1922–) was born in south London and established himself early as a comic novelist with *Lucky Jim* (1954), his first novel, about a young anti-Establishment university lecturer, Jim Dixon, which was taken as the expression of a new and critical social attitude as well as a remarkably funny work. There have been many novels since, including *That Uncertain Feeling* (1955), *Take a Girl Like You* (1960), *The Green Man* (1969), *Ending Up* (1974), *The Old Devils* (1986, Booker Prize) and *Difficulties With Girls* (1988), some of them displaying the darkness and unease underlying his natural instinct for comedy.

Amis has written only a small number of short stories, many about the wartime period, some playful experiments with science fiction. 'Interesting Things', from *My Enemy's Enemy* (1962), is a wry piece of social comedy. Like much of his work it is a look at the dull, commonplace, ordinary world, which – as Jim Dixon, 'Lucky Jim', shows us in Amis's brilliant and deeply funny novel – is seen as preferable to the world of false ideas or high pretensions. It is a story about boredom, and the endless human hope for 'interesting things'. Amis's alert attention to the way people dress, speak and reveal themselves as comic is all here, and so is his inimitable vernacular cadence ('He was older than her usual escorts, to start with, and to go on with there was something about that mackintosh hat and that string bag which made it hard to think of him putting his arm round anyone, except perhaps his mother'). Amis has been thought the natural successor, in British comic fiction, of Evelyn Waugh; and so he is.

Gloria Davies crossed the road towards the Odeon on legs that weaved a little, as if she was tipsy or rickety. She wasn't either really; it was just the high-heeled shoes, worn for the first time specially for today. The new hoop earrings swayed from her lobes, hitting her rhythmically on the jaws as she walked. No. They were wrong. They had looked fine in her bedroom mirror, but they were wrong, somehow. She whipped them off and stuffed them into her handbag. Perhaps there'd be a chance to try them again later, when it was the evening. They might easily make all the difference then.

She stopped thinking about the earrings when she found she couldn't see Mr Huws-Evans anywhere in the crowd of people waiting for their friends on the steps of the Odeon. She knew at once then that he hadn't really meant it. After all, what could an Inspector of Taxes (Assessment Section) see in an eighteen-year-old comptometer operator? How stuck-up she'd been, congratulating herself on being the first girl in the office Mr Huws-Evans had ever asked out. Just then a tall man who'd been standing close by took off his beige mackintosh hat with a drill-like movement, keeping his elbow close to his chest. It was Mr Huws-Evans.

'Hello, Gloria,' he said. He watched her for a bit, a smile showing round the curly stem of the pipe he was biting. Then he added: 'Didn't you recognize me, Gloria?'

'Sorry, Mr Huws-Evans, I sort of just didn't see you.' The hat and the pipe had put her off completely, and she was further confused by being called Gloria twice already.

He nodded, accepting her apology and explanation. He put his hat on again with a ducking gesture, then removed his pipe. 'Shall we go in? Don't want to miss the news.'

While Mr Huws-Evans bought two two-and-fourpennies Gloria noticed he was carrying a string bag full of packets of potato crisps. She wondered why he was doing that.

It was very dark inside the cinema itself, and Mr Huws-Evans had to click his fingers for a long time, and tremendously loudly, before an usherette came. The Odeon was often full on a Saturday when the football team was playing away, and Gloria and Mr Huws-Evans couldn't help pushing past a lot of people to get to their seats. A good deal of loud sighing, crackling of sweet-packets and uncoiling of embraces marked their progress. At last they were settled in full view of the screen, on which the Duke of Edinburgh was playing polo. Mr Huws-Evans asked Gloria loudly whether she could see all right, and when she whispered that she could he offered her a chocolate. 'They're rather good,' he said.

Almost nothing happened while the films were shown. The main feature was on first. As soon as Gloria could tell that it was old-fashioned she was afraid she wouldn't enjoy it. Nobody did anything in it, they just talked.

Some of the talking made Mr Huws-Evans laugh for a long time at a time, and once or twice he nudged Gloria. When he did this she laughed too, because it was up to her to be polite and not spoil his pleasure. The film ended with a lot of fuss about a Gladstone bag and people falling into each other's arms in a daft, put-on way.

Gloria kept wondering if Mr Huws-Evans was going to put his arm round her. She'd never yet gone to the pictures in male company without at least this happening, and usually quite a lot more being tried on, but somehow Mr Huws-Evans didn't seem the man for any of that. He was older than her usual escorts, to start with, and to go on with there was something about that mackintosh hat and that string bag which made it hard to think of him putting his arm round anyone, except perhaps his mother. Once she caught sight of his hand dangling over the arm of the seat towards her, and she moved her own hand carefully so that he could take hold of it easily if he wanted to, but he didn't. He leaned rather closer to her to light her cigarettes than he strictly needed to, and that was all.

After a pair of tin gates had been shown opening in a slow and dignified way, there was about half an hour of advertisements while everybody whistled the tunes that were playing. The cereals and the detergents came up, then a fairly long and thorough episode about razor-blades. During it Mr Huws-Evans suddenly said: 'It's a damned scandal, that business.'

'What's that, then?'

'Well, all this business about the modern shave. All these damned gadgets and things. It's just a way of trying to get you to use a new blade every day, that's all.'

'Oh, I get you. You mean because the –'

'Mind you, with the kind of blade some of these firms turn out you've got to use a new blade. I grant them that.' He laughed briefly. 'If you don't want to skin yourself getting the beard off, that is. And of course they don't give a damn how much they spend on publicity. It's all off tax. Doesn't really cost them a bean.'

Gloria was going to say 'How's that, then?' but Mr Huws-Evans's manner, that of one with a comprehensive explanation on instant call, warned her not to. She said instead: 'No, of course it doesn't.'

He looked at her with mingled scepticism and wistfulness, and ended the conversation by saying violently: 'Some of these firms.'

While the lights went down again, Gloria thought about this brief exchange. It was just the kind of talk older men went in for, the sort of thing her father discussed with his buddies when they called to take him down to the pub, things to do with the Government and pensions and jobs and the Russians, things that fellows who went dancing never mentioned. She saw, on the other hand, that that kind of talk wasn't only tied up in some way with getting old, it also had to do with money and a car, with speaking properly and with being important. So a girl would show herself up for a lump with no conversation and bad manners if she gave away to an older man the fact that uninteresting things didn't interest her. Next time Mr Huws-Evans got on to them she must do better.

The second film promised to be full of interesting things. There were some lovely dresses, the star looked just like another star Gloria had often wished she looked like, and there was a scene in a kind of flash nightclub with dim lights, men in tail coats and a modern band. The star was wearing a terrific evening dress with sequins and had a white fur round her shoulders. A man with a smashing profile sitting at the bar turned and saw her. Her eyes met his for a long moment. Gloria swallowed and leaned forward in her seat.

Mr Huws-Evans nudged Gloria and said: 'Don't think much of this, do you? What about some tea?'

'Oh, we haven't got to go yet, have we?'

'Well, we don't want to sit through this, do we?'

Gloria recollected herself. 'No, right you are, then.'

They moved effortfully back along the row, taking longer this time because some of the embraces were slower in uncoiling. In the foyer, Gloria said: 'Well, thank you very much, Mr Huws-Evans, I enjoyed the film ever so much,' but he wasn't listening; he was looking wildly about as if he'd just found himself in a ladies' cloakroom, and beginning to say: 'The crisps. I've left them inside.'

'Never mind, don't you worry, it won't take a minute fetching them. I don't mind waiting at all.'

He stared out at her from under the mackintosh hat, which he'd pulled down for some reason so that it hid his eyebrows. 'I shan't be able to remember the seat. You come too, Gloria. Please.'

After a lot more finger-clicking inside they found the row. In the beam of the usherette's torch Gloria saw that their seats were already occupied. Even more slowly than before, Mr Huws-Evans began shuffling sidelong away from her; there was some disturbance. Gloria, waiting in the aisle, turned and looked at the screen. The man with the profile was dancing with the star now and all the other people had gone back to their tables and were watching them. Gloria watched them too, and had forgotten where she was when a moderate uproar slowly broke out and slowly moved towards her. It was Mr Huws-Evans with the crisps, which were rustling and crunching like mad. Men's voices were denouncing him, some of them loudly and one of the loud ones using words Gloria didn't like, in fact one word was the word she called 'that word'. Her cheeks went hot. Mr Huws-Evans was saying things like 'Very sorry, old boy' and 'Hurts me as much as it hurts you,' and every so often he laughed cheerily. Everywhere people were calling 'Ssshh.' Gloria couldn't think of anything to do to help.

A long time later they were outside again. It was clear at once that the rain had stopped holding off hours ago. Mr Huws-Evans took her arm and said they'd better run for it, and that was what they did. They ran a long way for it, and fast too, so that the high heels were doing some terrible slipping and skidding. Opposite Woolworth's Gloria nearly did the splits, but Mr Huws-Evans prevented that, and was just as effective when she started a kind of sliding football tackle towards a lady in bifocal glasses carrying a little boy. That was just outside Bevan & Bevan's, and Gloria didn't mind it much because she'd guessed by now that they were going to Dalessio's, a fairly flash Italian restaurant frequented by the car-owning classes – unless, of course, they were making for Cwmbwrla or Portardulais on foot.

There was a queue in Dalessio's and Gloria panted out the news that she was going to the cloakroom, where there was another, but shorter, queue. While she waited her turn she felt her hair, which must have been looking dreadful, and wondered about her face, to which she'd applied some of the new liquid make-up everyone was talking about. She was glad to find, in due time, that she hadn't been looking too bad. Touching up with the liquid stuff didn't quite provide the amazing matt finish the advertisements described, in fact she wondered if she didn't look a bit like one of the waxworks she'd seen that time in Cardiff, but there was no time to redo it and it must surely wear off a little after a bit. She gazed longingly at the earrings in her bag, and at the new mascara kit, but these must certainly wait. Taking a last peep at herself, she reflected gratefully, as her father had often exhorted her to do, that she was very lucky to be quite pretty and have all that naturally curly naturally blond hair.

Mr Huws-Evans had a table for two when she joined him. He took the bag of crisps off her chair and laid them reverently at his side. Gloria thought he seemed very attached to them. What did he want them for, and so many of them too? It was a puzzle. Perhaps he guessed her curiosity, because he said: 'They're for the party. They said I was to get them.'

'Oh, I see. Who'll be there? At the party? You did tell me when you asked me, but I'm afraid I've forgotten.'

'Not many people you'll know, I'm afraid. There'll be Mr Pugh, of course, from Allowances, and his wife, and Miss Harry from Repayments, and my brother – you've met him, haven't you? – and my dentist and his, er, and his friend, and two or three of my brother's friends. About a dozen altogether.'

'It sounds lovely,' Gloria said. A little tremor of excitement ran through her; then she remembered about poise. She arranged herself at the table like one of the models who showed off jewellery on TV, and purposely took a long while deciding what to have when the waitress came, though she'd known ever since passing Bevan & Bevan's that she was going to have mixed grill, with French fried potatoes. She was soon so lost in thoughts of the party and in enjoying eating that it was like a voice in a dream when Mr Huws-Evans said:

'Of course, the real difficulties come when we have to decide whether something's income or capital.'

Gloria looked up, trying not to seem startled. 'Oh yes.'

'For instance,' Mr Huws-Evans went on, drawing a long fishbone from his mouth, 'take the case of a man who buys a house, lives in it for a bit and then sells it. Any profit he might make wouldn't be assessable. It's capital, not income.'

'So he wouldn't have to pay tax on it, is that right?'

'Now for goodness' sake don't go and get that mixed up with the tax on the property itself, the Schedule A tax.'

'Oh yes, I've heard of that. There were some figures I –'

'That still has to be paid.' He leaned forward in an emphatic way. 'Unless the man is exempt of course.'

'Oh yes.'

'Now it'd be much easier, as you can imagine, to catch him on the sale of several houses. But even then we'd need to show that there was a trade. If the chap buys them as investments, just to get the rents, well then you couldn't catch him if he sold out later at a profit. There'd be no trade, you see.'

'No.' Gloria swallowed a mushroom stalk whole. 'No trade.'

'That's right.' He nodded and seemed pleased, then changed his tone to nonchalant indulgence. 'Mind you, even the profit on an isolated transaction could be an income profit. There was the case of three chaps who bought some South African brandy, had it shipped over here and blended with French brandy, and sold it at a profit. But the court still said there was a trade. They'd set up a selling organization.'

'Ah, I get it.'

'You'll be perfectly all right just so long as you remember that income tax is a tax on income.'

Gloria felt a little dashed when Mr Huws-Evans found nothing to add to his last maxim. She hadn't spoken up enough and shown she was taking an interest. He couldn't just go on talking, with nobody helping to make it a proper conversation. And yet – what could she have said? It was so hard to think of things.

Mr Huws-Evans launched off again soon and she cheered up. He questioned her about herself and her parents and friends and what she did in the evenings. He watched her with his big brown eyes and tended to raise his eyebrows slowly when she got near the end of each bit she said. Then, before asking his next question, he'd let his eyes go vacant, and drop his jaw without opening his mouth at all, and nod slightly, as if each reply of hers was tying up, rather disturbingly, with some fantastic theory about her he'd originally made up for fun: that she was a Communist spy, say, or a goblin in human form. During all this he dismantled, cleaned, reassembled, filled and lit his pipe, finally tamping down the tobacco with his thumb and burning himself slightly.

At last it was time to go. In the street Gloria said: 'Well, thank you very much, Mr Huws-Evans, I enjoyed the food ever so much,' but he wasn't listening; he was rubbing his chin hard with some of his fingers, and beginning to say: 'Shave. Got to have a shave before the party. That blade this morning.'

They boarded a bus and went a long way on it. Mr Huws-Evans explained, quoting figures, that a taxi wasn't worth while and that he personally was damned if he was going to lay out all that cash on a car simply to make a splash and impress a few snobs. He paid the conductor with coins from a leather purse that did up with two poppers. This purse, Gloria thought, was somehow rather like the mackintosh hat and the string bag with the crisps. After doing up the purse and putting it safely away Mr Huws-Evans said that his digs, where the shave was going to happen, were quite near Mr Pugh's house, which was where the party was going to happen. He added that this would give them just nice time.

They got off the bus and walked for a few minutes. The rain had stopped and the sun was out. Gloria cheered up again, and didn't notice at first when Mr Huws-Evans suddenly stopped in the middle of the pavement. He was looking about in rather the same way as he'd done in the foyer of the Odeon. He said: 'Funny. I could have sworn.'

'What's the matter, then?'

'Can't seem to remember the right house. Ridiculous of me, isn't it? Just can't seem to remember at all.'

'Not your digs it isn't, where you can't remember, is it?'

'Well yes, my digs. This is it. No, there's no TV aerial.'

'Never mind, what's the number?'

'That's the silly part. I don't know the number.'

'Oh, but you must. How ever do you manage with letters and things? Come on, you must know. Try and think, now.'

'No good. I've never known it.'

'What?'

'Well, you see, the landlady's got one of those stamp things to stamp the address at the top of the notepaper and I always use that. And then when I get a letter I just see it's for me and that's all I bother about, see?' He said most of this over his shoulder in the intervals of trying to see through some lace curtains. Then he shook his head and walked on, only to bend forward slightly with hands on knees, like a swimmer waiting for the starting-pistol, and stare at a photograph of a terrier which someone had arranged, thoughtfully turned outward, on a windowsill. 'The number's got a three in it, I do know that,' he said then. 'At least I think so.'

'How do you manage as a rule?'

'I know the house, you see.'

Mr Huws-Evans now entered a front garden and put his eye to a gap in the curtains. Quite soon a man in shirtsleeves holding a newspaper twitched the curtain aside and stood looking at him. He was a big man with hair growing up round the base of his neck, and you could guess that he worked at some job where strength was important. Mr Huws-Evans came out of the garden, latching its gate behind him. 'I don't think that's the one,' he said.

'Come on, why not just knock somewhere and ask?'

'Can't do that. They'd think I was barmy.'

Eventually Mr Huws-Evans recognized his house by its bright red door. 'Eighty-seven,' he murmured, studying the number as he went in. 'I must remember that.'

Gloria sat in the sitting room, which had more books in it than she'd ever seen in a private house before, and looked at the book Mr Huws-Evans had dropped into her lap before going up to have his shave. It was called *Income Taxes in the Commonwealth*, and he'd said it would probably interest her.

She found it didn't do that and had gone to see if there were any interesting books in the bookcase when the door opened and an old lady looked in. She and Gloria stared at each other for about half a minute, and Gloria's cheeks felt hot again. The old lady's top lip had vertical furrows and there was something distrustful about her. She gave a few grunts with a puff of breath at the beginning of each one, and went out. Gloria didn't like to touch the bookcase now and told herself that the party would make everything worth while.

When Mr Huws-Evans came back he had a big red patch on his neck. 'These razor-blade firms,' he said bitterly, but made no objection when Gloria asked if she could go and wash her hands. He even came to the foot of the stairs to show her the right door.

The liquid make-up looked fine, the mascara went on like distemper on a wall and the earrings were just right now. She only hoped her white blouse and rust cocktail-length skirt, the only clothes she had that were at all evening, were evening enough. When she came out the old lady was there, about thirty inches away. This time she gave more puffing grunts than before and started giving them sooner. She was still giving them when Gloria went downstairs. But then Mr Huws-Evans, as soon as he saw her, jumped up and said: 'You look absolutely stunning, Gloria,' so that part was worth while.

After they'd left, what Gloria had been half-expecting all along happened, though not in the way she'd half-expected. It now appeared that they were much too early, and Mr Huws-Evans took her into a park for a sit-down. Before long he said: 'You know, Gloria, it means a lot to me, you coming out with me today.'

This was hard to answer, so she just nodded.

'I think you're the prettiest girl I've ever been out with.'

'Well, thank you very much, Mr Huws-Evans.'

'Won't you call me Waldo? I wish you would.'

'Oh no, I don't think I could, really.'

'Why not?'

'I . . . I don't think I know you well enough.'

He stared at her with the large brown eyes she'd often admired in the office, but which she now thought looked soft. Sadly, he said: 'If only you knew what I feel about you, Gloria, and how much you mean to me. Funny, isn't it? I couldn't have guessed what you were going to do to me, make me feel, I mean, when I first saw you.' He lurched suddenly towards her, but drew back at the last minute. 'If only you could feel for me just a tiny bit of what I feel for you, you've no idea what it would mean to me.'

An approach of this kind was new to Gloria and it flustered her. If, instead of all this daft talk, Mr Huws-Evans had tried to kiss her, she'd probably have let him, even in this park place; she could have handled that. But all he'd done was make her feel foolish and awkward. Abruptly, she stood up. 'I think we ought to be going.'

'Oh, not yet. Please. Please don't be offended.'

'I'm not offended, honest.'

He got up too and stood in front of her. 'I'd give anything in the world to think that you didn't think too hardly of me. I feel such a worm.'

'Now you're not to talk so silly.'

When it was much too late, Mr Huws-Evans did try to kiss her, saying as he did so: 'Oh, my darling.'

Gloria sidestepped him. 'I'm not your darling,' she said decisively.

After that neither spoke until they arrived at the house where the party was. Mr Huws-Evans's daft talk, Gloria thought, was to be expected from the owner of that mackintosh hat – which he still wore.

When Mr Huws-Evans's brother caught sight of her their eyes met for a long moment. It was because of him – she'd seen him once or twice when he called in at the office – that she'd accepted Mr Huws-Evans's invitation. Originally she'd intended just to look at him across the room while she let Mr Huws-Evans talk to her, but after what had happened she left Mr Huws-Evans to unpack his crisps and put them in bowls while the brother (it was funny to think that he was Mr Huws-Evans too, in a way) took her across the room, sat her on a sofa and started talking about interesting things.

MURIEL SPARK

A Member of the Family

Muriel Spark (1918–) was born in Edinburgh, and worked in political intelligence during the war. She has written many novels and stories, as well as plays, radio dramas, poetry and criticism. Her novels include *The Comforters* (1957), *Memento Mori* (1959), *The Prime of Miss Jean Brodie* (1961), *The Driver's Seat* (1970), *The Abbess of Crewe* (1974) and *A Far Cry from Kensington* (1988). In recent years she has lived in Rome, and she has won many international prizes and honours.

'A Member of the Family' comes from the story collection *Voices at Play* (1961). Like much of Muriel Spark's best work, it is a tale about emotional relations (and manipulations) that cunningly unfolds into a chilling and wonderful irony. Spark's splendidly detached vision, her deadly wit, and her gift for creating strange and remarkable human communities can generally be guaranteed to upturn the expectations of any of her more innocent protagonists. Such is the rather simple Trudy in the story, and this is a classic tale of comic surprise, leavened with the ironic detachment of a writer whose gift for malice often seems an essential part of both her moral and her Catholic religious insight.

'You must,' said Richard, suddenly, one day in November, 'come and meet my mother.'

Trudy, who had been waiting for a long time for this invitation, after all was amazed.

'I should like you,' said Richard, 'to meet my mother. She's looking forward to it.'

'Oh, does she know about me?'

'Rather,' Richard said.

'Oh!'

'No need to be nervous,' Richard said. 'She's awfully sweet.'

'Oh, I'm sure she is. Yes, of course, I'd love –'

'Come to tea on Sunday,' he said.

They had met the previous June in a lake town in southern Austria. Trudy had gone with a young woman who had a bed-sitting-room in Kensington just below Trudy's room. This young woman could speak German, whereas Trudy couldn't.

Bleilach was one of the cheaper lake towns; in fact, cheaper was a way of putting it: it was cheap.

'Gwen, I didn't realize it ever rained here,' Trudy said on their third day. 'It's all rather like Wales,' she said, standing by the closed double windows of their room regarding the downpour and imagining the mountains which indeed were there, but invisible.

'You said that yesterday,' Gwen said, 'and it was quite fine yesterday. Yesterday you said it was like Wales.'

'Well, it rained a bit yesterday.'

'But the sun was shining when you said it was like Wales.'

'Well, so it is.'

'On a much larger scale, I should say,' Gwen said.

'I didn't realize it would be so wet.' Then Trudy could almost hear Gwen counting twenty.

'You have to take your chance,' Gwen said. 'This is an unfortunate summer.'

The pelting of the rain increased as if in confirmation.

Trudy thought, I'd better shut up. But suicidally: 'Wouldn't it be better if we moved to a slightly more expensive place?' she said.

'The rain falls on the expensive places too. It falls on the just and the unjust alike.'

Gwen was thirty-five, a schoolteacher. She wore her hair and her clothes and her bit of lipstick in such a way that, standing by the window looking out at the rain, it occurred to Trudy like a revelation that Gwen had given up all thoughts of marriage. 'On the just and the unjust alike,' said Gwen, turning her maddening imperturbable eyes upon Trudy, as if to say, you are the unjust and I'm the just.

Next day was fine. They swam in the lake. They sat drinking apple juice under the red-and-yellow awnings on the terrace of their guesthouse and gazed at the innocent smiling mountain. They paraded – Gwen in her navy-blue shorts and Trudy in her puffy sunsuit – along the lake-side where marched also the lean brown camping youths from all over the globe, the fat print-frocked mothers and double-chinned fathers from Germany followed by their blonde sedate young, and the English women with their perms.

'There aren't any men about,' Trudy said.

'There are hundreds of men,' Gwen said, in a voice which meant, whatever do you mean?

'I really must try out my phrase-book,' Trudy said, for she had the feeling that if she were independent of Gwen as interpreter she might, as she expressed it to herself, have more of a chance.

'You might have more of a chance of meeting someone interesting that way,' Gwen said, for their close confinement by the rain had seemed to make her psychic, and she was continually putting Trudy's thoughts into words.

'Oh, I'm not here for that. I only wanted a rest, as I told you I'm not –'

'Goodness, Richard!'

Gwen was actually speaking English to a man who was not apparently accompanied by a wife or aunt or sister.

He kissed Gwen on the cheek. She laughed and so did he. 'Well, well,' he said. He was not much taller than Gwen. He had dark crinkly hair and a small moustache of a light brown. He wore bathing trunks and his large chest was impressively bronze. 'What brings you here?' he said to Gwen, looking meanwhile at Trudy.

He was staying at an hotel on the other side of the lake. Each day for the rest of the fortnight he rowed over to meet them at ten in the morning, sometimes spending the whole day with them. Trudy was charmed, she could hardly believe in Gwen's friendly indifference to him, notwithstanding he was a teacher at the same grammar school as Gwen, who therefore saw him every day.

Every time he met them he kissed Gwen on the cheek.

'You seem to be on very good terms with him,' Trudy said.

'Oh. Richard's an old friend. I've known him for years.'

The second week, Gwen went off on various expeditions of her own and left them together.

'This is quite a connoisseur's place,' Richard informed Trudy, and he pointed out why, and in what choice way, it was so, and Trudy, charmed, saw in the peeling pastel stucco of the little town, the unnecessary floral balconies, the bulbous Slovene spires, something special after all. She felt she saw, through his eyes, a precious rightness in the women with their grey skirts and well-filled blouses who trod beside their husbands and their clean children.

'Are they all Austrians?' Trudy asked.

'No, some of them are German and French. But this place attracts the same type.'

Richard's eyes rested with appreciation on the young noisy campers whose tents were pitched in the lake-side field. The campers were long-limbed and animal, brightly and briefly dressed. They romped like galvanized goats, yet looked surprisingly virtuous.

'What are they saying to each other?' she inquired of Richard when a group of them passed by, shouting some words and laughing at each other through glistening red lips and very white teeth.

'They are talking about their fast MG racing cars.'

'Oh, have they got racing cars?'

'No, the racing cars they are talking about don't exist. Sometimes they talk about their film contracts which don't exist. That's why they laugh.'

'Not much of a sense of humour, have they?'

'They are of mixed nationalities, so they have to limit their humour to jokes which everyone can understand, and so they talk about racing cars which aren't there.'

Trudy giggled a little, to show willing. Richard told her he was thirty-five, which she thought feasible. She volunteered that she was not quite twenty-two. Whereupon Richard looked at her and looked away, and looked again and took her hand. For, as he told Gwen afterwards, this remarkable statement was almost an invitation to a love affair.

Their love affair began that afternoon, in a boat on the lake, when, barefoot, they had a game of placing sole to sole, heel to heel. Trudy squealed, and leaned back hard, pressing her feet against Richard's.

She squealed at Gwen when they met in their room later on. 'I'm having a heavenly time with Richard. I do so much like an older man.'

Gwen sat on her bed and gave Trudy a look of wonder. Then she said, 'He's not much older than you.'

'I've knocked a bit off my age,' Trudy said. 'Do you mind not letting on?'

'How much have you knocked off?'

'Seven years.'

'Very courageous,' Gwen said.

'What do you mean?'

'That you are brave.'

'Don't you think you're being a bit nasty?'

'No. It takes courage to start again and again. That's all I mean. Some women would find it boring.'

'Oh, I'm not an experienced girl at all,' Trudy said. 'Whatever made you think I was experienced?'

'It's true,' Gwen said, 'you show no signs of having profited by experience. Have you ever found it a successful tactic to remain twenty-two?'

'I believe you're jealous,' Trudy said. 'One expects this sort of thing from most older women, but somehow I didn't expect it from you.'

'One is always learning,' Gwen said.

Trudy fingered her curls. 'Yes, I have got a lot to learn from life,' she said, looking out of the window.

'God,' said Gwen, 'you haven't begun to believe that you're still twenty-two, have you?'

'Not quite twenty-two is how I put it to Richard,' Trudy said, 'and yes, I do feel it. That's my point. I don't feel a day older.'

The last day of their holidays Richard took Trudy rowing on the lake, which reflected a grey low sky.

'It looks like Windermere today, doesn't it?' he said.

Trudy had not seen Windermere, but she said, yes it did, and gazed at him with shining twenty-two-year-old eyes.

'Sometimes this place,' he said, 'is very like Yorkshire, but only when the weather's bad. Or, over on the mountain side, Wales.'

'Exactly what I told Gwen,' Trudy said. 'I said Wales, I said, it's like Wales.'

'Well, of course, there's quite a difference, really. It –'

'But Gwen simply squashed the idea. You see, she's an older woman, and being a schoolmistress – it's so much different when a man's a teacher – being a woman teacher, she feels she can treat me like a kid. I suppose I must expect it.'

'Oh well –'

'How long have you known Gwen?'

'Several years,' he said. 'Gwen's all right, darling. A great friend of my mother, is Gwen. Quite a member of the family.'

Trudy wanted to move her lodgings in London but she was prevented from doing so by a desire to be near Gwen, who saw Richard daily at school, and who knew his mother so well. And therefore Gwen's experience of Richard filled in the gaps in his life which were unknown to Trudy and which intrigued her.

She would fling herself into Gwen's room. 'Gwen, what d'you think? There he was waiting outside the office and he drove me home, and he's calling for me at seven, and next weekend . . .'

Gwen frequently replied, 'You are out of breath. Have you got heart trouble?' – for Gwen's room was only on the first floor. And Trudy was furious with Gwen on these occasions for seeming not to understand that the breathlessness was all part of her only being twenty-two, and excited by the boyfriend.

'I think Richard's so exciting,' Trudy said. 'It's difficult to believe I've only known him a month.'

'Has he invited you home to meet his mother?' Gwen inquired.

'No – not yet. Oh, do you think he will?'

'Yes, I think so. One day I'm sure he will.'

'Oh, do you mean it?' Trudy flung her arms girlishly round Gwen's impassive neck.

'When is your father coming up?' Gwen said.

'Not for ages, if at all. He can't leave Leicester just now, and he hates London.'

'You must get him to come and ask Richard what his intentions are. A young girl like you needs protection.'

'Gwen, don't be silly.'

Often Trudy would question Gwen about Richard and his mother.

'Are they well off? Is she a well-bred woman? What's the house like? How long have you known Richard? Why hasn't he married before? The mother, is she –'

'Lucy is a marvel in her way,' Gwen said.

'Oh, do you call her Lucy? You must know her awfully well.'

'I'm quite,' said Gwen, 'a member of the family in my way.'

'Richard has often told me that. Do you go there *every* Sunday?'

'Most Sundays,' Gwen said. 'It is often very amusing, and one sometimes sees a fresh face.'

'Why,' Trudy said, as the summer passed and she had already been away for several weekends with Richard, 'doesn't he ask me to meet his mother? If my mother were alive and living in London I know I would have asked him home to meet her.'

Trudy threw out hints to Richard. 'How I wish you could meet my father. You simply must come up to Leicester in the Christmas holidays and stay with him. He's rather tied up in Leicester and never leaves it. He's an insurance manager. The successful kind.'

'I can't very well leave Mother at Christmas,' Richard said, 'but I'd love to meet your father some other time.' His tan had worn off, and Trudy thought him more distinguished and at the same time more unattainable than ever.

'I think it only right,' Trudy said in her young way, 'that one should introduce the man one loves to one's parents' – for it was agreed between them that they were in love.

But still, by the end of October, Richard had not asked her to meet his mother.

'Does it matter all that much?' Gwen said.

'Well, it would be a definite step forward,' Trudy said. 'We can't go on being just friends like this. I'd like to know where I stand with him. After all, we're in love and we're both free. Do you know, I'm beginning to think he hasn't any serious intentions after all. But if he asked me to meet his mother it would be a sort of sign, wouldn't it?'

'It certainly would,' Gwen said.

'I don't even feel I can ring him up at home until I've met his mother. I'd feel shy of talking to her on the phone. I must meet her. It's becoming a sort of obsession.'

'It certainly is,' Gwen said. 'Why don't you just say to him, "I'd like to meet your mother"?'

'Well, Gwen, there are some things a girl can't say.'

'No, but a woman can.'

'Are you going on about my age again? I tell you, Gwen, I feel twenty-two. I think twenty-two. I am twenty-two so far as Richard's concerned. I don't think really you can help me much. After all, you haven't been successful with men yourself, have you?'

'No,' Gwen said, 'I haven't. I've always been on the old side.'

'That's just my point. It doesn't get you anywhere to feel old and think old. If you want to be successful with men you have to hang on to your youth.'

'It wouldn't be worth it at the price,' Gwen said, 'to judge by the state you're in.'

Trudy started to cry and ran to her room, presently returning to ask Gwen questions about Richard's mother. She could rarely keep away from Gwen when she was not out with Richard.

'What's his mother really like? Do you think I'd get on with her?'

'If you wish I'll take you to see his mother one Sunday.'

'No, no,' Trudy said. 'It's got to come from him if it has any meaning. The invitation must come from Richard.'

Trudy had almost lost her confidence, and in fact had come to wonder if Richard was getting tired of her, since he had less and less time to spare for her, when unexpectedly and yet so inevitably, in November, he said, 'You must come and meet my mother.'

'Oh!' Trudy said.

'I should like you to meet my mother. She's looking forward to it.'

'Oh, does she know about me?'

'Rather.'

'Oh!'

*

'It's happened. Everything's all right,' Trudy said breathlessly.

'He has asked you home to meet his mother,' Gwen said without looking up from the exercise book she was correcting.

'It's important to me, Gwen.'

'Yes, yes,' Gwen said.

'I'm going on Sunday afternoon,' Trudy said. 'Will you be there?'

'Not till suppertime,' Gwen said. 'Don't worry.'

'He said, "I want you to meet Mother. I've told her all about you." '

'All about you?'

'That's what he said, and it means so much to me, Gwen. So much.'

Gwen said, 'It's a beginning.'

'Oh, it's the beginning of everything. I'm sure of that.'

Richard picked her up in his Singer at four on Sunday. He seemed preoccupied. He did not, as usual, open the car door for her, but slid into the driver's seat and waited for her to get in beside him. She fancied he was perhaps nervous about her meeting his mother for the first time.

The house on Campion Hill was delightful. They must be very *comfortable*, Trudy thought. Mrs Seeton was a tall, stooping woman, well dressed and preserved, with thick steel-grey hair and large light eyes. 'I hope you'll call me Lucy,' she said. 'Do you smoke?'

'I don't,' said Trudy.

'Helps the nerves,' said Mrs Seeton, 'when one is getting on in life. You don't need to smoke yet awhile.'

'No,' Trudy said. 'What a lovely room, Mrs Seeton.'

'*Lucy*,' said Mrs Seeton.

'Lucy,' Trudy said, very shyly, and looked at Richard for support. But he was drinking the last of his tea and looking out of the window as if to see whether the sky had cleared.

'Richard has to go out for supper,' Mrs Seeton said, waving her cigarette holder very prettily. 'Don't forget to watch the time, Richard. But Trudy will stay to supper with me, I *hope*. Trudy and I have a lot to talk about, I'm sure.' She looked at Trudy and very faintly, with no more than a butterfly-flick, winked.

Trudy accepted the invitation with a conspiratorial nod and a slight squirm in her chair. She looked at Richard to see if he would say where he was going for supper, but he was gazing up at the top pane of the window, his fingers tapping on the arm of the shining Old Windsor chair on which he sat.

Richard left at half past six, very much more cheerful in his going than he had been in his coming.

'Richard gets restless on a Sunday,' said his mother.

'Yes, so I've noticed,' Trudy said, so that there should be no mistake about who had been occupying his recent Sundays.

'I dare say now you want to hear all about Richard,' said his mother in a secretive whisper, although no one was in earshot. Mrs Seeton giggled through her nose and raised her shoulders all the way up her long neck till they almost touched her earrings.

Trudy vaguely copied her gesture. 'Oh, yes,' she said, 'Mrs Seeton.'

'Lucy. You must call me Lucy, now, you know. I want you and me to be friends. I want you to feel like a member of the family. Would you like to see the house?'

She led the way upstairs and displayed her affluent bedroom, one wall of which was entirely covered by mirror, so that, for every photograph on her dressing-table of Richard and Richard's late father, there were virtually two photographs in the room.

'This is Richard on his pony, Lob. He adored Lob. We all adored Lob. Of course, we were in the country then. This is Richard with Nana. And this is Richard's father at the outbreak of war. What did you do in the war, dear?'

'I was at school,' Trudy said, quite truthfully.

'Oh, then you're a teacher, too?'

'No, I'm a secretary. I didn't leave school till after the war.'

Mrs Seeton said, looking at Trudy from two angles, 'Good gracious me, how deceiving. I thought you were about Richard's age, like Gwen. Gwen is such a dear. This is Richard as a graduate. Why he went into schoolmastering I don't know. Still, he's a very good master. Gwen always says so, quite definitely. Don't you adore Gwen?'

'Gwen is a good bit older than me,' Trudy said, being still upset on the subject of age.

'She ought to be here any moment. She usually comes for supper. Now I'll show you the other rooms and Richard's room.'

When they came to Richard's room his mother stood on the threshold and, with her finger to her lips for no apparent reason, swung the door open. Compared with the rest of the house this was a bleak, untidy, almost schoolboy's room. Richard's green pyjama trousers lay on the floor where he had stepped out of them. This was a sight familiar to Trudy from her several weekend excursions with Richard, of late months, to hotels up the Thames valley.

'So untidy,' said Richard's mother, shaking her head woefully. 'So untidy. One day, Trudy, dear, we must have a real chat.'

Gwen arrived presently, and made herself plainly at home by going straight into the kitchen to prepare a salad. Mrs Seeton carved slices of cold meat while Trudy stood and watched them both, listening to a conversation between them which indicated a long intimacy. Richard's mother seemed anxious to please Gwen.

'Expecting Grace tonight?' Gwen said.

'No, darling, I thought perhaps *not tonight*. Was I right?'

'Oh, of course, yes. Expecting Joanna?'

'Well, as it's Trudy's *first* visit, I thought perhaps not –'

'Would you,' Gwen said to Trudy, 'lay the table, my dear. Here are the knives and forks.'

Trudy bore these knives and forks into the dining room with a sense of having been got rid of with a view to being talked about.

At supper, Mrs Seeton said, 'It seems a bit odd, there only being the three of us. We usually have such jolly Sunday suppers. Next week, Trudy, you must come and meet the whole crowd – mustn't she, Gwen?'

'Oh yes,' Gwen said, 'Trudy must do that.'

Towards half past ten Richard's mother said, 'I doubt if Richard will be back in time to run you home. Naughty boy, I daren't think what he gets up to.'

On the way to the bus stop Gwen said, 'Are you happy now that you've met Lucy?'

'Yes, I think so. But I think Richard might have stayed. It would have been nice. I dare say he wanted me to get to know his mother by myself. But in fact I felt the need of his support.'

'Didn't you have a talk with Lucy?'

'Well yes, but not much really. Richard probably didn't realize you were coming to supper. Richard probably thought his mother and I could have a heart-to-heart –'

'I usually go to Lucy's on Sunday,' Gwen said.

'Why?'

'Well, she's a friend of mine. I know her ways. She amuses me.'

During the week Trudy saw Richard only once, for a quick drink.

'Exams,' he said. 'I'm rather busy, darling.'

'Exams in November? I thought they started in December.'

'Preparation for exams,' he said. 'Preliminaries. Lots of work.' He took her home, kissed her on the cheek and drove off.

She looked after the car, and for a moment hated his moustache. But she pulled herself together and, recalling her youthfulness, decided she was too young really to judge the fine shades and moods of a man like Richard.

He picked her up at four o'clock on Sunday.

'Mother's looking forward to seeing you,' he said. 'She hopes you will stay for supper.'

'You won't have to go out, will you, Richard?'

'Not tonight, no.'

But he did have to go out to keep an appointment of which his mother reminded him immediately after tea. He had smiled at his mother and said, 'Thanks.'

Trudy saw the photograph album, then she heard how Mrs Seeton had met Richard's father in Switzerland, and what Mrs Seeton had been wearing at the time.

At half past six the supper party arrived. There were three women, including Gwen. The one called Grace was quite pretty, with a bewildered air. The one called Iris was well over forty and rather loud in her manner.

'Where's Richard tonight, the old cad?' said Iris.

'How do I know?' said his mother. 'Who am I to ask?'

'Well, at least he's a hard worker during the week. A brilliant teacher,' said doe-eyed Grace.

'Middling as a schoolmaster,' Gwen said.

'Oh, Gwen! Look how long he's held down the job,' his mother said.

'I should think,' Grace said, 'he's wonderful with the boys.'

'Those Shakespearean productions at the end of the summer term are really magnificent,' Iris bawled. 'I'll hand him that, the old devil.'

'Magnificent,' said his mother. 'You must admit, Gwen –'

'Very middling performances,' Gwen said.

'I suppose you are right, but, after all, they are only schoolboys. You can't do much with untrained actors, Gwen,' said Mrs Seeton very sadly.

'I adore Richard,' Iris said, 'when he's in his busy, occupied mood. He's so –'

'Oh yes,' Grace said, 'Richard is wonderful when he's got a lot on his mind.'

'I know,' said his mother. 'There was one time when Richard had just started teaching – I must tell you this story – he . . .'

Before they left Mrs Seeton said to Trudy, 'You will come with Gwen next week, won't you? I want you to regard yourself as one of us. There are two other friends of Richard's I do want you to meet. Old friends.'

On the way to the bus Trudy said to Gwen, 'Don't you find it dull going to Mrs Seeton's every Sunday?'

'Well, yes, my dear young thing, and no. From time to time one sees a fresh face, and then it's quite amusing.'

'Doesn't Richard ever stay at home on a Sunday evening?'

'No, I can't say he does. In fact, he's very often away for the whole weekend. As you know.'

'Who are these women?' Trudy said, stopping in the street.

'Oh, just old friends of Richard's.'

'Do they see him often?'

'Not now. They've become members of the family.'

JOHN UPDIKE

The Bulgarian Poetess

John Updike (1932–), born in Shillington, Pennsylvania, has been one of the most prolific, vivid and responsive recorders of contemporary American middle-class and literary life. A regular contributor to the *New Yorker*, he has, since the end of the 1950s, produced many novels, including *Rabbit, Run* (1960), *Couples* (1968), *A Month of Sundays* (1975), *Roger's Version* (1986), and *The Witches of Eastwick* (1984), as well as many collections of short stories and essays, poetry, and a number of notable parodies.

'The Bulgarian Poetess' comes from *Bech: A Book* (1970), a group of tales about a literary alter ego. Henry Bech, author of *Travel Light* and *Think Big*, a novel in progress, is a very anxious well-known writer, Jewish American (Updike is not), travelling on an official tour in eastern Europe in the Khrushchev era. The story has all Updike's observant wit and his fascination with the happenings of the modern literary life – where, as Bech says elsewhere in the book, 'Envied like Negroes, disbelieved in like angels, we veer between the harlotry of the lecture platform and the torture of the writing desk.' It also has his warm and pleasant sentimentality, as well as his sharp insight into the Cold War political mood.

'**Y**our poems. Are they difficult?'

She smiled and, unaccustomed to speaking English, answered carefully, drawing a line in the air with two delicately pinched fingers holding an imaginary pen. 'They are difficult – to write.'

He laughed, startled and charmed. 'But not to read?'

She seemed puzzled by his laugh, but did not withdraw her smile, though its corners deepened in a defensive, feminine way. 'I think,' she said, 'not so very.'

'Good.' Brainlessly he repeated 'Good,' disarmed by her unexpected quality of truth. He was, himself, a writer, this fortyish young man, Henry Bech, with his thinning curly hair and melancholy Jewish nose, the author of one good book and three others, the good one having come first. By a kind of oversight, he had never married. His reputation had grown while his powers declined. As he felt himself sink, in his fiction, deeper and deeper into eclectic sexuality and bravura narcissism, as his search for plain truth carried him further and further into treacherous realms of fantasy and, lately, of silence, he was more and more thickly hounded by homage, by flat-footed exegetes, by arrogantly worshipful undergraduates who had hitch-hiked a thousand miles to touch his hand, by querulous translators, by election to honorary societies, by invitations to lecture, to 'speak', to 'read', to participate in symposia trumped up by ambitious girlie magazines in shameless conjunction with venerable universities. His very government, in airily unstamped envelopes from Washington, invited him to travel, as an ambassador of the arts, to the other half of the world, the hostile, mysterious half. Rather automatically, but with some faint hope of shaking himself loose from the burden of himself, he consented, and found himself floating, with a passport so stapled with visas it fluttered when pulled from his pocket, down into the dim airports of Communist cities.

He arrived in Sofia the day after a mixture of Bulgarian and African students had smashed the windows of the American legation and ignited an overturned Chevrolet. The cultural officer, pale from a sleepless night of guard duty, tamping his pipe with trembling fingers, advised Bech to stay out of crowds and escorted him to his hotel. The lobby was swarming with Negroes in black wool fezzes and pointed European shoes. Insecurely disguised, he felt, by an astrakhan hat purchased in Moscow, Bech passed through to the elevator, whose operator addressed him in German. '*Ja, vier,*' Bech answered, '*danke,*' and telephoned, in his bad French, for dinner to be brought up to his room. He remained there all night, behind a locked door, reading Hawthorne. He had lifted a paperback collection of short stories from a legation windowsill littered with broken glass. A few curved bright crumbs fell from between the pages on to his blanket. The image of Roger Malvin lying alone, dying, in the forest – 'Death would come like the slow approach of a corpse, stealing gradually towards him through the forest, and showing its ghastly and motionless features from behind a nearer and yet a nearer tree' – frightened him. Bech fell asleep early and suffered from swollen, homesick dreams. It had been the first day of Hanukkah.

In the morning, venturing downstairs for breakfast, he was surprised to find the restaurant open, the waiters affable, the eggs actual, the coffee hot, though syrupy. Outside, Sofia was sunny and (except for a few dark glances at his big American shoes) amenable to his passage along the streets. Lozenge-patterns of pansies, looking flat and brittle as pressed flowers, had been set in the public beds. Women with a touch of Western *chic* walked hatless in the park behind the mausoleum of Georgi Dimitrov. There was a mosque, and an assortment of trolley cars salvaged from the remotest corner of Bech's childhood, and a tree that talked – that is, it was so full of birds that it swayed under their weight and emitted volumes of chirping sound like a great leafy loudspeaker. It was the inverse of his hotel, whose silent walls presumably contained listening microphones. Electricity was somewhat enchanted in the Socialist world. Lights flickered off untouched and radios turned themselves on. Telephones rang in the dead of the night and breathed wordlessly in his ear. Six weeks ago, flying from New York City, Bech had expected Moscow to be a blazing counterpart and instead saw, through the plane window, a skein of hoarded lights no brighter, on that vast black plain, than a girl's body in a dark room.

Past the talking tree was the American legation. The sidewalk, heaped with broken glass, was roped off, so that pedestrians had to detour into the gutter. Bech detached himself from the stream, crossed the little barren of pavement, smiled at the Bulgarian militiamen who were sullenly guarding the jewel-bright heaps of shards, and pulled open the bronze door. The cultural officer was crisper after a normal night's sleep. He clenched his pipe in his teeth and handed Bech a small list. 'You're to meet with the Writers' Union at eleven. These are writers you might ask to see. As far as we can tell, they're among the more progressive.'

Words like 'progressive' and 'liberal' had a somewhat reversed sense in this world. At times, indeed, Bech felt he had passed through a mirror, a dingy flecked mirror that reflected feebly the capitalist world; in its dim depths everything was similar but left-handed. One of the names ended in '-ova.' Bech said, 'A woman.'

'A poetess,' the cultural officer said, sucking and tamping in a fury of bogus efficiency. 'Very popular, apparently. Her books are impossible to buy.'

'Have you read anything by these people?'

'I'll be frank with you. I can just about make my way through a newspaper.'

'But you always know what a newspaper will say anyway.'

'I'm sorry, I don't get your meaning.'

'There isn't any.' Bech didn't quite know why the Americans he met irritated him – whether because they garishly refused to blend into this shadow-world or because they were always so solemnly sending him on ridiculous errands.

At the Writers' Union, he handed the secretary the list as it had been handed to him, on US legation stationery. The secretary, a large stooped man with the hands of a stonemason, grimaced and shook his head but obligingly reached for the telephone. Bech's meeting was already waiting in another room. It was the usual one, the one that, with small differences, he had already attended in Moscow and Kiev, Yerevan and Alma-Ata, Bucharest and Prague: the polished oval table, the bowl of fruit, the morning light, the gleaming glasses of brandy and mineral water, the lurking portrait of Lenin, the six or eight patiently sitting men who would leap to their feet with quick blank smiles. These men would include a few literary officials, termed 'critics', high in the Party, loquacious and witty and destined to propose a toast to international understanding; a few selected novelists and poets, mustachioed, smoking, sulking at this invasion of their time; a university professor, the head of the Anglo-American Literature Department, speaking in a beautiful withered English of Mark Twain and Sinclair Lewis; a young interpreter with a moist handshake; a shaggy old journalist obsequiously scribbling notes; and, on the rim of the group, in chairs placed to suggest that they had invited themselves, one or two gentlemen of ill-defined status, fidgety and tieless, maverick translators who would turn out to be the only ones present who had ever read a word by Henry Bech.

Here this type was represented by a stout man in a tweed coat leather-patched at the elbows in the British style. The whites of his eyes were distinctly red. He shook Bech's hand eagerly, made of it almost an embrace of reunion, bending his face so close that Bech could distinguish the smells of tobacco, garlic, cheese, and alcohol. Even as they were seating themselves around the table, and the Writers' Union chairman, a man elegantly bald, with very pale eyelashes, was touching his brandy glass as if to lift it, this anxious red-eyed interloper blurted at Bech, 'Your *Travel Light* was so marvelous a book. The motels, the highways, the young girls with their lovers who were motor-cyclists, so marvelous, so American, the youth, the adoration for space and speed, the barbarity of the advertisements in neon lighting, the very poetry. It takes us truly into another dimension.'

Travel Light was the first novel, the famous one. Bech disliked discussing it. 'At home,' he said, 'it was criticized as despairing.'

The man's hands, stained orange with tobacco, lifted in amazement and plopped noisily to his knees. 'No, no, a thousand times. Truth, wonder, terror even, vulgarity, yes. But despair, no, not at all, not one iota. Your critics are dead wrong.'

'Thank you.'

The chairman softly cleared his throat and lifted his glass an inch from the table, so that it formed with its reflection a kind of playing card.

Bech's admirer excitedly persisted. 'You are not a *wet* writer, no. You are a dry writer, yes? You have the expressions, am I wrong in English, dry, hard?'

'More or less.'

'I want to translate you!'

It was the agonized cry of a condemned man, for the chairman coldly lifted his glass to the height of his eyes, and like a firing squad the others followed suit. Blinking his white lashes, the chairman gazed mistily in the direction of the sudden silence, and spoke in Bulgarian.

The young interpreter murmured in Bech's ear, 'I wish to propose now, ah, a very brief toast. I know it will seem doubly brief to our honored American guest, who has so recently enjoyed the, ah, hospitality of our Soviet comrades.' There must have been a joke here, for the rest of the table laughed. 'But in seriousness permit me to say that in our country we have seen in years past too few Americans, ah, of Mr Bech's progressive and sympathetic stripe. We hope in the next hour to learn from him much that is interesting and, ah, socially useful about the literature of his large country, and perhaps we may in turn inform him of our own proud literature, of which perhaps he knows regrettably little. Ah, so let me finally, then, since there is a saying that too long a courtship spoils the marriage, offer to drink, in our native plum brandy *slivovica*, ah, firstly to the success of his visit and, in the second place, to the mutual increase of international understanding.'

'Thank you,' Bech said and, as a courtesy, drained his glass. It was wrong; the others, having merely sipped, stared. The purple burning revolved in Bech's stomach and a severe distaste for himself, for his role, for this entire artificial and futile process, focused into a small brown spot on a pear in the bowl so shiningly posed before his eyes.

The red-eyed fool smelling of cheese was ornamenting the toast. 'It is a personal honor for me to meet the man who, in *Travel Light*, truly added a new dimension to American prose.'

'The book was written,' Bech said, 'ten years ago.'

'And since?' A slumping, mustached man sat up and sprang into English. 'Since, you have written what?'

Bech had been asked that question often in these weeks and his answer had grown curt. 'A second novel called *Brother Pig*, which is St Bernard's expression for the body.'

'Good. Yes, and?'

'A collection of essays and sketches called *When the Saints*.'

'I like the title less well.'

'It's the beginning of a famous Negro song.'

'We know the song,' another man said, a smaller man, with the tense, dented mouth of a hare. He lightly sang, 'Lordy, I just want to be in that number.'

'And the last book,' Bech said, 'was a long novel called *The Chosen* that took five years to write and that nobody liked.'

'I have read reviews,' the red-eyed man said. 'I have not read the book. Copies are difficult here.'

'I'll give you one,' Bech said.

The promise seemed, somehow, to make the recipient unfortunately conspicuous; wringing his stained hands, he appeared to swell in size, to intrude grotesquely upon the inner ring, so that the interpreter took it upon himself to whisper, with the haste of an apology, into Bech's ear, 'This gentleman is well known as the translator into our language of *Alice in Wonderland*.'

'A marvelous book,' the translator said, deflating in relief, pulling at his pockets for a cigarette. 'It truly takes us into another dimension. Something that must be done. We live in a new cosmos.'

The chairman spoke in Bulgarian, musically, at length. There was polite laughter. Nobody translated for Bech. The professorial type, his hair like a flaxen toupee, jerked forward. 'Tell me, is it true, as I have read' – his phrases whistled slightly, like rusty machinery – 'that the stock of Sinclair Lewis has plummeted under the Salinger wave?'

And so it went, here as in Kiev, Prague, and Alma-Ata, the same questions, more or less predictable, and his own answers, terribly familiar to him by now, mechanical, stale, irrelevant, untrue, claustrophobic. Then the door opened. In came, with the rosy air of a woman fresh from a bath, a little breathless, having hurried, hatless, a woman in a blond coat, her hair also blond. The secretary, entering behind her, seemed to make a cherishing space around her with his large curved hands. He introduced her to Bech as Vera Something-ova, the poetess he had asked to meet. None of the others on the list, he explained, had answered their telephones.

'Aren't you kind to come?' As Bech asked it, it was a genuine question, to which he expected some sort of an answer.

She spoke to the interpreter in Bulgarian. 'She says,' the interpreter told Bech, 'she is sorry she is so late.'

'But she was just called!' In the warmth of his confusion and pleasure Bech turned to speak directly to her, forgetting he would not be understood. 'I'm terribly sorry to have interrupted your morning.'

'I am pleased,' she said, 'to meet you. I heard of you spoken in France.'

'You speak English!'

'No. Very little amount.'

'But you *do*.'

A chair was brought for her from a corner of the room. She yielded her coat, revealing herself in a suit also blond, as if her clothes were an aspect of a total consistency. She sat down opposite Bech, crossing her legs. Her legs were visibly good; her face was perceptibly broad. Lowering her lids, she tugged her skirt to the curve of her knee. It was his sense of her having hurried, hurried to *him*, and of being, still, graciously flustered, that most touched him.

He spoke to her very clearly, across the fruit, fearful of abusing and breaking the fragile bridge of her English. 'You are a poetess. When I was young, I also wrote poems.'

She was silent so long he thought she would never answer; but then she smiled and pronounced, 'You are not old now.'

'Your poems. Are they difficult?'

'They are difficult – to write.'

'But not to read?'

'I think – not so very.'

'Good. Good.'

Despite the decay of his career, Bech had retained an absolute faith in his instincts; he never doubted that somewhere an ideal course was open to him and that his intuitions were pre-dealt clues to his destiny. He had loved, briefly or long, with or without consummation, perhaps a dozen women; yet all of them, he now saw, shared the trait of approximation, of narrowly missing an undisclosed prototype. The surprise he felt did not have to do with the appearance, at last, of this central woman; he had always expected her to appear. What he had not expected was her appearance here, in this remote and abused nation, in this room of morning light, where he discovered a small knife in his fingers and on the table before him, golden and moist, a precisely divided pear.

Men traveling alone develop a romantic vertigo. Bech had already fallen in love with a freckled embassy wife in Prague, a buck-toothed chanteuse in Rumania, a stolid Mongolian sculptress in Kazakhstan. In the Tretyakov Gallery he had fallen in love with a recumbent statue, and at the Moscow Ballet School with an entire roomful of girls. Entering the room, he had been struck by the aroma, tenderly acrid, of young female sweat. Sixteen and seventeen, wearing patchy practice suits, the girls were twirling so strenuously their slippers were unraveling. Demure student faces crowned the unconscious insolence of their bodies. The room was doubled in depth by a floor-to-ceiling mirror. Bech was seated on a bench at its base. Staring above his head, each girl watched herself with frowning eyes frozen, for an instant in the turn, by the imperious delay and snap of her head. Bech tried to remember the lines of Rilke that expressed it, this snap and delay: *did not the drawing remain / that the dark stroke of your eyebrow / swiftly wrote on the wall of its own turning?* At one point the teacher, a shapeless old Ukrainian lady with gold canines, a *prima* of the thirties, had arisen and cried something translated to Bech as, 'No, no, the arms free, *free!*' And in demonstration she had executed a rapid series of pirouettes with such proud effortlessness that all the girls, standing this way and that like deer along the wall, had applauded. Bech had loved them for that. In all his loves, there was an urge to rescue – to rescue the girls from the slavery of their exertions, the statue from the cold grip of its own marble, the embassy wife from her boring and unctuous husband, the chanteuse from her nightly humiliation (she could not sing), the Mongolian from her stolid race. But the Bulgarian poetess presented herself to him as needing nothing, as being complete, poised, satisfied, achieved. He was aroused and curious and, the next day, inquired about her of the man with the vaguely contemptuous mouth of a hare – a novelist turned playwright and scenarist, who accompanied him to the Rila Monastery. 'She lives to write,' the playwright said. 'I do not think it is healthy.'

Bech said, 'But she seems so healthy.' They stood beside a small church with whitewashed walls. From the outside it looked like a hovel, a shelter for pigs or chickens. For five centuries the Turks had ruled Bulgaria, and the Christian churches, however richly adorned within, had humble exteriors. A peasant woman with wildly snarled hair unlocked the door for them. Though the church could hardly ever have held more than thirty worshippers, it was divided into three parts, and every inch of wall was covered with eighteenth-century frescoes. Those in the narthex depicted a Hell where the devils wielded scimitars. Passing through the tiny nave, Bech peeked through the iconostasis into the screened area that, in the symbolism of Orthodox architecture, represented the next, the hidden world – Paradise. He glimpsed a row of books, an easy chair, a pair of ancient oval spectacles. Outdoors again, he felt released from the unpleasantly tight atmosphere of a children's book. They were on the side of a hill. Above them was a stand of pines whose trunks were shelled with ice. Below them sprawled the monastery, a citadel of Bulgarian national feeling during the years of the Turkish Yoke. The last monks had been moved out in 1961. An aimless soft rain was falling in these mountains, and there were not many German tourists today. Across the valley, whose little silver river still turned a water wheel, a motionless white horse stood silhouetted against a green meadow, pinned there like a brooch.

'I am an old friend of hers,' the playwright said. 'I worry about her.'

'Are the poems good?'

'It is difficult for me to judge. They are very feminine. Perhaps shallow.'

'Shallowness can be a kind of honesty.'

'Yes. She is very honest in her work.'

'And in her life?'

'As well.'

'What does her husband do?'

The other man looked at him with parted lips and touched his arm, a strange Slavic gesture, communicating an underlying racial urgency, that Bech no longer shied from. 'But she has no husband. As I say, she is too much for poetry to have married.'

'But her name ends in "-ova".'

'I see. You are mistaken. It is not a matter of marriage; I am Petrov, my unmarried sister is Petrova. All females.'

'How stupid of me. But I think it's such a pity, she's so charming.'

'In America, only the uncharming fail to marry?'

'Yes, you must be very uncharming not to marry.'

'It is not so here. The Government indeed is alarmed; our birth rate is one of the lowest in Europe. It is a problem for economists.'

Bech gestured at the monastery. 'Too many monks?'

'Not enough, perhaps. With too few of monks, something of the monk enters everybody.'

The peasant woman, who seemed old to Bech but who was probably younger than he, saw them to the edge of her domain. She huskily chattered in what Petrov said was very amusing rural slang. Behind her, now hiding in her skirts and now darting away, was her child, a boy not more than three. He was faithfully chased, back and forth, by a small white pig, who moved, as pigs do, on tiptoe, with remarkably abrupt changes of direction. Something in the scene, in the open glee of the woman's parting smile and the unselfconscious way her hair thrust out from her head, something in the mountain mist and spongy rutted turf into which frost had begun to break at night, evoked for Bech a nameless absence to which was attached, like a horse to a meadow, the image of the poetess, with her broad face, her good legs, her Parisian clothes, and her sleekly brushed hair. Petrov, in whom he was beginning to sense, through the wraps of foreignness, a clever and kindred mind, seemed to have overheard his thoughts, for he said, 'If you would like, we could have dinner. It would be easy for me to arrange.'

'With her?'

'Yes, she is my friend, she would be glad.'

'But I have nothing to say to her. I'm just curious about such an intense conjunction of good looks and brains. I mean, what does a soul do with it all?'

'You may ask her. Tomorrow night?'

'I'm sorry, I can't. I'm scheduled to go to the ballet, and the next night the legation is giving a cocktail party for me, and then I fly home.'

'Home? So soon?'

'It does not feel soon to me. I must try to work again.'

'A drink, then. Tomorrow evening before the ballet? It is possible? It is not possible.'

Petrov looked puzzled, and Bech realized that it was his fault, for he was nodding to say Yes, but in Bulgarian nodding meant No, and a shake of the head meant Yes. 'Yes,' he said. 'Gladly.'

The ballet was entitled *Silver Slippers*. As Bech watched it, the word 'ethnic' kept coming to his mind. He had grown accustomed, during his trip, to this sort of artistic evasion, the retreat from the difficult and disappointing present into folk-dance, folk-tale, folk-song, with always the implication that, beneath the embroidered peasant costume, the folk was really one's heart's own darling, the proletariat.

'Do you like fairy-tales?' It was the moist-palmed interpreter who accompanied him to the theatre.

'I *love* them,' Bech said, with a fervor and gaiety lingering from the previous hour. The interpreter looked at him anxiously, as when Bech had swallowed the brandy in one swig, and throughout the ballet kept murmuring explanations of self-evident events on the stage. Each night, a princess would put on silver slippers and dance through her mirror to tryst with a wizard, who possessed a magic stick that she coveted, for with it the world could be ruled. The wizard, as a dancer, was inept, and once almost dropped her, so that anger flashed from her eyes. She was, the princess, a little redhead with a high round bottom and a frozen pout and beautiful free arm motions, and Bech found it oddly ecstatic when, preparatory to her leap, she would dance toward the mirror, an empty oval, and another girl, identically dressed in pink, would emerge from the wings and perform as her reflection. And when the princess, haughtily adjusting her cape of invisibility, leapt through the oval of gold wire, Bech's heart leapt backward into the enchanted hour he had spent with the poetess.

Though the appointment had been established, she came into the restaurant as if, again, she had been suddenly summoned and had hurried. She sat down between Bech and Petrov slightly breathless and fussed, but exuding, again, that impalpable warmth of intelligence and virtue.

'Vera, Vera,' Petrov said.

'You hurry too much,' Bech told her.

'Not so very much,' she said.

Petrov ordered her a cognac and continued with Bech their discussion of the newer French novelists. 'It is tricks,' Petrov said. 'Good tricks, but tricks. It does not have enough to do with life, it is too much verbal nervousness. Is that sense?'

'It's an epigram,' Bech said.

'There are just two of their number with whom I do not feel this: Claude Simon and Samuel Beckett. You have no relation, Bech, Beckett?'

'None.'

Vera said, 'Nathalie Sarraute is a very modest woman. She felt motherly to me.'

'You have met her?'

'In Paris I heard her speak. Afterward there was the coffee. I liked her theories, of the, oh, *what*? Of the *little* movements within the heart.' She delicately measured a pinch of space and smiled, through Bech, back to herself.

'Tricks,' Petrov said. 'I do not feel this with Beckett; there, in a low form, believe it or not, one has human content.'

Bech felt duty-bound to pursue this, to ask about the theatre of the absurd in Bulgaria, about abstract painting (these were the touchstones of 'progressiveness'; Russia had none, Rumania some, Czechoslovakia plenty), to subvert Petrov. Instead, he asked the poetess, 'Motherly?'

Vera explained, her hands delicately modeling the air, rounding into nuance, as it were, the square corners of her words. 'After her talk, we – talked.'

'In French?'

'And in Russian.'

'She knows Russian?'

'She was born Russian.'

'How is her Russian?'

'Very pure but – old-fashioned. Like a book. As she talked, I felt in a book, safe.'

'You do not always feel safe?'

'Not always.'

'Do you find it difficult to be a woman poet?'

'We have a tradition of woman poets. We have Elisaveta Bagriana, who is very great.'

Petrov leaned toward Bech as if to nibble him. 'Your own works? Are they influenced by the *nouvelle vague*? Do you consider yourself to write anti-*romans*?'

Bech kept himself turned toward the woman. 'Do you want to hear about how I write? You don't, do you?'

'Very much yes,' she said.

He told them, told them shamelessly, in a voice that surprised him with its steadiness, its limpid urgency, how once he had written, how in *Travel Light* he had sought to show people skimming the surface of things with their lives, taking tints from things the way that objects in a still life color one another, and how later he had attempted to place beneath the melody of plot a counter-melody of imagery, interlocking images which had risen to the top and drowned his story, and how in *The Chosen* he had sought to make of this confusion the theme itself, an epic theme, by showing a population of characters whose actions were all determined, at the deepest level, by nostalgia, by a desire to get back, to dive, each, into the springs of their private imagery. The book probably failed; at least, it was badly received. Bech apologized for telling all this. His voice tasted flat in his mouth; he felt a secret intoxication and a secret guilt, for he had contrived to give a grand air, as of an impossibly noble and quixotically complex experiment, to his failure when at bottom, he suspected, a certain simple laziness was the cause.

Petrov said, 'Fiction so formally sentimental could not be composed in Bulgaria. We do not have a happy history.'

It was the first time Petrov had sounded like a Communist. If there was one thing that irked Bech about these people behind the mirror, it was their assumption that, however second-rate elsewhere, in suffering they were supreme. He said, 'Believe it or not, neither do we.'

Vera calmly intruded. 'Your personae are not moved by love?'

'Yes, very much. But as a form of nostalgia. We fall in love, I tried to say in the book, with women who remind us of our first landscape. A silly idea. I used to be interested in love. I once wrote an essay on the orgasm – you know the word? –'

She shook her head. He remembered that it meant Yes.

'– on the orgasm as perfect memory. The one mystery is, what are we remembering?'

She shook her head again, and he noticed that her eyes were gray, and that in their depths his image (which he could not see) was searching for the thing remembered. She composed her fingertips around the brandy glass and said, 'There is a French poet, a young one, who has written of this. He says that never else do we, do we so gather up, collect into ourselves, oh –' Vexed, she spoke to Petrov in rapid Bulgarian.

He shrugged and said, 'Concentrate our attention.'

'– concentrate our attention,' she repeated to Bech, as if the words, to be believed, had to come from her. 'I say it foolish – foolishly – but in French it is very well put and – *correct*.'

Petrov smiled neatly and said, 'This is an enjoyable subject for discussion, love.'

'It remains,' Bech said, picking his words as if the language were not native even to him, 'one of the few things that still deserve meditation.'

'I think it is good,' she said.

'Love?' he asked, startled.

She shook her head and tapped the stem of her glass with a fingernail, so that Bech had an inaudible sense of ringing, and she bent as if to study the liquor, so that her entire body borrowed a rosiness from the brandy and burned itself into Bech's memory – the silver gloss of her nail, the sheen of her hair, the symmetry of her arms relaxed on the white tablecloth, everything except the expression on her face.

Petrov asked aloud Bech's opinion of Dürrenmatt.

Actuality is a running impoverishment of possibility. Though he had looked forward to seeing her again at the cocktail party and had made sure that she was invited, when it occurred, though she came, he could not get to her. He saw her enter, with Petrov, but he was fenced in by an attaché of the Yugoslav Embassy and his burnished Tunisian wife; and, later, when he was worming his way toward her diagonally, a steely hand closed on his arm and a rasping American female told him that her fifteen-year-old nephew had decided to be a writer and desperately needed advice. Not the standard crap, but real brass-knuckles advice. Bech found himself balked. He was surrounded by America: the voices, the narrow suits, the watery drinks, the clatter, the glitter. The mirror had gone opaque and gave him back only himself. He managed, in the end, as the officials were thinning out, to break through and confront her in a corner. Her coat, blond, with a rabbit collar, was already on; from its side pocket she pulled a pale volume of poems in the Cyrillic alphabet. 'Please,' she said. On the flyleaf she had written, 'to H. Beck, sincerelly, with bad spellings but much' – the last word looked like 'leave' but must have been 'love'.

'Wait,' he begged, and went back to where his ravaged pile of presentation books had been and, unable to find the one he wanted, stole the legation library's jacketless copy of *The Chosen*. Placing it in her expectant hands, he told her, 'Don't look,' for inside he had written, with a drunk's stylistic confidence,

Dear Vera Glavanakova –

It is a matter of earnest regret for me that you and I must live on opposite sides of the world.

MARY LAVIN

My Vocation

Mary Lavin (1912–) was born in Massachusetts but moved to Ireland with her family in 1923. She has written two novels, but is above all known for her short stories, which number more than a hundred and have been collected in various volumes, from the early rural stories *Tales from Bective Bridge* (1942) to *A Family Likeness and Other Stories* (1985). She lives in Dublin and is a noted figure in the rich and often comic Irish tradition of short fiction, which includes the writing of Frank O'Connor, Liam O'Flaherty, Sean O'Faolain and Edna O'Brien.

'My Vocation', taken from *Collected Stories, Volume Two* (1964), is one of her comic tales, part of a writing range which has always embraced wide and varied aspects of experience. Nearly all Mary Lavin's tales are set in Ireland, in Dublin or in small villages, and they frequently deal with unhappy and frustrated characters for whom life is a source of dismay and disappointment. They also deal with a world where the Catholic religion is important – though, as in the present story, it does not always provide the answer to the human problems and troubled lives which Lavin portrays with both irony and compassion.

I'm not married yet, but I'm still in hopes. One thing is certain though: I was never cut out to be a nun in the first place. Anyway, I was only thirteen when I got the Call, and I think if we were living out here in Crumlin at the time, in the new houses that the Government gave us, I'd never have got it at all, because we hardly ever see nuns out here, somehow, and a person wouldn't take so much notice of them out here anyway. It's so airy, you know, and they blow along in their big white bonnets and a person wouldn't take any more notice of them than the seagulls that blow in from the sea. And then, too, you'd never get near enough to them out here to get the smell of them.

It was the smell of them I used to love in the Dorset Street days, when they'd stop us in the street to talk to us, when we'd be playing hopscotch on the path. I used to push up as close to them as possible and take big sniffs of them. But that was nothing to when they came up to the room to see Mother. You'd get it terribly strong then.

'What smell are you talking about?' said my father one day when I was going on about them after they went. 'That's no way to talk about people in Religious Orders,' he said. 'There's no smell at all off the like of them.'

That was right, of course, and I saw where I was wrong. It was the no-smell that I used to get, but there were so many smells fighting for place in Dorset Street, fried onions, and garbage, and the smell of old rags, that a person with no smell at all stood out a mile from everybody else. Anyone with an eye in their head could see that I didn't mean any disrespect. It vexed me shockingly to have my father think such a thing. I told him so, too, straight out.

'And if you want to know,' I finished up, 'I'm going to be a nun myself when I get big.'

But my father only roared laughing.

'Do you hear that?' he said, turning to Mother. 'Isn't that a good one? She'll be joining the same order as you, I'm thinking.' And he roared out laughing again: a very common laugh I thought, even though he was my father.

And he was nothing to my brother Paudeen.

'We'll be all right if it isn't the Order of Mary Magdalen that one joins,' he said.

What do you make of that for commonness? Is it any wonder I wanted to get away from the lot of them?

He was always at me, that fellow, saying I was cheapening myself, and telling Ma on me if he saw me as much as lift my eye to a fellow passing me in the street.

'She's mad for boys, that one,' he used to say. And it wasn't true at all. It wasn't my fault if the boys were always after me, was it? And even if I felt a bit sparky now and then, wasn't that the kind that always became nuns? I never saw a plain-looking one, did you? I never did. Not in those days, I mean. The ones that used to come visiting us in Dorset Street were all gorgeous-looking, with pale faces and not a rotten tooth in their heads. They were twice as good-looking as the Tiller Girls in the Gaiety. And on Holy Thursday, when we were doing the Seven Churches, and we used to cross over the Liffey to the south side to make up the number, I used to go into the Convent of the Reparation just to look at the nuns. You see them inside in a kind of little golden cage, back of the altar in their white habits with blue sashes and their big silver beads dangling down by their side. They were like angels: honest to God. You'd be sure of it if you didn't happen to hear them give an odd cough now and again, or a sneeze.

It was in there with them I'd like to be, but Sis – she's my girlfriend – she told me they were all ladies, titled ladies too, some of them, and I'd have to be a lay sister. I wasn't having any of that, thank you. I could have gone away to domestic service any day if that was only all the ambition I had. It would have broken my mother's heart to see me scrubbing floors and the like. She never sank that low, although there were fourteen of them in the family, and only eleven of us. She was never anything less than a wards' maid in the Mater Hospital, and they're sort of nurses, if you like, and when she met my father she was after getting an offer of a great job as a barmaid in Geary's of Parnell Street. She'd never have held with me being a lay sister.

'I don't hold with there being any such things as lay sisters at all,' she said. 'They're not allowed a hot jar in their beds, I believe, and they have to sit at the back of the chapel with no red plush on their kneeler. If you ask me, it's a queer thing to see the Church making distinctions.'

She had a great regard for the Orders that had no lay sisters at all, like the Little Sisters of the Poor, and the Visiting Sisters.

'Oh, they're the grand women!' she said.

You'd think then, wouldn't you, that she'd be glad when I decided to join them. But she was as much against me as any of them.

'Is it you?' she cried. 'You'd want to get the impudent look taken off your face if that's the case!' she said, tightly.

I suppose it was the opposition that nearly drove me mad. It made me dead set on going ahead with the thing.

You see, they never went against me in any of the things I was going to be before that. The time I said I was going to be a Tiller Girl in the Gaiety, you should have seen the way they went on: all of them. They were dead keen on the idea.

'Are you tall enough though – that's the thing?' said Paudeen.

And the tears came into my mother's eyes.

'That's what I always wanted to be when I was a girl,' she said, and she dried her eyes and turned to my father. 'Do you think there is anyone you could ask to use his influence?' she said. Because she was always sure and certain that influence was the only thing that would get you any job.

But it wasn't influence in the Tiller Girls: it was legs. And I knew that, and my legs were never my strong point, so I gave up that idea.

Then there was the time I thought I'd like to be a waitress, even though I wasn't a blonde, said Paudeen morosely.

But you should see the way they went on then too.

'A packet of henna would soon settle the hair question,' said my mother.

'Although I'm sure some waitresses are good girls,' she said. 'It all depends on a girl herself, and the kind of a home she comes from.'

They were doubtful if I'd get any of these jobs, but they didn't raise any obstacles, and they didn't laugh at me like they did in this case.

'And what will I do for money,' said my father, 'when they come looking for your dowry? If you haven't an education you have to have money, going into those convents.'

But I turned a deaf ear to him.

'The Lord will provide,' I said. 'If it's His will for me to be a nun He'll find a way out of all difficulties,' I said grandly, and in a voice I imagined to be as near as I could make it to the ladylike voices of the Visiting Sisters.

But I hadn't much hope of getting into the Visiting Sisters. To begin with, they always seemed to take it for granted I'd get married.

'I hope you're a good girl,' they used to say to me, and you'd know by the way they said it what they meant. 'Boys may like a fast girl when it comes to having a good time, but it's the modest girl they pick when it comes to choosing a wife,' they said. And suchlike things. They were always harping on the one string. Sure they'd never get over it if I told them what I had in mind. I'd never have the face to tell them!

And then one day what did I see but an advertisement in the paper.

'Wanted, Postulants,' it said, in big letters, and then underneath in small letters, there was the address of the Reverend Mother you were to apply to, and in smaller letters still, at the very bottom, were the words that made me sit up and take notice. 'No Dowry,' they said.

'That's me,' said I, and there and then I up and wrote off to them, without as much as saying a word to anyone only Sis.

Poor Sis: you should have seen how bad she took it.

'I can't believe it,' she said over and over again, and she threw her arms around me and burst out crying. She was always a good sort, Sis.

Every time she looked at me she burst out crying. And I must say that was more like the way I expected people to take me. But as a matter of fact Sis started the ball rolling, and it wasn't long after that everyone began to feel bad, because you see, the next thing that happened was a telegram arrived from the Reverend Mother in answer to my letter.

'It can't be for you,' said my mother, as she ripped it open. 'Who'd be sending you a telegram?'

And I didn't know who could have sent it either until I read the signature. It was Sister Mary Alacoque.

That was the name of the nun in the paper.

'It's for me all right,' I said then. 'I wrote to her,' I said and I felt a bit awkward.

My mother grabbed back the telegram.

'Glory be to God!' she said, but I don't think she meant it as a prayer. 'Do you see what it says? "Calling to see you this afternoon, Deo Gratias." What on earth is the meaning of all this?'

'Well,' I said defiantly, 'when I told you I was going to be a nun you wouldn't believe me. Maybe you'll believe it when I'm out among the savages!' I added. Because it was a missionary order: that's why they didn't care about the dowry. People are always leaving money in their wills to the Foreign Missions, and you don't need to be too highly educated to teach savages, I suppose.

'Glory be to God!' said my mother again. And then she turned on me. 'Get up out of that and we'll try and put some sort of front on things before they get here: there'll be two of them, I'll swear. Nuns never go out alone. Hurry up, will you?'

Never in your life did you see anyone carry on like my mother did that day. For the few hours that remained of the morning she must have worked like a lunatic, running mad around the room, shoving things under the bed, and ramming home the drawers of the chest, and sweeping things off the seats of the chairs.

'They'll want to see a chair they can sit on, anyway,' she said. 'And I suppose we'll have to offer them a bite to eat.'

'Oh, a cup of tea,' said my father.

But my mother had very grand ideas at times.

'Oh, I always heard you should give monks or nuns a good meal,' she said. 'They can eat things out in the world that they can't eat in the convent. As long as you don't ask them. Don't say will you or won't you! Just set it in front of them – that's what I always heard.'

I will say this for my mother, she has a sense of occasion, because we never heard any of this lore when the Visiting Sisters called, or even the Begging Sisters, although you'd think they could do with a square meal by the look of them sometimes.

But no: there was never before seen such a fuss as she made on this occasion.

'Run out to Mrs Mullins in the front room and ask her for the lend of her brass fender,' she cried, giving me a push out the door. 'And see if poor Mr Duffy is home from work – he'll be good enough to let us have a chair, I'm sure, the poor soul, the one with the plush seat,' she cried, coming out to the landing after me, and calling across the well of the stairs.

As I disappeared into Mrs Mullins's I could see her standing in the doorway as if she was trying to make up her mind about something. And sure enough, when I came out lugging the fender with me, she ran across and took it from me.

'Run down to the return room, like a good child,' she said, 'and ask old Mrs Dooley for her tablecloth – the one with the lace edging she got from America.' And as I showed some reluctance, she caught my arm. 'You might give her a wee hint of what's going on. Won't everyone know it as soon as the nuns arrive, and it'll give her the satisfaction of having the news ahead of everyone else.'

But it would be hard to say who had the news first because I was only at the foot of the steps leading to the return room when I could hear doors opening in every direction on our own landing, and the next minute you'd swear they were playing a new kind of postman's knock, in which each one carried a piece of furniture round with him, by the way our friends and neighbours were rushing back and forth across the landing; old Ma Dunne with her cuckoo clock, and young Mrs McBride, that shouldn't be carrying heavy things at all, with our old wicker chair that she was going to exchange for the time with a new one of her own. And I believe she wanted to get her piano rolled in to us too, only there wasn't time!

That was the great thing about Dorset Street: you could meet any and all occasions, you had so many friends at your back. And you could get anything you wanted, all in a few minutes, without anyone outside the landing being any the wiser.

My mother often said it was like one big happy family, that landing – including the return room, of course.

The only thing was everyone wanted to have a look at the room.

'We'll never get shut of them before the nuns arrive,' I thought.

'Isn't this the great news entirely,' said old Mrs Dooley, making her way up the stairs as soon as I told her. And she rushed up to my mother and kissed her. 'Not but that you deserve it,' she said. 'I never knew a priest or a nun yet that hadn't a good mother behind them!' And then Mrs McBride coming out, she drew her into it. 'Isn't that so, Mrs McBride?' she cried. 'I suppose you heard the news?'

'I did indeed,' said Mrs McBride. 'Not that I was surprised,' she said, but I think she only wanted to let on she was greater with us than she was, because as Sis could tell you, there was nothing of the Holy Molly about me – far from it.

What old Mr Duffy said was more like what you'd expect.

'Well, doesn't that beat all!' he cried, hearing the news as he came up the last step of the stairs. 'Ah, well, I always heard it's the biggest divils that make the best saints, and now I can believe it!'

He was a terribly nice old man.

'And is it the Foreign Missions?' he asked, calling me to one side, 'because if that's the case I want you to know you can send me raffle tickets for every draw you hold, and I'll sell the lot for you and get the stubs back in good time, with the money along with it in postal orders. And what's more –' he was going on, when Mrs Mullins let out a scream:

'You didn't tell me it was the Missions,' she cried. 'Oh, God help you, you poor child!' And she threw up her hands. 'How will any of us be saved at all at all with the like of you going to the ends of the earth where you'll never see a living soul only blacks till the day you die! Oh, glory be to God. And to think we never knew who we had in our midst!'

In some ways it was what I expected, but in another way I'd have liked it if they didn't all look at me in such a pitying way.

And old Mrs Dooley put the lid on it.

'A saint – that's what you are, child,' she cried, and she caught my hand and pulled me down close to her – she was a low butt of a little woman. 'They tell me it's out to the poor lepers you're going?'

That was the first I heard about lepers, I can tell you. And I partly guessed the poor old thing had picked it up wrong, but all the same I put a knot in my handkerchief to remind me to ask where I was going.

And I may as well admit straight out, that I wasn't having anything to do with any lepers. I hadn't thought of backing out of the thing entirely at that time, but I was backing out of it if it was to be lepers!

The thought of the lepers gave me the creeps, I suppose. Did you ever get the feeling when a thing was mentioned that you *had* it? Well, that was the way I felt. I kept going over to the basin behind the screen (Mrs McBride's) and washing my hands every minute, and as for spitting out, my throat was raw by the time I heard the cab at the door.

'Here they come,' cried my father, raising his hand like the starter at the dog track.

'Out of this, all of you,' cried Mrs Mullins, rushing out and giving an example to everyone.

'Holy God!' said my mother, but I don't think that was meant to be a prayer either.

But she had nothing to be uneasy about: the room was gorgeous.

That was another thing: I thought they'd be delighted with the room. We never did it up any way special for the Visiting Sisters, but they were always saying how nice we kept it: maybe that was only to encourage my mother, but all the same it was very nice of them. But when the two Recruiting Officers arrived (it was my father called them that after they went), they didn't seem to notice the room at all in spite of what we'd done to it.

And do you know what I heard one of them say to the other?

'It seems clean, anyway,' she said.

Now I didn't like that 'seems'. And what did she mean by the 'anyway' I'd like to know?

It sort of put me off from the start – would you believe that? That, and the look of them. They weren't a bit like the Visiting Sisters – or even the Begging Sisters; who all had lovely figures – like statues. One of them was thin all right, but I didn't like the look of her all the same. She didn't look thin in an ordinary way; she looked worn away, if you know what I mean? And the other one was fat. She was so fat I was afraid if she fell on the stairs she'd start to roll like a ball.

She was the boss: the fat one.

And do you know one of the first things she asked me? You'd never guess. I don't even like to mention it. She caught a hold of my hair.

'I hope you keep it nice and clean,' she said.

What do you think of that? I was glad my mother didn't hear her. My mother forgets herself entirely if she's mad about anything. She didn't hear it, though. But I began to think to myself that they must have met some very low-class girls if they had to ask *that* question. And wasn't that what you'd think?

Then the worn-looking one said a queer thing, not to me, but to the other nun.

'She seems strong, anyway,' she said. And there again I don't think she meant my health. I couldn't help putting her remark alongside the way she was so worn-looking, and I began to think I'd got myself into a nice pickle.

But I was prepared to go through with it all the same. That's me: I have great determination although you mightn't believe it. Sis often says I'd have been well able for the savages if I'd gone on with the thing.

But I didn't.

I missed it by a hair's breadth, though. I won't tell you all the interview, but at the end of it anyway they gave me the name of the Convent where I was to go for Probation, and they told me the day to go, and they gave me a list of clothes I was to get.

'Will you be able to pay for them?' they said, turning to my father. They hadn't taken much notice of him up to that.

I couldn't help admiring the way he answered.

'Well, I managed to pay for plenty of style for her up to now,' he said, 'and seeing that this mourning outfit is to be the last I'll be asked to pay for, I think I'll manage it all right. Why?'

I admired the 'why?'

'Oh, we have to be ready for all eventualities,' said the fat one.

Sis and I nearly died laughing afterwards thinking of those words. But I hardly noticed them at the time, because I was on my way out the door to order a cab. They had asked me to get one and they had given me so many instructions that I was nearly daft.

They didn't want a flighty horse, and they didn't want a cab that was too high up off the ground, and I was to pick a cabby that looked respectable.

Now at this time, although there were still cabs to be hired, you didn't have an almighty great choice, and I knew I had my work cut out for me to meet all their requirements.

But I seemed to be dead in luck in more ways than one, because when I went to the cab-stand there, among the shiny black cabs, with big black horses that rolled their eyes at me, there was one old cab and it was all battered and green-mouldy. The cabby too looked about as mouldy as the cab. And as for the horse – well, wouldn't anyone think that he'd be mouldy too. But as a matter of fact the horse wasn't mouldy in any way. Indeed, it was due to the way he bucketed it about that the old cab was so racked-looking: it was newer than the others I believe, and as for the cabby, I believe it was the horse had him so bad-looking. That horse had the heart scalded in him.

But it was only afterwards I heard all this. I thought I'd done great work, and I went up and got the nuns, and put them into it and off they went, with the thin one waving to me.

It was while I was still waving that I saw the horse starting his capers.

My first thought was to run, but I thought I'd have to face them again, so I didn't do that. Instead, I ran after the cab and shouted to the driver to stop.

Perhaps that was what did the damage. Maybe I drove the horse clean mad altogether, because the next thing he reared up and let his hindlegs fly. There was a dreadful crash and a sound of splintering, and the next thing I knew the bottom of the cab came down on the road with a clatter. I suppose it had got such abuse from that animal from time to time it was on the point of giving way all the time.

It was a miracle for them they weren't let down on the road – the two nuns. It was a miracle for me too in another way because if they did I'd have to go and pick them up and I'd surely be drawn deeper into the whole thing.

But that wasn't what happened. Off went the horse, as mad as ever down the street, rearing and leaping, but the nuns must have got a bit of a warning and held on to the sides, because the next thing I saw, along with the set of four feet under the horse, was four more feet showing out under the body of the cab, and running for dear life.

Honest to God, I started to laugh. Wasn't that awful? They could have been killed, and I knew it, although as a matter of fact someone caught hold of the cab before it got to Parnell Street and they were taken out of it and put into another cab. But once I started to laugh I couldn't stop, and in a way – if you can understand such a thing – I laughed away my vocation. Wasn't that awful?

Not but that I have a great regard for nuns even to this day, although, mind you, I sometimes think the nuns that are going nowadays are not the same as the nuns that were going in our Dorset Street days. I saw a terribly plain-looking one the other day in Cabra Avenue. But all the same, they're grand women! I'm going to make a point of sending all my kids to school with the nuns anyway, when I have them. But of course it takes a fellow with a bit of money to educate his kids nowadays. A girl has to have an eye to the future, as I always tell Sis – she's my girlfriend, you remember.

Well, we're going out to Dollymount this afternoon, Sis and me, and you'd never know who we'd pick up. So long for the present!

DONALD BARTHELME

To London and Rome

Donald Barthelme (1933–89), born in Philadelphia and raised in Texas, worked as director of the Museum of Contemporary Art in Houston before becoming known as a writer of self-mocking short fiction, much of it for the pages of the *New Yorker*. His first story collection, *Come Back Dr Caligari* (1964), used experimental techniques to overlay a world of cultural fragments and 'nostalgia', and subsequent collections like *City Life* (1970), *Sadness* (1972) and *Great Days* (1979) made use of ever more experimental techniques, including visual collage.

Barthelme once said 'Fragments are the only form I trust', and his work, like that of Raymond Queneau, generally examines the workings of fiction itself: its typical tales and images, its appearance on the page, the emotions it tries to raise, its structures of beginning, middle, and end. The earlyish 'To London and Rome', with its playful inner story and its equally playful outer frame, is Barthelme at his best. He engages us enough in the plot to make us think about his characters, and their often troubled emotional lives; he constantly reminds us that characters are words put down on a page, and products of a linguistic illusion. This has been aptly called 'metafiction', and Barthelme is not only one of its best but also one of its most comic practitioners. He is a parodist, parodying writing itself. But his parodic method actually has the power to move us, as well as tease us constantly with its lively, knowing, sophisticated intelligence. Barthelme's many stories are now gathered in two collections, *Sixty Stories* (1985) and *Forty Stories* (1987) – bringing together some of the best post-modern comic experimentation we have.

Do you know what I want more than anything else?
Alison asked.

THERE WAS A
BRIEF PAUSE

What? I said.

A sewing machine Alison said, with buttonhole-making attachments.

THERE WAS A
LONG PAUSE

There are so many things I could do with it for instance fixing up last year's fall dresses and lots of other things.

THERE WAS A
TREMENDOUS
PAUSE DURING
WHICH I BOUGHT
HER A NECCHI
SEWING MACHINE

Wonderful! Alison said sitting at the controls of the Necchi and making buttonholes in a copy of the New York *Times* Sunday Magazine. Her eyes glistened. I had also bought a two-year subscription to *Necchi News* because I could not be sure that her interest would not be held for that long at least.

THERE WAS A
PAUSE BROKEN
ONLY BY THE
HUMMING OF THE
NECCHI

Then I bought her a purple Rolls which we decided to park on the street because our apartment building had no garage. Alison said she absolutely loved the Rolls! and gave me an enthusiastic kiss. I paid for the car with a check drawn on the First City Bank.

THERE WAS AN
INTERVAL

Peter Alison said, what do you want to do now?
Oh I don't know I said.

THERE WAS A
LONG INTERVAL

Well we can't simply sit around the apartment Alison said so we went to the races at Aqueduct where I bought a racehorse that was running well out in front of the others. What a handsome racehorse! Alison said delightedly. I paid for the horse with a check on the Capital National Bank.

THERE WAS AN
INTERMISSION
BETWEEN RACES
SO WE WENT
AROUND TO THE
STABLES AND
BOUGHT A HORSE
TRAILER

The trailer was attached by means of a trailer hitch, which I bought when it became clear that the trailer could not be hitched up without one, to the back of our new Rolls. The horse's name was Dan and I bought a horse blanket, which he was already wearing but which did not come with him, to keep him warm.

He *is* beautiful Alison said.
A front-runner too I said.

THERE WAS AN
INTERVAL OF
SEVERAL DAYS.
THEN ALISON
AND I DROVE THE
CAR WITH THE
TRAILER UP THE

After stopping for lunch at Howard Johnson's where we fed Dan some fried clams which he seemed to like very much Alison said: Do you know what we've completely forgotten? I knew that there was something but although I thought hard I could not imagine what it was.

169

RAMP INTO THE
PLANE AND WE
FLEW BACK TO
MILWAUKEE

ON THE
DOORSTEP OF THE
NEW HOUSE THE
PIANO MOVERS
PAUSED FOR A
GLASS OF COLD
WATER

THERE WAS
AN UNCOM-
FORTABLE
SILENCE

A SILENCE
FREIGHTED
WITH SEXUAL
SIGNIFICANCE
ENSUED. THEN
WE WENT TO BED
FIRST HOWEVER
ORDERING A
PIANO TEACHER
AND A PIANO
TUNER FOR THE
EARLY MORNING

A SILENCE

There's no place to keep him in our apartment building! Alison said triumphantly, pointing at Dan. She was of course absolutely right and I hastily bought a large three-story house in Milwaukee's best suburb. To make the house more comfortable I bought a concert grand piano.

Here are some little matters which you must attend to Alison said, handing me a box of bills. I went through them carefully, noting the amounts and thinking about money.

What in the name of God is this! I cried, holding up a bill for $1600 from the hardware store.

Garden hose Alison said calmly.

It was clear that I would have to remove some money from the State Bank & Trust and place it in the Municipal National and I did so. The pilot of the airplane which I had bought to fly us to Aqueduct, with his friend the pilot of the larger plane I had bought to fly us back, appeared at the door and asked to be paid. The pilots' names were George and Sam. I paid them and also bought from Sam his flight jacket, which was khaki-colored and pleasant-looking. They smiled and saluted as they left.

Well I said looking around the new house, we'd better call a piano teacher because I understand that without use pianos tend to fall out of tune.

Not only pianos Alison said giving me an exciting look.

The next day Mr Washington from the Central National called to report an overdraft of several hundred thousand dollars for which I apologized. Who was that on the telephone? Alison asked. Mr Washington from the bank I replied. Oh Alison said, what do you want for breakfast? What have you got? I asked. Nothing Alison said, we'll have to go out for breakfast.

So we went down to the drugstore where Alison had eggs sunny-side-up and I had buckwheat cakes with sausage. When we got back to the house I noticed that there were no trees surrounding it, which depressed me.

Have you noticed I asked, that there are no trees?

Yes Alison said, I've noticed.

<table>
<tr><td>

A PROLONGED
SILENCE

A TERRIBLE
SILENCE

ABSOLUTE SILENCE
FOR ONE MINUTE

SHORT SILENCE

SILENTLY WE
REGARDED THE
TWO MEN WHO
SAT ON THE
SOFA

THERE WAS A
SHAMEFACED
SILENCE

WE CONSIDERED
THE PROBLEM IN
SILENCE

THERE WAS A
JOYFUL SILENCE
AS BUSTER AND
SLIM TRIED TO
DIGEST THE
GOOD NEWS

THE SOUND OF
THE FLUTE
FILLED THE
SILENT HALLWAY

</td><td>

In fact Alison said, the treelessness of this house almost makes me yearn for our old apartment building.

There at least one could look at the large plants in the lobby.

As soon as we go inside I said, I will call the tree service and buy some trees.

Maples I said.

Oh Peter what a fine idea Alison said brightly. But who are these people in our living room?

Realizing that the men were the piano teacher and the piano tuner we had requested, I said: Well did you try the piano?

Yep the first man said, couldn't make heads or tails out of it.

And you? I asked, turning to the other man.

Beats me he said with a mystified look.

What seems to be the difficulty? I asked.

Frankly the piano teacher said, this isn't my real line of work. *Really* he said, I'm a jockey.

How about you? I said to his companion.

Oh I'm a bona fide piano tuner all right the tuner said. It's just that I'm not very good at it. Never was and never will be.

I have a proposition to make I announced. What is your name? I asked, nodding in the direction of the jockey.

Slim he said, and my friend here is Buster.

Well Slim I said, we need a jockey for our racehorse, Dan, who will fall out of trim without workouts. And Buster, you can plant the maple trees which I have just ordered for the house.

I settled on a salary of $12,000 a year for Slim and a slightly smaller one for Buster. This accomplished I drove the Rolls over to Courtlandt Street to show it to my mistress, Amelia.

When I knocked at the door of Amelia's apartment she refused to open it. Instead she began practicing scales on her flute. I knocked again and called out: Amelia!

I knocked again but Amelia continued to play. So I sat down on the steps and began to read the newspaper which was lying on the floor, knocking at intervals and at the same time wondering about the psychology of Amelia.

</td></tr>
</table>

171

Montgomery Ward I noticed in the newspaper was at 40½. Was Amelia being adamant I considered, because of Alison?

Amelia I said at length (through the door), I want to give you a nice present of around $5500. Would you like that?

Do you mean it? she said.

Certainly I said.

Can you afford it? she asked doubtfully.

I have a new Rolls I told her, and took her outside where she admired the car at great length. Then I gave her a check for $5500 on the Commercial National for which she thanked me. Back in the apartment she gracefully removed her clothes and put the check in a book in the bookcase. She looked very pretty without her clothes, as pretty as ever, and we had a pleasant time for an hour or more. When I left the apartment Amelia said Peter, I think you're a very pleasant person which made me feel very good and on the way home I bought a new gray Dacron suit.

Where have you been? Alison said, I've been waiting lunch for hours. I bought a new suit I said, how do you like it? Very nice Alison said, but hurry I've got to go shopping after lunch. Shopping! I said, I'll go with you!

So we ate a hasty lunch of vichyssoise and ice-cream and had Buster drive us in the Rolls to the Federated Department Store where we bought a great many things for the new house and a new horse blanket for Dan.

Do you think we ought to buy uniforms for Buster and Slim? Alison asked and I replied that I thought not, they didn't seem the sort who would enjoy wearing uniforms.

I think they ought to wear uniforms Alison said firmly.

No I said, I think not.

Uniforms with something on the pocket Alison said. A crest or something.

No.

Instead of uniforms I bought Slim a Kaywoodie pipe and some pipe tobacco, and bought Buster a large sterling silver cowboy belt buckle and a belt to go with it.

SILENTLY I WONDERED WHAT TO DO

AN INTERMINABLE SILENCE. THEN AMELIA HOLDING THE FLUTE OPENED THE DOOR

WHEN I GAVE THE SALESMAN A CHECK ON THE MEDICAL NATIONAL HE PAUSED, FROWNED, AND SAID: 'THIS IS A NEW BANK ISN'T IT?'

A FROSTY SILENCE

DEAD SILENCE

THERE WAS AN INTERVAL DURING WHICH I SENT A CHECK

FOR $500,000 TO
THE MUSEUM OF
MODERN ART

Buster was very pleased with his sterling silver belt buckle and said that he thought Slim would be pleased too when he saw the Kaywoodie pipe which had been bought for him. You were right after all Alison whispered to me in the back seat of the Rolls.

Alison decided that she would make a pie for supper, a chocolate pie perhaps, and that we would have Buster and Slim and George and Sam the pilots too if they were in town and not flying. She began looking in her recipe book while I read the *Necchi News* in my favorite armchair.

Then Slim came in from the garage with a worried look. Dan he said is not well.

A STUNNED
PAUSE

Everyone was thrown into a panic by the thought of Dan's illness and I bought some Kaopectate which Slim however did not believe would be appropriate. The Kaopectate was $0.98 and I paid for it with a check on the Principal National. The delivery boy from the drugstore, whose name was Andrew, suggested that Dan needed a doctor. This seemed sensible so I tipped Andrew with a check on the Manufacturers' Trust and asked him to fetch the very best doctor he could find on such short notice.

WE LOOKED AT
ONE ANOTHER IN
WORDLESS FEAR

Dan was lying on his side in the garage, groaning now and then. His face was a rich gray color and it was clear that if he did not have immediate attention, the worst might be expected.

PAUSING ONLY TO
WHIP A FRESH
CHECKBOOK FROM
THE DESK DRAWER,
I BOUGHT A LARGE
HOSPITAL
NEARBY FOR $1.5
MILLION

Peter for God's sake do something for this poor horse! Alison cried.

We sent Dan over in his trailer with strict instructions that he be given the best of everything. Slim and Buster accompanied him and when Andrew arrived with the doctor I hurried them off to the hospital too. Concern for Dan was uppermost in my mind at that moment.

RETURNING TO
THE LIVING-
ROOM, ALISON
HESITATED

The telephone rang and Alison answered.

Then she said: It's some girl, for you.

As I had thought it might be, it was Amelia. I told her about Dan's illness. She was very concerned and asked if I thought it would be appropriate if she went to the hospital.

A MOMENT OF
INDECISION

You don't think it would be appropriate Amelia said.

FOLLOWED BY A
PAINFUL SILENCE

THE
CONVERSATION
LAPSED

AN HIATUS
FILLED WITH
DOUBT AND
SUSPICION

No Amelia I said truthfully, I don't.

Then Amelia said that this indication of her tiny status in all our lives left her with nothing to say.

To cheer her up I said I would visit her again in the near future. This pleased her and the exchange ended on a note of warmth. I knew however that Alison would ask questions and I returned to the living room with some anxiety.

But now the pilots George and Sam rushed in with good news indeed. They had gotten word of Dan's illness over the radio they said, and filled with concern had flown straight to the hospital, where they learned that Dan's stomach had been pumped and all was well. Dan was resting easily George and Sam said, and could come home in about a week.

Oh Peter! Alison exclaimed in a pleased way, our ordeal is over. She kissed me with abandon and George and Sam shook hands with each other and with Andrew and Buster and Slim, who had just come in from the hospital. To celebrate we decided that we would all fly to London and Rome on a Viscount jet which I bought for an undisclosed sum and which Sam declared he knew how to fly very well.

CLIVE SINCLAIR

Uncle Vlad

Clive Sinclair (1948–) was born in London, and began writing fiction when a student at the University of East Anglia. His first novel *Bibliosexuality* appeared in 1973; other novels include *Blood Libels* (1985), *Cosmetic Effects* (1989) and *Augustus Rex* (1992). He has also produced two noted collections of stories, *Hearts of Gold* (1979), which won the Somerset Maugham Award, and *Bedbugs* (1982). His stories display both his experiences as a writer in America (he taught at the University of California, Santa Cruz) and his Anglo-Jewish background. He was also for a time literary editor of the *Jewish Chronicle*, and was chosen one of the 'Best of Young British Novelists' in 1983.

'Uncle Vlad', from the early collection *Hearts of Gold*, shows both Sinclair's gift for macabre parody and his taste for complex literary illusion. Vlad, after all, reminds us not just of Vlad the Impaler, and the Dracula legend, so important to popular fiction, but of Vladimir Nabokov, the great and teasing writer of modern fictional play. The butterflies here come from Nabokov, the Dracula theme from Bram Stoker, and the story is a fine example of what Sinclair himself calls 'bibliosexuality', the preoccupation of the writer with both bookishness and erotic energy – with, in fact, the sexy play of story.

A small puff of powder cleared and I saw my aunt touch my uncle on his white cheek with such exquisite precision that she left lip marks like the wings of a ruby butterfly. I watched her for nine times nine swings of the golden pendulum as she walked from guest to guest leaving behind trails of the silver dust that sparkled in the lamplight. It was as though the entire effort of her toilet was not so much designed to establish a character as to create an impression that would leave a colourful insignia on the memory. Her voice floated on her breath, a soft wind that bent and bared the necks of her listeners before her; I heard her whisper imaginary family secrets to an English aesthete who made notes behind her back:

'I believe that Lupus thinks that Vlad married me on purely scientific principles as the best specimen he could find of a modern butterfly.'

The aesthete laughed. 'Well, Countess,' he said, 'I hope he won't stick pins into you.'

Then they both swirled away in a creamy whirl of silk out into the milky way of moonlight and left behind the delicate blooms and rouged cheeks. Uncle Vlad smiled at my aunt's joke and followed her silhouette as it flitted among the lace curtains, but he remained where he was, still standing beneath the candelabra, wax dripping on to his white hair, holding several glass jars, some containing ether, others containing frantic beating moths, one containing champagne.

Our family is old and distinguished, descended from the ancient mountain lords down into a lowland mansion. Uncle Vlad, tall and grand, the head of the house, is himself called after our most famous ancestor Vled the Impaler, who finally drove the Turks from Europe, so named because of his sanguine habit of tossing Turkish captives into the air and catching them on the point of a spear. We have a portrait in the Great Hall of Vled standing in a full field of flowers amid the dying Turks who, pierced through the middle, and waving their arms and legs, look like a multitude of ecstatic butterflies. Beneath this scene in now smoked grey this legend is painted in Roman print – *Vled I called The Impaler*. 'Vlad' is the modern corruption of the venerable Vled, the result of an obscure etymological whim. However, there is no disguising the physical similarities; it is all but impossible to detect a difference between the painting of Vled and the face of Uncle Vlad. Uncle Vlad is an honoured lepidopterist, but, as a rule, does not sail about honey fields in short trousers; instead he goes out at night and gathers moths by candlelight. He exchanges these easily, because of his skill and their unique paleness, for the more brightly coloured varieties, which he mounts, simply, by driving a needle through their bodies. Uncle Vlad's pursuit is looked upon with much interest by the distant Viennese branch of our family which maintains, to a doctor, that it is a genuine genetic manifestation of his more barbaric prototype; while another more émigré branch claims that Uncle Vlad is a veritable paragon of the pattern of behaviourism in that, having seen the painting of Vled at an early age, he has ever since sought to realize the contents within the limitations of his own civilized environment. Uncle Vlad believes greatly in tradition.

Every year, on a fixed day, the entire family gathers at our home to celebrate the generations with a gorgeous extravagance. My uncle and aunt occupy weeks in anticipation of the fantastic evening, working and reworking menus, always seeking a sublime gastronomic equilibrium, so that the discards look like nothing more than the drafts of meticulous lyric poems. And what poets they are! Garbure Béarnaise, Truites au Bleu, Grives au Genièvre, Canard au Sang, Crêpes Flambés aux Papillons. They strive to astonish the most sophisticated taste, the only applause they seek is the thick sound of the satisfied tongue clapping the palatine papillae. Once Uncle Vlad said to my aunt, at the supreme moment before the food is collected, 'Should we not share the secrets of our art with the swine that starve?' And she replied, 'Let them eat words.'

Our family is proud and jealous of its dark arboreal rebus.

This year, being the first congregation since my coming of age, I was permitted to help in the preparations. On the eve, I went out alone into the nocturnal wood, carrying my rods and nets, and followed the overgrown path to the gilt river. And there I sat in silence for many hours until my nets were full, very content, for there are few sights more beautiful than that of the silver fish struggling in the moonlight. I left the fish where they were, because it was vital to keep them alive, and commenced the journey back, proud that I had completed my task so well. But I had gone no more than a kilometre towards the residence when I heard a rustling of dead leaves and the final cry of a bird in pain. I pushed my way through the bushes in the direction of the sound and came into the perfect circle of a moonbright glade. The air was full of the melodious song of a score or more of thrushes. The birds were all on the ground, trapped in Uncle Vlad's subtle snares, and they did not look real but seemed to be some eccentric ornament of the night.

Uncle Vlad himself, dressed by the shadows as a harlequin, was stepping among the thrushes and killing them one by one by gently pressing their soft necks between his thumb and forefinger. Each death, save for the single scream and the frightened flap of the wings, was conducted in complete silence: until the survivors sang again. Uncle Vlad saw me and allowed me to help.

'My boy,' he whispered to me as we worked, 'how was the fishing?'

'It was good, Uncle,' I replied, 'I caught twenty trout.'

When we had finished Uncle Vlad collected all the tight bodies into a little bundle and opened a sack of the finest silk. But before he dropped the birds into it he bit off their heads. Fine tributaries of blood ran from his swelling lips.

'The thrushes always come to this spot,' he said, 'they cannot resist my special snails.'

The kitchen was already full with the shadowy figures of our servants when we returned, and my aunt was throwing resinous logs into the dancing flames. One of the anonymous cooks was apparent through a vaporous curtain of steam, stirring a dull copper soup-pot bubbling with boiling water and vegetables.

'There must be no garlic in the Garbure Béarnaise!' Uncle Vlad called out as we entered.

'Of course not, my dear,' replied my aunt. 'Did you do well?'

Uncle Vlad emptied his bag out on to the ancient wooden table, and at once long fingers fluttered out of the obscurity and plucked the feathers from the bodies. Then the birds were split open with sharp knives and stuffed till they were full with peppercorn and juniper. When this was done to the satisfaction of my uncle the breasts were sewn up, and the birds wrapped in slices of pork lard, and bound, ready to be cooked.

'We shall eat well tomorrow,' said my aunt to me.

Exactly one hour before we were due to dine, when all our guests were safely arrived, we killed the ducks. We took seven regal mallards from the lake and suffocated them by wringing their necks and pressing their breasts. The carcasses were given to the cooks, under the supervision of my aunt, to dress and draw, while Uncle Vlad and I went out with a large tank to collect the patient trout. And when we carried it back into the kitchen the oval tank seemed to have a shining lid, so full was it with fish. The remains of the ducks were ready in the great meat press waiting only for my uncle to add his libation of red wine. Then the press was turned and the blood and wine was caught as it ran, by Uncle Vlad, in goblets of gold and poured into a silver bowl. Pure vinegar was heated in large pans, over the oven, until it boiled.

'Throw in the fish while they still live,' ordered my aunt, 'and let them cook until they shrivel and turn steel blue.'

Thus everything was made complete, and we went into the incandescent dining room to join our guests.

The English aesthete, protégé of my blond cousin Adorian, and Madeleine, adored but adopted daughter of the childless union of the Count Adolphus and the Countess Ada, were the only visitors I did not recognize from an earlier year.

'My dear, you look absolutely *ravissant*,' said myopic Countess Ada, 'you simply must meet Madeleine.'

However, before that happened the implacable gong gave out with sonorous tidings of the approaching pabulum and, at the sound, we all took our places, according to the established decorum, at the ebony table. I sat in velvet, as always, between my aunt and the ageing mistress, so old as to have been long accepted as a second or rather parallel wife, of General X. The Garbure Béarnaise was served in ochre bowls of rough clay, the Truites au Bleu came on dishes of silver garlanded with circles of lemon and round potatoes, and the Grives au Genièvre were carried high on plates of the finest porcelain. The bones crunched deliciously beneath white teeth, knives and forks flashed like smiles as they moved, faces shone, and the wine glowed like a living thing in the crystal glasses. Then amid a fanfare of the oohs and aahs of aroused and admiring appetites the Canard au Sang was brought on and, as Uncle Vlad flamed the pieces of meat with the sauce of blood and wine and a bottle of cognac, I looked toward Madeleine for the first time.

Her face was the shape of a slightly more serious moon than our own, and her nocturnal hair was as black as the ravens that fly in the hills beyond our lands. She seemed to be searching some distant horizon, for her crescent eyebrows hovered like the wings of a gliding bird, and her mouth was slightly open as if she were holding the most delicate bird's egg between her lips. When she noticed that I was regarding her so curiously she smiled a little and she blushed.

As was the custom, after the main course, our smooth glasses were filled with champagne, and we left the decadent table, before the dessert was served. The wonders of our cuisine were praised, by a familiar chorus, to the heights of our moulded ceilings; but my aunt went outside with the English aesthete to discuss synaesthesia, and Uncle Vlad took the opportunity to catch some moths. I looked for Madeleine, but I could not find her.

'I say, young fellow,' mumbled ancient Count Adolphus through his moustaches, 'have you seen Madeleine yet?'

But I did not see Madeleine again until the butterflies burst into ardent applause when we all sat down for the Crêpes aux Papillons. There was something indescribably wonderful, that night, in watching those blazing palettes puff away in smoke; it was very much as if the colours evaporated into the air and were absorbed by our breath. The crêpes too seemed suffused with this vibrant energy; it must be said, Uncle Vlad had created the most brilliant dessert of his life. I wondered afterwards if the extraordinary vitality had communicated itself to Madeleine, if her cheeks had grown roses, but when I looked I saw that she was already walking away from the table.

'I do believe that that young lady has dropped her handkerchief,' observed the mistress of General X. 'If I were you, young man, I should return it to her.'

I nodded. I could hear the violins beginning to play discordant themes in the ballroom.

The dance opened with a grand flourish of wind instruments and took off around the room on the resonant wings of the flutes and strings, and joined, in counterpoint, the butterflies released simultaneously by Uncle Vlad. My uncle and aunt, as much concerned with the macula lutea as with the more alimentary organs, had carefully planned to fill in the musical space with the most unusual sights. A pellucid cube of the purest crystal was suspended from the centre of the ceiling and rotated on a fixed cycle by means of a concealed clockwork motor, creating an optical illusion, for in each of the faces a single eye was carved, and in each of the eyes a prism had been planted; so that, as it revolved above the dancing floor, it caught the occasional beam of light and projected visionary rainbows. Benevolent Uncle Vlad, having led the dancers with my aunt in an energetic pas de deux, stood resting against an ormolu commode, pouring out tall glasses of punch from a commodious bowl, happily recording the performance of his decorated insects.

'Ah, Nephew,' he remarked as I emerged from among a crowd of dancers, 'have you noticed that spinal quiver in the little beasts when a certain note is sounded, high C, I believe?'

'As a matter of fact I have not,' I replied. 'I am trying to find Madeleine to return a handkerchief.'

Countess Ada and Count Adolphus came capering by and called out, 'She is beside the flowers in the garden.'

Madeleine was standing all alone beneath the moon, in the centre of a crazy path, skirted by a row of yellow gaslights and ghostly trees. As I approached nearer to her, along that long lane, I fancied that she was looking, as if fascinated, at the illuminated cupolas, each of which was nightly adorned with the tingling jewellery of bats. And I was reminded what a newcomer Madeleine really was, for this singular display was almost a family phenomenon; indeed, by coincidence, all true members of our family have a small but distinctive brown birthmark on the cheek that is said to resemble two open wings. Poor General X, as a result of this, was forced to grow a bushy beard, not because of his military manner, nor because of his virile dignity, but because he developed an unfortunate twitch.

'Hello,' I spoke into the night, 'hello.' I do not think that I have seen anyone look so beautiful as Madeleine looked at that moment with the full curve of her throat outlined against the blackness as if by the inspired stroke of an artist's brush.

She jumped a little, like a sleeper awakened, and turned towards me. Her brown eyes were excited and shining like an Indian summer. 'The night is so wonderful,' she said, 'I feel enchanted.'

'Let us walk together,' I replied, 'and I will show you the garden.'

Madeleine took my arm and in the instant that I felt the warm flesh of her own bare arm brush carelessly against my cold hand I experienced a sensation I can only call an emotional tickle; as if some hitherto secret nerve-end had been suddenly revealed and stimulated. That arm of hers was a marvellous thing, it was no single colour but a multitude of hues and tints, and covered with the finest down, except inside the elbow, where the smooth skin was pale and shy and utterly desirable. The flowers were everywhere but the famous roses were all spaced out before the french windows, so that they encircled the building like some blooming necklace. Madeleine reached out to pick one of the blossoms but managed only to prick her finger. She gave a little cry, and stared at the finger which was rapidly dropping beads of blood.

'Let me see,' I said, 'I know how to make it better.' And I took the wounded finger between my thumb and forefinger and squeezed it, very carefully, until the last few drops of blood came like red flowers, then I carried it to my lips and sucked away any hurt. I bandaged the flushed tip with Madeleine's own handkerchief.

She smiled.

'Will you dance?' I asked.

The slight dizziness I had felt when I tended Madeleine's hurt was heightened by our mazy movement around the dance floor to the sound of a jazzy waltz; though it was not, in fact, at all an unpleasant feeling, rather like being drunk on champagne bubbles.

'Look!' shouted Countess Ada to my aunt. 'Look who Madeleine is dancing with.'

Madeleine coloured slightly, which only made her the more radiant, then as she raised her face to me the spectrum burst all over her, and all else retreated into spectral shades. In the magic of that moment I completely forgot that the entire illusion was due to the clever artifice of my uncle and aunt and quite unconsciously pulled Madeleine closer to me, she responded with a shiver along her back, as if she were waving invisible wings, and I drifted over a dreamlike sea holding on to Madeleine's warm body. I have no idea how long that moment lasted, but in those seconds or minutes I experienced an extraordinary sensation: my senses were literally magnified, I saw her skin as mixtures of pure colour, I felt her every movement; the beat of her heart, the air in her lungs, the blood in her veins. But Madeleine suddenly broke the spell.

'Oh, no!' she cried. 'We have danced over a butterfly.'

When, at last, a sliver of sun shone through the lead-light windows and exploded over the trumpet section, the dancers all leaned against one another and walked from the floor into the corridors and dimness of the receding night. I led Madeleine by the hand to her chamber.

'I must sleep now,' she said, 'but we will meet again in the afternoon?'

'Yes, you must sleep,' I replied as I touched her tired eyelids with my fingertips, 'but I will plan a picnic for when you awaken, and I will show you the ruined castle of Vled.' I returned to the ballroom to find my uncle and aunt, to congratulate them upon their success, and found them both upon their knees collecting up the bruised bodies of the fallen butterflies. I joined them, to complete the family group, crawling about as if we were posing for a portrait of a surreal autumn in a sparkling land of leaves without trees.

'Your designs were wonderful, the execution was superb,' I said to them both, 'even I ignored the methods for the sake of the effect.'

'Everything worked perfectly,' agreed my aunt, 'and what is more you and Madeleine liked each other.'

'Yes, I wanted to speak to you about that,' I began. 'I have asked Madeleine to come with me beyond the woods, and I would like to take some food and wine with us,' I paused, 'so will you be kind enough to show me the cellars?'

Uncle Vlad looked very pleased with himself and beamed at my aunt as if all credit for my request was owed to him. 'Of course, with pleasure,' he replied, with that smile of his, and added: 'Tell me, Nephew, do you intend to kiss her?'

No light at all came into the cellars except, that is, from the illumined rectangle at the head of the stairs, where the old oaken door was left open. I had never been into the cellars before, so it was all strange to me, but Uncle Vlad walked among the rows upon rows of green bottles as if this weird underwater world were his natural habitat.

'We are standing directly beneath our small lake,' he informed me. 'The cellars were designed that way deliberately so as to control the air temperature in here.'

Soon I was moving about freely on my own, and the longer I remained in the cellars the more I felt that I too belonged to this profound environment, that I was in truth the nephew of my uncle. The air was rich with the smells of the earth, the cellars were like a distillation of night and the world, the essence of the veil, the antithesis of those bright tedious rooms where everything is visible at once, where you forget that you are breathing. There should be an art to capturing beauty; it becomes merely banal when it is not hunted. Uncle Vlad emerged from the depths of a particularly dusty rack of vintage carrying two bottles of red wine by their swans' necks, one in each hand.

'These should be just the thing,' he said as he rubbed a label, 'Château Margaux.'

Then we went much deeper, beyond where the wine was stored, until we came to a dank natural cave which smelled very strongly of pelardon.

Uncle Vlad picked up a few small rounds of the aged goats' cheese, carefully wrapped and tied in dusky vine leaves, and weighed them in his hands. 'Perfect,' he adjudged, 'just ripe. Now all you require is some pâté de foie gras.'

'You must beware of the sun,' said Madeleine, regarding my pale complexion with some concern, 'I do not want you to burn because of showing me the castle.'

She gave me her straw bonnet to wear, and the blue ribbons flew in the breeze on the slope of the hill. Lupus, the great dog, ran on through the waving corn and the poppies and waited for us, barking, at the start of the woods. Several birds flew out in a straight line squawking with alarm. The woods were much cooler and greener than the sandy daylight, a delightful diurnal anachronism, an Eden free from gardeners; what is more, I knew all the paths. Lupus darted ahead and chased rabbits through the undergrowth; usually he caught them. I carried the picnic on my back in a creamy satchel made from a pelt of the softest goatskin, and led Madeleine by the hand, watching all the tonal variations that the light and the shade of the sun and the different leaves made over her body. It seemed that the life in her had come to the surface and was showing itself in this ebb and flow of moving colours. I chose the spot very carefully and spread a chequered cloth over the ground, and I put out all the food on it in the crafty design of a rather ingenious checkmate. We sat beneath the tall trees in the long grass. The picnic was excellent; the pâté provided the expected largesse, the cheese had just the right temperament, and I continually filled the glasses with the flowing wine. Madeleine ate a yellow pear for her dessert, and the juice dripped from her fingers; her black hair was just touching emerald leaves, also pear-shaped, and the attracted flies flew round her head like a halo.

'That was a lovely picnic,' she said, smiling. 'What shall we do now?'

'I must tell you something, Madeleine,' I confessed, by way of a reply, after some assumed consideration. 'I dabble in paronomasia.'

Madeleine put down the core of the pear. 'I thought that the game would be chess,' she gave me a sly smile, 'but now I suppose that it will be a crossword puzzle, am I right?'

She was right, of course. Nevertheless, I took a black crayon from the satchel and wrote on the white squares of the cloth – *many alive devils enliven living even in novel evils.*

'Oh, well,' laughed Madeleine, 'we all have our acrostics to bear.'

I don't know why, it certainly was not because Madeleine had beaten me at my own game, but her response made me shiver. Madeleine must have noticed because she touched my cheek with her lips.

'You are cold,' she said.

'There,' I said after we pushed through the last of the overgrown bushes, 'is Vled's castle.'

The ruined keep stood erect and solitary on the motte in melancholy grandeur. Ravens flew about the grey merlons in great circles. As we watched, the setting sun shone red through holes in the broken walls giving the whole, for a brief while, the appearance of a cavernous skull with bloodshot sockets. Although I had seen the same sight many times it still exerted over me an irresistible and hypnotic fascination; as if there really were some powerful force behind those empty carmine eyes. Then the sun deepened to purple and streaks of fiery clouds opened labial wounds in the sky. The castle looked even blacker, and all the more compelling. Madeleine did not blink, she stood transfixed, staring into the approaching gloom; her eyes reflected what she saw. I felt her hand tighten in mine and grow colder all the time; her entire being seemed frozen on the threshold of an irreversible event like a reluctant swimmer poised on the edge of a diving board. I touched her left breast with my right hand, just enough to feel the flesh.

'Will you go in, Madeleine?' I asked. She came without a word.

The graves of my ancestors were all covered with historic weeds, and the moat was dry, but a wooden table and twelve wooden chairs remained within the hollow keep. We walked through the grounds with all the care and respect due to fallen stones and came into the dining hall. It was evening. I lit many candles and covered the table with the chequered cloth and spread out upon it the remains of the picnic; there were a few cheeses, a little pâté, much fruit, and most of a bottle of wine, so that I was able to compose a creditable still life. It glowed in the glimmering light. On the walls beside where Madeleine sat there was the famed mural which represented, in picturesque detail, the narrative of Vled's many military victories; also, by way of interludes, either for himself or the spectator, the artist had included the faded delights of Vled's more carnal conquests. Even as I looked a single moonbeam suddenly shot as swift as an arrow through a crack in the annals and flashed directly on to Madeleine's face and neck.

'This is the most extraordinary supper,' she murmured, very coyly, 'that I have ever eaten.' She smiled across at me and I saw at once, in the luminous night, that her upper lip was shaped exactly like the famous longbow old Vled had used to lick the Turks. It quivered a little beneath my gaze, and the more I studied that priceless object the more I was filled with an increasing need to make it mine. I wanted to taste that secret egg. Then the light changed, or she moved. I followed the graceful arch of her neck to where her ear disappeared among her rich hair and I felt again, though I knew not why, that I had to possess that mysterious lobe that hung so full like a liquid jewel. Madeleine became in that chance instant of illumination a collection of individual treasures and temptations; I had never done it before, but I knew then that I had to kiss her. My desire was inevitable, as inevitable as the flame that burned above the candle.

In the courtyard beyond the keep, in the centre of a thirsty fountain, a small statue of Cupid was slowly falling to pieces.

There is an old belief in our family to the effect that any passion, if held strongly enough, can so influence the prevailing atmosphere as to establish conditions favourable for the realization of that same passion. It happened in the gathering night that Madeleine got up from her place at a table of crumbling foods and walked towards me, slowly, languorously, through the undulant waves and splashes of candlelight and wax. I couldn't take my eyes from her mouth; the tongue was just visible through the open lips; the teeth looked sharp and white. I rose too, unawares, in a state of hard anticipation. We met, quickly, flesh against flesh; and I knew, by a kind of ecstatic instinct, exactly what I had to do.

I put my hands on Madeleine's hot cheeks, making a prize cup of my hands and her cervix, and tilted her head to one side. She looked at me with a sleepy look, and half closed her eyes. Her lips started to move. I placed my face on Madeleine's offered neck and began to kiss her, moving my tongue over her smooth skin, seeking, seeking, pressing, until I could feel the blood pumping through her jugular vein. Then I took a roll of the powdered flesh between my lips so that it was pressed against my teeth. I had to hold Madeleine tight, for her whole body was swept again and again with a series of short but violent tremors. I could feel her breathing right into my ear, her warm breath came in gasps and clung to me for a few seconds before vanishing. I sank my teeth into the skin and pushed, harder, harder – suddenly a great wave seized me and with a convulsive spasm of my cervical spine I bit deeper into Madeleine's vein. Then my mouth was filled with her blood and I think I heard her shriek of pleasure through my own blaze of delight.

It was a perfect kiss! I kissed Madeleine until I had to stop for breath; by then she was quite relaxed, and the arms which had clutched me so firmly hung limp by her sides. I carried her gently to the table and rolled her over the chequered cloth so that she finished on her back. Her arms got in a bit of a tangle, so I straightened them out for her. And I leaned back in a chair, well satisfied. As I did so a rather large *acherontia atropos* flew into a candle flame and fell burning on to Madeleine's cheek. She was too weak to brush it off; her hands fluttered as vainly as the moth's wings.

'Madeleine,' I whispered in her ear as I blew off the ashes, 'now you are really one of the family.'

MILAN KUNDERA

Nobody Will Laugh

Milan Kundera (1929–), who was born in Brno, Czechoslovakia, taught film at the Academy of Music and Arts in Prague, and published fiction. After the Prague Spring of 1968 his books were banned and blacklisted by the Marxist authorities, and he moved to Paris in the 1970s, becoming a French citizen as well as an internationally famed author. His novels, all written with a sense of the importance of human love and with a wonderful lightness of touch, include *The Joke* (1969 in English), *The Book of Laughter and Forgetting* (1980 in English), and *The Unbearable Lightness of Being* (1984 in English).

'Nobody Will Laugh', from Kundera's only story collection, *Laughable Loves* (1974), was one of his banned works, written in Prague before 1968. Like much of his writing, it touches on the question of both the importance of, and the dangerous nature of, laughter and humour. In *The Joke*, it is a careless piece of humour that gets the central character into trouble with the authorities; the same thing happened to Kundera himself. Yet, his fiction suggests, humour is also what enables us to get free of the totalitarian world. In 'Nobody Will Laugh', the joke, or trick, of the story backfires. It is the Kafkaesque difficulties of living in a totalitarian state that create the atmosphere of suspicion and deception on which the whole story turns, as Dr Klima attempts to survive in his job and protect his sexual adventuring. He is finally rejected by everyone as a result of his trickeries, but he has learned his lesson. For even his own tale is after all not tragic, but 'of the comic variety'.

'Pour me some more slivovitz,' said Klara, and I wasn't against it. It was by no means unusual for us to open a bottle and this time there was a genuine excuse for it. That day I had received a considerable sum for the last part of a study, which was being published in installments by a professional visual arts magazine.

Publishing the study hadn't been so easy – what I'd written was polemical and controversial. That's why my studies had previously been rejected by *Visual Arts Journal*, where the editors were old and cautious, and had then been published only in a minor rival periodical, where the editors were younger and not so conservative.

The mailman brought the payment to the university along with another letter; an unimportant letter; in the morning in the first flush of beatitude I had hardly read the letter. But now at home, when it was approaching midnight and the wine was nearly gone, I took it off the table to amuse us.

'Esteemed comrade and if you will permit the expression – my colleague!' I read aloud to Klara. 'Please excuse me, a man whom you have never met, for writing to you. I am turning to you with a request that you should read the enclosed article. True, I do not know you, but I respect you as a man whose judgments, reflections, and conclusions astonish me by their agreement with the results of my own research; I am completely amazed by it. Thus, for example, even though I bow before your conclusions and your excellent comparative analysis, I wish to call attention emphatically to the thought that Czech art has always been close to the people. I voiced this opinion before reading your treatise. I could prove this quite easily, for among other things, I even have witnesses. However, this is only marginal, for your treatise . . .' There followed further praise of my excellence and then a request. Would I kindly write a review of his article, that is, a specialist's evaluation for *Visual Arts Journal*, where they had been underestimating and rejecting his article for more than six months. They had told him that my opinion would be decisive, so now I had become the writer's only hope, a single light in an otherwise total darkness.

We made fun of Mr Zaturetsky, whose aristocratic name fascinated us. But it was just fun; fun that meant no harm, for the praise which he had lavished on me, along with the excellent slivovitz, softened me. It softened me so that in those unforgettable moments I loved the whole world. However, out of the whole world, especially Klara, because she was sitting opposite me, while the rest of the world was hidden from me by the walls of my Vrshovits attic. And because at that moment I didn't have anything to reward the world with, I rewarded Klara; at least with promises.

Klara was a twenty-year-old girl from a good family. What am I saying, from a good family? From an excellent family! Her father had been a bank manager, and some time in the fifties, as a representative of the upper bourgeoisie, had been exiled to the village of Chelakovits, which was some distance from Prague. As a result, his daughter had a bad party record and worked as a seamstress in a large Prague dress factory. I can't bear prejudice. I don't believe that the extent of a father's property can leave its mark on his child's genes. I ask you, who today is really a plebeian and who is a patrician? Everything has been mixed up and has changed places so completely, that it's sometimes difficult to understand anything in terms of sociological concepts. I was far from feeling that I was sitting opposite a class enemy; on the contrary, I was sitting opposite a beautiful seamstress and trying to make her like me more by telling her light-heartedly about the advantages of a job I'd promised to get her through connections. I assured her that it was absurd for such a pretty girl to lose her beauty over a sewing machine, and I decided that she should become a model.

Klara didn't offer any resistance and we spent the night in happy understanding.

2

Man passes through the present with his eyes blindfolded. He is permitted merely to sense and guess at what he is actually experiencing. Only later when the cloth is untied can he glance at the past and find out *what* he has experienced and what meaning it has had.

That evening I thought I was drinking to my successes and didn't in the least suspect that it was the prelude to my undoing.

And because I didn't suspect anything I woke up the next day in a good mood, and while Klara was still breathing contentedly by my side, I took the article, which was attached to the letter, and skimmed through it with amused indifference.

It was called 'Mikolash Alesh, Master of Czech Drawing', and it really wasn't worth even the half-hour of inattention that I devoted to it. It was a collection of platitudes heaped together with no sense of continuity and without the least intention of advancing through them some original thought.

Quite clearly it was pure nonsense. The very same day Dr Kalousek, the editor of *Visual Arts Journal* (in other respects an unusually hostile man), confirmed my opinion over the telephone; he called me at the university: 'Say, did you get that treatise from the Zaturetsky guy? . . . Then take care of it. Five lecturers have already cut him to pieces, but he keeps on bugging us; he's got it into his head that you're the only genuine authority. Tell him in two sentences that it's crap, you know how to do that, you know how to be really venomous; and then we'll all have some peace.'

But something inside me protested: why should *I* have to be Mr Zaturetsky's executioner? Was *I* the one receiving an editor's salary for this? Besides, I remembered very well that they had refused my article at *Visual Arts Journal* out of overcautiousness; what's more, Mr Zaturetsky's name was firmly connected in my mind with Klara, slivovitz, and a beautiful evening. And finally, I shan't deny it, it's human – I could have counted on one finger the people who think me 'a genuine authority': why should I lose this only one?

I closed the conversation with some clever vaguery, which Kalousek considered a promise and I, an excuse. I put down the receiver firmly convinced that I would never write the review for Mr Zaturetsky.

Instead I took some writing paper out of the drawer and wrote a letter to Mr Zaturetsky, in which I avoided any kind of judgment of his work, excusing myself by saying that my opinions on nineteenth-century art were commonly considered devious and eccentric, and therefore my intercession – especially with the editors of *Visual Arts Journal* – would harm rather than benefit his cause. At the same time, I overwhelmed Mr Zaturetsky with friendly loquacity, from which it was impossible not to detect approval on my part.

As soon as I had put the letter in the mailbox I forgot Mr Zaturetsky. But Mr Zaturetsky did not forget me.

3

One day when I was about to end my lecture – I lecture at college in the history of art – there was a knock at the door; it was our secretary, Mary, a kind elderly lady, who occasionally prepares coffee for me, and says that I'm out when there are undesirable female voices on the telephone. She put her head in the doorway and said that some gentleman was looking for me.

I'm not afraid of gentlemen and so I took leave of the students and went good-humoredly out into the corridor. A smallish man in a shabby black suit and a white shirt bowed to me. He very respectfully informed me that he was Zaturetsky.

I invited the visitor into an empty room, offered him an armchair, and began pleasantly discussing everything possible with him, for instance what a bad summer it was and what exhibitions were on in Prague. Mr Zaturetsky politely agreed with all of my chatter, but he soon tried to apply every remark of mine to his article, which lay invisibly between us like an irresistible magnet.

'Nothing would make me happier than to write a review of your work,' I said finally, 'but as I explained to you in the letter, I am not considered an expert on the Czech nineteenth century, and, in addition, I'm on bad terms with the editors of *Visual Arts Journal*, who take me for a hardened modernist, so that a positive review from me could only harm you.'

'Oh, you're too modest,' said Mr Zaturetsky. 'How can you, who are such an expert, judge your own standing so blackly! In the editors' office they told me that everything depends on your review. If you support my article they'll publish it. You are my only recourse. It's the work of three years of study and three years of toil. Everything is now in your hands.'

How carelessly and from what bad masonry does a man build his excuses! I didn't know how to reply to Mr Zaturetsky. I involuntarily looked at his face and noticed there not only small, ancient, and innocent spectacles staring at me, but also a powerful, deep vertical wrinkle on his forehead. In a brief moment of clairvoyance a shiver shot down my spine. This wrinkle, concentrated and stubborn, betrayed not only the intellectual torment which its owner had gone through over Mikolash Alesh's drawings, but also unusually strong willpower. I lost my presence of mind and failed to find any clever excuse. I knew that I wouldn't write the review, but I also knew that I didn't have the strength to say so to this pathetic little man's face.

And then I began to smile and promise something vague. Mr Zaturetsky thanked me and said that he would come again soon. We parted smiling.

In a couple of days he did come. I cleverly avoided him, but the next day I was told that he was searching for me again at the university. I realized that bad times were on the way; I went quickly to Mary so as to take appropriate steps.

'Mary dear, I beg you, if that man should come looking for me again, say that I've gone to do some research in Germany and I'll be back in a month. And you should know about this: I have, as you know, all my lectures on Tuesday and Wednesday. I'll shift them secretly to Thursday and Friday. Only the students will know about this, don't tell anyone, and leave the schedule uncorrected. I'll have to disobey the rules.'

4

Indeed Mr Zaturetsky did soon come back to look me up and was miserable when the secretary informed him that I'd suddenly gone off to Germany. 'But this is not possible. Mr Klima has to write a review about me. How could he go away like this?' 'I don't know,' said Mary. 'However, he'll be back in a month.' 'Another month . . .' moaned Mr Zaturetsky. 'And you don't know his address in Germany?' 'I don't,' said Mary.

And then I had a month of peace, but the month passed more quickly than I expected and Mr Zaturetsky stood once again in the office. 'No, he still hasn't returned,' said Mary, and when she met me later about something she asked me imploringly: 'Your little man was here again, what in heaven's name should I tell him?' 'Tell him, Mary, that I got jaundice and am in the hospital in Jena.' 'In the hospital!' cried Mr Zaturetsky, when Mary told him the story a few days later. 'It's not possible! Don't you know that Mr Klima has to write a review about me?' 'Mr Zaturetsky,' said the secretary reproachfully, 'Mr Klima is lying in a hospital somewhere abroad seriously ill, and you think only about your review.' Mr Zaturetsky backed down and went away, but two weeks later was once again in the office: 'I sent a registered letter to Mr Klima in Jena. It is a small town, there can only be one hospital there, and the letter came back to me!' 'Your little man is driving me crazy,' said Mary to me the next day. 'You mustn't get angry with me, what could I say to him? I told him that you've come back. You must deal with him by yourself now.'

I didn't get angry with Mary. She had done what she could. Besides, I was far from considering myself beaten. I knew that I was not to be caught. I lived under cover all the time. I lectured secretly on Thursday and Friday; and even Tuesday and Wednesday, crouching in the doorway of a house opposite the school, I would rejoice at the sight of Mr Zaturetsky, who kept watch in front of the school waiting for me to come out. I longed to put on a bowler hat and stick on a beard. I felt like Sherlock Holmes or the Invisible Man, who strides stealthily; I felt like a little boy.

One day, however, Mr Zaturetsky finally got tired of keeping watch and jumped on Mary. 'Where exactly does Comrade Klima lecture?' 'There's the schedule,' said Mary, pointing to the wall, where the times of all the lectures were laid out in exemplary fashion on a large, checkered board.

'I see that,' said Mr Zaturetsky, refusing to be put off. 'Only Comrade Klima never lectures here on either Tuesday or Wednesday. Is he reported sick?'

'No,' said Mary hesitantly. And then the little man turned again on Mary. He reproached her for the confusion in the schedule. He inquired ironically how it was that she didn't know where every teacher was at a given time. He told her that he was going to complain about her. He shouted. He said that he was also going to complain about Comrade Assistant Klima, who wasn't lecturing, although he was supposed to be. He asked if the dean was in.

Unfortunately, the dean was in. Mr Zaturetsky knocked on his door and went in. Ten minutes later he returned to Mary's office and demanded the address of my apartment.

'Twenty Skalnik Street in Litomyshl,' said Mary. 'In Prague, Mr Klima only has a temporary address and he doesn't want it disclosed . . .' 'I'm asking you to give me the address of Assistant Klima's Prague apartment,' cried the little man in a trembling voice.

Somehow Mary lost her presence of mind. She gave him the address of my attic, my poor little refuge, my sweet den, in which I would be caught.

5

Yes, my permanent address is in Litomyshl; there I have my mother, my friends, and memories of my father; I flee from Prague, as often as I can, and write at home in my mother's small apartment. So it happened that I kept my mother's apartment as my permanent residence and in Prague I didn't manage to get myself a proper bachelor's apartment, as you're supposed to do, but lived in Vrshovits in lodgings, in a small, completely private attic, whose existence I concealed as much as possible. I didn't register anywhere so as to prevent unnecessary meetings between undesirable guests and my various transient female roommates or visitors, whose comings and goings, I confess, were sometimes most disorganized. For precisely these reasons I didn't enjoy the best reputation in the house. Also, during my stays in Litomyshl I had several times lent my cozy little room to friends, who amused themselves only too well there, and didn't allow anyone in the house to get a wink of sleep. All this scandalized some of the occupants, who conducted a quiet war against me. Sometimes they had the local committee express unfavorable opinions of me and they even handed in a complaint to the apartment office.

At that time it was inconvenient for Klara to get to work from such a distance as Chelakovits, and so she began to stay overnight at my place. At first she stayed timidly and as an exception, then she left one dress, then several dresses, and within a short time my two suits were stuffed into a corner of the wardrobe, and my little room was transformed into a woman's boudoir.

I really liked Klara; she was beautiful; it pleased me that people turned their heads when we went out together; she was at least thirteen years younger than me, which increased the students' respect for me; I had a thousand reasons for taking good care of her. But I didn't want it to be known that she was living with me. I was afraid of rumors and gossip about us in the house; I was afraid that someone would start attacking my good old landlord, who lived for the greater part of the year outside Prague, was discreet, and didn't concern himself about me; I was afraid that one day he would come to me, unhappy and with a heavy heart, and ask me to send the young lady away for the sake of his good name.

Klara had been strictly ordered not to open the door to anyone.

One day she was alone in the house. It was a sunny day and rather stuffy in the attic. She was lounging almost naked on my couch, occupying herself with an examination of the ceiling, when suddenly there was a pounding on the door.

There was nothing alarming in this. I didn't have a bell, so anyone who came had to knock. So Klara wasn't going to let herself be disturbed by the noise and didn't stop examining the ceiling. But the pounding didn't cease; on the contrary, it went on with imperturbable persistence. Klara was getting nervous. She began to imagine a man standing behind the door, a man who slowly and significantly turns up the lapels of his jacket, and who will later pounce on her demanding why she hadn't opened the door, what she was concealing, and whether she was registered. A feeling of guilt seized her; she lowered her eyes from the ceiling and tried to think where she had left her dress lying. But the pounding continued so stubbornly, that in the confusion she found nothing but my raincoat hanging in the hall. She put it on and opened the door.

Instead of an evil, querying face, she only saw a little man, who bowed: 'Is Mr Klima at home?' 'No, he isn't.' 'That's a pity,' said the little man and apologized for having disturbed her. 'The thing is that Mr Klima has to write a review about me. He promised me and it's very urgent. If you would permit it, I could at least leave him a message.'

Klara gave him paper and pencil, and in the evening I read that the fate of the article about Mikolash Alesh was in my hands alone, and that Mr Zaturetsky was waiting most respectfully for my review and would try to look me up again at the university.

6

The next day, Mary told me how Mr Zaturetsky had threatened her, and how he had gone to complain about her; her voice trembled and she was on the verge of tears; I flew into a rage. I realized that the secretary, who until now had been laughing at my game of hide-and-seek (though I would bet anything that she did what she did out of kindness toward me, rather than simply from a sense of fun), was now feeling hurt and conceivably saw me as the cause of her troubles. When I also included the exposure of my attic, the ten-minute pounding on the door, and Klara's fright – my anger grew to a frenzy.

As I was walking back and forth in Mary's office, biting my lips, boiling with rage and thinking about revenge, the door opened and Mr Zaturetsky appeared.

When he saw me a glimmer of happiness flashed over his face. He bowed and greeted me. He had come a little prematurely, he had come before I had managed to consider my revenge.

He asked if I had received his message yesterday.

I was silent. He repeated his question. 'I received it,' I replied.

'And will you, please, write the review?'

I saw him in front of me: sickly, obstinate, beseeching. I saw the vertical wrinkle – etched on his forehead, the line of a single passion – I examined this line and grasped that it was a straight line determined by two points, my review and his article; that beyond the vice of this maniacal straight line nothing existed in his life but saintly asceticism; and then a spiteful trick occurred to me.

'I hope that you understand that after yesterday I can't speak to you,' I said.

'I don't understand you.'

'Don't pretend. She told me everything. It's unnecessary for you to deny it.'

'I don't understand you,' repeated the little man once again; but this time more decidedly.

I assumed a genial, almost friendly tone. 'Look here, Mr Zaturetsky, I don't blame you. I chase women as well and I understand you. In your position I would have tried to seduce a beautiful girl like that, if I'd found myself alone in an apartment with her and she'd been naked beneath a man's raincoat.'

'This is an outrage!' The little man turned pale.

'No, it's the truth, Mr Zaturetsky.'

'Did the lady tell you this?'

'She has no secrets from me.'

'Comrade Assistant, this is an outrage! I'm a married man. I have a wife! I have children!' The little man took a step forward, so that I had to step back.

'So much the worse for you, Mr Zaturetsky.'

'What do you mean, so much the worse?'

'I think being married must be a drawback to chasing women.'

'Take it back!' said Mr Zaturetsky menacingly.

'Well, all right,' I conceded, 'the matrimonial state need not always be an obstacle. Sometimes it can, on the contrary, excuse all sorts of things. But it makes no difference. I've already told you that I'm not angry with you and I understand you quite well. There's only one thing I don't understand. How can you still want a review from a man whose woman you've been trying to make?'

'Comrade Assistant! Dr Kalousek, the editor of the magazine of the Academy of Sciences, *Visual Arts Journal*, is asking you for this review. And you must write the review!'

'The review or the woman. You can't ask for both.'

'What kind of behavior is this, comrade!' screamed Mr Zaturetsky in desperate anger.

The odd thing is that I suddenly felt that Mr Zaturetsky had really wanted to seduce Klara. Seething with rage, I shouted, 'You have the audacity to tell me off? You who should humbly apologize to me in front of my secretary.'

I turned my back on Mr Zaturetsky, and, confused, he staggered out.

'Well then,' I sighed with relief like a general after the victorious conclusion of a hard campaign, and I said to Mary, 'Perhaps he won't want a review by me any more.'

Mary smiled and after a moment timidly asked, 'Just why is it you don't want to write this review?'

'Because, Mary my dear, what he's written is the most awful crap.'

'Then why don't you write in your review that it's crap?'

'Why should I write it? Why do I have to antagonize people?' – but hardly had I said this when I realized that Mr Zaturetsky was my enemy all the same and that my struggle not to write the review was an aimless and absurd struggle – unfortunately, there was nothing I could do either to stop it or to back down.

Mary was looking at me with an indulgent smile, as women look upon the foolishness of children; then the door opened and there stood Mr Zaturetsky with his arm raised. 'It's not me! It's you who will have to apologize,' he shouted in a trembling voice and disappeared again.

7

I don't remember exactly when, perhaps that same day or perhaps a few days later, we found an envelope in my mailbox without an address.

Inside there was a letter in a clumsy, almost primitive handwriting:

Dear Madame:
Present yourself at my house on Sunday regarding the insult to my husband. I shall be at home all day. If you don't present yourself, I shall be forced to take measures. Anna Zaturetsky, 14 Dalimilova Street, Prague 3.

Klara was scared and began saying something about my guilt. I waved my hand, declaring that the purpose of life is to give amusement, and if life is too lazy for this, there is nothing left but to help it along a little. Man must constantly saddle events, those swift mares without which he would be dragging his feet in the dust like a weary footslogger. When Klara said that she didn't want to saddle any events, I assured her that she would never meet Mr or Mrs Zaturetsky, and that the event into whose saddle I had jumped, I'd take care of with one hand tied behind my back.

In the morning when we were leaving the house, the porter stopped us. The porter wasn't an enemy. Prudently, I had once bribed him with a fifty-crown bill, and I had lived until this time in the agreeable conviction that he'd learned not to know anything about me, and didn't add fuel to the fire, which my enemies in the house kept alight.

'Some couple was here looking for you yesterday,' he said.

'What sort of couple?'

'A little guy with a woman.'

'What did the woman look like?'

'Two heads taller. Terribly energetic. A stern woman. She was asking about all sorts of things.' He turned to Klara. 'Chiefly about you. Who you are and what your name is.'

'Good heavens, what did you say to her?' exclaimed Klara.

'What could I say? How do I know who comes to see Mr Klima? I told her that a different person comes every evening.'

'Great!' I laughed and drew ten crowns from my pocket. 'Just go on talking like that.'

'Don't be afraid,' I then said to Klara, 'you won't go anywhere on Sunday and nobody will find you.'

And Sunday came, and after Sunday, Monday, Tuesday, Wednesday; nothing happened. 'You see,' I said to Klara. But then came Thursday. I was lecturing to my students at the customary secret lecture about how feverishly and in what an atmosphere of unselfish camaraderie the young Fauvists had liberated color from its former impressionistic character, when Mary opened the door and whispered to me, 'The wife of that Zaturetsky is here.' 'But I'm not here,' I said, 'just show her the schedule!' But Mary shook her head. 'I showed her, but she peeped into your office and saw your raincoat on the stand. Just then Assistant Professor Zeleny came by and assured her that it was yours. So now she's sitting in the corridor waiting.'

Had fate been able to pursue me more systematically, it is quite possible that I would have been a success. A blind alley is the place for my best inspirations. I said to my favorite student:

'Be so kind as to do me a small favor. Run to my office, put on my raincoat, and go out of the building in it. Some woman will try to prove that you are me, and your task will be not to admit it at any price.'

The student went off and returned in about a quarter of an hour. He told me that the mission had been completed, the coast was clear, and the woman was out of the building.

This time then I had won. But then came Friday, and in the afternoon Klara returned from work trembling almost like a leaf.

The polite gentleman who received customers in the tidy office of the dress factory had suddenly opened the door leading to the workroom, where my Klara and fifteen other seamstresses were sitting over their sewing machines, and cried:

'Does any one of you live at 5 Pushkin Street?'

Klara knew that it concerned her, because 5 Pushkin Street was my address. However, well-advised caution kept her quiet, for she knew that her living with me was a secret and that nobody knew anything about it.

'You see, that's what I've been telling her,' said the polished gentleman when none of the seamstresses spoke up, and he went out again. Klara learned later that a strict female voice on the telephone had made him search through the directory of employees, and had talked for a quarter of an hour trying to convince him there must be a woman employee from 5 Pushkin Street in the factory.

The shadow of Mrs Zaturetsky was cast over our idyllic room.

'But how could she have found out where you work? After all, here in the house nobody knows about you!' I yelled.

Yes, I was really convinced that nobody knew about us. I lived like an eccentric who thinks that he lives unobserved behind a high wall, while all the time one detail escapes him: the wall is made of transparent glass.

I had bribed the porter not to reveal that Klara lived with me, I had forced Klara into the most troublesome inconspicuousness and concealment and, meanwhile, the whole house knew about her. It was enough that once she had entered into an ill-advised conversation with a woman on the second floor – and they got to know where Klara was working.

Without suspecting it we had been living exposed for quite some time. What remained concealed from our persecutors was merely Klara's name and then one small detail: that she lived with me unregistered. These two were the final and only secrets behind which, for the time being, we eluded Mrs Zaturetsky, who launched her attack so consistently and methodically that I was horror-struck.

I understood that it was going to be tough. The horse of my story was damnably saddled.

8

This was on Friday. And when Klara came back from work on Saturday, she was trembling again. Here is what had happened:

Mrs Zaturetsky had set out with her husband for the factory. She had called beforehand and asked the manager to allow her and her husband to visit the workshop, to examine the faces of the seamstresses. It's true that this request astonished the comrade manager, but Mrs Zaturetsky put on such an air that it was impossible to refuse. She said something vague about an insult, about a ruined existence, and about court. Mr Zaturetsky stood beside her, frowned, and was silent.

They were shown into the workroom. The seamstresses raised their heads indifferently, and Klara recognized the little man; she turned pale and with conspicuous inconspicuousness quickly went on with her needlework.

'Here you are,' exclaimed the manager with ironic politeness to the stiff-looking pair. Mrs Zaturetsky realized that she must take the initiative and she urged her husband: 'Well look!' Mr Zaturetsky assumed a scowl and looked around. 'Is it one of them?' whispered Mrs Zaturetsky.

Even with his glasses Mr Zaturetsky couldn't see clearly enough to examine the large room, which in any case wasn't easy to survey, full as it was of piled-up junk and dresses hanging from long horizontal bars, with fidgety seamstresses, who didn't sit neatly with their faces toward the door, but in various positions; they were turning round, getting up and down, and involuntarily averting their faces. Therefore, Mr Zaturetsky had to step forward and try not to skip anyone.

When the women understood that they were being examined by someone, and in addition by someone so unsightly and unattractive, they felt vaguely insulted, and sneers and grumbling began to be heard. One of them, a robust young girl, impertinently burst out:

'He's searching all over Prague for the shrew who made him pregnant!'

The noisy, ribald mockery of the women overwhelmed the couple; they stood downcast, and then became resolute with a peculiar sort of dignity.

'Ma'am,' the impertinent girl yelled again at Mrs Zaturetsky, 'you look after your little son badly! I would never have let such a nice little boy out of the house.'

'Look some more,' she whispered to her husband, and sullenly and timidly he went forward step by step as if he were running the gauntlet, but firmly all the same – and he didn't miss a face.

All the time the manager was smiling noncommittally; he knew his women and he knew that you couldn't do anything with them; and so he pretended not to hear their clamor, and he asked Mr Zaturetsky, 'Now please tell me, what is this woman supposed to look like?'

Mr Zaturetsky turned to the manager and spoke slowly and seriously: 'She was beautiful . . . She was very beautiful . . .'

Meanwhile Klara crouched in a corner, setting herself off from all the playful women by her agitation, her bent head, and her dogged activity. Oh, how badly she feigned her inconspicuousness and insignificance! And Mr Zaturetsky was only a little way away from her; in the next minute he must look into her face.

'That isn't much, when you only remember that she was beautiful,' said the polite comrade manager to Mr Zaturetsky. 'There are many beautiful women. Was she short or tall?'

'Tall,' said Mr Zaturetsky.

'Was she brunette or blonde?' Mr Zaturetsky thought a moment and said, 'She was blonde.'

This part of the story could serve as a parable on the power of beauty. When Mr Zaturetsky had seen Klara for the first time at my place, he was so dazzled that he actually hadn't seen her. Beauty created before her some opaque screen. A screen of light, behind which she was hidden as if beneath a veil.

For Klara is neither tall nor blonde. Only the inner greatness of beauty lent her in Mr Zaturetsky's eyes a semblance of great physical size. And the glow, which emanates from beauty, lent her hair the appearance of gold.

And so when the little man finally approached the corner where Klara, in a brown work smock, was huddled over a shirt, he didn't recognize her, because he had never seen her.

9

When Klara had finished an incoherent and barely intelligible account of this event I said, 'You see, we're lucky.'

But amid sobs Klara said to me, 'What kind of luck? If they didn't find me today, they'll find me tomorrow.'

'I should like to know how.'

'They'll come here for me, to your place.'

'I won't let anyone in.'

'And what when they send the police?'

'Come now, I'll make a joke of it. After all, it was just a joke and fun.'

'Today there's no time for jokes, today everything gets serious. They'll say that I wanted to blacken his reputation. When they take a look at him, how could they ever believe that he was capable of trying to seduce a woman?'

'You're right, Klara,' I said, 'they'll probably lock you up. But look, Karel Havlichek Borovsky was also in jail and think how far he got; you must have learned about him in school.'

'Stop chattering,' said Klara. 'You know it looks bad for me. I'll have to go before the disciplinary committee and I'll have it on my record, and I'll never get out of the workshop. Anyway, I'd like to know what's happening about the modeling job you promised me. I can't sleep at your place any longer. I'll always be afraid that they're coming for me. Today I'm going back to Chelakovits.' This was one conversation.

And that afternoon after a departmental meeting I had a second.

The chairman of the department, a gray-haired art historian and a wise man, invited me into his office.

'I hope you know that you haven't helped yourself with that study that has just come out,' he said to me.

'Yes, I know,' I replied.

'Many of our professors think that it applies to them and the dean thinks that it was an attack on his views.'

'What can be done about it?' I said.

'Nothing,' replied the professor, 'but your three-year period as a lecturer has expired and candidates will compete to fill the position. It is customary for the committee to give the position to someone who has already taught in the school, but are you so sure that this custom will be upheld in your case? But this is not what I wanted to speak about. So far it has spoken in your favor that you lectured regularly, that you were popular with the students, and that you taught them something. But now you can't even rely on this. The dean has informed me that for the last three months you haven't lectured at all. And quite without excuse. Well, this in itself would be enough for immediate dismissal.'

I explained to the professor that I hadn't missed a single lecture, that it had all been a joke, and I told him the whole story about Mr Zaturetsky and Klara.

'Fine, I believe you,' said the professor, 'but what does it matter if I believe you? Today the whole school says that you don't lecture and don't do anything. It has already been discussed at the union meeting and yesterday they took the matter to the board of regents.'

'But why didn't they speak to me about it first?'

'What should they speak to you about? Everything is clear to them. Now they are only looking back over your whole performance trying to find connections between your past and your present.'

'What can they find bad in my past? You know yourself how much I like my work! I've never shirked! My conscience is clear.'

'Every human life has many aspects,' said the professor. 'The past of each one of us can be just as easily arranged into the biography of a beloved statesman as into that of a criminal. Only look thoroughly at yourself. Nobody is denying that you like your work. But what if it served you above all as an opportunity for escape? You weren't often seen at meetings and when you did come, for the most part, you were silent. Nobody really knew what you thought. I myself remember that several times when a serious matter was being discussed you suddenly made a joke, which caused embarrassment. This embarrassment was of course immediately forgotten, but today, when it is retrieved from the past, it acquires a particular significance. Or remember how various women came looking for you at the university and how you refused to see them. Or else your last article, about which anyone who wishes can allege that it was written from suspicious premises. All these, of course, are isolated facts; but just look at them in the light of today's offense, and they suddenly unite into a totality of significant testimony about your character and attitude.'

'But what sort of offense? Everything can be explained so easily! The facts are quite simple and clear!'

'Facts mean little compared to attitudes. To contradict rumor or sentiment is as futile as arguing against a believer's faith in the Immaculate Conception. You have simply become a victim of faith, Comrade Assistant.'

'There's a lot of truth in what you say,' I said, 'but if a sentiment has arisen against me like an act of faith, I shall fight faith with reason. I shall explain before everyone the things that took place. If people are human they will have to laugh at it.'

'As you like. But you'll learn either that people aren't human or that you don't know what humans are like. They will not laugh. If you place before them everything as it happened, it will then appear that not only did you fail to fulfill your obligations as they were indicated on the schedule – that you did not do what you should have done – but on top of this, you lectured secretly, that is, you did what you shouldn't have done. It will appear that you insulted a man who was asking for your help. It will appear that your private life is not in order, that you have some unregistered girl living with you, which will make a very unfavorable impression on the female chairman of the union. The issue will become confused and God knows what further rumors will arise. Whatever they are they will certainly be useful to those who have been provoked by your views, but were ashamed to be against you on account of them.'

I knew that the professor wasn't trying to alarm or deceive me. In this matter, however, I considered him a crank and didn't want to give myself up to his skepticism. The scandal with Mr Zaturetsky made me go cold all over, but it hadn't tired me out yet. For I had saddled this horse myself, so I couldn't let it tear the reins from my hands and carry me off wherever it wished. I was prepared to engage in a contest with it. And the horse did not avoid the contest. When I reached home, there in the mailbox was a summons to a meeting of the local committee, and I had no doubt as to what it was about.

10

I was not mistaken. The local committee, which was in session in what had been a store, was seated around a long table. The members assumed a gloomy expression when I came in. A grizzled man with glasses and a receding chin pointed to a chair. I said thank you, sat down, and this man took the floor. He informed me that the local committee had been watching me for some time, that it knew very well that I led an irregular private life; that this did not produce a good impression in my neighborhood; that the tenants from my apartment house had already complained about me once, when they couldn't sleep because of the uproar in my apartment; that all this was enough for the local committee to have formed a proper conception of me. And now, on top of all this, Comrade Madame Zaturetsky, the wife of a scientific worker, had turned to them for help. Six months ago I should have written a review about her husband's scientific work, and I hadn't done so, even though I well knew that the fate of the said work depended on my review.

'What the devil d'you mean by scientific work!' I interrupted the man with the little chin: 'It's a patchwork of plagiarized thoughts.'

'That is interesting, comrade.' A fashionably dressed blonde of about thirty now joined in the discussion; on her face was permanently glued a beaming smile. 'Permit me a question; what is your field?'

'I am an art theoretician.'

'And Comrade Zaturetsky?'

'I don't know. Perhaps he's trying at something similar.'

'You see,' the blonde turned enthusiastically to the remaining members, 'Comrade Klíma sees a worker in the same field as a competitor and not as a comrade. This is the way that almost all our intellectuals think today.'

'I shall continue,' said the man with the receding chin. 'Comrade Madame Zaturetsky told us that her husband visited your apartment and met some woman there. It is said that this woman accused Mr Zaturetsky of wanting to molest her sexually. Comrade Madame Zaturetsky has in her hand documents which prove that her husband is not capable of such a thing. She wants to know the name of this woman who accused her husband, and to transfer the matter to the disciplinary section of the people's committee, because she claims this false accusation has damaged her husband's good name.'

I tried again to cut this ridiculous affair short. 'Look here, comrades,' I said, 'it isn't worth all the trouble. It's not a question of damaged reputation. The work is so weak that no one else could recommend it either. And if some misunderstanding occurred between this woman and Mr Zaturetsky, it shouldn't really be necessary to summon a meeting.'

'Fortunately, it is not you who will decide about our meetings, comrade,' replied the man with the receding chin. 'And when you now assert that Comrade Zaturetsky's work is bad, then we must look upon this as revenge. Comrade Madame Zaturetsky gave us a letter to read, which you wrote after reading her husband's work.'

'Yes. Only in that letter I didn't say a word about what the work was like.'

'That is true. But you did write that you would be glad to help him; in this letter it is clearly implied that you respect Comrade Zaturetsky's work. And now you declare that it's a patchwork. Why didn't you say it to his face?'

'Comrade Klima has two faces,' said the blonde.

At this moment an elderly woman with a permanent wave joined the discussion (she had an expression of self-sacrificing good will in examining the lives of others); she passed at once to the heart of the matter. 'We would need to know, comrade, who this woman was whom Mr Zaturetsky met at your home.'

I understood unmistakably that it wasn't within my power to remove the senseless gravity from the whole affair, and that I could dispose of it in only one way: to confuse the traces, to lure them away from Klara, to lead them away from her as the partridge leads the hound away from its nest, offering its own body for the sake of its young.

'It's a bad business, I don't remember her name,' I said.

'How is it that you don't remember the name of the woman you live with?' questioned the woman with the permanent wave.

'At one time, I used to write all this down, but then it occurred to me that it was stupid and I dropped it. It's hard for a man to rely on his memory.'

'Perhaps, Comrade Klima, you have an exemplary relationship with women,' said the blonde.

'Perhaps I could remember, but I should have to think about it. Do you know when it was that Mr Zaturetsky visited me?'

'That was . . . wait a moment,' the man with the receding chin looked at his papers, 'the fourteenth, on Wednesday afternoon.'

'On Wednesday . . . the fourteenth . . . wait . . .' I held my head in my hand and did some thinking. 'Oh I remember. That was Helena.' I saw that they were all hanging expectantly on my words.

'Helena what?'

'What? I'm sorry, I don't know. I didn't want to ask her that. As a matter of fact, speaking frankly, I'm not even sure that her name was Helena. I only called her that because her husband seemed to me to be like red-haired Menelaus. But anyway she very much liked being called that. On Tuesday evening I met her in a wine-shop and managed to talk to her for a while, when her Menelaus went to the bar to drink a cognac. The next day she came to my place and was there the whole afternoon. Only I had to leave her in the evening for a couple of hours, I had a meeting at the university. When I returned she was disgusted because some little man had molested her and she thought that I had put him up to it; she took offense and didn't want to know me any more. And so, you see, I didn't even manage to learn her correct name.'

'Comrade Klíma, whether you are telling the truth or not,' went on the blonde, 'it seems to me to be absolutely incomprehensible that you can educate our youth. Does our life really inspire in you nothing but the desire to carouse and abuse women? Be assured, we shall give our opinion about this in the proper places.'

'The porter didn't speak about any Helena,' broke in the elderly lady with the permanent wave, 'but he did inform us that some unregistered girl from the dress factory has been living with you for a month. Don't forget, comrade, that you are in lodgings. How can you imagine that someone can live with you like this? Do you think that your house is a brothel?'

There flashed before my eyes the ten crowns which I'd given to the porter a couple of days ago, and I understood that the encirclement was complete. And the woman from the local committee continued: 'If you don't want to tell us her name, the police will find it out.'

11

The ground was slipping away beneath my feet. At the university I began to sense the malicious atmosphere which the professor had told me about. For the time being, I wasn't summoned to any interviews, but here and there I caught an allusion, and now and then Mary let something out, for the teachers drank coffee in her office and didn't watch their tongues. In a couple of days the selection committee, which was collecting evidence on all sides, was to meet. I imagined that its members had read the report of the local committee, a report about which I knew only that it was secret and that I couldn't refer to it.

There are moments in life when a man retreats defensively, when he must give ground, when he must surrender less important positions in order to protect the more important ones. But should it come to the very last, the most important one, at this point a man must halt and stand firm if he doesn't want to begin life all over again with idle hands and a feeling of being shipwrecked.

It seemed to me that this single, most important position was my love. Yes, in those troubled days I suddenly began to realize that I loved my fragile and unfortunate seamstress, who had been both beaten and pampered by life, and that I clung to her.

That day I met Klara at the museum. No, not at home. Do you think that home was still home? Is home a room with glass walls? A room observed through binoculars? A room where you must keep your beloved more carefully hidden than contraband?

Home was not home. There we felt like housebreakers who might be caught at any minute. Footsteps in the corridor made us nervous; we kept expecting someone to start pounding on the door. Klara was commuting from Chelakovits and we didn't feel like meeting in our alienated home for even a short while. So I had asked an artist friend to lend me his studio at night. That day I had got the key for the first time.

And so we found ourselves beneath a high roof in Vinohrady, in an enormous room with one small couch and a huge, slanting window, from which we could see all the lights of Prague. Amid the many paintings propped against the walls, the untidiness, and the carefree artist's squalor, a blessed feeling of freedom returned to me. I sprawled on the couch, pushed in the corkscrew and opened a bottle of wine. I chattered gaily and freely, and was looking forward to a beautiful evening and night.

However, the pressure, which I no longer felt, had fallen with its full weight on Klara.

I have already mentioned how Klara without any scruples and with the greatest naturalness had lived at one time in my attic. But now, when we found ourselves for a short time in someone else's studio, she felt put out. More than put out: 'It's humiliating,' she said.

'What's humiliating?' I asked her.

'That we have to borrow an apartment.'

'Why is it humiliating that we have to borrow an apartment?'

'Because there's something humiliating about it,' she replied.

'But we couldn't do anything else.'

'I guess,' she replied, 'but in a borrowed apartment I feel like a whore.'

'Good God, why should you feel like a whore in a *borrowed* apartment? Whores mostly operate in their own apartments, not in borrowed ones –'

It was futile to attack with reason the stout wall of irrational feelings that, as is known, is the stuff of which the female mind is made. From the beginning our conversation was ill-omened.

I told Klara what the professor had said, I told her what had happened at the local committee, and I was trying to convince her that in the end we would win if we loved each other and were together.

Klara was silent for a while and then said that I myself was guilty.

'Will you at least help me to get away from those seamstresses?'

I told her that this would have to be, at least temporarily, a time of forbearance.

'You see,' said Klara, 'you promised and in the end you do nothing. I won't be able to get out, even if somebody else wanted to help me, because I shall have my reputation ruined on your account.'

I gave Klara my word that the incident with Mr Zaturetsky couldn't harm her.

MILAN KUNDERA

'I also don't understand,' said Klara, 'why you won't write the review. If you'd write it, then there'd be peace at once.'

'It's too late, Klara,' I said. 'If I write this review they'll say that I'm condemning the work out of revenge and they'll be still more furious.'

'And why must you condemn it? Write a favorable review!'

'I can't, Klara. This work is thoroughly absurd.'

'So what? Why are you being truthful all of a sudden? Wasn't it a lie when you told the little man that they don't think much of you at *Visual Arts Journal*? And wasn't it a lie when you told the little man that he had tried to seduce me? And wasn't it a lie when you invented Helena? When you've told so many lies, what does it matter if you tell one more and praise him in the review? That's the only way you can smooth things out.'

'You see, Klara,' I said, 'you think that a lie is a lie and it would seem that you're right. But you aren't. I can invent anything, make a fool of someone, carry out hoaxes and practical jokes – and I don't feel like a liar and I don't have a bad conscience. These lies, if you want to call them that, represent myself as I really am. With such lies I'm not simulating anything, with such lies I am in fact speaking the truth. But there are things which I can't lie about, things I've penetrated, whose meaning I've grasped, which I love and take seriously. It's impossible, don't ask me to do it, I can't.'

We didn't understand each other.

But I really loved Klara and decided to do everything so that she would have nothing to reproach me for. The following day I wrote a letter to Mrs Zaturetsky, saying that I would expect her the day after tomorrow at two o'clock in my office.

12

True to her terrifying methodicalness, Mrs Zaturetsky knocked precisely at the appointed time. I opened the door and asked her in.

Then I finally saw her. She was a tall woman, very tall with a thin peasant's face and pale blue eyes. 'Take off your things,' I said, and with awkward movements she took off a long, dark coat, narrow at the waist and oddly styled, a coat which God knows why evoked the image of an ancient greatcoat.

I didn't want to attack at once; I wanted my adversary to show me her cards first. After Mrs Zaturetsky sat down, I got her to speak by making a remark or two.

'Mr Klima,' she said in a serious voice, but without any aggressiveness, 'you know why I was looking for you. My husband has always respected you very much as a specialist and as a man of character. Everything depended on your review and you didn't want to do it for him. It took my husband three years to write this study. His life was harder than yours. He was a teacher, he commuted daily twenty miles outside Prague. Last year I forced him to stop that and devote himself to research.'

'Mr Zaturetsky isn't employed?' I asked.

'No . . .'

'What does he live on?'

'For the time being I have to work hard myself. This research, Mr Klima, is my husband's passion. If you knew how he studied everything. If you knew how many pages he rewrote. He always says that a real scholar must write three hundred pages so as to keep thirty. And on top of it, this woman. Believe me, Mr Klima, I know him, I'm sure he didn't do it, so why did this woman accuse him? I don't believe it. Let her say it before me and before him. I know women, perhaps she likes you very much and you don't care for her. Perhaps she wanted to make you jealous. But you can believe me, Mr Klima, my husband would never have dared!'

I was listening to Mrs Zaturetsky, and all at once something strange happened to me: I ceased being aware that this was the woman for whose sake I should have to leave the university, and that this was the woman who caused the tension between myself and Klara, and for whose sake I'd wasted so many days in anger and unpleasantness. The connection between her and the incident, in which we'd both played a sad role, suddenly seemed vague, arbitrary, accidental, and not our fault. All at once I understood that it had only been my illusion that we ourselves saddle events and control their course. The truth is that they aren't *our* stories at all, that they are foisted upon us from somewhere *outside*; that in no way do they represent us; that we are not to blame for the queer path that they follow. They carry us away, since they are controlled by some *other* forces; no, I don't mean by supernatural forces, but by human forces, by the forces of those people who, when they unite, unfortunately still remain mutually *alien*.

When I looked at Mrs Zaturetsky's eyes it seemed to me that these eyes couldn't see the consequences of my actions, that these eyes weren't seeing at all, that they were merely swimming in her face; that they were only stuck on.

'Perhaps you're right, Mrs Zaturetsky,' I said in a conciliatory tone. 'Perhaps my girl didn't speak the truth, but you know how it is when a man's jealous . . . I believed her and was carried away. This can happen to anyone.'

'Yes, certainly,' said Mrs Zaturetsky and it was evident that a weight had been lifted from her heart. 'When you yourself see it, it's good. We were afraid that you believed her. This woman could have ruined my husband's whole life. I'm not speaking of the moral light it casts upon him.

But my husband swears by your opinion. The editors assured him that it depended on you. My husband is convinced that if his article were published, he would finally be recognized as a scientific worker. I ask you, now that everything has been cleared up, will you write this review for him? And can you do it quickly?'

Now came the moment to avenge myself on everything and appease my rage, only at this moment I didn't feel any rage, and when I spoke it was only because there was no escaping it: 'Mrs Zaturetsky, there is some difficulty regarding the review. I shall confess to you how it all happened. I don't like to say unpleasant things to people's faces. This is my weakness. I avoided Mr Zaturetsky, and I thought that he would figure out why I was avoiding him. His paper is weak. It has no scientific value. Do you believe me?'

'I find it hard to believe. I can't believe you,' said Mrs Zaturetsky.

'Above all, this work is not original. Please understand, a scholar must always arrive at something new; a scholar can't copy what we already know, what others have written.'

'My husband definitely didn't copy.'

'Mrs Zaturetsky, you've surely read this study . . .' I wanted to continue, but Mrs Zaturetsky interrupted me: 'No, I haven't.' I was surprised. 'You will read it then for yourself.'

'I can't see,' said Mrs Zaturetsky. 'I see only light and shadow, my eyes are bad. I haven't read a single line for five years, but I don't need to read to know if my husband's honest or not. This can be recognized in other ways. I know my husband, as a mother her children, I know everything about him. And I know that what he does is always honest.'

I had to undergo worse. I read aloud to Mrs Zaturetsky paragraphs from Mateychek, Pechirka, and Michek, whose thoughts and formulations Mr Zaturetsky had taken over. It wasn't a question of willful plagiarism, but rather an unconscious submission to those authorities who inspired in Mr Zaturetsky a feeling of sincere and inordinate respect. But anyone who had seen these passages compared must have understood that no serious scholarly magazine could publish Mr Zaturetsky's work.

I don't know how much Mrs Zaturetsky concentrated on my exposition, how much of it she followed and understood; she sat humbly in the armchair, humbly and obediently like a soldier, who knows that he may not leave his post. It took about half an hour for us to finish. Mrs Zaturetsky got up from the armchair, fixed her transparent eyes upon me, and in a dull voice begged my pardon; but I knew that she hadn't lost faith in her husband and she didn't reproach anyone except herself for not knowing how to resist my arguments, which seemed obscure and unintelligible to her. She put on her military raincoat and I understood that this woman was a soldier in body and spirit, a sad and loyal soldier, a soldier tired from long marches, a soldier who doesn't understand the sense of an order and yet carries it out without objections, a soldier who goes away defeated but without dishonor.

After she'd gone, something remained in my office of her weariness, her loyalty, and her sadness. I suddenly forgot myself and my sorrows. The sorrow which seized me at that moment was purer, because it didn't issue from within me, but flowed from without, from afar.

13

'So now you don't have to be afraid of anything,' I said to Klara, when later in the Dalmatian wine-shop I repeated to her my conversation with Mrs Zaturetsky.

'I didn't have anything to fear anyhow,' replied Klara with a self-assurance that astonished me.

'How's that, you didn't? If it wasn't for you I wouldn't have met Mrs Zaturetsky at all!'

'It's good that you did meet her, because what you did to them was cruel. Dr Kalousek said that it's hard for an intelligent man to understand this.'

'When did you meet Kalousek?'

'I've met him,' said Klara.

'And did you tell him everything?'

'What? Is it a secret perhaps? Now I know exactly what you are.'

'Hm.'

'May I tell you what you are?'

'Please.'

'A stereotyped cynic.'

'You got that from Kalousek.'

'Why from Kalousek? Do you think that I can't figure it out for myself? You actually think that I'm not capable of forming an opinion about you. You like to lead people by the nose. You promised Mr Zaturetsky a review.'

'I didn't promise him a review.'

'That's one thing. And you promised me a job. You used me as an excuse to Mr Zaturetsky, and you used Mr Zaturetsky as an excuse to me. But you may be sure that I'll get that job.'

'Through Kalousek?' I tried to be scornful.

'Not from you. You've gambled so much away and you don't even know yourself how much.'

'And do you know?'

'Yes. Your contract won't be renewed and you'll be glad if they'll let you in some gallery as a clerk. But you must realize that all this was only your own mistake. If I can give you some advice: another time be honest and don't lie, because a man who lies can't be respected by any woman.'

She got up, gave me (clearly for the last time) her hand, turned, and left.

Only after a while did it occur to me (in spite of the chilly silence which surrounded me) that my story was not of the tragic sort, but rather of the comic variety.

At any rate that afforded me some comfort.

(Translated by Suzanne Rappaport)

BERYL BAINBRIDGE

The Longstop

Beryl Bainbridge (1934–) was born in Liverpool and trained as a dancer. She has written several television screenplays and many novels, including *Harriet Said* (1972), *The Dressmaker* (1973), *Injury Time* (1977), *Young Adolf* (1978), an account of Adolf Hitler's time as a young man in Liverpool, and *An Awfully Big Adventure* (1989). A number of these are set in Liverpool, and most of them are hilarious.

'The Longstop', from her story collection *Mum and Mr Armitage*, is a story of vivid reminiscence, a comic anecdote about a fading northern culture, its odd customs and snobberies, its constant social or physical disasters. Like a good deal of this author's work, it goes back to the world of Liverpool at war, as seen through the eyes of childhood and from the malicious viewpoint of black comedy. Beryl Bainbridge has explained, 'I write about the sort of childhood I had, my parents, the landscape I grew up in.' But she renders it with a wonderful comic vividness comparable to that of another deeply talented northern writer, the playwright Alan Bennett.

Words and cricket seem to go together. Whenever I watch the game, by mistake, on television, I think it's not true that you can't get blood from a stone.

I only ever played the game once myself, in the park with some evacuees from Bootle. I was allowed to join in because I held a biscuit tin filled with shortbread that my mother had baked. They said I could have a turn if I gave them a biscuit afterwards. I didn't make any runs because I never hit the ball, and when I kept my promise and began to open the tin the evacuees knocked me over and took every piece of shortbread. They threw the tin over the wall into the gentlemen's lavatory. I had to tell my mother a six-foot-high naughty man with a Hitler moustache had chased me; she would have slapped me for playing with evacuees.

Mr Baines, who was my maternal grandfather, was a lover of cricket. Mr Jones, my father, didn't care for the game. He cared even less for my grandfather. In his humble estimation Mr Baines was a mean old bugger, a fifth columnist, and, following his self-confessed denouncing of a neighbour in Norris Green for failing to draw his curtains against the blackout, a Gauleiter into the bargain. He was also a lounge lizard, a term never satisfactorily explained, though it was true that my grandfather fell asleep between meals.

Apart from words, my father was keen on sailing ships. He subscribed to a monthly magazine on the subject. If he was to be believed, he had, when no more than a child, sailed as a cabin boy to America. In middle age, his occupation a commercial traveller, he prowled the deserted shore beyond the railway line, peering of an evening through the barbed-wire entanglements at the oil tankers and the black destroyers that crawled along the bleak edge of the Irish Sea; it was a gloomy mystery to him where that fearless lad before the mast had gone.

Every week Mr Baines came for Sunday dinner. There had been a moment at the outbreak of the war when he had contemplated coming to live with us, but after three days he returned home. He said he preferred to take his chances with the Luftwaffe. His conversation during the meal was always about cricket, and mostly to do with a man called Briggs. Briggs, he said, had just missed greatness by a lack of seriousness. If only Briggs had taken batting more seriously he would have been, make no bones about it, the best all-round cricketer in England since W. G. Grace. Briggs, he informed us, took bowling and fielding in deadly earnest, but as a batsman he was a disaster; he seemed far more anxious to amuse the crowd than to improve his average.

Nobody listened to my grandfather, certainly not my father who was often heard to remark quite loudly that, had he been in control, he wouldn't give the old skinflint the time of day, let alone Sunday dinner, world without end.

However, one particular Sunday in the summer of 1944, Mr Baines, without warning, excelled himself when describing a cricketer called Ranjitsinhji.

'Just to set eyes on him,' said Mr Baines, 'was a picture in motion. The way his shirt ballooned –'

'A black chappie,' my father exclaimed, taken aback at my grandfather speaking civilly of a foreigner.

'An Indian prince,' said Mr Baines. He was equally taken aback at being addressed in the middle of his monologue. He was used to conversing uninterrupted throughout the devouring of the black-market roast pork.

'They're two a penny,' my father said.

'More potatoes?' asked my mother, worriedly.

'Even when it wasn't windy,' continued Mr Baines, 'his shirt ballooned. Whether half a gale was blowing on the Hove ground or there wasn't enough breeze to shift the flag at Lord's, the fellow's shirt flapped like the mainsail of a six-tonner on the Solent.'

'Blithering rubbish,' said my father. He stabbed at a sprout on his plate as though it was alive.

My mother told Mr Baines that they played cricket in the park every Sunday afternoon. Not a proper team, just old men and young lads. Not what he was used to, of course. 'But,' she said, eyeing my father contemptuously, 'it will do us good to get out into the pure air.'

She didn't mean my father to come. We were never a family who went anywhere together. My father's opinion, had he voiced it, would have been that the family who stood together fell out together. Often we would attempt an outing, but between the closing of the back door and the opening of the front gate, misunderstandings occurred and plans were abruptly abandoned. She was astonished when, having washed up and taken off her pinny, she found my father in the hall putting on his trilby hat. She didn't like it, you could tell. Her mouth went all funny and the lipstick ran down at one corner. Shoulder to shoulder, more or less, we set off for the park.

I wanted to nip over the garden fence and through the blackberry bushes into Brows Lane, but my mother said my grandfather wasn't about to nip anywhere, not at his age. We trotted him down the road past the roundabout and the Council offices. The brass band was practising in the hut behind the fire station. When he heard the music, Mr Baines began to walk with his arms held stiffly at his sides, only the band kept stopping and starting and the tune came in bits, and after a little while he gave up playing at soldiers and shuffled instead. My father looked at the ground all the time; there was a grey splodge on the brim of his hat where a pigeon had done its business.

The park was quite grand, even though it had lost its ornamental gates at the entrance. My mother said they'd been removed to make into tanks. My father swore they were mouldering away in a brickfield down by the Docks, along with his mother's copper kettle and a hundred thousand front railings. The park had a pavilion, a sort of hunting lodge with mullioned windows and a thatched roof. People were worried about incendiary bombs. The park keeper kept his grass roller inside and buckets of water. In front of the pavilion was a sunken bowling green, and beyond that a miniature clock-golf course. We used to ride our bikes up and down the bumps. Behind the pavilion, within a roped enclosure, was a German Messerschmitt. It had been there for two years. It hadn't crash-landed anywhere near our village; it was on loan. The park keeper was always telling the Council to tell someone to come back for it. At first we had all run round it and shuddered, but after a few weeks we hardly noticed it any more. It just perched there, propped on blocks, one wing tipped up to the sky, the cockpit half burned away, its melted hood glittering beetle-black in the sunlight.

When he saw the aeroplane, my father cried out, 'Good Lord, look at that!' He flung his arms out theatrically and demanded, 'Why wasn't I told?'

No one took any notice of him; he was always showing off. He stared up at the plane with an expression both fearful and excited, as though the monster was still flying through the air and he might yet be machine-gunned where he stood.

My mother and Mr Baines sat on wooden chairs pressed against the privet hedge. My mother was worried in case we were too near the wicket. She was forever ducking and flinching, mistaking the white clouds that bowled across the sky for an oncoming ball. It wasn't an exciting game as far as I could tell but my grandfather sat on the edge of his chair and didn't fall asleep once. There was a man fielding who was almost as old as Mr Baines, and when the bowler was rubbing the ball up and down the front of his trousers preparing to run, the old man rested in a deck-chair on the pitch. The butcher's boy from the village shop was crouching down behind the wicket wearing a tin hat and smoking a cigarette.

'That fellow,' said Mr Baines, pointing at the elderly batsman in Home Guard uniform, 'is taking a risk. If he misses the ball he'll be out leg before or he'll get his skull stove in.'

'Heavens,' cried my mother, cringing backwards on her chair.

'Briggs used to play that sort of stroke,' said Mr Baines. 'Of course, he knew what he was doing.'

My father came and sat down beside him. He said: 'I never knew it was there. I never knew.' He still looked excited. He'd taken his hat off and there was a mark all round his forehead.

'As soon as he saw what ball it was,' Mr Baines said, 'he'd stand straight in front of the wicket and wait until it looked as if it would go straight through his body –'

'I never knew,' repeated my father. 'I never even guessed.' He was very unobservant. He'd been morosely loping to and from the railway station night and morning for twenty years and never bothered to look through the trees.

'Be quiet,' said my mother. 'We're concentrating.'

'At the last moment,' Mr Baines said, 'Briggs would hook it. Glorious stroke. Poetry in motion.'

'If I could have served,' remarked my father, 'I would have chosen the Merchant Navy.'

'Mind you,' Mr Baines said. 'It had to be a fast ball.'

'Failing that, I think I'd have fancied the Air Force,' said my father.

There wasn't anything one could reply to that piece of poppy-cock. If my father had been healthy enough to join up, he wouldn't have been any use. When Wilfred Pickles said on the wireless, 'And how old are you, luv? Ninety-seven!', my father had to blow his nose from emotion. If he happened to hear 'When the lights go on again all over the world' on Forces' Favourites, he had to go out into the scullery to take a grip on himself. According to my mother, Auntie Doris had turned him into a cissy. He was a terrible cry-baby. He cried one time when the cat went missing. My mother said that most of the time his carrying on like that was misplaced. Once he went all over Southport pressing shilling pieces into the hands of what he called 'our gallant boys in blue'. They were soldiers from the new hospital down by the Promenade. My father told them he was proud of them, that they were the walking wounded; he had a field day with his handkerchief. Afterwards it turned out there was nothing wrong with them, nothing wounded that is, it wasn't that sort of hospital. They were soldiers all right, my mother said, but they'd all caught a nasty disease from just being in the Army, not from fighting or anything gallant like that, and it was certainly nothing to be proud of.

'I'm not criticizing,' said Mr Baines, looking at the fielder resting in his deck-chair, 'but these fellows lack self-discipline. The true sportsman is a trained athlete. He dedicates himself to the game. Only way to succeed. Same with anything in all walks of life – cotton, fishing, banking, shipping –'

'Doesn't he ever get tired of his own voice?' said my father savagely.

I sat on the grass with my back propped against my mother's knees. I could feel her trembling from indignation. My grandfather began to clap, slapping the palms of his hands together above my head as the elderly batsman left the crease and began to trail towards the pavilion. Mr Baines was the only one applauding; there were few spectators and most of those had swivelled round the other way to look at the bowling green. The new batsman was younger and he had a gammy leg. When he heard Mr Baines clapping he glared at him, thinking he was being made fun of.

'One time,' said Mr Baines, 'Briggs got stale. The Lancashire committee suggested that he should take a week's holiday. He went to a remote village in Wiltshire –'

'Don't think I don't know what the old beggar's getting at,' said my father. 'Talking about cotton like that. Did he think I wanted to come a cropper in cotton –'

'Word got round as it will,' Mr Baines said. 'Second day there a fellow came up to Briggs and asked him how much he'd take for playing in a local match. Ten pound, said Briggs, thinking that would be prohibitive –'

The park was shimmering in sunshine. You couldn't see the boundary by the poplar trees; all the leaves were reflecting like bits of glass. The man with the gammy leg was out almost at once. I didn't know why, the bails were still standing. I couldn't follow the rules. A fat man came out in a little peaked cap. I could hear the dull clop of the ball against the bat and the click of the bowls on the green as they knocked against each other. Behind me the voices went on and on, another game in progress, more dangerous than either cricket or bowls, and the rules were always changing.

'Briggs's side lost the toss,' said Mr Baines, 'and he had to begin the bowling. His first ball was hit out of the ground for six –'

'If I'd had any appreciation all these years,' my father said, 'things might have been different. When I think how I tramp from door to door in all weathers while you and your blasted Dad put your feet up –'

'Finally he had two wickets for a hundred and fifty runs. The crowd was looking quite nasty,' Mr Baines said. 'But what finished them off was that when he went in to bat he was bowled second ball.'

'All I needed was a few bob at the right moment,' said my father. 'Just a few measly quid and the old skinflint wouldn't put his hand in his pocket –'

'Don't speak about him like that,' cried my mother. 'I won't have him called names.'

'Only a stalwart policeman and the train to London saved him from a jolly good hiding,' said Mr Baines. 'He never tried village cricket again.'

'If you'd been any proper sort of woman,' groaned my father, 'you'd have been a helpmate.'

'Be quiet,' my mother cried. 'Shut your mouth.'

'You've only been a bloody hindrance,' my father shouted. He jumped up and knocked over his chair. He walked away in the direction of the aeroplane, leaving his hat on the grass.

'What's up?' I asked. Though I knew. 'Is he off home, then?'

'Ssh,' said my mother. 'He's gone for a widdle.' Her voice was all choked.

'Don't upset yourself,' said Mr Baines. 'It's not worth it.'

'He sickens me,' my mother said. 'Sickens me. Whimpering over the least thing when inside he's like a piece of rock. He's hard. He's got no pity for man nor beast.'

'Don't waste your tears,' said Mr Baines. 'You can't get blood from a stone.'

At that moment the ball flew past the wicket and striking the ground rolled to my grandfather's feet. He leapt up and striding to the side of the pitch chucked the ball at the batsman. He didn't exactly bowl it; he sort of dipped one shoulder and flung the ball like a boy skimming a stone on water. The batsman, taken by surprise at such an accurate throw, swung his bat. The scarlet ball shot over Mr Baines's shoulder and went like a bullet from a gun after my father.

When we ran up to him he was stood there in the shadow of the Messerschmitt with his hand clutched to the side of his head. The ball hadn't hit him full on, merely grazed the side of his temple. But he was bleeding like a pig.

'That's a turn-up for the book,' said Mr Baines.

PETER CAREY

American Dreams

Peter Carey (1943–) was born in Bacchus Marsh, Victoria, in Australia (birthplace of an earlier Australian writer, Frank Hardy). He worked for a time in advertising, and then brought out an acclaimed and often bitter collection of stories, *The Fat Man in History*, in 1974. He is today one of Australia's leading novelists, his works including *Bliss* (1981), *Illywhacker* (1985), and the remarkable *Oscar and Lucinda* (1988) which won the Booker Prize for Fiction.

'American Dreams' comes from his first collection, *The Fat Man in History*, a volume of surreal tales that captures the flavour of a rapidly changing Australia. The story, written during the 1970s, ironically explores Australian fantasies about approaching Americanization (Carey once commented on the way Australians were drugged out by their desire to believe in newness). If this is the first irony, the second comes from what happens when Mr Gleason's surreal warning to his fellow small-town citizens is finally unveiled. The change he has presumably meant to halt is hastened, and his miniature world becomes preferred to a real one. Some elements of this story (one of Carey's best) recur in his novel *Oscar and Lucinda*, also a strange mixture of surrealism and vivid Australian history.

No one can, to this day, remember what it was we did to offend him. Dyer the butcher remembers a day when he gave him the wrong meat and another day when he served someone else first by mistake. Often when Dyer gets drunk he recalls this day and curses himself for his foolishness. But no one seriously believes that it was Dyer who offended him.

But one of us did something. We slighted him terribly in some way, this small meek man with the rimless glasses and neat suit who used to smile so nicely at us all. We thought, I suppose, he was a bit of a fool and sometimes he was so quiet and grey that we ignored him, forgetting he was there at all.

When I was a boy I often stole apples from the trees at his house up in Mason's Lane. He often saw me. No, that's not correct. Let me say I often sensed that he saw me. I sensed him peering out from behind the lace curtains of his house. And I was not the only one. Many of us came to take his apples, alone and in groups, and it is possible that he chose to exact payment for all these apples in his own peculiar way.

Yet I am sure it wasn't the apples.

What has happened is that we all, all eight hundred of us, have come to remember small transgressions against Mr Gleason who once lived amongst us.

My father, who has never borne malice against a single living creature, still believes that Gleason meant to do us well, that he loved the town more than any of us. My father says we have treated the town badly in our minds. We have used it, this little valley, as nothing more than a stopping place. Somewhere on the way to somewhere else. Even those of us who have been here many years have never taken the town seriously. Oh yes, the place is pretty. The hills are green and the woods thick. The stream is full of fish. But it is not where we would rather be.

For years we have watched the films at the Roxy and dreamed, if not of America, then at least of our capital city. For our own town, my father says, we have nothing but contempt. We have treated it badly, like a whore. We have cut down the giant shady trees in the main street to make doors for the schoolhouse and seats for the football pavilion. We have left big holes all over the countryside from which we have taken brown coal and given back nothing.

The commercial travellers who buy fish and chips at George the Greek's care for us more than we do, because we all have dreams of the big city, of wealth, of modern houses, of big motor-cars: American Dreams, my father has called them.

Although my father ran a petrol station he was also an inventor. He sat in his office all day drawing strange pieces of equipment on the back of delivery dockets. Every spare piece of paper in the house was covered with these little drawings and my mother would always be very careful about throwing away any piece of paper no matter how small. She would look on both sides of any piece of paper very carefully and always preserved any that had so much as a pencil mark.

I think it was because of this that my father felt that he understood Gleason. He never said as much, but he inferred that he understood Gleason because he, too, was concerned with similar problems. My father was working on plans for a giant gravel crusher, but occasionally he would become distracted and become interested in something else.

There was, for instance, the time when Dyer the butcher bought a new bicycle with gears, and for a while my father talked of nothing else but the gears. Often I would see him across the road squatting down beside Dyer's bicycle as if he were talking to it.

We all rode bicycles because we didn't have the money for anything better. My father did have an old Chev truck, but he rarely used it and it occurs to me now that it might have had some mechanical problem that it was impossible to solve, or perhaps it was just that he was saving it, not wishing to wear it out all at once. Normally, he went everywhere on his bicycle and, when I was younger, he carried me on the crossbar, both of us dismounting to trudge up the hills that led into and out of the main street. It was a common sight in our town to see people pushing bicycles. They were as much a burden as a means of transport.

Gleason also had his bicycle and every lunchtime he pushed and pedalled it home from the shire offices to his little weatherboard house out at Mason's Lane. It was a three-mile ride and people said that he went home for lunch because he was fussy and wouldn't eat either his wife's sandwiches or the hot meal available at Mrs Lessing's café.

But while Gleason pedalled and pushed his bicycle to and from the shire offices everything in our town proceeded as normal. It was only when he retired that things began to go wrong.

Because it was then that Mr Gleason started supervising the building of the wall around the two-acre plot up on Bald Hill. He paid too much for this land. He bought it from Johnny Weeks, who now, I am sure, believes the whole episode was his fault, firstly for cheating Gleason, secondly for selling him the land at all. But Gleason hired some Chinese and set to work to build his wall. It was then that we knew that we'd offended him. My father rode all the way out to Bald Hill and tried to talk Mr Gleason out of his wall. He said there was no need for us to build walls. That no one wished to spy on Mr Gleason or whatever he wished to do on Bald Hill. He said no one was in the least bit interested in Mr Gleason. Mr Gleason, neat in a new sportscoat, polished his glasses and smiled vaguely at his feet. Bicycling back, my father thought that he had gone too far. Of course we had an interest in Mr Gleason. He pedalled back and asked him to attend a dance that was to be held on the next Friday, but Mr Gleason said he didn't dance.

'Oh well,' my father said, 'any time, just drop over.'

Mr Gleason went back to supervising his family of Chinese labourers on his wall.

Bald Hill towered high above the town and from my father's small filling-station you could sit and watch the wall going up. It was an interesting sight. I watched it for two years, while I waited for customers who rarely came. After school and on Saturdays I had all the time in the world to watch the agonizing progress of Mr Gleason's wall. It was as painful as a clock. Sometimes I could see the Chinese labourers running at a jog-trot carrying bricks on long wooden planks. The hill was bare, and on this bareness Mr Gleason was, for some reason, building a wall.

In the beginning people thought it peculiar that someone would build such a big wall on Bald Hill. The only thing to recommend Bald Hill was the view of the town, and Mr Gleason was building a wall that denied that view. The topsoil was thin and bare clay showed through in places. Nothing would ever grow there. Everyone assumed that Gleason had simply gone mad and after the initial interest they accepted his madness as they accepted his wall and as they accepted Bald Hill itself.

Occasionally someone would pull in for petrol at my father's filling-station and ask about the wall and my father would shrug and I would see, once more, the strangeness of it.

'A house?' the stranger would ask. 'Up on that hill?'

'No,' my father would say, 'chap named Gleason is building a wall.'

And the strangers would want to know why, and my father would shrug and look up at Bald Hill once more. 'Damned if I know,' he'd say.

Gleason still lived in his old house at Mason's Lane. It was a plain weatherboard house with a rose garden at the front, a vegetable garden down the side, and an orchard at the back.

At night we kids would sometimes ride out to Bald Hill on our bicycles. It was an agonizing, muscle-twitching ride, the worst part of which was a steep, unmade road up which we finally pushed our bikes, our lungs rasping in the night air. When we arrived we found nothing but walls. Once we broke down some of the brickwork and another time we threw stones at the tents where the Chinese labourers slept. Thus we expressed our frustration at this inexplicable thing.

The wall must have been finished on the day before my twelfth birthday. I remember going on a picnic birthday party up to Eleven Mile Creek and we lit a fire and cooked chops at a bend in the river from where it was possible to see the walls on Bald Hill. I remember standing with a hot chop in my hand and someone saying, 'Look, they're leaving!'

We stood on the creek-bed and watched the Chinese labourers walking their bicycles slowly down the hill. Someone said they were going to build a chimney up at the mine at A1 and certainly there is a large brick chimney there now, so I suppose they built it.

When the word spread that the walls were finished most of the town went up to look. They walked around the four walls which were as interesting as any other brick walls. They stood in front of the big wooden gates and tried to peer through, but all they could see was a small blind wall that had obviously been constructed for this special purpose. The walls themselves were ten feet high and topped with broken glass and barbed wire. When it became obvious that we were not going to discover the contents of the enclosure, we all gave up and went home.

Mr Gleason had long since stopped coming into town. His wife came instead, wheeling a pram down from Mason's Lane to Main Street and filling it with groceries and meat (they never bought vegetables, they grew their own) and wheeling it back to Mason's Lane. Sometimes you would see her standing with the pram halfway up the Gell Street hill. Just standing there, catching her breath. No one asked her about the wall. They knew she wasn't responsible for the wall and they felt sorry for her, having to bear the burden of the pram and her husband's madness. Even when she began to visit Dixon's hardware and buy plaster of Paris and tins of paint and water-proofing compound, no one asked her what these things were for. She had a way of averting her eyes that indicated her terror of questions. Old Dixon carried the plaster of Paris and the tins of paint out to her pram for her and watched her push them away. 'Poor woman,' he said, 'poor bloody woman.'

From the filling-station where I sat dreaming in the sun, or from the enclosed office where I gazed mournfully at the rain, I would see, occasionally, Gleason entering or leaving his walled compound, a tiny figure way up on Bald Hill. And I'd think 'Gleason', but not much more.

Occasionally strangers drove up there to see what was going on, often egged on by locals who told them it was a Chinese temple or some other silly thing. Once a group of Italians had a picnic outside the walls and took photographs of each other standing in front of the closed door. God knows what they thought it was.

But for five years between my twelfth and seventeenth birthdays there was nothing to interest me in Gleason's walls. Those years seem lost to me now and I can remember very little of them. I developed a crush on Susy Markin and followed her back from the swimming pool on my bicycle. I sat behind her in the pictures and wandered past her house. Then her parents moved to another town and I sat in the sun and waited for them to come back.

We became very keen on modernization. When coloured paints became available the whole town went berserk and brightly coloured houses blossomed overnight. But the paints were not of good quality and quickly faded and peeled, so that the town looked like a garden of dead flowers. Thinking of those years, the only real thing I recall is the soft hiss of bicycle tyres on the main street. When I think of it now it seems very peaceful, but I remember then that the sound induced in me a feeling of melancholy, a feeling somehow mixed with the early afternoons when the sun went down behind Bald Hill and the town felt as sad as an empty dance hall on a Sunday afternoon.

And then, during my seventeenth year, Mr Gleason died. We found out when we saw Mrs Gleason's pram parked out in front of Phonsey Joy's Funeral Parlour. It looked very sad, that pram, standing by itself in the windswept street. We came and looked at the pram and felt sad for Mrs Gleason. She hadn't had much of a life.

Phonsey Joy carried old Mr Gleason out to the cemetery by the Parwan railway station and Mrs Gleason rode behind in a taxi. People watched the old hearse go by and thought, 'Gleason', but not much else.

And then, less than a month after Gleason had been buried out at the lonely cemetery by the Parwan railway station, the Chinese labourers came back. We saw them push their bicycles up the hill. I stood with my father and Phonsey Joy and wondered what was going on.

And then I saw Mrs Gleason trudging up the hill. I nearly didn't recognize her, because she didn't have her pram. She carried a black umbrella and walked slowly up Bald Hill and it wasn't until she stopped for breath and leaned forward that I recognized her.

'It's Mrs Gleason,' I said, 'with the Chinese.'

But it wasn't until the next morning that it became obvious what was happening. People lined the main street in the way they do for a big funeral but, instead of gazing towards the Grant Street corner, they all looked up at Bald Hill.

All that day and all the next people gathered to watch the destruction of the walls. They saw the Chinese labourers darting to and fro, but it wasn't until they knocked down a large section of the wall facing the town that we realized there really was something inside. It was impossible to see what it was, but there was something there. People stood and wondered and pointed out Mrs Gleason to each other as she went to and fro supervising the work.

And finally, in ones and twos, on bicycles and on foot, the whole town moved up to Bald Hill. Mr Dyer closed up his butcher shop and my father got out the old Chev truck and we finally arrived up at Bald Hill with twenty people on board. They crowded into the back tray and hung on to the running boards and my father grimly steered his way through the crowds of bicycles and parked just where the dirt track gets really steep. We trudged up this last steep track, never for a moment suspecting what we would find at the top.

It was very quiet up there. The Chinese labourers worked diligently, removing the third and fourth walls and cleaning the bricks which they stacked neatly in big piles. Mrs Gleason said nothing either. She stood in the only remaining corner of the walls and looked defiantly at the townspeople who stood open-mouthed where another corner had been.

And between us and Mrs Gleason was the most incredibly beautiful thing I had ever seen in my life. For one moment I didn't recognize it. I stood open-mouthed, and breathed the surprising beauty of it. And then I realized it was our town. The buildings were two feet high and they were a little rough but very correct. I saw Mr Dyer nudge my father and whisper that Gleason had got the faded 'U' in the BUTCHER sign of his shop.

I think at that moment everyone was overcome with a feeling of simple joy. I can't remember ever having felt so uplifted and happy. It was perhaps a childish emotion but I looked up at my father and saw a smile of such warmth spread across his face that I knew he felt just as I did. Later he told me that he thought Gleason had built the model of our town just for this moment, to let us see the beauty of our own town, to make us proud of ourselves and to stop the American Dreams we were so prone to. For the rest, my father said, was not Gleason's plan and he could not have foreseen the things that happened afterwards.

I have come to think that this view of my father's is a little sentimental and also, perhaps, insulting to Gleason. I personally believe that he knew everything that would happen. One day the proof of my theory may be discovered. Certainly there are in existence some personal papers, and I firmly believe that these papers will show that Gleason knew exactly what would happen.

We had been so overcome by the model of the town that we hadn't noticed what was the most remarkable thing of all. Not only had Gleason built the houses and the shops of our town, he had also peopled it. As we tiptoed into the town we suddenly found ourselves. 'Look,' I said to Mr Dyer, 'there you are.'

And there he was, standing in front of his shop in his apron. As I bent down to examine the tiny figure I was staggered by the look on its face. The modelling was crude, the paintwork was sloppy, and the face a little too white, but the expression was absolutely perfect: those pursed, quizzical lips and the eyebrows lifted high. It was Mr Dyer and no one else on earth.

And there beside Mr Dyer was my father, squatting on the footpath and gazing lovingly at Mr Dyer's bicycle's gears, his face marked with grease and hope.

And there was I, back at the filling-station, leaning against a petrol pump in an American pose and talking to Brian Sparrow who was amusing me with his clownish antics.

Phonsey Joy standing beside his hearse. Mr Dixon sitting inside his hardware store. Everyone I knew was there in that tiny town. If they were not in the streets or in their backyards they were inside their houses, and it didn't take very long to discover that you could lift off the roofs and peer inside.

We tiptoed around the streets peeping into each other's windows, lifting off each other's roofs, admiring each other's gardens, and, while we did it, Mrs Gleason slipped silently away down the hill towards Mason's Lane. She spoke to nobody and nobody spoke to her.

I confess that I was the one who took the roof from Cavanagh's house. So I was the one who found Mrs Cavanagh in bed with young Craigie Evans.

I stood there for a long time, hardly knowing what I was seeing. I stared at the pair of them for a long, long time. And when I finally knew what I was seeing I felt such an incredible mixture of jealousy and guilt and wonder that I didn't know what to do with the roof.

Eventually it was Phonsey Joy who took the roof from my hands and placed it carefully back on the house, much, I imagine, as he would have placed the lid on a coffin. By then other people had seen what I had seen and the word passed around very quickly.

And then we all stood around in little groups and regarded the model town with what could only have been fear. If Gleason knew about Mrs Cavanagh and Craigie Evans (and no one else had), what other things might he know? Those who hadn't seen themselves yet in the town began to look a little nervous and were unsure of whether to look for themselves or not. We gazed silently at the roofs and felt mistrustful and guilty.

We all walked down the hill then, very quietly, the way people walk away from a funeral, listening only to the crunch of the gravel under our feet while the women had trouble with their high-heeled shoes.

The next day a special meeting of the shire council passed a motion calling on Mrs Gleason to destroy the model town on the grounds that it contravened building regulations.

It is unfortunate that this order wasn't carried out before the city newspapers found out. Before another day had gone by the Government had stepped in.

The model town and its model occupants were to be preserved. The Minister for Tourism came in a large black car and made a speech to us in the football pavilion. We sat on the high, tiered seats eating potato chips while he stood against the fence and talked to us. We couldn't hear him very well, but we heard enough. He called the model town a work of art and we stared at him grimly. He said it would be an invaluable tourist attraction. He said tourists would come from everywhere to see the model town. We would be famous. Our businesses would flourish. There would be work for guides and interpreters and caretakers and taxi-drivers and people selling soft drinks and ice-creams.

The Americans would come, he said. They would visit our town in buses and in cars and on the train. They would take photographs and bring wallets bulging with dollars. American dollars.

We looked at the minister mistrustfully, wondering if he knew about Mrs Cavanagh, and he must have seen the look because he said that certain controversial items would be removed, had already been removed. We shifted in our seats, like you do when a particularly tense part of a film has come to its climax, and then we relaxed and listened to what the minister had to say. And we all began, once more, to dream our American Dreams.

We saw our big smooth cars cruising through cities with bright lights. We entered expensive nightclubs and danced till dawn. We made love to women like Kim Novak and men like Rock Hudson. We drank cocktails. We gazed lazily into refrigerators filled with food and prepared ourselves lavish midnight snacks which we ate while we watched huge television sets on which we would be able to see American movies free of charge and for ever.

The minister, like someone from our American Dreams, re-entered his large black car and cruised slowly from our humble sports ground, and the newspapermen arrived and swarmed over the pavilion with their cameras and notebooks. They took photographs of us and photographs of the models up on Bald Hill. And the next day we were all over the newspapers. The photographs of the model people side by side with photographs of the real people. And our names and ages and what we did were all printed there in black and white.

They interviewed Mrs Gleason but she said nothing of interest. She said the model town had been her husband's hobby.

We all felt good now. It was very pleasant to have your photograph in the paper. And, once more, we changed our opinion of Gleason. The shire council held another meeting and named the dirt track up Bald Hill 'Gleason Avenue'. Then we all went home and waited for the Americans we had been promised.

It didn't take long for them to come, although at the time it seemed an eternity, and we spent six long months doing nothing more with our lives than waiting for the Americans.

Well, they did come. And let me tell you how it has all worked out for us.

The Americans arrive every day in buses and cars and sometimes the younger ones come on the train. There is now a small airstrip out near the Parwan cemetery and they also arrive there, in small aeroplanes. Phonsey Joy drives them to the cemetery where they look at Gleason's grave and then up to Bald Hill and then down to the town. He is doing very well from it all. It is good to see someone doing well from it. Phonsey is becoming a big man in town and is on the shire council.

On Bald Hill there are half a dozen telescopes through which the

Americans can spy on the town and reassure themselves that it is the same down there as it is on Bald Hill. Herb Gravney sells them ice-creams and soft drinks and extra film for their cameras. He is another one who is doing well. He bought the whole model from Mrs Gleason and charges five American dollars admission. Herb is on the council now too. He's doing very well for himself. He sells them the film so they can take photographs of the houses and the model people and so they can come down to the town with their special maps and hunt out the real people.

To tell the truth most of us are pretty sick of the game. They come looking for my father and ask him to stare at the gears of Dyer's bicycle. I watch my father cross the street slowly, his head hung low. He doesn't greet the Americans any more. He doesn't ask them questions about colour television or Washington DC. He kneels on the footpath in front of Dyer's bike. They stand around him. Often they remember the model incorrectly and try to get my father to pose in the wrong way. Originally he argued with them, but now he argues no more. He does what they ask. They push him this way and that and worry about the expression on his face which is no longer what it was.

Then I know they will come to find me. I am next on the map. I am very popular for some reason. They come in search of me and my petrol pump as they have done for four years now. I do not await them eagerly because I know, before they reach me, that they will be disappointed.

'But this is not the boy.'

'Yes,' says Phonsey, 'this is him all right.' And he gets me to show them my certificate.

They examine the certificate suspiciously, feeling the paper as if it might be a clever forgery. 'No,' they declare. (Americans are so confident.) 'No,' they shake their heads, 'this is not the real boy. The real boy is younger.'

'He's older now. He used to be younger.' Phonsey looks weary when he tells them. He can afford to look weary.

The Americans peer at my face closely. 'It's a different boy.'

But finally they get their cameras out. I stand sullenly and try to look amused as I did once. Gleason saw me looking amused but I can no longer remember how it felt. I was looking at Brian Sparrow. But Brian is also tired. He finds it difficult to do his clownish antics and to the Americans his little act isn't funny. They prefer the model. I watch him sadly, sorry that he must perform for such an unsympathetic audience.

The Americans pay one dollar for the right to take our photographs. Having paid the money they are worried about being cheated. They spend their time being disappointed and I spend my time feeling guilty that I have somehow let them down by growing older and sadder.

ANGELA CARTER

The Kitchen Child

Angela Carter (1940–92), one of the most interesting of recent British writers, was born in Eastbourne, Sussex, and lived for a time in Japan. She taught creative writing at Sheffield, Brown University in Rhode Island, and East Anglia, and wrote much fine criticism, social commentary, and analysis of folk-tale and fairy-story. She published her first novel *Shadow Dance* in 1966. Many others followed, culminating in her two finest, *Nights at the Circus* (1984) and *Wise Children* (1991), but all were noted for her vivid and surreal power of imagination. She also published several volumes of short stories – *Fireworks: Nine Profane Pieces* (1974), *The Bloody Chamber* (1979), feminist reworkings of fairy-stories, *Black Venus* (1985), and the excellent posthumous collection, *American Ghosts and Old World Wonders* (1993).

'The Kitchen Child', from *Black Venus*, displays Angela Carter's comic energy and the lighter side of her vivid imagination. The kitchen child who tells the story has had a magic beginning to his life, having come into the world while his mother, a cook in the remarkably rendered kitchen of a great English house, is seduced and impregnated in the most unusual circumstances. The story has an elegant shape and a wonderful outcome; it is also, like much of Carter's work, a magnificent exotic commentary on a world already much used in far more familiar ways by many other writers.

233

'Born in a trunk', they say when a theatrical sups grease-paint with mother's milk, and if there be a culinary equivalent of the phrase then surely I merit it, for was I not conceived the while a soufflé rose? A lobster soufflé, very choice, twenty-five minutes in a medium oven.

And the very first soufflé that ever in her life as cook me mam was called upon to make, ordered up by some French duc, house guest of Sir and Madam, me mam pleased as punch to fix it for him since few if any *fins becs* pecked their way to our house, not even during the two weeks of the Great Grouse Shoot when nobs rolled up in droves to score the feathered booty of the skies. Especially not then. Palates like shoe leather. 'Pearls before swine,' my mother would have said as she reluctantly sent the four-and-twenty courses of her Art up to the dining room, except that pigs would have exhibited more gourmandise. I tell you, the English country house, yes! that's the place for grub; but, only when Sir and Madam are *pas chez lui*. It is the staff who keep up the standards.

For Madam would touch nothing but oysters and grapes on ice three times a day, due to the refinement of her sensibility, while Sir fasted until a devilled bone at sundown, his tongue having been burned out by curry when he was governing a bit of Poonah. (I reckon those Indians hotted up his fodder out of spite. Oh, the cook's vengeance, when it strikes – terrible!) And as for the Shooters of Grouse, all they wanted was sandwiches for hors d'oeuvres, sandwiches for entrées, followed by sandwiches, sandwiches, sandwiches, and their hip flasks kept replenished, oh, yes, wash it down with the amber fluid and who can tell how it tastes?

So me mam took great pains with the construction of this, her very first lobster soufflé, sending the boy who ground knives off on his bike to the sea, miles, for the beast itself and then the boiling of it alive, how it come squeaking piteously crawling out of the pot etc. etc. etc. so me mam all a-flutter before she so much as separated the eggs.

Then, just as she bent over the range to stir the flour into the butter, a pair of hands clasped tight around her waist. Thinking, at first, it was but kitchen horseplay, she twitched her ample hips to put him off as she slid the egg yolks into the roux. But as she mixed in the lobster meat, diced up, all nice, she felt those hands stray higher.

That was when too much cayenne went in. She always regretted that.

And as she was folding in the toppling contents of the bowl of beaten egg-white, God knows what it was he got up to but so much so she flings all into the white dish with abandon and:

'To hell with it!'

Into the oven goes the soufflé; the oven door slams shut.

I draw a veil.

'But, mam!' I often begged her. '*Who was that man?*'

235

'Lawks a mercy, child,' says she. 'I never thought to ask. I were that worried the wallop I give the oven door would bring the soufflé down.'

But, no. The soufflé went up like a montgolfier and, as soon as its golden head knocked imperiously against the oven door, she bust through the veil I have discreetly drawn over this scene of passion and emerged, smoothing her apron, in order to extract the exemplary dish amidst oohs and aahs of the assembled kitchen staff, some forty-five in number.

But not quite exemplary. The cook met her match in the eater. The housekeeper brings his plate herself, slaps it down. 'He said: "Trop de cayenne," and scraped it off his plate into the fire,' she announces with a gratified smirk. She is a model of refinement and always very particular about her aspirates. She hiccups. She even says the 'h' in 'hic'.

My mother weeps for shame.

'What we need here is a congtinental – hic – chef to improve le ton,' menaces the housekeeper, tossing me mam a killing look as she sweeps out the door for me mam is a simple Yorkshire lass for all she has magic in her fingers but no room for two queens in this hive, the housekeeper hates her. And the housekeeper is pricked perpetually by the fancy for the importation of a Carême or a Soyer with moustaches like hat-racks to croquembouche her and milly filly her as is all the rage.

'For isn't it Alberlin, chef to the dear Devonshires; and Crépin, at the Duchess of Sutherland's. Then there's Labalme, with the Duke of Beaufort's household, doncherno . . . and the Queen, bless her, has her Ménager . . . while we're stuck with that fat cow who can't speak nothing but broad Yorkshire, never out of her carpet slippers . . .'

Conceived upon a kitchen table, born upon a kitchen floor; no bells rang to welcome me but, far more aptly, my arrival heralded by a bang! bang! bang! on every skillet in the place, a veritable fusillade of copper-bottom kitchen tympani; and the merry clatter of ladle against dish-cover; and the very turnspit dogs all went: 'Bow wow!'

It being, as you might yourself compute, a good three months off October, Sir and Madam being in London the housekeeper maintains a fine style all by herself, sitting in her parlour partaking of the best Bohea from a Meissen cup, to which she adds a judicious touch of rum from the locked bottles to which she's forged a key in her ample leisure. The housekeeper's little skivvy, that she keeps to fetch, carry and lick boot, just topping the teacup up with old Jamaica, all hell breaks loose below stairs as if a Chinese orchestra started up its woodblocks and xylophones, crash, wallop.

'What on earth are the – hic – lower ordures up to?' elocutes the housekeeper in ladylike and dulcet tones, giving the ear of the skivvy a quick but vicious tug to jerk the gossip out of her.

'Oh, madamissima!' quavers the poor little skivvyette. ''Tis nobbut the cook's babby!'

'The cook's baby?!?'

Due to my mother's corpulence, which is immense, she's round as the 'o' in 'obese', and the great loyalty and affection towards her of all the kitchen staff, the housekeeper knew nothing of my imminence but, amid her waxing wroth, also glad to hear it, since she thought she spied a way to relieve my mother of her post due to this unsolicited arrival and then nag Sir and Madam to get in some mincing and pomaded gent to *chaudfroid* and *gêlée* and butter up. Belowstairs she descends forthwith, a stately yet none too stable progress due to the rum with a dash of tea she sips all day, the skivvy running in front of her to throw wide the door.

What a spectacle greets her! Raphael might have sketched it, had he been in Yorkshire at the time. My mother, wreathed in smiles, enthroned on a sack of spuds with, at her breast, her babe, all neatly swaddled in a new-boiled pudding cloth and the entire kitchen brigade arranged around her in attitudes of adoration, each brandishing a utensil and giving out therewith that merry rattle of the ladles, yours truly's first lullaby.

Alas, my cradle song soon peters out in the odd thwack and tinkle as the housekeeper casts her coldest eye.

'What's – hic – this?'

'A bonny boy!' croons me mam, planting a smacking kiss on the tender forehead pressed against her pillowing bosom.

'Out of the house for this!' cries the housekeeper. 'Hic,' she adds.

But what a clang and clamour she unleashes with that demand; as if she'd let off a bomb in a hardware store, for all present (except my mother and myself) attack their improvised instruments with renewed vigour, chanting in unison:

'The kitchen child! The kitchen child! You can't turn out the kitchen child!'

And that was the truth of the matter; who else could I claim as my progenitor if not the greedy place itself, that, if it did not make me, all the same, it caused me to be made? Not one scullery-maid nor the littlest vegetable boy could remember who or what it was which visited my mother that soufflé morning, every hand in the kitchen called to cut sandwiches, but some fat shape seemed to have haunted the place, drawn to the kitchen as a ghost to the dark; had not that gourmet duc kept a gourmet valet? Yet his outlines melt like aspic in the heat from the range.

'The kitchen child!'

The kitchen brigade made such a din that the housekeeper retreated to revive herself with another tot of rum in her private parlour, for, faced with a mutiny amongst the pans, she discovered little valour in her spirit and went to sulk in her tent.

The first toys I played with were colanders, egg whisks and saucepan lids. I took my baths in the big tureen in which the turtle soup was served.

They gave up salmon until I could toddle because, as for my crib, what else but the copper salmon kettle? And this kettle was stowed way up high on the mantelshelf so I could snooze there snug and warm out of harm's way, soothed by the delicious odours and appetizing sounds of the preparation of nourishment, and there I cooed my way through babyhood above that kitchen as if I were its household deity high in my tiny shrine.

And, indeed, is there not something holy about a great kitchen? Those vaults of soot-darkened stone far above me, where the hams and strings of onions and bunches of dried herbs dangle, looking somewhat like the regimental banners that unfurl above the aisles of old churches. The cool, echoing flags scrubbed spotless twice a day by votive persons on their knees. The scoured gleam of row upon row of metal vessels dangling from hooks or reposing on their shelves till needed with the air of so many chalices waiting for the celebration of the sacrament of food. And the range like an altar, yes, an altar, before which my mother bowed in perpetual homage, a fringe of sweat upon her upper lip and fire glowing in her cheeks.

At three years old she gave me flour and lard and straight away I invented shortcrust. I being too little to manage the pin, she hoists me on her shoulders to watch her as she rolls out the dough upon the marble slab, then sets me to stamp out the tartlets for myself, tears of joy at my precocity trickling down her cheeks, lets me dollop on the damson jam and lick the spoon for my reward. By three and a half, I've progressed to rough puff and, after that, no holding me. She perches me on a tall stool so I can reach to stir the sauce, wraps me in her pinny that goes round and round and round me thrice, tucks it in at the waist else I trip over it headfirst into my own Hollandaise. So I become her acolyte.

Reading and writing come to me easy. I learn my letters as follows: A for asparagus, *asperges au beurre fondue* (though never, for my mother's sake, with a *sauce bâtarde*); B for *boeuf*, baron of, roasted mostly, with a *pouding Yorkshire* patriotically sputtering away beneath it in the dripping pan; C for carrots, *carrottes, chouxfleur, Camembert* and so on, right down to Zabaglione, although I often wonder what use the X might be, since it figures in no cook's alphabet.

And I stick as close to that kitchen as the croûte to a pâté or the mayonnaise to an oeuf. First, I stand on that stool to my saucepans; then on an upturned bucket; then on my own two feet. Time passes.

Life in this remote mansion flows by a tranquil stream, only convulsing into turbulence once a year and then for two weeks only, but that fuss enough, the Grouse Shoot, when they all come from town to set us by the ears.

Although Sir and Madam believe their visit to be the very and unique reason for the existences of each and every one of us, the yearly climacteric of our beings, when their staff, who, as far as *they* are concerned, sleep out a hibernation the rest of the year, now spring to life like Sleeping Beauty when her prince turns up, in truth, we get on so well without them during the other eleven and a half months that the arrival of Themselves is a chronic interruption of our routine. We sweat out the fortnight of their presence with as ill a grace as gentlefolk forced by reduced circumstances to take paying guests into their home, and as for haute cuisine, forget it; sandwiches, sandwiches, sandwiches, all they want is sandwiches.

And never again, ever again, a special request for a soufflé, lobster or otherwise. Me mam always a touch broody come the Grouse Shoot, moody, distracted, and, even though no order came, nevertheless, every year, she would prepare her lobster soufflé all the same, send the grinding boy off for the lobster, boil it alive, beat the eggs, make the panada etc. etc. etc., as if the doing of the thing were a magic ritual that would raise up out of the past the great question mark from whose loins her son had sprung so that, perhaps, she could get a good look at his face, this time. Or, perhaps, there was some other reason. But she never said either way. In due course, she could construct the airiest, most savoury soufflé that ever lobster graced; but nobody arrived to eat it and none of the kitchen had the heart. So, fifteen times in all, the chickens got that soufflé.

Until, one fine October day, the mist rising over the moors like the steam off a consommé, the grouse taking last hearty meals like condemned men, my mother's vigil was at last rewarded. The house-party arrives and as it does we hear the faint, nostalgic wail of an accordion as a closed barouche comes bounding up the drive all festooned with the *lys de France*.

Hearing the news, my mother shakes, comes over queer, has to have a sit-down on the marble pastry slab whilst I, oh, I prepare to meet my maker, having arrived at the age when a boy most broods about his father.

But what's this? Who trots into the kitchen to pick up the chest of ice the duc ordered for the bottles he brought with him but a beardless boy of my own age or less! And though my mother tries to quiz him on the whereabouts of some other hypothetical valet who, once upon a time, might possibly have made her hand tremble so she lost control of the cayenne, he claims he cannot understand her Yorkshire brogue, he shakes his head, he mimes incomprehension. Then, for the third time in all her life, my mother wept.

First, she wept for shame because she'd spoiled a dish. Next, she wept for joy, to see her son mould the dough. And now she weeps for absence.

But still she sends the grinding boy off for a lobster, for she must and will prepare her autumn ritual, if only as a wake for hope or as the funeral baked meats. And, taking matters into my own hands, I use the quickest method, the dumb waiter, above stairs to make a personal inquiry of this duc as to where his staff might be.

The duc, relaxing before dinner, popping a cork or two, is wrapped up in a velvet quilted smoking jacket much like the coats they put on very well-bred dogs, warming his slippered (Morocco) feet before the blazing fire and singing songs to himself in his native language. And I never saw a fatter man; he'd have given my mother a stone or two and not felt the loss. Round as the 'o' in 'rotund'. If he's taken aback by the apparition of this young chef out of the panelling, he's too much of a gent to show it by a jump or start, asks, what can he do for me? nice as you like and, in my best culinary French, my *petit poi de française*, I stammer out:

'The valet de chambre who accompanied you (garni de) those many years past of your last visit –'

'Ah! Jean-Jacques!' he readily concurs. 'Le pauvre,' he adds.

He squints lugubriously down his museau.

'Une crise de foie. Hélas, il est mort.'

I blanche like an endive. He, being a perfect gentleman, offers me a restorative snifter of his bubbly, brought as it has been all the way from his own cellars, he don't trust Sir's incinerated tastes, and I can feel it put hairs on my chest as it goes eructating down. Primed by another bottle, in which the duc joins me with that easy democratic affability which is the mark of all true aristocrats, I give him an account of what I take to be the circumstances of my conception, how his defunct valet wooed and won my mother in the course of the cooking of a lobster soufflé.

'I well remember that soufflé,' says the duc. 'Best I ever eat. Sent my compliments to the chef by way of the concierge, only added the advice of a truly exigeant gourmet to go easy on the cayenne, next time.'

So that was the truth of it! The spiteful housekeeper relaying only half the message!

I then relate the touching story, how, every Grouse Shoot after, my mother puts up a lobster soufflé in (I believe) remembrance of Jean-Jacques, and we share another bottle of bubbly in memory of the departed until the duc, exhibiting all the emotion of a tender sensibility, says through a manly tear:

'Tell you what, me lad, while your maman is once again fixing me up this famous lobster soufflé, I shall myself, as a tribute to my ex-valet, slip down –'

'Oh, sir!' I stammer. 'You are too good!'

Forthwith I speed to the kitchen to find my mother just beginning the béchamel. Presently, as the butter melts like the heart of the duc melted when I told him her tale, the kitchen door steals open and in tippytoes Himself. Never a couple better matched for size, I must say. The kitchen battalion all turn their heads away, out of respect for this romantic moment, but I myself, the architect of it, cannot forbear to peep.

He creeps up behind her, his index finger pressed to his lips to signify caution and silence, and extends his arm, and, slowly, slowly, slowly, with infinite delicacy and tact, he lets his hand adventure athwart her flank. It might have been a fly alighting on her bum. She flicks a haunch, like a mare in the field, unmoved, shakes in the flour. The duc himself quivers a bit. An expression as of a baby in a sweetie shop traverses his somewhat Bourbonesque features. He is attempting to peer over her shoulder to see what she is up to with her *batterie de cuisine* but his *embonpoint* gets in the way.

Perhaps it is to shift her over a bit, or else a genuine tribute to her large charms, but now, with immense if gigantic grace, he *gooses* her.

My mother fetches out a sigh, big enough to blow away the beaten egg-whites but, great artist that she is, her hand never trembles, not once, as she folds in the yolks. And when the ducal hands stray higher – not a mite of agitation stirs the spoon.

For it is, you understand, the time for seasoning. And in goes just sufficient cayenne, this time. Not a grain more. Huzzah! This soufflé will be – I flourish the circle I have made with my thumb and forefinger, I simulate a kiss.

The egg-whites topple into the panada; the movements of her spoon are quick and light as those of a bird caught in a trap. She upturns all into the soufflé dish.

He tweaks.

And *then* she cries: 'To hell with it!' Departing from the script, my mother wields her wooden spoon like a club, brings it, smack! down on to the duc's head with considerable force. He drops on to the flags with a low moan.

'Take that,' she bids his prone form. Then she smartly shuts the soufflé in the oven.

'How could you!' I cry.

'Would you have him spoil my soufflé? Wasn't it touch and go, last time?'

The grinding boy and I get the duc up on the marble slab, slap his face, dab his temples with the oven cloth dipped in chilled chablis, at long last his eyelids flicker, he comes to.

'Quelle femme,' he murmurs.

My mother, crouching over the range stopwatch in hand, pays him no heed.

'She feared you'd spoil the soufflé,' I explain, overcome with embarrassment.

'What dedication!'

The man seems awestruck. He stares at my mother as if he will never get enough of gazing at her. Bounding off the marble slab as sprightly as a man his size may, he hurls himself across the kitchen, falls on his knees at her feet.

'I beg you, I implore you –'

But my mother has eyes only for the oven.

'*Here* you are!' Throwing open the door, she brings forth the veritable queen of all the soufflés, that spreads its archangelic wings over the entire kitchen as it leaps upwards from the dish in which the force of gravity alone confines it. All present (some forty-seven in number – the kitchen brigade with the addition of me, plus the duc) applaud and cheer.

The housekeeper is mad as fire when my mother goes off in the closed barouche to the duc's very own regal and French kitchen but she comforts herself with the notion that now she can persuade Sir and Madam to find her a spanking new chef such as Soyer or Carême to twirl their moustaches in her direction and *gâteau Saint-Honoré* her on her birthday and indulge her in not infrequent *babas au rhum*. But – I am the only child of my mother's kitchen and now I enter into my inheritance; besides, how can the housekeeper complain? Am I not the youngest (Yorkshire born) French chef in all the land?

For am I not the duc's stepson?

WOODY ALLEN

The Kugelmass Episode

Woody Allen (1935–) was born in Brooklyn and, after being expelled from New York and City Universities, turned to writing as a career, initially for television and comedians and subsequently for the screen and stage. He has written and directed twenty-two films, two of which – *Annie Hall* (1977) and *Hannah and Her Sisters* (1986) – won Academy Awards for the best original screenplay, and two others – *Crimes and Misdemeanors* (1989) and *Alice* (1990) – were nominated in the same category.

A frequent contributor to the *New Yorker*, Woody Allen is also noted for his humorous fiction, which has included *Getting Even* (1971), *Without Feathers* (1978), *Side Effects* (1980) and *The Lunatics' Tale* (1986). 'The Kugelmass Episode', from his very funny collection *Side Effects*, is, as you would expect, a bravura comic performance. His unhappily married Professor Kugelmass is a professor of literature whose sexual fantasies lie with the great literary heroines, and now comes his opportunity to fulfil them. Woody Allen's Manhattan wit is all here, and the story also shows up the links between his works and the tradition of Jewish literary humour – already well established in this volume.

Kugelmass, a professor of humanities at City College, was unhappily married for the second time. Daphne Kugelmass was an oaf. He also had two dull sons by his first wife, Flo, and was up to his neck in alimony and child support.

'Did I know it would turn out so badly?' Kugelmass whined to his analyst one day. 'Daphne had promise. Who suspected she'd let herself go and swell up like a beach ball? Plus she had a few bucks, which is not in itself a healthy reason to marry a person, but it doesn't hurt, with the kind of operating nut I have. You see my point?'

Kugelmass was bald and as hairy as a bear, but he had soul.

'I need to meet a new woman,' he went on. 'I need to have an affair. I may not look the part, but I'm a man who needs romance. I need softness, I need flirtation. I'm not getting younger, so before it's too late I want to make love in Venice, trade quips at '21,' and exchange coy glances over red wine and candlelight. You see what I'm saying?'

Dr Mandel shifted in his chair and said, 'An affair will solve nothing. You're so unrealistic. Your problems run much deeper.'

'And also this affair must be discreet,' Kugelmass continued. 'I can't afford a second divorce. Daphne would really sock it to me.'

'Mr Kugelmass –'

'But it can't be anyone at City College, because Daphne also works there. Not that anyone on the faculty at CCNY is any great shakes, but some of those coeds . . .'

'Mr Kugelmass –'

'Help me. I had a dream last night. I was skipping through a meadow holding a picnic basket and the basket was marked "Options." And then I saw there was a hole in the basket.'

'Mr Kugelmass, the worst thing you could do is act out. You must simply express your feelings here, and together we'll analyze them. You have been in treatment long enough to know there is no overnight cure. After all, I'm an analyst, not a magician.'

'Then perhaps what I need is a magician,' Kugelmass said, rising from his chair. And with that he terminated his therapy.

A couple of weeks later, while Kugelmass and Daphne were moping around in their apartment one night like two pieces of old furniture, the phone rang.

'I'll get it,' Kugelmass said. 'Hello.'

'Kugelmass?' a voice said. 'Kugelmass, this is Persky.'

'Who?'

'Persky. Or should I say The Great Persky?'

'Pardon me?'

'I hear you're looking all over town for a magician to bring a little exotica into your life? Yes or no?'

'S-h-h,' Kugelmass whispered. 'Don't hang up. Where are you calling from, Persky?'

Early the following afternoon, Kugelmass climbed three flights of stairs in a broken-down apartment house in the Bushwick section of Brooklyn. Peering through the darkness of the hall, he found the door he was looking for and pressed the bell. I'm going to regret this, he thought to himself.

Seconds later, he was greeted by a short, thin, waxy-looking man.

'*You're* Persky the Great?' Kugelmass said.

'The Great Persky. You want a tea?'

'No, I want romance. I want music. I want love and beauty.'

'But not tea, eh? Amazing. OK, sit down.'

Persky went to the back room, and Kugelmass heard the sounds of boxes and furniture being moved around. Persky reappeared, pushing before him a large object on squeaky roller-skate wheels. He removed some old silk handkerchiefs that were lying on its top and blew away a bit of dust. It was a cheap-looking Chinese cabinet, badly lacquered.

'Persky,' Kugelmass said, 'what's your scam?'

'Pay attention,' Persky said. 'This is some beautiful effect. I developed it for a Knights of Pythias date last year, but the booking fell through. Get into the cabinet.'

'Why, so you can stick it full of swords or something?'

'You see any swords?'

Kugelmass made a face and, grunting, climbed into the cabinet. He couldn't help noticing a couple of ugly rhinestones glued on to the raw plywood just in front of his face. 'If this is a joke,' he said.

'Some joke. Now, here's the point. If I throw any novel into this cabinet with you, shut the doors, and tap it three times, you will find yourself projected into that book.'

Kugelmass made a grimace of disbelief.

'It's the emess,' Persky said. 'My hand to God. Not just a novel, either. A short story, a play, a poem. You can meet any of the women created by the world's best writers. Whoever you dreamed of. You could carry on all you like with a real winner. Then when you've had enough you give a yell, and I'll see you're back here in a split second.'

'Persky, are you some kind of outpatient?'

'I'm telling you it's on the level,' Persky said.

Kugelmass remained skeptical. 'What are you telling me – that this cheesy home-made box can take me on a ride like you're describing?'

'For a double sawbuck.'

Kugelmass reached for his wallet. 'I'll believe this when I see it,' he said.

Persky tucked the bills in his pants pocket and turned toward his bookcase. 'So who do you want to meet? Sister Carrie? Hester Prynne? Ophelia? Maybe someone by Saul Bellow? Hey, what about Temple Drake? Although for a man your age she'd be a workout.'

'French. I want to have an affair with a French lover.'

'Nana?'

'I don't want to have to pay for it.'

'What about Natasha in *War and Peace*?'

'I said French. I know! What about Emma Bovary? That sounds to me perfect.'

'You got it, Kugelmass. Give me a holler when you've had enough.' Persky tossed in a paperback copy of Flaubert's novel.

'You sure this is safe?' Kugelmass asked as Persky began shutting the cabinet doors.

'Safe. Is anything safe in this crazy world?' Persky rapped three times on the cabinet and then flung open the doors.

Kugelmass was gone. At the same moment, he appeared in the bedroom of Charles and Emma Bovary's house at Yonville. Before him was a beautiful woman, standing alone with her back turned to him as she folded some linen. I can't believe this, thought Kugelmass, staring at the doctor's ravishing wife. This is uncanny. I'm here. It's her.

Emma turned in surprise. 'Goodness, you startled me,' she said. 'Who are you?' She spoke in the same fine English translation as the paperback.

It's simply devastating, he thought. Then, realizing that it was he whom she had addressed, he said, 'Excuse me. I'm Sidney Kugelmass. I'm from City College. A professor of humanities. CCNY? Uptown. I – oh, boy!'

Emma Bovary smiled flirtatiously and said, 'Would you like a drink? A glass of wine, perhaps?'

She is beautiful, Kugelmass thought. What a contrast with the troglodyte who shared his bed! He felt a sudden impulse to take this vision into his arms and tell her she was the kind of woman he had dreamed of all his life.

'Yes, some wine,' he said hoarsely. 'White. No, red. No, white. Make it white.'

'Charles is out for the day,' Emma said, her voice full of playful implication.

After the wine, they went for a stroll in the lovely French countryside. 'I've always dreamed that some mysterious stranger would appear and rescue me from the monotony of this crass rural existence,' Emma said, clasping his hand. They passed a small church. 'I love what you have on,' she murmured. 'I've never seen anything like it around here. It's so . . . so modern.'

'It's called a leisure suit,' he said romantically. 'It was marked down.' Suddenly he kissed her. For the next hour they reclined under a tree and whispered together and told each other deeply meaningful things with their eyes. Then Kugelmass sat up. He had just remembered he had to meet Daphne at Bloomingdale's. 'I must go,' he told her. 'But don't worry, I'll be back.'

'I hope so,' Emma said.

He embraced her passionately, and the two walked back to the house. He held Emma's face cupped in his palms, kissed her again, and yelled, 'OK, Persky! I got to be at Bloomingdale's by three thirty.'

There was an audible pop, and Kugelmass was back in Brooklyn.

'So? Did I lie?' Persky asked triumphantly.

'Look, Persky, I'm right now late to meet the ball and chain at Lexington Avenue, but when can I go again? Tomorrow?'

'My pleasure. Just bring a twenty. And don't mention this to anybody.'

'Yeah. I'm going to call Rupert Murdoch.'

Kugelmass hailed a cab and sped off to the city. His heart danced on point. I am in love, he thought, I am the possessor of a wonderful secret. What he didn't realize was that at this very moment students in various classrooms across the country were saying to their teachers, 'Who is this character on page 100? A bald Jew is kissing Madame Bovary?' A teacher in Sioux Falls, South Dakota, sighed and thought, Jesus, these kids, with their pot and acid. What goes through their minds!

Daphne Kugelmass was in the bathroom accessories department at Bloomingdale's when Kugelmass arrived breathlessly. 'Where've you been?' she snapped. 'It's four thirty.'

'I got held up in traffic,' Kugelmass said.

Kugelmass visited Persky the next day, and in a few minutes was again passed magically to Yonville. Emma couldn't hide her excitement at seeing him. The two spent hours together, laughing and talking about their different backgrounds. Before Kugelmass left, they made love. 'My God, I'm doing it with Madame Bovary!' Kugelmass whispered to himself. 'Me, who failed freshman English.'

As the months passed, Kugelmass saw Persky many times and developed a close and passionate relationship with Emma Bovary. 'Make sure and always get me into the book before page 120,' Kugelmass said to the magician one day. 'I always have to meet her before she hooks up with this Rodolphe character.'

'Why?' Persky asked. 'You can't beat his time?'

'Beat his time. He's landed gentry. Those guys have nothing better to do than flirt and ride horses. To me, he's one of those faces you see in the pages of *Women's Wear Daily*. With the Helmut Berger hairdo. But to her he's hot stuff.'

'And her husband suspects nothing?'

'He's out of his depth. He's a lackluster little paramedic who's thrown in his lot with a jitterbug. He's ready to go to sleep by ten, and she's putting on her dancing shoes. Oh, well . . . See you later.'

And once again Kugelmass entered the cabinet and passed instantly to the Bovary estate at Yonville. 'How you doing, cupcake?' he said to Emma.

'Oh, Kugelmass,' Emma sighed. 'What I have to put up with. Last night at dinner, Mr Personality dropped off to sleep in the middle of the dessert course. I'm pouring my heart out about Maxim's and the ballet, and out of the blue I hear snoring.'

'It's OK, darling. I'm here now,' Kugelmass said, embracing her. I've earned this, he thought, smelling Emma's French perfume and burying his nose in her hair. I've suffered enough. I've paid enough analysts. I've searched till I'm weary. She's young and nubile, and I'm here a few pages after Léon and just before Rodolphe. By showing up during the correct chapters, I've got the situation knocked.

Emma, to be sure, was just as happy as Kugelmass. She had been starved for excitement, and his tales of Broadway night life, of fast cars and Hollywood and TV stars, enthralled the young French beauty.

'Tell me again about O. J. Simpson,' she implored that evening, as she and Kugelmass strolled past Abbé Bournisien's church.

'What can I say? The man is great. He sets all kinds of rushing records. Such moves. They can't touch him.'

'And the Academy Awards?' Emma said wistfully. 'I'd give anything to win one.'

'First you've got to be nominated.'

'I know. You explained it. But I'm convinced I can act. Of course, I'd want to take a class or two. With Strasberg maybe. Then, if I had the right agent –'

'We'll see, we'll see. I'll speak to Persky.'

That night, safely returned to Persky's flat, Kugelmass brought up the idea of having Emma visit him in the big city.

'Let me think about it,' Persky said. 'Maybe I could work it. Stranger things have happened.' Of course, neither of them could think of one.

'Where the hell do you go all the time?' Daphne Kugelmass barked at her husband as he returned home late that evening. 'You got a chippie stashed somewhere?'

'Yeah, sure, I'm just the type,' Kugelmass said wearily. 'I was with Leonard Popkin. We were discussing Socialist agriculture in Poland. You know Popkin. He's a freak on the subject.'

'Well, you've been very odd lately,' Daphne said. 'Distant. Just don't forget about my father's birthday. On Saturday?'

'Oh, sure, sure,' Kugelmass said, heading for the bathroom.

'My whole family will be there. We can see the twins. And Cousin Hamish. You should be more polite to Cousin Hamish – he likes you.'

'Right, the twins,' Kugelmass said, closing the bathroom door and shutting out the sound of his wife's voice. He leaned against it and took a deep breath. In a few hours, he told himself, he would be back in Yonville again, back with his beloved. And this time, if all went well, he would bring Emma back with him.

At three fifteen the following afternoon, Persky worked his wizardry again. Kugelmass appeared before Emma, smiling and eager. The two spent a few hours at Yonville with Binet and then remounted the Bovary carriage. Following Persky's instructions, they held each other tightly, closed their eyes, and counted to ten. When they opened them, the carriage was just drawing up at the side door of the Plaza Hotel, where Kugelmass had optimistically reserved a suite earlier in the day.

'I love it! It's everything I dreamed it would be,' Emma said as she swirled joyously around the bedroom, surveying the city from their window. 'There's F.A.O. Schwarz. And there's Central Park, and the Sherry is which one? Oh, there – I see. It's too divine.'

On the bed there were boxes from Halston and Saint Laurent. Emma unwrapped a package and held up a pair of black velvet pants against her perfect body.

'The slacks suit is by Ralph Lauren,' Kugelmass said. 'You'll look like a million bucks in it. Come on, sugar, give us a kiss.'

'I've never been so happy!' Emma squealed as she stood before the mirror. 'Let's go out on the town. I want to see *Chorus Line* and the Guggenheim and this Jack Nicholson character you always talk about. Are any of his flicks showing?'

'I cannot get my mind around this,' a Stanford professor said. 'First a strange character named Kugelmass, and now she's gone from the book. Well, I guess the mark of a classic is that you can reread it a thousand times and always find something new.'

The lovers passed a blissful weekend. Kugelmass had told Daphne he would be away at a symposium in Boston and would return Monday. Savoring each moment, he and Emma went to the movies, had dinner in Chinatown, passed two hours at a discothèque, and went to bed with a TV movie. They slept till noon on Sunday, visited SoHo, and ogled celebrities at Elaine's. They had caviar and champagne in their suite on Sunday night and talked until dawn. That morning, in the cab taking them to Persky's apartment, Kugelmass thought, It was hectic, but worth it. I can't bring her here too often, but now and then it will be a charming contrast with Yonville.

At Persky's, Emma climbed into the cabinet, arranged her new boxes of clothes neatly around her, and kissed Kugelmass fondly. 'My place next time,' she said with a wink. Persky rapped three times on the cabinet. Nothing happened.

'Hmm,' Persky said, scratching his head. He rapped again, but still no magic. 'Something must be wrong,' he mumbled.

'Persky, you're joking!' Kugelmass cried. 'How can it not work?'

'Relax, relax. Are you still in the box, Emma?'

'Yes.'

Persky rapped again – harder this time.

'I'm still here, Persky.'

'I know, darling. Sit tight.'

'Persky, we *have* to get her back,' Kugelmass whispered. 'I'm a married man, and I have a class in three hours. I'm not prepared for anything more than a cautious affair at this point.'

'I can't understand it,' Persky muttered. 'It's such a reliable little trick.'

But he could do nothing. 'It's going to take a little while,' he said to Kugelmass. 'I'm going to have to strip it down. I'll call you later.'

Kugelmass bundled Emma into a cab and took her back to the Plaza. He barely made it to his class on time. He was on the phone all day, to Persky and to his mistress. The magician told him it might be several days before he got to the bottom of the trouble.

'How was the symposium?' Daphne asked him that night.

'Fine, fine,' he said, lighting the filter end of a cigarette.

'What's wrong? You're as tense as a cat.'

'Me? Ha, that's a laugh. I'm as calm as a summer night. I'm just going to take a walk.' He eased out the door, hailed a cab, and flew to the Plaza.

'This is no good,' Emma said. 'Charles will miss me.'

'Bear with me, sugar,' Kugelmass said. He was pale and sweaty. He kissed her again, raced to the elevators, yelled at Persky over a payphone in the Plaza lobby, and just made it home before midnight.

'According to Popkin, barley prices in Krakow have not been this stable since 1971,' he said to Daphne, and smiled wanly as he climbed into bed.

The whole week went by like that. On Friday night, Kugelmass told Daphne there was another symposium he had to catch, this one in Syracuse. He hurried back to the Plaza, but the second weekend there was nothing like the first. 'Get me back into the novel or marry me,' Emma told Kugelmass. 'Meanwhile, I want to get a job or go to class, because watching TV all day is the pits.'

'Fine. We can use the money,' Kugelmass said. 'You consume twice your weight in room service.'

'I met an Off Broadway producer in Central Park yesterday, and he said I might be right for a project he's doing,' Emma said.

'Who is this clown?' Kugelmass asked.

'He's not a clown. He's sensitive and kind and cute. His name's Jeff Something-or-Other, and he's up for a Tony.'

Later that afternoon, Kugelmass showed up at Persky's drunk.

'Relax,' Persky told him. 'You'll get a coronary.'

'Relax. The man says relax. I've got a fictional character stashed in a hotel room, and I think my wife is having me tailed by a private shamus.'

'OK, OK. We know there's a problem.' Persky crawled under the cabinet and started banging on something with a large wrench.

'I'm like a wild animal,' Kugelmass went on. 'I'm sneaking around town, and Emma and I have had it up to here with each other. Not to mention a hotel tab that reads like the defense budget.'

'So what should I do? This is the world of magic,' Persky said. 'It's all nuance.'

'Nuance, my foot. I'm pouring Dom Pérignon and black eggs into this little mouse, plus her wardrobe, plus she's enrolled at the Neighborhood Playhouse and suddenly needs professional photos. Also, Persky, Professor Fivish Kopkind, who teaches Comp Lit and who has always been jealous of me, has identified me as the sporadically appearing character in the Flaubert book. He's threatened to go to Daphne. I see ruin and alimony jail. For adultery with Madame Bovary, my wife will reduce me to beggary.'

'What do you want me to say? I'm working on it night and day. As far as your personal anxiety goes, that I can't help you with. I'm a magician, not an analyst.'

By Sunday afternoon, Emma had locked herself in the bathroom and refused to respond to Kugelmass's entreaties. Kugelmass stared out the window at the Wollman Rink and contemplated suicide. Too bad this is a low floor, he thought, or I'd do it right now. Maybe if I ran away to Europe and started life over . . . Maybe I could sell the *International Herald Tribune*, like those young girls used to.

The phone rang. Kugelmass lifted it to his ear mechanically.

'Bring her over,' Persky said. 'I think I got the bugs out of it.'

Kugelmass's heart leapt. 'You're serious?' he said. 'You got it licked?'

'It was something in the transmission. Go figure.'

'Persky, you're a genius. We'll be there in a minute. Less than a minute.'

Again the lovers hurried to the magician's apartment, and again Emma Bovary climbed into the cabinet with her boxes. This time there was no kiss. Persky shut the doors, took a deep breath, and tapped the box three times. There was the reassuring popping noise, and when

Persky peered inside, the box was empty. Madame Bovary was back in her novel. Kugelmass heaved a great sigh of relief and pumped the magician's hand.

'It's over,' he said. 'I learned my lesson. I'll never cheat again, I swear it.' He pumped Persky's hand again and made a mental note to send him a necktie.

Three weeks later, at the end of a beautiful spring afternoon, Persky answered his doorbell. It was Kugelmass, with a sheepish expression on his face.

'OK, Kugelmass,' the magician said. 'Where to this time?'

'It's just this once,' Kugelmass said. 'The weather is so lovely, and I'm not getting any younger. Listen, you've read *Portnoy's Complaint?* Remember The Monkey?'

'The price is now twenty-five dollars, because the cost of living is up, but I'll start you with one freebie, due to all the trouble I caused you.'

'You're good people,' Kugelmass said, combing his few remaining hairs as he climbed into the cabinet again. 'This'll work all right?'

'I hope. But I haven't tried it much since all that unpleasantness.'

'Sex and romance,' Kugelmass said from inside the box. 'What we go through for a pretty face.'

Persky tossed in a copy of *Portnoy's Complaint* and rapped three times on the box. This time, instead of a popping noise there was a dull explosion, followed by a series of crackling noises and a shower of sparks. Persky leapt back, was seized by a heart attack, and dropped dead. The cabinet burst into flames, and eventually the entire house burned down.

Kugelmass, unaware of this catastrophe, had his own problems. He had not been thrust into *Portnoy's Complaint*, or into any other novel, for that matter. He had been projected into an old textbook, *Remedial Spanish*, and was running for his life over a barren, rocky terrain as the word *tener* ('to have') – a large and hairy irregular verb – raced after him on its spindly legs.

ADAM MARS-JONES

Lantern Lecture

Adam Mars-Jones (1954–), who was born in London, studied at Cambridge and the University of Virginia. He has published three short-story collections: *Lantern Lecture and Other Stories* (1981), which won the Somerset Maugham Award, *The Darker Proof: Stories from a Crisis* (1987), written with Edmund White and concerned with the crisis of Aids, and *Monopolies of Loss* (1992). He is also the editor of *Mae West Is Dead: Recent Lesbian and Gay Fiction* (1983), and he was selected one of the twenty 'Best of Young British Writers' in both 1983 and 1993.

'Lantern Lecture' comes from the first collection and was written in 1979. A highly precise and ironic piece about an eccentric landowner from a household in decline, it teasingly plays with time and narrative order. Thus in many of the two-paragraph, present-tense sections that make up the narrative, we find ourselves suddenly jolted back to a previous time, or forward to the future – as if the slides of the lantern lecture we are hearing have been confused or placed in unusual order. The story, about Philip Yorke from birth to the memorial service following his death, shows all of Mars-Jones's wry sense of human absurdity, as well as his technical wit and cunning.

1 905. The Yorkes' second child becomes Philip Scott at a private ceremony in the Saloon. His father takes from its place the miniature cabinet he brought back from his visit to the Holy Land as a young man. The six vessels inside it contain Jordan water; when the first seals are broken, a terrible smell announces itself, and the entire batch proves to be tainted. The tall windows are kept open until the air clears. A manservant meanwhile fetches more modest water from the lake in front of the house, so that the ceremony can go ahead.

1978. A Memorial Service for Philip Yorke is held at Marchwiel Church. The fame of his house and of his own appearances on television attracts a large crowd. The overflow is awkwardly accommodated in the adjoining Church Hall, by chance the site of Philip's last magic-lantern lecture only weeks before his death. A loudspeaker rigged up at the last moment relays the full reverent cabaret from the church.

Mrs Yorke relieves the nursemaid of Philip's perambulator for a few minutes. As she pushes it through the celebrated Park, she passes a group of villagers; they acknowledge her pleasantly. To her, they look undernourished; she is sad to see so many afflicted with limps. Can nothing be done to eliminate rickets and the dreadful suffering it causes? The villagers move on, heading for the woods on the estate, where they will remedy their undernourishment by poaching. The guns they carry inside their trouser-legs give their gait a stiff-jointed awkwardness.

For posterity Philip tape-records reminiscences of his mother and father, rambles through the park, and his popular guided tours of the house; in different versions anecdotes are transferred from Dutch tallboy to Chinese cabinet and back again. Dates, of the Dutch cabinet and the Chinese tallboy, wander unsupervised from century to century; Simons and Philips run together in a hereditary blur. Philip enacts on his side of the velvet rope all the indulgences his audience is denied by the Trust's watchful care. He leaps on to the drying-frames, turns every available handle, raps each surface, and sets all the music boxes going. He encourages children to duck under the barrier and helps them to fill their mouths with the tiny wooden animals of the complete Noah's Ark set. Laughing, he becomes the agent of laughter in others, even when they are unsure if the house is the best part of the man, or the other way about. Philip records clocks and bells, even the Ram before its final retirement from service; tapes and recorder end up in his bicycle basket, and are in due course stolen from there.

With help from his nanny, Philip writes a letter prescribing the cake he wants for his fifth birthday. It is to have two layers of almond filling and hundreds of *silver bobels* on top: he includes a drawing to show how it should look. A footman takes the letter to Cook, who will supervise construction and delivery.

Opening a drawer in search of some lost correspondence, Philip finds a crust of bread and a length of fish which he instantly eats, between one murmured any-good-not-much and the next. The fish has been giving off a dim green light in the dark drawer; the bread, a faint fizzing. Philip's diet is in theory based on the Disciples', but in practice on condensed milk and the Abbey Crunch biscuit, not available to the first Faithful. Philip's dog Trixie shares in his regime, taking her cue from her master's contentment and not realizing how many nutrients she is being denied.

The money which Erddig Hall represents and monumentalizes comes from coal. Bersham colliery can be seen from the house, across a little valley; the house itself is perched on a huge pillar of coal. Later generations of Yorkes, named in alternation Simon and Philip, create no additional wealth and marry just well enough to keep the estate going as before. They never have enough money to replace the furnishings with more up-to-date styles and fabrics, so the eighteenth-century interiors remain untouched for the lifetime of the house. On a smaller scale the family motto becomes Never Throw Anything Away, and every broken toy of Philip's childhood finds its haphazard way into storage.

Faithfully Philip loads his car with firewood and takes it to Miss Richards' cottage on the estate. She gives him a good welcome and shows him where to stack it, next to the piles of previous years. These have now overflowed the shed, and take up much space in the pantry and spare rooms; but Miss Richards insists, in spite of the meagreness of her pension, on buying coal and burning that instead. As a result she spends almost nothing on necessities. But in her mind, wood is a fuel associated exclusively with servants, and there seems to be no way of letting her know that social history is carrying on without her. Philip hopes that in the end she will be forced to burn wood simply to dispose of it; but that point is a long way off yet.

Mr and Mrs Yorke are sitting at their ease in the Chinese Room when they hear a sharp cracking sound from the Saloon. The glass of a mirrored table-top is parting. 'What is that terrible noise?' cries Mrs Yorke, and is answered by a sweet calm voice saying, only me Philip breaking the table with my little hammer.

A silken rope keeps the public at a distance from the frailer treasures. Philip worries that paying visitors can't see the obsessive craftsmanship which has gone into the mother-of-pearl pagoda, three foot high, constructed by a lady's-maid in the eighteenth century. At each corner of each tier is suspended, on a hook of silver wire, a daintily-carved lantern like a miniature earring. Philip stands next to the showcase and makes a series of plump little jumps. The case trembles with each impact, but a tiny clashing can be heard in the intervals, and tiny lanterns can be seen swinging madly from their hooks. The Trust officials concentrate on their smiles.

On their Saturdays Simon and Philip make tours of the county, setting out from Erddig with a sixpence each. They start their trip on bicycles, and change to train barge tram and bus before arriving in Wrexham with tuppence in hand, which they spend on sweets and a visit to the pictures.

In a succession of dying cars Philip potters through the countryside on errands so small that no one else would hear their call. He buys hardware in tiny quantities, so that he can have the pleasure of buying again soon, and so that the surplus from a completed project can't suggest another one no different. His energy is distributed through his life with absolute evenness; he plans from hour to hour as an artist would measure from one exhibition to the next. In the restlessness of his temperament he resembles Picasso, except for the life's-work. He hears of a blacksmith somewhere round Chirk who will make new spokes for penny-farthings, and sets out in search of him. He devises the Yorke Remote Wasp Destroyer, for those awkward places under floorboards and eaves. He knocks together his own cat-ladders, and does repairs on the slate roofs of tenants' farms. He strings all the light-bulbs in his houses at head-height so he can change them without a stepladder. He shops in Ruabon High Street, but shuns the Co-Op after a hitch-hiker informs him that a fraction of the profits ends up in the coffers of the Labour Party. The same source mischievously tells him that APT, the name of a rival shopping chain, stands for 'Aristocratic Purchasing Trust'. Believing that this organization subsidizes the landed gentry, Philip takes his custom there.

House guests arrive at Erddig for the shooting season. The Yorkes do no shooting themselves, but put their servants at the disposal of the visiting guns, just as they serve meat to their guests though themselves vegetarian. Soon the game-larder, a slatted cage high on a wall outside the kitchen, is full of plump brown bodies. The ripening pheasants are dated in the customary way; to indicate 'shot on a Monday', the extreme-left claw is twisted off (extreme-*right* from the bird's point of view), and so on along the stiffening feet for the rest of the week. Philip intensifies his horror and his panic by climbing a stepladder until he can smell their deadness, see every dead detail.

Philip boycotts the world when it falls short of humane standards. He hears that a newly-established dairy in the area has bribed local boys to break the bottles of its rivals, and so gained control of the market; instantly and forever he changes to condensed milk in tins. Trixie finds herself making the same dietetic protest against thuggery.

Philip reads Theology at Corpus Christi, Cambridge. It is his intention to enter the Church, but he hesitates to do so before he has met people at large and learned how they live and work. His small private income allows this to become a lifelong hesitation.

All Philip's mending jobs on his clothes are carried out in scarlet thread, the only colour for which he can find biblical authority. The bright stitches stand out oddly against the sombre weave of the suits he picks up at jumble sales in Liverpool. The massive turn-ups delight him, since from their fuzzy contents – biscuit crumbs, sand, slate chips, and straw – he can reconstruct a day which has otherwise vanished from his mind. Everyone he meets is offered a similar suit from his next Liverpool expedition.

Serving his country in the war, Philip is puzzled about Scripture. He knows that if a man compel thee to walk with him a mile, you should go with him twain, but can't make up his mind whether the crucial element is twice-duty or duty-plus-one. Deciding, he re-enlists for a single additional year.

Philip's new little flat opens on to the servants' gallery, where the tourists gather to admire the old photos and poems. They ambush Philip as he wanders out, or knock on his door to say how much they liked seeing him on the TV. His performances in the documentaries don't satisfy him (he makes no attempt to cash the cheques he is sent in payment), but he doesn't say so now. Nor for instance does he say that to him the new dovecote looks like a bus shelter. Once he has been spotted or dug out by visitors, he feels he has an obligation to put on a good show by guiding their tour. He rewards himself with a large tea in the canteen, formerly the stables, where he places his order in a stage whisper since he gets everything at half-price. This always delights and amazes him, though seeing that the Trust's employees all enjoy the same concession, it could just as easily seem an indignity as a privilege.

Philip takes train-and-bicycle tours of Spain, and soon learns to refine his packing to the point of nonexistence. He brings only a pair of paper underpants to wear while he washes his more substantial ones, and an extra sock so that each day one is fresh, one is being washed, and one is in its second day of service, though transferred for variety's sake to the other foot. He starts his cycling in the south, so that prevailing winds will give him a little help, and the sun will not often be in his eyes. He conceives a passion for Franco and for Franco's Spain, largely because under this regime the trains never exceed sixteen miles an hour, and he can touch seventeen on the Ladies' All-Steel of 1937. If he misses a train he can rely on beating it to the next station, his big knees grazing the handlebars each time he pedals.

Finding a stack of unused traveller's cheques at the back of a kitchen cupboard, Philip makes a final trip to Spain, vaguely expecting to die there. Spain after Franco displeases him, now that the trains are well-scheduled and elusive. His Spanish is luckily not fluent enough for him to communicate his displeasure to the natives, and he returns home without expressing it.

Philip spends much time writing huge plays on biblical themes (Scene: The Camp of the Assyrians); but the genre at which, unconsciously, he excels, is the last-will-and-testament. In his hands the will becomes a literary form as tightly liberating as the haiku, the sonnet, the limerick. Its givens are the crudenesses of posthumous bribery and revenge, of I-told-you-so and you-never-suspected, but all is transformed into a delicate series of exclusions and caprices. As the will-sequence grows, subtle fluctuations (the constantly halving and doubling bequests to Bertram 'Hoohah' Heyhoe) stand out with poignance against the massive reversals (vast properties transferred from Mother Church to Welsh Language Society).

The handover of Erddig and nine hundred acres to the National Trust is accomplished at last seven years after Philip's inheritance; a large plot of land is sold to endow it, and a suite of seven rooms is converted and set aside for the Trust's administrator. Philip for his part chooses an old pantry as the site of his new flat. He feels that it was his hard-hitting wills which did the trick in the end; the Trust people played hard-to-get until he started bequeathing the property wholesale to the Welsh Nationalists. *Then* they sat up and took notice In A Big Way. Now Philip conceives irrational but splendid little hatreds for the Trust's representatives, pompous go-getters to a man. They are determined at all costs to humour the Last Squire, colourful character that he is, thus rendering him monochrome in their presence. Unwittingly Philip escalates his nuisance-value by continuing to clean the drains and to service the Ram, improvising repairs even as the Trust moves in to make its thorough restorations. Then Philip decides to outlive Mr Powell-Jones, the Trust's caretaker, so as to replace him with a pro-Yorke friend; he assumes this will be easy, since Mr Powell-Jones is not a teetotaller, and is therefore in Philip's eyes being visibly eaten away by The Drink.

Simon on his travels dislikes the French, tolerates the Belgians, and thoroughly approves of the Germans. He staffs Erddig with German maids, who arrive with hand-luggage and leave, after a few months, with packing cases.

Philip is intensively cultivated by his acquaintances for a few weeks each year, just before the International Music Eisteddfod in Llangollen, for which Philip always makes block bookings. He feels obliged to play up to his position as Squire and prominent (non-Welsh-speaking) Welshman, though the music is of no interest to him. His acquaintances court him and his tickets with cakes and confections, soon realizing that he is a soft touch who can be won with almost any soft plateful.

Simon Yorke's betrothed fails to attend the wedding. Simon allows himself to become embittered, and makes no further attempt to carry on the line. He stays in the big house but takes no care of it, living almost entirely on meringues. Philip has made his home in Plas Noble, and the two brothers see each other only rarely; when they do they are out of sympathy, now that they are cultivating incompatible manias. Simon becomes obsessed with buying back the land his father and grandfather let go; even in his last years he devotes himself to this unreal expansion.

On Simon's death in 1966 Philip inherits Erddig and its park, plus extensive property in Ruabon and Wrexham, all of it in a state of near-dereliction. This ruinous inheritance suits him perfectly; Plas Noble by itself wasn't big enough to generate the disorders which are the units of Yorke activity. The whole estate, though, is one huge deranged machine perfectly corresponding to Philip's need for unlikely projects. The contents of Erddig alone are worth a rough million pounds, so Philip buys a gun and sleeps with it under his pillow, unpredictably varying the site of his bed. He has a single power-point installed, into which he plugs a standard lamp and two hundred feet of extension flex. Carrying it, he walks past mirrors which return light of a different date. The State Bed goes to the Victoria and Albert, to be restored and then exhibited for a few years. Underneath the roof-leaks Philip rigs up funnels which decant into hosepipes suspended on slings of string and thrust out of the nearest window. He constructs a burglar alarm for the back door; round the doorknob a length of string – at its other end the tethered leg of a tottering table – on the table-top a pile of empty soup tins – within earshot of the tins a watchful Trixie, ready to tear at intruders with her loose teeth.

Moments after he signs his Unilateral Declaration of Independence Ian Smith receives a letter from Philip, by way of Rhodesia House in London. Philip explains to Mr Smith that he is altogether right, and that the better sort of people in Britain will be vocal in their support of him. Mr Smith makes no reply, perhaps waiting for other better-sort-of-people to co-ordinate their battle cry.

The *Liverpool Post* publishes a letter from Philip on the subject of getting the economy back on its feet. He advocates the dropping of sanctions against Rhodesia, and proposes a World Tour (permanent and compulsory) by The Beatles as the other half of his remedial package.

Philip retains in Britain driving quirks he has picked up in Spain. The Spanish custom is to sound the horn whenever the road is visible for less than a hundred metres ahead; in the twisting lanes of Wales this applies almost the whole time. The English horn-blast says only I-am-here, with various shades of irony and understatement. Very different are Philip's Hispanic inflections, which range from I-am-here-and-I-may-as-well-enjoy-myself, all the way to Madonna-I-invoke-you-send-angry-angels-to-my-aid.

For several years Philip drives a bus full of tourists in a venture he calls 'Spain on a Penny a Mile'. Travellers of limited means, for whom holidays abroad are still very much dangerous mysteries, entrust themselves to his driving skills and his international savoir-faire. Philip for his part makes no preparations whatever. His customers assume that a fixed itinerary and a planned series of reliable hotels are keeping them safe from enteritis and anarchy, while Philip drives more or less on whim, assuming that Spain will be Spain whichever way she is sliced, and that Franco's Paradise will make itself apparent no matter what. As evening falls he halts the bus and deserts his charges to ask passers-by, preferably children, where to eat and where to stay, and where to point the bus next day. He writes this information on his left palm and returns to his party in innocence and triumph. Any criticism of the choices which emerge in this way he disarms by murmuring 'Any Good? Not Much' at appropriate moments, without leaving space between question and answer for anyone else's contribution.

Philip continues to rent out the three-bedroomed houses in the Tai Clawdd terrace for three pounds a week. This represents better and better value as the years go by, but the residents never adjust to Philip's behaving as if barriers between landlord and tenant had no existence. They would rather pay more for the knowledge that no hitch-hiker befriended by Philip will spend the evening watching their colour television instead of Philip's own sets, which are eccentric and black-and-white. Being mostly miners, active or retired, they could well afford a higher rent. Their winters are made pleasant by free coal from the colliery, supplied on condition they don't sell it or give any away; they burn it freely, even on warm late-summer nights, for the sheer fun and focus of it. Then one morning they are embarrassed to see that Philip has spotted their ash-buckets, and is picking out half-burnt coals to heat his own sitting room. After this they feel obliged to fill the buckets with fresh coal under a thin top-dressing of ash. Philip retrieves the glossy nuggets with abstract pleasure and gratitude, as if he has found a way of digging up potatoes where none have been planted.

At some stage before the formation of the National Coal Board in 1948, inroads are made into the coal column underlying Erddig, in breach of the long-standing agreement. The result is a deafening crack and an eventual subsidence, from one side of the house to the other, of eleven feet. The roof is ruptured, and rain pours directly on to the State Bed of antique Chinese silk. Multiple cracks appear in the walls, and in the hand-painted wallpapers which cover them.

Philip befriends a charismatic ewe from the flock of sheep which he uses to keep the wilderness of the lawns in check. He names her Auntie, and she soon learns to seek him out in the house; Trixie wearily learns to ignore her, never suspecting that this newcomer might be the protein missing from her life. When the National Trust begins to put the estate in order, Auntie is moved, along with her peer group, to Pentreclawdd Farm a little way away; but she continues for a long while to come to Philip's call, though increasingly baffled by her own response.

The friends Philip has made at Cambridge, from his college, his subject, and his interest in rowing, keep in touch for several years. Then they stop making the effort as their careers diverge conclusively from his, which shows no signs of orthodox advance.

Philip's eye-catching mildness in the television documentaries *Last Squire of Erddig* and *House That Coal Built* impresses Pam Ayres, a young comedienne preparing her first television series. She sees entertainment potential in his musical saw and his entrenched innocence; she invites him to London for an audition. Philip is flustered by a bona fide appointment, and arrives late. Nervously he unpacks his saw and wipes the bow with chalk; but when he turns to his music case he finds it contains only two long-superseded versions of his will, and a draft of his biblical play *Out of Egypt*. His attempt to perform without the music is something of a disaster; but Miss Ayres locates another saw-player for her series, so all is well.

For several seasons Philip runs a private theatre at Bexhill-on-Sea. Friends from Cambridge make up the cast, while Philip always plays the juvenile lead, a role for which he has no qualification other than the excellence of his wardrobe. Advertisements for forthcoming productions, *The Ghost Train*, *Lady Precious Stream*, are painted on the panels of Philip's Bull-Nosed Cowley which he and Mrs Caradoc Evans, known as the Countess Barzinska, drive round the county to spread the news. On stage Philip is supremely himself, his blandness undisturbed by lines learned and gestures rehearsed; he is diffused and not focused by the attention of an audience. He projects no Other-Self across the footlights, and strips even the big scene in *While Parents Sleep* of its tenseness and power to shock.

*

A hitch-hiking student extends his thumb doubtfully in front of Philip's car; very little more would be needed to stop it for ever. There is a bicycle lying loosely on its roof-rack, like the lifeboat on a liner. All the lights and signals on one side (plus one windscreen wiper) are out of action; it has had a stroke or something quite similar, but it hasn't bounced back the way Philip did after his. Philip tells him that since it says Morris on the car's bonnet and Austin on the boot, it must be a Mostyn. Wanting only a lift to Llangollen, the student finds himself diverted to a farm, where the two of them feed a pair of half-wild cats, and Philip makes kissing noises over the fence at a flock of unamused sheep. Then Philip leads him to a privy, in which three ancient motor-bikes stand rusting. Philip wheels out a massive Matchless and fiddles with it until his hands are covered with petrol; then he straddles it and asks to be pushed down the path. When the engine roars, Philip shouts at his helper to hop on; then as if two on a bike wasn't a quorum, he shouts at a farm-worker in the distance to join them. Getting no answer, Philip sets off across the bumpy field anyway. After this experience with the bike, the hitch-hiker is relieved when their next stop in the car is only a church. Philip rattles the collection-box, wonders aloud if the Catholics have raided it, and stuffs it with money. There is money everywhere about his person: statements of dividend on stock (in tobacco firms and distilleries mainly, wickedness at second-hand), and plenty of cash. Today The Yorke Is *Very* Rich, Philip murmurs; he has notes salted away in different pockets, in wallets and envelopes, loose or tied with rubber bands, like a squirrel with an autumn of foresight and a winter of forgetfulness compressed into each transaction. From church Philip briefly rejoins the route for Llangollen to buy a rum-and-raisin choc-ice, then turns right round to pick up some clean clothes from the launderette at Rhosllanerchrugog. By this time the hitch-hiker is reconciled to rambling strangeness, and makes no more protest than the wasted mongrel in the back seat. The party ends up in a terraced house in Ruabon, where amongst other places Philip is based; the hitch-hiker has to duck as he enters, to avoid low-slung light-bulbs. Philip starts a fire and ignites the chimney, or so a policeman knocking at the front door tells him. He makes coffee with water straight out of the hot tap and pronounces it wonderful. An elderly man arrives and immediately retires to the front room to sort out Philip's correspondence; Philip is capable of ignoring any number of Stamped Self-Addressed Envelopes, and without Brownie's visits every few months his affairs would simply seize up. Brownie will accept only a cup of hot water, believing everything else in the world to be an irritant, and leaves as soon as the job is done. The hiker is retained to help with the task of making up a double bed with single-size fitted sheets. Then Philip makes supper of instant soup, ice-cream, and biscuits, murmuring If It's Wet It's Clean as he pulls plates from a greasy sink. He shows off his most prized possession, a pewter plate-holder he prefers to anything on show to the public at Erddig. He explains that he likes living here better than in the big house, because You Can't Live off a View; and paintings and mirrors are wonderful but they can't stop you from burning your hands. The hitch-hiker spends a miserable night between the nylon sheets he has helped, inadequately, to fix up; but Philip's morning porridge restores him. Philip insists on giving him some money when he goes, but salves wounded pride by calling it a loan; he writes 4 Tai Clawdd Ruabon, the address to which it should be returned, on each banknote.

Philip's Cambridge friends have persuaded him to take them out on his motor-cycle to Fen Ditton to watch the boat races. Sedately Philip pulls on his crash helmet, his gauntlets and goggles. A saw protrudes weirdly from the saddlebag. Two of his friends cling on as pillion-passengers on the heavy machine; the third hanger-on is towed behind them on a bicycle, at the end of a piece of string.

Philip makes a day trip to Shrewsbury for the Flower Show, on a Senior Citizen's concessionary ticket. He stays to watch the fireworks and misses the last train home. He makes cheery gestures with his thumb as he starts walking, and is soon given a lift by a passing driver. The car radio is playing, and no conversation suggests itself; Philip absently studies the slick layout of the dashboard, which he much likes. The driver's hand, overshooting the gear-lever, alights on his thigh and is not retrieved. Philip goes very white then very red; he turns his head to look out of the window and says with brightness, 'Why don't I get out here?' Hearing no answer, he reaches for the door-handle and tugs at it. The car slows down to let him out, then parks round the next corner so that the driver can lie in wait. Walking into ambush, Philip has his glasses and a front tooth broken before his shouts scare his attacker off. At the police station he is able to give no helpful particulars of the driver or the car; all he can describe is the slick layout of the dashboard, which he much likes.

Philip's absent-minded progress towards puberty is arrested by an untimely and severe bout of mumps when he is twelve; German measles complicates his case. Thereafter his manner has a puzzled boyishness, as he waits for the world to take on a fuller focus. When sickness strikes tenants or neighbours or servants, Mr Yorke sends them the family music box to enliven their convalescence, but to Philip he reads his most recent pieces of poetry. They commemorate in doggerel the virtues and foibles of the servants, and will be typed up and hung on the wall outside the servants' hall along with photographs of their subjects. Mr Yorke's grandfather started this custom with painted portraits, but help is so hard to keep these days that photographs and verses make more sense. Philip dozes off as the good-natured cadences overlap each other good-naturedly in his father's good-natured voice.

For his magic-lantern lectures about his house and history, Philip asks a tenth of the takings towards new bulbs, and a tithe to be given to Marchwiel Church. His audience today is from the Women's Institute, translated by the wonder of Welsh into Merchedd-y-Fawr, Ladies-of-the-Dawn. The walls of the hall are a dark grey, so Philip has asked the vicar's permission to paint them white for the show, promising to return them to grey the day after. When the vicar refuses, Philip instead brings a huge roll of off-white canvas to do duty as a screen. The opticon is perched on a tall stack of chairs, Philip on another behind it. His commentary is prompted by the images as they appear, in an order which becomes abstract even when it follows chronology. His listeners sigh with pleasure when the lantern projects a slide in gorgeous colour; Philip then explains that this is a view of Lake Geneva he picked up cheap on his travels. The combination of showmanship and absence of mind provokes a puzzled laughter. Family anecdotes encode the family character. The antique pattern-slides, rotating panes of latticed lozenges in primary colours, are a great success; but the biggest triumph is the final lantern-slide. This is a rendering, painted on glass, of an old man in bed; Philip works a sliding panel which puts the beard through the motions of open-mouthed snoring. Then with the slowness of vegetable growth, he pulls a second tab to introduce a mouse at the edge of the sheet. Still more slowly, with flirtatious pauses and retreats, he brings the mouse up to the bewhiskered brink, then makes it scuttle inside. The audience is wild with joy; two children in the front row overheat and have to be taken outside to recover.

Mr Yorke delights his tenants and their families with a Christmas magic-lantern show. A small oil lamp flickering in the dense warmth is enough to project the photographic images and the abstract designs of coloured glass. Little Philip loses all sense of time. The lights go up again; but it is some moments before the spectators realize that thanks to the heavy deposits of soot on their faces, they look less like an audience than a troupe of nigger minstrels, performers in their own right.

Prince Charles arrives to open Erddig to the public. When he sees the bicycle collection, he asks if he can have a go on one of the penny-farthings. Philip, who has made regular appearances on these wheeled grotesques at fairs and fêtes until very recently, gives him a few hints and warns him that it's a tricky business. To start, you must run at the machine and trust it to do the right thing, while to slow down and stop you must exert backwards pressure on the pedals; the brake will tend to tip you and the frame over the big front wheel. Charles coasts for a few feet, and is then photographed toppling sideways by the massed gentlemen-of-the-press. Philip feels that to expose the Heir to the Throne to such indignity must amount to high treason, though it is if anything good public relations; so he withdraws to the house at Tai Clawdd to contemplate suicide. Instead he decides to present the Prince with the offending bicycle, and spends six weeks, while the Palace reassures him with mounting tact, grooming it for its new home.

Philip learns to ride a bicycle almost as soon as he can walk. His first machine has little supplementary wheels, to be removed once the novice's sense of balance is securely established, and soon he joins Simon on his larger two-wheeler, Mrs Yorke on the old bike (one of the first with a free wheel) to which she will always be faithful, and Mr Yorke on his favourite 'farthing-penny', which has taken him as far as Rhyl.

In sleep Philip achieves an ecstatic attention which bypasses the humdrum middleman of memory. Almost every evening, at the cottage of his tenant-farmer friends young Mr and Mrs Morgan, he falls asleep in front of the television set. The armchair is firm and massive; here he is a household god who only needs to work shifts. The Morgans call him Mr Phil, and at intervals empty and refill the tea mug on the chair-arm, so he will have something to wake up to. At home Philip falls asleep twice while Eartha Kitt sings 'Mack the Knife' on the radio, proving it to be one of his favourite songs, and three times during his record of Churchill's Speeches, thus strongly reaffirming his loyalty. At the Wrexham Odeon he sleeps through all but fifteen minutes of *What's Up Doc?*.

Mr and Mrs Yorke take a picnic out in the park, near the Cup-and-Saucer. Simon toddles freely, while Philip sucks up sunlight like a thick pink-and-white plant. His hands clench and unclench, but he means nothing by this. He is forming tiny sentences of gesture, but everything within range of the big heartbeat is too big to be grasped by hands or lost from them. The world-pulse which enfolds him comes from the automatic pumping system called the Ram. Water from a stream is divided as it runs down a circular weir, the Cup-and-Saucer; then the force of one part is used to pump the other half up to the house. The Ram's rebounding diaphragm gives a double thud. Philip has never yet been out of earshot of the Ram, and from where he lies can see nothing but Yorkes and their mild plenty.

During the sermon in Pen-y-cae Church, Philip's sleep is interrupted from within. He goes very red then very white; his arm drops to his side, the fist unclenching.

The Yorkes' noisy second child becomes quiet Philip Scott at a private ceremony in the Saloon. His father takes from its place the miniature cabinet he brought back from his visit to the Holy Land as a young man.

The six vessels inside it contain Jordan water; when the first seals are broken, a terrible smell announces itself, and the entire batch proves to be tainted. The tall windows are kept open until the air clears. A manservant meanwhile fetches more modest water from the lake in front of the house, so that the ceremony can go ahead.

MARGARET ATWOOD

Lives of the Poets

Margaret Atwood (1939–) was born in Ottawa, Ontario, and is one of Canada's leading writers. She has taught widely, and won many prizes. Her many and varied novels include *The Edible Woman* (1969), *Surfacing* (1972), *Bodily Harm* (1981), *The Handmaid's Tale* (1986), and *Cat's Eye* (1988). She has published several works of criticism, including an important study of Canadian literature, and a number of volumes of short stories (including *Dancing Girls*, 1977; *Bluebeard's Egg*, 1983; *Wilderness Tips*, 1991; *Good Bones*, 1992), a form at which she excels.

'Lives of the Poets', from *Dancing Girls*, displays the mixture of pain and strong comic vitality that typifies much of Margaret Atwood's writing. There is a vivid portrait of the underlying truths of a literary tour – the mixture of momentary fame and general neglect, the contrast between respect as a poet and the dull and ordinary troubles that workaday poets are heir to. Like many of the heroines in Atwood's hard, ironic and often very funny stories, Julia is afflicted by the familiar sense of homelessness and sexual disappointment and betrayal, but is struggling with her feeling of being a victim. Perhaps poetry or her strength will defeat it – 'words swarming behind her eyes like spring bees' – and the polite world of poetry readings will explode into something else.

L ying on the bathroom floor of this anonymous hotel room, my feet upon the edge of the bathtub and a cold wet washcloth balled at the back of my neck. Bloody nosebleed. A good adjective, it works, as the students say in those creative writing classes that are sometimes part of the package. So colourful. Never had a nosebleed before, what are you supposed to do? An ice cube would be nice. Image of the Coke-and-ice machine at the end of the hall, me streaking toward it, a white towel over my head, the bloodstain spreading through it. A hotel guest opens his room door. Horrors, an accident. Stabbed in the nose. Doesn't want to get involved, the room door shuts, my quarter jams the machine. I'll stick with the washcloth.

The air's too dry, that must be it, nothing to do with me or the protests of the soggy body. Osmosis. Blood to the outside because there's not enough water vapour; they keep the radiators going full blast and no switch to shut them off. Cheapskates, why couldn't I stay at the Holiday Inn? Instead it's this one, pseudo-Elizabethan motifs tacked to a mouse-eaten frame, somebody's last-ditch attempt to make something out of this corner of the woods. The outskirts of Sudbury, nickel-smelting capital of the world. Can we show you around? they said. I'd like to see the slag heaps, and the places where the vegetation has all been scorched off. Oh, ha-ha, they said. It's growing back, they raised the stacks. It's turning into quite a, you know, civilized place. I used to like it, I said, it looked like the moon. There's something to be said for a place where absolutely nothing grows. Bald. Dead. Clean as a bone. Know what I mean? Furtive glances at one another, young beardy faces, one pipesmokes, they write footnotes, on their way up, why do we always get stuck with the visiting poet? Last one threw up on the car rug. Just wait till we get tenure.

Julia moved her head. The blood trickled gently down the back of her throat, thick and purple-tasting. She had been sitting there in front of the phone, trying to figure out the instructions for calling long-distance through the hotel operator, when she'd sneezed and the page in front of her had suddenly been spattered with blood. Totally unprovoked. And Bernie would be hanging around at home, waiting for her to call. In two hours she had to give the reading. A gracious introduction, she would rise and move to the microphone, smiling, she would open her mouth and blood would start to drip from her nose. Would they clap? Would they pretend not to notice? Would they think it was part of the poem? She would have to start rooting around in her purse for a Kleenex, or, better still, she'd faint, and someone else would have to cope. (But everyone would think she was drunk.) How upsetting for the committee. Would they pay her anyway? She could imagine them discussing it.

She raised her head a little, to see if it had stopped. Something that felt like a warm slug crawled down towards her upper lip. She licked, tasting salt. How was she going to get to the phone? On her back, crawling supine across the floor, using her elbows and pushing with her feet, a swimming motion, like a giant aquatic insect. She shouldn't be calling Bernie, she should be calling a doctor. But it wasn't serious enough. Something like this always happened when she had to give a reading, something painful but too minor for a doctor. Besides, it was always out of town, she never knew any doctors. Once it was a bad cold; her voice had sounded as if it was coming through a layer of mud. Once her hands and ankles had swelled up. Headaches were standard: she never got headaches at home. It was as if something was against these readings and was trying to keep her from giving them. She was waiting for it to take a more drastic form, paralysis of the jaw muscles, temporary blindness, fits. This was what she thought about during the introductions, always: herself on a stretcher, the waiting ambulance, then waking up, safe and cured, with Bernie sitting beside the bed. He would smile at her, he would kiss her forehead, he would tell her – what? Some magical thing. They had won the Wintario Lottery. He'd been left a lot of money. The gallery was solvent. Something that would mean she didn't have to do this any more.

That was the problem: they needed the money. They had always needed the money, for the whole four years they had lived together, and they still needed it. At first it hadn't seemed so important. Bernie was on a grant then, painting, and after that he got a renewal. She had a part-time job, cataloguing in a library. Then she had a book published, by one of the medium-sized houses, and got a grant herself. Of course she quit her job, to make the best use of the time. But Bernie ran out of money, and he had trouble selling paintings. Even when he did sell one, the dealer got most of it. The dealer system was wrong, he told her, and he and two other painters opened a co-operative artists' gallery which, after a lot of talk, they decided to call The Notes from Underground. One of the other painters had money, but they didn't want to take advantage of him; they would go strict thirds. Bernie explained all this to her; and he was so enthusiastic it had seemed natural to lend him half of her grant money, just to get things going. As soon as they began to show a profit, he said, he would pay her back. He even gave her two shares in the gallery. They hadn't started to show a profit yet, though, and, as Bernie pointed out, she didn't really need the money back right at the moment. She could get some more. She now had a reputation; a small one, but still, she could earn money easier and faster than he could, travelling around and giving readings on college campuses. She was 'promising', which meant that she was cheaper than those who were more than promising. She got enough invitations to keep them going, and though she debated the merits of each one with Bernie, hoping he would veto, he had never yet advised her to turn one down. But to be fair, she had never told him quite how much she hated it, the stares of the eyes, her own voice detached and floating, the one destructive question that was sure to lurk there among all the blank ones. *I mean, do you really think you have anything to say?*

Deep in February, deep in the snow, bleeding on the tiles of this bathroom floor. By turning her head she could see them, white hexagons linked like a honeycomb, with a single black tile at regular intervals.

For a measly hundred and twenty-five dollars – but it's half the rent, don't forget that – and twenty-five a day for expenses. Had to take the morning plane, no seats in the afternoon, who the hell goes to Sudbury in February? A bunch of engineers. Practical citizens, digging out the ore, making a bundle, two cars and a swimming pool. They don't stay at this place, anyway. Dining room at lunchtime almost empty. Just me and a very old man who talked to himself out loud. What's wrong with him? I said to the waitress. Is he crazy? In a whisper I said it. It's OK, he's deaf, she said. No, he's just lonely, he's been real lonely ever since his wife died. He lives here. I guess it's better than an old-age home, you know? There are more people here in the summertime. And we get a lot of men who're separating from their wives. You can always tell them, by what they order.

Didn't pursue that. Should have though, now I'll never know. What they order. Was looking as usual for the cheapest thing on the menu. Need that whole hundred and twenty-five, why waste it on food? This food. The menu a skewed effort to be Elizabethan, everything spelled with an *e* at the end. Got the Anne Boleyn Special, a hamburger with no bun, garnished with a square of red Jell-O and followed by 'a glass of skime milke'. Do they know that Anne Boleyn's head was cut off? Is that why the hamburger has no bun? What goes on in people's minds? Everyone thinks writers must know more about the inside of the human head, but that is wrong. They know less, that's why they write. Trying to find out what everyone else takes for granted. The symbolism of the menu, for God's sake, why am I even thinking about it? The menu has no symbolism, it's just some dimwit's ill-informed attempt to be cute. Isn't it?

You're too complicated, Bernie used to tell her, when they were still stroking and picking at each other's psyches. You should take it easy. Lie back. Eat an orange. Paint your toenails.

All very well for him.

Maybe he wasn't even up yet. He used to take naps in the afternoons, he'd be lying there under the heaped-up blankets of their Queen Street West apartment (over the store that had once sold hardware but was now a weaving boutique, and the rent was climbing), face down, arms flung out to either side, his socks on the floor where he'd discarded them, one after the other, like deflated feet or stiffened blue footprints leading to the bed. Even in the mornings he would wake up slowly and fumble his way to the kitchen for some coffee, which she would already have made. That was one of their few luxuries, real coffee. She'd have been up for hours, crouching at the kitchen table, worrying away at a piece of paper, gnawing words, shredding the language. He would place his mouth, still full of sleep, on hers, and perhaps pull her back into the bedroom and down into the bed with him, into that liquid pool of flesh, his mouth sliding over her, furry pleasure, the covers closing over them as they sank into weightlessness. But he hadn't done that for some time. He had been waking earlier and earlier; she, on the other hand, had been having trouble getting out of bed. She was losing that compulsion, that joy, whatever had nagged her out into the cold morning air, driven her to fill all those notebooks, all those printed pages. Instead she would roll herself up in the blankets after Bernie got up, tucking in all the corners, muffling herself in wool. She had begun to have the feeling that nothing was waiting for her outside the bed's edge. Not emptiness but nothing, the zero with legs in the arithmetic book.

'I'm off,' he'd say to her groggy bundled back. She'd be awake enough to hear this; then she would lapse back into a humid sleep. His absence was one more reason for not getting up. He would be going to The Notes from Underground, which was where he seemed to spend most of his time now. He was pleased with the way it had been going, they'd had several interviews in the papers, and it was easy for her to understand how something could be thought of as a qualified success and still not make money, since the same thing had happened to her book. But she worried a little because he wasn't doing very much painting any more. His last picture had been a try at Magic Realism. It was her, sitting at the kitchen table, wrapped in the plaid rug off the foot of the bed, with her hair in a sleazy bun at the back of her neck, looking like some kind of famine victim. Too bad the kitchen was yellow; it made her skin green. He hadn't finished it though. Paperwork, he would say. That was what he spent his morning at the gallery doing, that and answering the phone. The three of them were supposed to take turns and he should have been off at twelve, but he usually ended up there in the afternoons, too. The gallery had attracted a few younger painters, who sat around drinking plastic cups of Nescafé and cans of beer and arguing about whether or not anyone who bought a share in the gallery should be able to have a show there and whether the gallery should take commissions, and if not how it was going to survive. They had various schemes, and they'd recently hired a girl to do public relations, posters and mailings and bothering the media. She was free-lance and did it for two other small galleries and one commercial photographer. She was just starting out, Bernie said. She talked about building them up. Her name was Marika; Julia had met her at the gallery, back in the days when she'd been in the habit of dropping around in the afternoons. That seemed a long time ago.

Marika was a peach-cheeked blonde, about twenty-two or three, anyway no more than five or six years younger than Julia. Although her name suggested the exotic, a Hungarian perhaps, her accent was flat Ontario and her last name was Hunt. Either a fanciful mother or a name-changing father, or perhaps Marika had adopted the name herself. She had been very friendly to Julia. 'I've read your book,' she said. 'I don't find time to read too many books, but I got yours out of the library because of Bernie. I didn't think I was going to like it, but actually it's quite good.' Julia was grateful, Bernie said too grateful, to people who said they liked her work or who had even read it. Nevertheless, she heard a voice inside her head saying, *Piss right off.* It was the way Marika offered her compliment: like a biscuit to a dog, part reward, part bribe, and condescending.

Since then they'd had coffee together several times. It was always Marika who dropped over, on some errand or other from Bernie. They sat in the kitchen and talked, but no real connections were made. They were like two mothers at a birthday party, sitting on the sidelines while their children whooped and gobbled: they were polite to each other, but the real focus of their attention was elsewhere. Once Marika had said, 'I've always thought I might like to write myself,' and Julia had felt a small red explosion at the back of her neck and had almost thrown her cup of coffee at her, until she realized Marika didn't mean it that way, she was just trying to appear interested. 'Aren't you afraid you'll run out of material?'

'Not material, energy,' she'd said, making it sound like a joke; but it had been true, that was her fear. Weren't they the same thing? 'According to Einstein,' she said, and Marika, having missed the connection, gave her a funny look and changed the subject to films.

The last time Marika came over, Julia wasn't even out of bed. She had no excuse, no explanation. She almost told her to go away, but Bernie needed his black notebook, the one with the phone numbers, so she had to let her in. Marika leaned in the bedroom doorway, trim in her little layered look, dangling her hand-woven bag, while Julia, with unwashed hair straggling over the shoulders of her nightgown, moss-mouthed and blurry-minded, knelt on the floor and scrabbled through Bernie's discarded pockets. For the first time in their life she wished he would bloody well pick up his clothes. She felt exposed by them, though she shouldn't, they weren't her clothes, she hadn't dropped them. Marika exuded surprise, embarrassment and a certain glee, as if Bernie's dirty socks and trampled jeans were Julia's soft underbelly, which she'd always wanted to get a look at.

'I don't know where he's put it,' Julia said, irritated. 'He's supposed to pick them up himself,' and added, far too defensively she knew, 'We share everything.'

'Of course, with your work and all,' Marika said. She was scanning the room, the greyish bed, Julia's sweater slumped in the corner chair, the avocado with brown-edged leaves on the windowsill, their only plant. She'd grown it from the pit of a celebration avocado – she could no longer remember the reason for the rejoicing – but there was something wrong with it. Tea-leaves, you were supposed to put tea-leaves on them, or was it charcoal?

The notebook was finally under the bed. Julia pulled it out; a dustball clung to it. She saw in her mind a small plaque, like the ones on historical houses: DUSTBALL. *Once the property of Julia Morse, Poetess.* With a few bored schoolchildren looking at it through the glass of a case. That was the future, if there was a future, if she kept on writing, if she became at least marginally significant, an obligatory footnote in someone's thesis. Fragments left over after the general decay, classified, gathering dust, like the vertebrae of dinosaurs. Bloodless.

She handed the notebook over. 'Would you like some coffee?' she asked, in a voice meant to discourage.

'I don't want to put you out,' Marika said, but she had some anyway, chatting brightly about their plans for a collective show, to be called 'Up from Under'. Her eyes shifted around the kitchen, taking in the dripping tap, the smelly cloth draped over it, the ancient toaster with the crumbs around its base like the debris from a tiny landslide. 'I'm really glad we can be friends,' she said just before leaving. 'Bernie says we have nothing in common, but I think we get on real well. They're mostly men down there.' This could have been some ersatz variety of women's lib, Julia thought, but it wasn't: Marika's voice stank of bridge club. 'Real well.' How incongruous, with those three-inch platforms, that trendy bum. Marika's visits made her feel like a welfare case. She wondered how she could get her to stop coming, without being too rude. She begrudged the time, too, she could be using it for work. Though increasingly there was no work.

Bernie didn't seem to notice that she was doing next to nothing. He no longer asked to read what she might have written during the day. When he came home for dinner he would talk obsessively about the gallery, eating plate after plate of spaghetti and, it seemed to her, whole loaves of bread. His appetite had increased, and they had recently begun to argue about the food bills and who was supposed to do the cooking and shopping. In the beginning they had shared everything, that was the agreement. Julia wanted to point out that since he was now eating twice as much as she was, he really ought to do more of the shopping and pay more than half, but she felt it would be mingy of her to say this.

Especially since, whenever they talked about money, he would say, 'Don't worry, you'll get paid off,' as if she begrudged him the gallery loan. Which she supposed she did.

What time is it? Lift the wrist: six thirty. The blood seems to have slowed down, but it's still there, a thickening like sludge at the back of the throat. A teacher, once, in public school, who came into the classroom with her teeth outlined in blood. She must have been to the dentist and then not checked in the mirror, but we were all so afraid of her none of us said anything and we spent the afternoon drawing three tulips in a vase, presided over by that bloodthirsty smile. Have to remember to brush my teeth and clean my face carefully, a drop of blood on the chin might be disturbing to the audience. Blood, the elemental fluid, the juice of life, by-product of birth, prelude to death. The red badge of courage. The people's flag. Maybe I could get a job writing political speeches, if all else fails. But when it comes out of your nose, not magic or even symbolic, just ridiculous. Pinned by the nose to the geometric net of this bathroom floor. Don't be completely stupid, get started. Stand up carefully: if the blood keeps flowing, call off the reading and get on the plane. (Leaving a trail of clots?) I could be home tonight. Bernie's there now, waiting for me to call, it's past the time.

She pulled herself up, slowly, holding on to the sink, and walked into the bedroom with her head tilted back precariously. She groped for the phone and picked it up. She dialled 0 and got the operator to place the call for her. She listened to the outer-space noises the phone made, anticipating Bernie's voice, feeling his tongue already on the inside of her mouth. They would go to bed and after that they would have a late supper, the two of them in the kitchen with the gas oven lit and open to keep them warm, the way they used to. (Her mind skipped the details of what they would eat. She knew there had been nothing in the refrigerator when she left but a couple of ageing wieners. Not even any buns.) Things would get better, time would reverse itself, they would talk, she would tell him how much she had missed him (for surely she had been away much longer than a day), silence would open, language would flow again.

The line was busy.

She did not want to think about her disappointment. She would phone later. There was no more blood, though she could feel it crusted inside her head. So she would stay, she would do the reading, she would collect the fee and use it to pay the rent. What else was possible?

It was dinnertime and she was hungry, but she couldn't afford another meal. Sometimes they took the poet out for dinner, sometimes they gave a party afterwards where she could fill up on crackers and cheese. Here there was nothing. They picked her up at the airport, that was it. She could tell there had been no posters, no advance publicity. A small audience, nervous because they were there and nobody else was, caught out attending the wrong reading. And she didn't even look like a poet, she was wearing a neat navy-blue pantsuit, easy for stairs and cars. Maybe a robe would help, something flowing and ethereal. Bangles, a scarf?

She sat on the edge of the straight-backed chair, facing a picture of two dead ducks and an Irish setter. There was time to be filled. No television set. Read the Gideon Bible? No, nothing too strenuous, she didn't want to start bleeding again. In half an hour they would come to pick her up. Then the eyes, the polite hands, the fixed smiles. Afterwards everyone would murmur. 'Don't you feel exposed up there?' a young girl had asked her once. 'No,' she'd said, and she didn't, it wasn't her, she read only her most soothing poems, she didn't want to disturb anyone. But they distrusted her anyway. At least she never got drunk beforehand the way a lot of the others did. She wanted to be nice, and everyone approved of that.

Except the few hungry ones, the ones who wanted to know the secret, who believed there was a secret. They would straggle up afterwards, she knew, hanging around the edges, behind the murmuring committee members, clutching little packets of poems, extending them to her gingerly, as if the pages were raw flesh they could not bear to have touched. She could remember when she had felt like that. Most of the poems would be dismal, but now and then there would be one that had something, the energy, the thing that could not be defined. *Don't do it*, she wanted to tell them, *don't make the mistake I made*. But what was her mistake? Thinking she could save her soul, no doubt. By the word alone.

Did I really believe that? Did I really believe that language could seize me by the hair and draw me straight up, out into the free air? But if you stop believing, you can't do it any longer, you can't fly. So I'm stuck here on this chair. A *sixty-year-old smiling public man*. Crisis of faith? Faith in what? Resurrection, that's what is needed. Up from under. Get rid of these haunts, these fictions, *he said, she said*, counting up points and grievances; the dialogues of shadows. Otherwise there will be nothing left but the rest of my life. Something is frozen.

Bernie, save me.

He was so nice this morning, before she left. The phone again, the voice flies through the darkness of space. Hollow ringing, a click.

'Hi.' A woman's voice, Marika, she knew who it would be.

'Could I please speak to Bernie?' Stupid to act as though she didn't recognize the voice.

'Hi, Julia,' Marika said. 'Bernie's not here right now. He had to go away for a couple of days, but he knew you'd be calling tonight so he asked me to come over. So you wouldn't worry or anything. He said to have a good reading, and don't forget to water the plant when you get back.'

'Oh, thanks, Marika,' she said. As if she was his secretary, leaving her with messages for the idiot wife while he . . . She couldn't ask where he had gone. She herself went away, why couldn't he? If he wanted her to know where, he'd tell her. She said goodbye. As she put down the phone, she thought she heard something. A voice, a laugh?

He hasn't gone anywhere. He's there, in the apartment. I can see it, it must have been going on for weeks, months, down at the gallery, *I've read your book*, checking out the competition. I must be feeble-minded, everyone knew but me. Trotting over to have coffee with me, casing the joint. Hope they have the grace to change the sheets. Didn't have the guts to talk to me himself, water the plant my ass, it's dead anyway. Melodrama in a parking lot, long stretches of asphalt with here and there a splotch of crushed animal, is that what my life has become?

Rock bottom in this room among the slag heaps, outer space, on the dead moon, with two slaughtered ducks and a stuffed dog, why did you have to do it that way, when I'm out here, you know it cripples me, these ordeals, walking through the eyes, couldn't you have waited? You set it up so well, I'll come back and yell and scream, and you'll deny it all, you'll look at me, very cool, and say, *What are you talking about?* And what will I be talking about, maybe I'm wrong, I'll never know. Beautiful.

It's almost time.

They will arrive, the two young men who are polite and who do not yet have tenure. She will get into the front seat of their Volvo, and all the way to the reading, as they drive between the snowdrifts piled halfway up the telephone poles, the two young men will discuss the virtues of this car and the relative virtues of the car belonging to the one who is not driving but who is sitting in the back seat with his legs doubled like a grasshopper's.

She will not be able to say anything at all. She will watch the snow coming at the windshield and being wiped away by the windshield wipers, and it will be red, it will be like a solid red wall. A violation, that is what she hates, they had promised never to lie.

Stomach full of blood, head full of blood, burning red, she can feel it at last, this rage that has been going on for a long time, energy, words swarming behind her eyes like spring bees. Something is hungry, something is coiling itself. A long song coils and uncoils itself just in front of the windshield, where the red snow is falling, bringing everything to life. They park the virtuous car and she is led by the two young men into the auditorium, grey cinder-block, where a gathering of polite faces waits to hear the word. Hands will clap, things will be said about her, nothing astonishing, she is supposed to be good for them, they must open their mouths and take her in, like vitamins, like bland medicine. No. No sweet identity, she will clench herself against it. She will step across the stage, words coiled, she will open her mouth and the room will explode in blood.

GARRISON KEILLOR

The Royal Family

Garrison Keillor (1942–), born in Minnesota, became famous for his story-telling on the National Public Radio programme *A Prairie Home Companion* before he began to write down his tales of the imaginary Lake Wobegon, Minnesota, in such volumes as *Happy to Be Here* (1982), *Lake Wobegon Days* (1985) and *Leaving Home* (1987).

'The Royal Family', from *Leaving Home*, is a typical Wobegon tale of fortune and misfortune in small-town midwestern America – pioneer land where, Keillor says, 'we had to stop short of the destination we dreamed of and we have to look to others to cross those mountains that stopped us and make the home that we tried so hard to reach'. Keillor's work goes back to the American tradition of oral frontier humour, developed by many nineteenth-century writers from Josh Billings to Mark Twain, and still alive in what he calls 'kitchen talk'. He has been called 'the best humorous writer to have come out of America since James Thurber' and, like Thurber, he brings a modern wit and irony to a traditional American subject and landscape. His stories are, he tells us, 'written for my voice, which is flat and slow. There are long pauses in them and sentences that trail off into the raspberry bushes.'

race Tollefson graduated from Lake Wobegon High School in 1938, a thespian and debater and member of the Order of the Shining Star, a quiet and sensible girl who surprised everyone and ran off with a man by the name of Alex Campbell. He was a handsome green-eyed fellow, the driver of a 1936 Singer coupe, who performed magic tricks with quarters and napkins, told jokes and tossed kids in the air, and seemed to have no prospect in this world. He kept a bottle of whiskey in the trunk of his car and he laughed too loud. The Tollefsons were united in opposition to him but Grace married him and moved to Saint Paul. Years went along, and people heard bits of news that she wasn't entirely happy with him. A child came along, and another. And a third. He left her in 1948. As some people told it, he came home drunk and she locked him out, but it didn't matter. There was nothing for her to do but get a ride back home and live off the charity of her family and the Lutheran church.

Her younger brother Lawrence bought her an old green mobile home and moved it into the yard behind his house, next to the garden. Lutheran ladies came and cleaned it up and donated old furniture, a three-legged table, a very nice green sofa with large holes chewed out of it, some rickety chairs, a reproduction of Larsson's *The Last Supper*. People were nice to them, as you'd be nice to anybody who was very peculiar. Divorce in that town was as odd as a purebred dog. Grace could see what people thought as she walked down the street: *We were right, we told you, now look at you.*

The oldest boy was Earl, her daughter was Marlys, and the little boy was Walter, who was only three and couldn't remember his father. When he asked his mother, she only said that Alex was a handsome man descended from Scottish nobility, that he had a weakness but it wasn't anybody's fault. When he asked his grandma Tollefson, she said, 'Huh! Those Campbells were all alike. There wasn't one of them worth mentioning. But it's not your fault, Walter. You didn't ask to be born into this world, now did you?' He didn't ask again.

It was hard living in a mobile home, living off contributions. At night, when the four of them cleared the supper table and did dishes, when she was feeling especially sad, Grace said, 'Well, what are we going to do when our ship comes in?' That was the cue to quit feeling sorry and to talk about what they'd do when they got rich. They'd have a big white brick mansion in Saint Paul with a stone wall around it, a crystal chandelier in the dining room, fireplaces in the bedrooms. Oriental rugs. A swimming pool. They'd have six servants, six ladies from the Lutheran church, to fix their meals and clean up. Earl had simple tastes and wanted a pony to ride bareback around the streets of Saint Paul and a .22 rifle. Marlys wanted a large dollhouse for her dolls, Mr and Mrs Parker Whitehurst and their children, Jacqueline, Lorraine, and Kathy.

Walter went along with what they wanted, but one thing he didn't say was that he hoped when the ship came in his father would be standing in the bow in a white uniform and a blue cap with gold braid.

One day they got a letter from a man in Philadelphia doing research on Scottish nobility, who asked who their ancestors were so he could look it up. He needed the information for a book he was writing. He enclosed a check for $15. So Grace wrote down what she knew about Alex's ancestors and sent it off and didn't think more of it until another letter arrived from Philadelphia five days later.

She opened the envelope. It was addressed to Mrs Grace Campbell, but the letter was addressed 'Your Royal Highness'. He wrote: 'Today is the happiest day of my life as I greet my one true Sovereign Queen.' And went on to say that their branch of the Campbell family was first in the line of succession of the House of Stewart, the Royal Family of Scotland. She passed it to the children and they each read it carefully, as if it were spun gold and if they dropped it, it would shatter into little pieces. She was quiet a long time. Then she said, 'It can't be true but we'll find out. Meanwhile, you're not to tell a soul. You don't tell anybody.' They promised.

A few days later, the Philadelphia man, whose name was D. R. Mackay, sent them a chart that unfolded bigger than their kitchen table. In the upper-left-hand corner were King James the Seventh, King James the Old Pretender, Prince Charles. There were several lines of counts and marquises, and in the lower-right-hand corner, skirting the clans of Keith and Ferguson, the lines led right straight to them: Earl, Marlys, and Walter. The Royal Family of Scotland living in Lake Wobegon in a green mobile home, furniture donated by the Lutheran church.

They were astounded beyond words. Disbelieving at first, afraid to put their weight on something so beautiful, afraid it was too good to be true, and then it took hold – this was grace, pure grace that God offered them. Not their will but His. Grace. Here they were in their same dismal place but everything had changed. They were different people. Their surroundings were the same, but they were different – and there were times in the months that followed when Walter wished he could tell somebody that he was a prince of Scotland, particularly his cousin Donna who lived in the house the Campbells lived behind and who made complex rules about who could play in her yard and for how long and what they had to do for her, as if she was royalty. Walter longed to tell her. One day D. R. Mackay wrote to Walter, 'Your Royal Highness: Discovering you and your family has been the happiest accomplishment of my life. And if God in His infinite wisdom should deny me the opportunity to meet you face to face on this Earth, I should still count myself the luckiest of men for this chance to play a part, however small, in restoring Scotland to her former greatness. Please know that you are in my thoughts and prayers every day. And that I will work with every ounce of my being to restore you from your sad exile to the land, the goods, and the reverence to which you, by the grace of God, are entitled.' A boy doesn't get a letter like that very often. He kept it under his mattress, he knew it by heart. He lay in bed and thought, over and over, 'the land, the goods, and the reverence to which you are entitled'.

The Tollefsons and other people in town, of course, had gotten wind of those letters from Philadelphia and were curious; they tried to pry the secret out of the children, but they wouldn't tell, and then some people began to resent them for keeping a secret. Lawrence said to Grace, 'You know, Grace, sometimes you act like you think you're too good to walk on the same ground with us.' She told him that she figured she was at least as good as anyone else. He said that if she was, maybe she'd like to try supporting herself. 'Gladly,' she replied.

They packed up to move back to Saint Paul. Lawrence packed their old donated furniture in a trailer but at the last minute Grace said, 'Take it off. I don't want to take that with me. That's not mine. That belongs to the church.'

'You might need it. Don't be so proud,' he said. She looked at him. She said, 'Lawrence, what I need in this life is understanding and love. And I need style. And I won't be carrying it with me from Lake Wobegon. I'm going to have to find it where I'm going.' The children sat in the back seat and looked at the neighbors who'd come to look at them as they left. Marlys held the Whitehursts on her lap. 'Someday, when we're the Royal Family, they'll have a parade here in our honor. And I'm not going to come,' she announced.

Life in Saint Paul has not been easy for them. Earl moved away a few years ago, he was tired of the whole business. He went to school to study bookkeeping and got a job in a salvage yard, as a bookkeeper. Grace had him sign a paper relinquishing all rights to succession. Marlys is twenty-four and still lives with her mother in their apartment near the State Fair grounds and so does Walter, a student at Hamline University. Over the years they've read all the histories of Scotland, learned its geography, and studied over and over the sad story of the House of Stewart, from which they're descended. That the English in 1688 overthrew their true and rightful king, James the Seventh, and brought in the Dutchman William of Orange, and when William and Mary bred no successor, the Stewarts were waiting in the wings, glad to forgive the English and come and be King and Queen again. But no, England sent to Germany for a motley bunch of princes from the House of Hanover. Brought them in and made them royalty. In 1746, Bonnie Prince Charlie came over from France and rallied his brave Highlanders and marched south into England and won battles against the English, then, for some reason, turned around and went back. And in April, at the Battle of Culloden, his army and his hopes were torn to shreds, and the Stewarts went over the hill into history.

Whenever Grace saw an article about Queen Elizabeth in the paper, she bit her lip and shook her head. Usurpers was what they were, all of them. *Germans*, sitting on the Royal Throne of Scotland. It wasn't right. It wasn't even decent.

Year after year, month after month, letters arrived from D. R. Mackay: he was forming a committee for the restoration of the House of Stewart to the throne, he was enlisting the help of other governments – secret meetings had been held and overtures made and some very encouraging signals had been received, *extremely* encouraging – he didn't want the Family to be troubled with details but he had been encouraged by the French, the Spanish, the Portuguese, and even the Americans had indicated an interest – so it could happen any time, they should prepare themselves. Whenever their faith was low, Grace read the letters out loud and she turned to Walter and said, 'Walter, tell us what it'll be like when we get the call.'

He said: 'It'll come at eight thirty in the evening on a summer day. August. We'll have eaten sweetcorn and tomatoes and hot dogs for supper, and the phone rings and they tell us to be on a plane the next morning. We'll be too excited to sleep. We'll go to the airport, exhausted, and get on the plane. Mother is wearing her good navy-blue dress, Marlys her silk bridesmaid dress from Nancy's wedding, I have my dark wool suit on. We land in Glasgow. There are huge crowds of people. Six men in blue pinstripe suits get on the plane, they're from Scotland Yard, they escort us to a helicopter. We fly to Holyrood Castle on High Street in Edinburgh. We're taken in to freshen up and have a light lunch and we can hear a low roar outside, and after a while we'll go up to the balcony – there is the balustrade, with thirteen microphones. And down there are a hundred thousand Scots. And we walk forward and speak.'

'You do it, Walter. I'm too nervous,' said Grace.

He often thought what he would say. Perhaps something humorous like 'How much is all this costing?' Or 'Nice to see ya.' But he'd aim for something royal and dignified. It was wonderful to imagine being restored and going to Scotland and being the Royal Family, though more modest than the Germans down in Buckingham Palace – they wouldn't need a private yacht or jet planes or new dresses to go off to fancy balls in – the Scottish Family didn't need all that. They'd be a good royal family, thrifty and sensible and plain. Having known poverty, they would eschew excess; whatever was satisfactory would be good enough.

Two weeks ago they received a telegram from their father, saying, 'Wire money. Five hundred dollars. Need desperately. Signed, Alex.' Grace didn't know what to do. Alex! What if he – Walter said, 'Don't do anything. If he can wire us, he can call us.' Three days later he called. Walter had never heard his father's voice. It said, 'Walter! This is wonderful. So good to talk to you. I think about you every day. How old are you?'

'Twenty-four, Dad.'

'My God. It doesn't seem that long ago.'

'Well, I get a year older every year, just like everybody else.'

'Walter,' he said, 'I need money. I don't need five hundred dollars. I need more like five thousand. I've been indicted for mail fraud. I didn't do anything wrong. Nothing to hurt people. But they want to put me away for ten, fifteen years, and Walter, I'm too old to go to prison. I gotta leave the country.'

'What is it you did?'

His father said, 'I was in the genealogy business. I made up family trees for people. But I can explain – let me tell you, son –' Walter's face went flat and numb. He said, 'You didn't! God. You did this to us. Why did you do this?'

'I meant to tell you before this. I really meant to tell you. It was meant as a gift, I wanted you to be proud. I knew how those Tollefsons would pity you – I wanted you to be so proud of the Campbell family that I wouldn't have to come crawling back. I hoped you would come and find me.'

Walter said he'd send him as much money as he could, and put down the phone. Grace said, 'You didn't tell him then about our secret.' Walter said, no, there'd be time to tell him later.

She said, 'Oh, Walter, what would I do without you? You're so strong. You're so good to me. You're a prince, you know. They can put a crown on a dog and call it a prince, but you are a prince through and through. They may not know it now, but they'll know it soon. Next year we'll be in Edinburgh with the bands playing and the flags flying and the crowds cheering.'

T. CORAGHESSAN BOYLE

Modern Love

T. Coraghessan Boyle (1948–) was born in Peekskill, New York, grandson of Irish immigrants, and he played drums in a rock band before publishing fiction. He teaches creative writing, and is known as one of the most innovative writers of his generation. His novels include *World's End* (1988), *East Is East* (1988) and *The Road to Wellville* (1993), about the American mania to live to be 110. He has published three volumes of stories: *Descent of Man* (1980), *Greasy Lake* (1985) and *If the River Was Whiskey* (1993), brought together as *The Collected Stories of T. Coraghessan Boyle* (1993).

'Modern Love', from the collection *Greasy Lake*, first appeared in *Playboy* magazine, and displays Boyle's skills as a contemporary satirist and his energetic comic invention. It is an ironic and wonderfully worked anecdote about the antiseptic nature of modern sexuality and gender relations, and reflects the preoccupation with health which has been a recurrent theme in Boyle's work. He is a writer of very varied tones, but one of them is satire, which has proved to be the impulse behind some of his best stories (see, for example, 'Dada', 'The Woman's Restaurant', or 'Hard Sell', about a PR man trying to improve the Ayatollah's image in America) and an important part of his contribution to contemporary writing.

There was no exchange of body fluids on the first date, and that suited both of us just fine. I picked her up at seven, took her to Mee Grop, where she meticulously separated each sliver of meat from her Phat Thai, watched her down four bottles of Singha at three dollars per, and then gently stroked her balsam-smelling hair while she snoozed through *The Terminator* at the Circle Shopping Center theater. We had a late-night drink at Rigoletto's Pizza Bar (and two slices, plain cheese), and I dropped her off. The moment we pulled up in front of her apartment she had the door open. She turned to me with the long, elegant, mournful face of her Puritan ancestors and held out her hand.

'It's been fun,' she said.

'Yes,' I said, taking her hand.

She was wearing gloves.

'I'll call you,' she said.

'Good,' I said, giving her my richest smile. 'And I'll call you.'

On the second date we got acquainted.

'I can't tell you what a strain it was for me the other night,' she said, staring down into her chocolate-mocha-fudge sundae. It was early afternoon, we were in Helmut's Olde Tyme Ice Cream Parlor in Mamaroneck, and the sun streamed through the thick frosted windows and lit the place like a convalescent home. The fixtures glowed behind the counter, the brass rail was buffed to a reflective sheen, and everything smelled of disinfectant. We were the only people in the place.

'What do you mean?' I said, my mouth glutinous with melted marshmallow and caramel.

'I mean Thai food, the seats in the movie theater, the *ladies' room* in that place for God's sake . . .'

'Thai food?' I wasn't following her. I recalled the maneuver with the strips of pork and the fastidious dissection of the glass noodles. 'You're a vegetarian?'

She looked away in exasperation, and then gave me the full, wide-eyed shock of her ice-blue eyes. 'Have you seen the Health Department statistics on sanitary conditions in ethnic restaurants?'

I hadn't.

Her eyebrows leapt up. She was earnest. She was lecturing. 'These people are refugees. They have – well, different standards. They haven't even been inoculated.' I watched her dig the tiny spoon into the recesses of the dish and part her lips for a neat, foursquare morsel of ice-cream and fudge.

'The illegals, anyway. And that's half of them.' She swallowed with an almost imperceptible movement, a shudder, her throat dipping and rising like a gazelle's. 'I got drunk from fear,' she said. 'Blind panic. I couldn't help thinking I'd wind up with hepatitis or dysentery or dengue fever or something.'

'Dengue fever?'

'I usually bring a disposable sanitary sheet for public theaters – just think of who might have been in that seat before you, and how many times, and what sort of nasty festering little cultures of this and that there must be in all those ancient dribbles of taffy and Coke and extra-butter popcorn – but I didn't want you to think I was too extreme or anything on the first date, so I didn't. And then the *ladies' room* ... You don't think I'm overreacting, do you?'

As a matter of fact, I did. Of course I did. I liked Thai food – and sushi and ginger crab and greasy souvlaki at the corner stand too. There was the look of the mad saint in her eye, the obsessive, the mortifier of the flesh, but I didn't care. She was lovely, wilting, clear-eyed, and pure, as cool and matchless as if she'd stepped out of a Pre-Raphaelite painting, and I was in love. Besides, I tended a little that way myself. Hypochondria. Anal retentiveness. The ordered environment and alphabetized books. I was a thirty-three-year-old bachelor, I carried some scars and I read the newspapers – herpes, Aids, the Asian clap that foiled every antibiotic in the book. I was willing to take it slow. 'No,' I said, 'I don't think you're overreacting at all.'

I paused to draw in a breath so deep it might have been a sigh. 'I'm sorry,' I whispered, giving her a dog-like look of contrition. 'I didn't know.'

She reached out then and touched my hand – touched it, skin to skin – and murmured that it was all right, she'd been through worse. 'If you want to know,' she breathed, 'I like places like this.'

I glanced around. The place was still empty, but for Helmut, in a blinding white jumpsuit and toque, studiously polishing the tile walls. 'I know what you mean,' I said.

We dated for a month – museums, drives in the country, French and German restaurants, ice-cream emporia, fern bars – before we kissed. And when we kissed, after a showing of *David and Lisa* at a revival house all the way up in Rhinebeck and on a night so cold no run-of-the-mill bacterium or commonplace virus could have survived it, it was the merest brushing of the lips. She was wearing a big-shouldered coat of synthetic fur and a knit hat pulled down over her brow and she hugged my arm as we stepped out of the theater and into the blast of the night. 'God,' she said, 'did you see him when he screamed "You touched me!"? Wasn't that priceless?' Her eyes were big and she seemed weirdly excited. 'Sure,' I said, 'yeah, it was great,' and then she pulled me close and kissed me. I felt the soft flicker of her lips against mine. 'I love you,' she said, 'I think.'

A month of dating and one dry fluttering kiss. At this point you might begin to wonder about me, but really, I didn't mind. As I say, I was willing to wait – I had the patience of Sisyphus – and it was enough just to be with her. Why rush things? I thought. This is good, this is charming, like the slow sweet unfolding of the romance in a Frank Capra movie, where sweetness and light always prevail. Sure, she had her idiosyncrasies, but who didn't? Frankly, I'd never been comfortable with the three-drinks-dinner-and-bed sort of thing, the girls who come on like they've been in prison for six years and just got out in time to put on their make-up and jump into the passenger seat of your car. Breda – that was her name, Breda Drumhill, and the very sound and syllabification of it made me melt – was different.

Finally, two weeks after the trek to Rhinebeck, she invited me to her apartment. Cocktails, she said. Dinner. A quiet evening in front of the tube.

She lived in Croton, on the ground floor of a restored Victorian, half a mile from the Harmon station, where she caught the train each morning for Manhattan and her job as an editor of *Anthropology Today*. She'd held the job since graduating from Barnard six years earlier (with a double major in Rhetoric and Alien Cultures), and it suited her temperament perfectly. Field anthropologists living among the River Dyak of Borneo or the Kurds of Kurdistan would send her rough and grammatically tortured accounts of their observations and she would whip them into shape for popular consumption. Naturally, filth and exotic disease, as well as outlandish customs and revolting habits, played a leading role in her rewrites. Every other day or so she'd call me from work and in a voice that could barely contain its joy give me the details of some new and horrific disease she'd discovered.

She met me at the door in a silk kimono that featured a plunging neckline and a pair of dragons with intertwined tails. Her hair was pinned up as if she'd just stepped out of the bath and she smelled of Noxzema and pHisoHex. She pecked my cheek, took the bottle of Vouvray I held out in offering, and led me into the front room. 'Chagas' disease,' she said, grinning wide to show off her perfect, outsized teeth.

'Chagas' disease?' I echoed, not quite knowing what to do with myself. The room was as spare as a monk's cell. Two chairs, a loveseat, and a coffee table, in glass, chrome, and hard black plastic. No plants ('God knows what sort of insects might live on them – and the *dirt*, the dirt has got to be crawling with bacteria, not to mention spiders and worms and things') and no rug ('A breeding ground for fleas and ticks and chiggers').

Still grinning, she steered me to the hard black plastic loveseat and sat down beside me, the Vouvray cradled in her lap. 'South America,' she whispered, her eyes leaping with excitement. 'In the jungle. These bugs –

295

assassin bugs, they're called – isn't that wild? These bugs bite you and then, after they've sucked on you a while, they go potty next to the wound. When you scratch, it gets into your bloodstream, and anywhere from one to twenty years later you get a disease that's like a cross between malaria and Aids.'

'And then you die,' I said.

'And then you die.'

Her voice had turned somber. She wasn't grinning any longer. What could I say? I patted her hand and flashed a smile. 'Yum,' I said, mugging for her. 'What's for dinner?'

She served a cold cream-of-tofu-carrot soup and little lentil-paste sandwiches for an appetizer and a garlic soufflé with biologically controlled vegetables for the entrée. Then it was snifters of cognac, the big-screen TV, and a movie called *The Boy in the Bubble*, about a kid raised in a totally antiseptic environment because he was born without an immune system. No one could touch him. Even the slightest sneeze would have killed him. Breda sniffled through the first half-hour, then pressed my hand and sobbed openly as the boy finally crawled out of the bubble, caught about thirty-seven different diseases, and died before the commercial break. 'I've seen this movie six times now,' she said, fighting to control her voice, 'and it gets to me every time. What a life,' she said, waving her snifter at the screen, 'what a perfect life. Don't you envy him?'

I didn't envy him. I envied the jade pendant that dangled between her breasts and I told her so.

She might have giggled or gasped or lowered her eyes, but she didn't. She gave me a long slow look, as if she were deciding something, and then she allowed herself to blush, the color suffusing her throat in a delicious mottle of pink and white. 'Give me a minute,' she said mysteriously, and disappeared into the bathroom.

I was electrified. This was it. Finally. After all the avowals, the pressed hands, the little jokes and routines, after all the miles driven, meals consumed, museums paced, and movies watched, we were finally, naturally, gracefully going to come together in the ultimate act of intimacy and love.

I felt hot. There were beads of sweat on my forehead. I didn't know whether to stand or sit. And then the lights dimmed, and there she was at the rheostat.

She was still in her kimono, but her hair was pinned up more severely, wound in a tight coil to the crown of her head, as if she'd girded herself for battle. And she held something in her hand – a slim package, wrapped in plastic. It rustled as she crossed the room.

'When you're in love, you make love,' she said, easing down beside me on the rock-like settee, '– it's only natural.' She handed me the package. 'I don't want to give you the wrong impression,' she said, her voice throaty and raw, 'just because I'm careful and modest and because there's so much, well, filth in the world, but I have my passionate side too. I do. And I love you, I think.'

'Yes,' I said, groping for her, the package all but forgotten.

We kissed. I rubbed the back of her neck, felt something strange, an odd sag and ripple, as if her skin had suddenly turned to Saran Wrap, and then she had her hand on my chest. 'Wait,' she breathed, 'the, the thing.'

I sat up. 'Thing?'

The light was dim but I could see the blush invade her face now. She was sweet. Oh, she was sweet, my Little Em'ly, my Victorian princess. 'It's Swedish,' she said.

I looked down at the package in my lap. It was a clear, skinlike sheet of plastic, folded up in its transparent package like a heavy-duty garbage bag. I held it up to her huge, trembling eyes. A crazy idea darted in and out of my head. No, I thought.

'It's the newest thing,' she said, the words coming in a rush, 'the safest . . . I mean, nothing could possibly –'

My face was hot. 'No,' I said.

'It's a condom,' she said, tears starting up in her eyes, 'my doctor got them for me, they're . . . they're Swedish.' Her face wrinkled up and she began to cry. 'It's a condom,' she sobbed, crying so hard the kimono fell open and I could see the outline of the thing against the swell of her nipples, 'a full-body condom.'

I was offended. I admit it. It wasn't so much her obsession with germs and contagion, but that she didn't trust me after all that time. I was clean. Quintessentially clean. I was a man of moderate habits and good health, I changed my underwear and socks daily – sometimes twice a day – and I worked in an office, with clean, crisp, unequivocal numbers, managing my late father's chain of shoe stores (and he died cleanly himself, of a myocardial infarction, at seventy-five). 'But Breda,' I said, reaching out to console her and brushing her soft, plastic-clad breast in the process, 'don't you trust me? Don't you believe in me? Don't you, don't you love me?' I took her by the shoulders, lifted her head, forced her to look me in the eye. 'I'm clean,' I said. 'Trust me.'

She looked away. 'Do it for me,' she said in her smallest voice, 'if you really love me.'

In the end, I did it. I looked at her, crying, crying for me, and I looked at the thin sheet of plastic clinging to her, and I did it. She helped me into the thing, poked two holes for my nostrils, zipped the plastic zipper up the back, and pulled it tight over my head. It fit like a wetsuit. And the whole thing – the stroking and the tenderness and the gentle yielding – was everything I'd hoped it would be.

Almost.

She called me from work the next day. I was playing with sales figures and thinking of her. 'Hello,' I said, practically cooing into the receiver.

'You've got to hear this.' Her voice was giddy with excitement.

'Hey,' I said, cutting her off in a passionate whisper, 'last night was really special.'

'Oh, yes,' she said, 'yes, last night. It was. And I love you. I do . . .' She paused to draw in her breath. 'But listen to this: I just got a piece from a man and his wife living among the Tuareg of Nigeria – these are the people who follow cattle around, picking up the dung for their cooking fires?'

I made a small noise of awareness.

'Well, they make their huts of dung too – isn't that wild? And guess what – when times are hard, when the crops fail and the cattle can barely stand up, you know what they eat?'

'Let me guess,' I said. 'Dung?'

She let out a whoop. 'Yes! Yes! Isn't it too much? They *eat* dung!'

I'd been saving one for her, a disease a doctor friend had told me about. 'Onchocerciasis,' I said. 'You know it?'

There was a thrill in her voice. 'Tell me.'

'South America and Africa both. A fly bites you and lays its eggs in your bloodstream and when the eggs hatch, the larvae – these little white worms – migrate to your eyeballs, right underneath the membrane there, so you can see them wriggling around.'

There was a silence on the other end of the line.

'Breda?'

'That's sick,' she said. 'That's really sick.'

But I thought –? I trailed off. 'Sorry,' I said.

'Listen,' and the edge came back into her voice, 'the reason I called is because I love you, I think I love you, and I want you to meet somebody.'

'Sure,' I said.

'I want you to meet Michael. Michael Maloney.'

'Sure. Who's he?'

She hesitated, paused just a beat, as if she knew she was going too far. 'My doctor.' she said.

You have to work at love. You have to bend, make subtle adjustments, sacrifices – love is nothing without sacrifice. I went to Dr Maloney. Why not? I'd eaten tofu, bantered about leprosy and bilharziasis as if I were immune, and made love in a bag. If it made Breda happy – if it eased the nagging fears that ate at her day and night – then it was worth it.

The doctor's office was in Scarsdale, in his home, a two-tone mock Tudor with a winding drive and oaks as old as my grandfather's Chrysler. He was a young man – late thirties, I guessed – with a red beard, shaved head, and a pair of over-sized spectacles in clear plastic frames. He took me right away – the very day I called – and met me at the door himself. 'Breda's told me about you,' he said, leading me into the floodlit vault of his office. He looked at me appraisingly a moment, murmuring 'Yes, yes' into his beard, and then, with the aid of his nurses, Miss Archibald and Miss Slivovitz, put me through a battery of tests that would have embarrassed an astronaut.

First, there were the measurements, including digital joints, maxilla, cranium, penis, and earlobe. Next the rectal exam, the EEG and urine sample. And then the tests. Stress tests, patch tests, reflex tests, lung-capacity tests (I blew up yellow balloons till they popped, then breathed into a machine the size of a Hammond organ), the X-rays, sperm count, and a closely printed, twenty-four-page questionnaire that included sections on dream analysis, genealogy, and logic and reasoning. He drew blood too, of course – to test vital-organ function and exposure to disease. 'We're testing for antibodies to over fifty diseases,' he said, eyes dodging behind the walls of his lenses. 'You'd be surprised how many people have been infected without even knowing it.' I couldn't tell if he was joking or not. On the way out he took my arm and told me he'd have the results in a week.

That week was the happiest of my life. I was with Breda every night, and over the weekend we drove up to Vermont to stay at a hygiene center her cousin had told her about. We dined by candlelight – on real food – and afterward we donned the Saran Wrap suits and made joyous, sanitary love. I wanted more, of course – the touch of skin on skin – but I was fulfilled and I was happy. Go slow, I told myself. All things in time. One night, as we lay entwined in the big white fortress of her bed, I stripped back the hood of the plastic suit and asked her if she'd ever trust me enough to make love in the way of the centuries, raw and unprotected. She twisted free of her own wrapping and looked away, giving me that matchless patrician profile. 'Yes,' she said, her voice pitched low, 'yes, of course. Once the results are in.'

'Results?'

She turned to me, her eyes searching mine. 'Don't tell me you've forgotten?'

I had. Carried away, intense, passionate, brimming with love, I'd forgotten.

'Silly you,' she murmured, tracing the line of my lips with a slim, plastic-clad finger. 'Does the name Michael Maloney ring a bell?'

*

And then the roof fell in.

I called and there was no answer. I tried her at work and her secretary said she was out. I left messages. She never called back. It was as if we'd never known one another, as if I were a stranger, a door-to-door salesman, a beggar on the street.

I took up a vigil in front of her house. For a solid week I sat in my parked car and watched the door with all the fanatic devotion of a pilgrim at a shrine. Nothing. She neither came nor went. I rang the phone off the hook, interrogated her friends, haunted the elevator, the hallway, and the reception room at her office. She'd disappeared.

Finally, in desperation, I called her cousin in Larchmont. I'd met her once – she was a homely, droopy-sweatered, baleful-looking girl who represented everything gone wrong in the genes that had come to such glorious fruition in Breda – and barely knew what to say to her. I'd made up a speech, something about how my mother was dying in Phoenix, the business was on the rocks, I was drinking too much and dwelling on thoughts of suicide, destruction, and final judgment, and I had to talk to Breda just one more time before the end, and did she by any chance know where she was? As it turned out, I didn't need the speech. Breda answered the phone.

'Breda, it's me,' I choked. 'I've been going crazy looking for you.'

Silence.

'Breda, what's wrong? Didn't you get my messages?'

Her voice was halting, distant. 'I can't see you anymore,' she said.

'Can't see me?' I was stunned, hurt, angry. 'What do you mean?'

'All those feet,' she said.

'Feet?' It took me a minute to realize she was talking about the shoe business. 'But I don't deal with anybody's feet – I work in an office. Like you. With air-conditioning and sealed windows. I haven't touched a foot since I was sixteen.'

'Athlete's foot,' she said. 'Psoriasis. Eczema. Jungle rot.'

'What is it? The physical?' My voice cracked with outrage. 'Did I flunk the damn physical? Is that it?'

She wouldn't answer me.

A chill went through me. 'What did he say? What did the son of a bitch say?'

There was a distant ticking over the line, the pulse of time and space, the gentle sway of Bell Telephone's hundred million miles of wire.

'Listen,' I pleaded, 'see me one more time, just once – that's all I ask. We'll talk it over. We could go on a picnic. In the park. We could spread a blanket and, and we could sit on opposite corners –'

'Lyme disease,' she said.

'Lyme disease?'

'Spread by tick bite. They're seething in the grass. You get Bell's palsy, meningitis, the lining of your brain swells up like dough.'

'Rockefeller Center then,' I said. 'By the fountain.'

Her voice was dead. 'Pigeons,' she said. 'They're like flying rats.'

'Helmut's. We can meet at Helmut's. Please. I love you.'

'I'm sorry.'

'Breda, please listen to me. We were so close –'

'Yes,' she said, 'we were close,' and I thought of that first night in her apartment, the boy in the bubble and the Saran Wrap suit, thought of the whole dizzy spectacle of our romance till her voice came down like a hammer on the refrain, 'but not that close.'

CLARE BOYLAN

The Stolen Child

Clare Boylan (1948–) was born and grew up in Dublin, which provides the setting for much of her fiction. She has worked widely as a journalist and her several novels include *Holy Pictures* (1983), *Last Resorts* (1986) and *Black Baby* (1989). She has written many short stories, collected in *A Nail on the Head* (1983) and *Concerning Virgins* (1989). She is also the editor of *The Agony and the Ego: The Art and Strategy of Fiction Writing Explored* (1993), a collection of essays by practising writers on their art.

'The Stolen Child' comes from *Writing on the Wall* and was originally written as a commentary on a painting, *L'Infirmière*, an idealized portrait of a mother and her child by the (childless) painter Beatrice How (1867–1932). Boylan remarks of the painting that it is only for the childless that the ideal of maternity really endures, and 'The Stolen Child' is a wicked treatment of that theme, cleverly told through the very distinctive and unnerving first-person voice of an aspiring mother who, when she commits the extreme offence and steals someone else's baby, quickly learns the darker lessons of motherhood. Like others of Boylan's stories, this is an unmasking of the strange, odd nature of maternal feeling, and the quirky if not menacing ways in which it expresses itself.

Women steal other people's husbands so why shouldn't they steal other people's babies? Mothers leave babies everywhere. They leave them with foreign students while they go out gallivanting, hand them over to strangers for years on end, who stuff them with dead languages and computer science. I knew a woman who left her baby on the bus. She was halfway down Grafton Street when she got this funny feeling and she said, 'Oh, my God, I've left my handbag,' and then with a surge of relief she felt the strap of her bag cutting into her wrist and remembered the baby.

I never wanted to steal another woman's husband. Whatever you might make of a man if you got him first-hand, there's no doing anything once some other woman's been at him, started scraping off the first layer of paint to see what's underneath, then decided she didn't like it, and left him like that all scratchy and patchy.

Babies come unpainted. They have their own smell, like new wood has. They've got no barriers. Mothers go at their offspring the way a man goes at a virgin, no shame or mercy. A woman once told me she used to bite her baby's bum when she changed its nappy. Other women have to stand back, but nature's nature.

Sometimes I dream of babies. Once there were two in a wooden cradle high up on a shelf. They had very small dark faces, like Russian icons, and I climbed on a chair to get at them. Then I saw their parents sitting up in bed, watching me. I have a dream about a little girl, three or four, who runs behind to catch up with me. She says nothing but her hand burrows into mine and her fingers tap on my palm. Now and then I have a baby in my sleep, although I don't remember anything about it. It's handed to me, and I know it's mine, and I just gaze into the opaque blueness of the eye that's like the sky, as if everything and nothing lies behind.

It comes over you like a craving. You stand beside a pram and stare the way a woman on a diet might stare at a bar of chocolate in a shop window. You can't say anything. It's taboo, like cannibalism. Your middle goes hollow and you walk away stiff-legged, as if you have to pee.

Or maybe you don't.

It happened just like that. I'd come out of the supermarket. There were three infants, left lying around in strollers. I stopped to put on my headscarf and I looked at the babies, the way people do. I don't know what did it to me, but I think it was the texture. There was this chrysalis look. I was wondering what they felt like. To tell the truth my mouth was watering just for a touch. Then one of them turned with jerky movements to look at me.

'Hello,' I said. She stirred in her blankets and blew a tiny bubble. She put out a toe to explore the air. She looked so new, so completely new, that I was mad to have her. It's like when you see some dress in a shop window and you have to have it because you think it will definitely change your life. Her skin was rose soft and I had a terrible urge to touch it. 'Plenty of time for that,' I thought as my foot kicked the brake of the pram.

Mothers don't count their blessings. They complain all the time and they resent women without children, as if they've got away with something. They see you as an alien species. Talk about a woman scorned! And it's not men who scorn you. They simply don't notice you at all. It's other women who treat you like the cat daring to look at the king. They don't care for women like me, they don't trust us. Well, I don't like them much either.

I was at the bus stop one day and this woman came along with a toddler by the hand and a baby in a push-car. 'Terrible day!' I said. Well it was. Cats and dogs. She gave me a look as if she was about to ask for a search warrant and then turned away and commenced a performance of pulling up hoods and shoving on mittens. It wasn't the rain. She didn't even notice the rain, soaked to the bone, hair stuck to her head like a bag of worms. She had all this shopping, spilling out of plastic bags, and she bent down and began undoing her parcels, arranging them in the tray underneath the baby's seat, as if to say to me, 'This is our world. We don't need your sort.' Not that I need telling.

It was a relief when the bus came – but that was short-lived. I don't know why mothers can't be more organized. She hoisted the toddler on to the platform and then got up herself, leaving the baby all alone in the rain to register its despair. 'You've forgotten the baby,' I said, and she gave me a very dirty look. She lunged outward and seized the handles of the pram and tried to manhandle it up after her, but it was too heavy. Sullen as mud, she plunged back out into the rain. This time the toddler was abandoned on the bus and it opened its little mouth and set up a pitiful screeching. She unstrapped the baby and sort of flung it up on the bus. Everyone was looking. Back she clambered, leaned out again and wrestled the pram on board, as if some sort of battle to the death was involved. I don't think the woman was in her right mind. Of course, half the groceries fell out into the gutter and the baby followed. 'You're going about that all wrong,' I told her, but she took no notice. The driver then woke up and said he couldn't take her as there was already one push-car on the bus. Do you think she apologized for keeping everyone waiting? No! She merely gave me a most unpleasant glance, as if I was the one to blame.

Walking away from the supermarket with someone else's child, I didn't feel guilty. I was cleansed, absolved of the guilt of not fitting in. I loved that baby. I felt connected to her by all the parts that unglamorous single women aren't supposed to have. I believed we were allies. She seemed to understand that I needed her more than her mother did and I experienced a great well of pity for her helplessness. She could do nothing without me and I would do anything in the world for her. I wheeled the pram out through the car park, not too quickly. Once I even stopped to settle her blankets. Oh, she was the sweetest thing. Several people smiled into the pram. When I gave her a little tickle, she laughed. I think I have a natural talent as a mother. I look at other women with their kids and think, 'She's doing that all wrong, she doesn't deserve to have her.' I notice things. The worst mothers are the ones with too many kids. Just like my mum. They bash them and yell at them and then they give them sweets. Just like this woman I saw watching me from the doorway of the supermarket. She seemed completely surrounded by children. There must have been seven of them. One kid was being belted by another and a third was scuttling off out under a car. And she just watched me intently with this pinched little face and I knew she was envying me my natural ease as a mother. I knew a widow once, used to leave her baby in the dog's basket with the dog when she went out to work.

And all this time, while I was pushing and plotting, where was her mother? She might have been in the newsagent's, flipping the pages of magazines, or giving herself a moustache of cappuccino in the coffee shop, or in the supermarket gazing at bloated purple figs and dreaming of a lover. Mothers, who swear that they would die in an instant for you, are never there when you need them. Luckily, there is frequently someone on hand, as for instance myself, who was now wheeling the poor little thing out of harm's way, and not, if you ask me, before time.

I can't remember ever being so happy. There was a sense of purpose, the feeling of being needed. And you'll laugh now, but for the first time in my life, looking into that sweet little face, I felt that I was understood.

When my mum died I got depressed and they sent me along to see a psychiatrist. He said to me, 'You're young. You have to make a life of your own.' I was furious. 'Hardly anyone makes a life of their own,' I told him. 'They get their lives made for them.' He asked me about my social life and I said I went to the pictures once in a while. 'You could put an advertisement in one of the personal columns,' he said.

'Advertisement for what?' I said.

'A companion,' he said.

'Just like that?' I must say I thought that was a good one. 'You put an advertisement in the paper and you get a companion?' I pictured a fattish little girl of about ten with long plaits.

'People do,' he promised me. 'Or you could go to an introduction agency.'

'And what sort of thing would you say in this advertisement?'

'You could say you were an attractive woman, early thirties, seeking kind gentleman friend, view to matrimony.'

I was so mad. I lashed out at him with my handbag. 'You said a companion. You never said anything about a gentleman friend.'

Well, I make out all right. I got a bit of part-time work and I took up a hobby. I became a shoplifter. Many people are compelled to do things that are outside their moral strictures in these straitened times, but personally I took to shoplifting like a duck to water. It gave me a lift and enabled me to sample a lot of interesting things. The trick is, you pay for the bulky items and put away the small ones, fork out for the sliced loaf, pinch the kiwi fruit, proffer for the potatoes, take the pâté, pay for the firelighters, stash the little tray of fillet steaks. In this way I added a lot of variety to my diet – lumpfish roe and anchovies and spiced olives and smoked salmon, although I also accumulated a lot of sliced bread. 'Use your imagination,' I told myself. 'There are other bulky items besides sliced loaves.'

Perhaps it was the pack of nappies in my trolley that did it. I hate waste. It also just happened that the first sympathetic face I saw that day (in years, in point of fact) was that tiny baby left outside in her pram to wave her toe around in the cold air, so I took her too.

I thought I'd call her Vera. It sounded like the name of a person who'd been around for a long time, or as if I'd called her after my mother. When I got home the first thing I did was to pick her up. Oh, she felt just lovely, like nothing at all. I went over to the mirror to see what kind of a pair we made. We looked a picture. She took years off my age.

Vera was looking around in a vaguely disgruntled way, as if she could smell burning. 'Milk,' I thought. 'She wants milk.' I kept her balanced on my arm while I warmed up some milk. It was a nice feeling, although inconvenient. I would have to get used to that. It was like smoking in the bath. I had to carry her back with the saucepan, and a spoon, and a dishtowel for a bib. Natural mothers don't have to ferret around with saucepans and spoons. They have everything to hand, inside their slip. I tried to feed her off a spoon but she blew at it instead of sucking. There was milk in my hair and on my cardigan and quite a lot of it went on the sofa, which is a kingfisher pattern, blue on cream. After a while she pushed the cup away and her face folded up as if she was going to cry. 'Oh, sorry, sweetheart,' I said. 'Who's a stupid mummy?' She needed her nappy changed.

To tell the truth I had been looking forward to this. Women complain about the plain duties of motherhood but to me she was like a present that was waiting to be unwrapped. I carried her back downstairs and filled a basin with warm water and put a lot of towels over my arm. How did I manage this, you ask? Well, a trail of water from kitchen to sofa tells the tale – but I managed the talc and the nappies and a sponge and all the other bits and pieces. I was proud of myself. I almost wished there was someone there to see.

By now Vera was a bit uneasy (perhaps I should have played some music, like women do to babies in the womb, but I don't know much about music). I took off the little pink jacket, the pink romper suit that was like a hot-water-bottle cover and then started to unwrap the nappy. A jet of water shot up into my eye. I was startled and none too pleased. I rubbed my eye and began again, removing all that soggy padding. Then I slammed it shut. The child looked gratified and started to chortle. Incredulous, I peeled the swaddling back once more. My jaw hung off its hinges. Growing out of the bottom of its belly was a wicked little ruddy horn. I found myself looking at balls as big as pomegranates and when I could tear my eyes away from them I had to look into his eye, a man's eye, already calculating and bargaining.

It was a boy. Who the hell wants a boy?

'Hypocrite!' I said to him. 'Going round with that nice little face.'

Vera stuck out his lower lip.

Imagine the nerve of the mother, dressing him up in pink, palming him off as a girl! Imagine, I could still be taken in by a man.

Now the problem with helping yourself to things, as opposed to coming by them lawfully, is that you have no redress. You have to take what you get. On the other hand, as a general rule, this makes you less particular. I decided to play it cool. 'The thing is, Vera,' I told him (I would change his name later. The shock was too great to adjust to all at once), 'I always thought of babies as female. It simply never occurred to me that they came in the potential rapist mode. Now, clearly there are points in your favour. You do look very nice with all your clothes on. On the other hand, I can't take to your sort as a species.'

I was quite pleased with that. I thought it very moderate and rational. Vera was looking at me in the strangest way, with a sweet, intent, intelligent look. Clearly he was concentrating. There is something to be said for the intelligent male. Maybe he and I would get along. 'The keynote,' I told him, 'is compromise. We'll have to give each other plenty of space.' Vera smiled. He looked relieved. It was a weight off my mind too. Then I got this smell. It dawned on me with horror the reason for his concentration. 'No!' I moaned. 'My mother's Sanderson!' I swooped on him and swagged him without looking too closely. His blue eyes no longer seemed opaque and new but very old and angry. He opened his mouth and began to bawl. Have you ever known a man who could compromise?

All that afternoon I gazed in wonder on the child who had melted my innards and compelled me to crime. Within the space of half an hour he had been transformed. His face took on the scalded red of a baboon's behind and he bellowed like a bull. His eyes were brilliant chips of ice behind a wall of boiling water. I got the feeling it wasn't even personal. It was just what he did whenever he thought of it. I changed his nappy and bounced him on my knee until his brains must have scrambled. I tried making him a mush of bread and milk and sugar, which he scarcely touched, yet still managed to return in great quantity over my ear. With rattling hands I strapped him into the stroller and took him for a walk. Out of doors the noise became a metallic booming. People glared at me and moved away and crows fell off their perches in the trees. Everything seemed distorted by the sound. I felt quite mad with tiredness. My legs seemed to be melting and when I looked at the sky the clouds had a fizzing, dangerous look. I wanted to lie flat on the pavement. You can't when you're a mother. Your life's not your own any more. I realized now that the mother-and-child unit is not the one I imagined but a different kind in which she exists to keep him alive and he exists to keep her awake.

I hadn't had a cup of tea all day, or a pee. When I got home there was a note on the door. It was from my landlord, asking had I a child concealed on the premises. Concealment, I mirthlessly snorted, would be a fine thing. He said it was upsetting the other tenants and either it went or I did.

I crept in to turn on the news. By now Vera would be reported missing. His distraught mother would come on the telly begging whoever had him to please let her have her baby back. It was difficult to hear above the infant shrieks but I could see Bill Clinton's flashing teeth and bodies in the streets in Bosnia and men in suits at EEC summits. I watched until the weatherman had been and gone. Vera and I wept in unison. Was this what they meant by bonding?

Some time in the night the crying stopped. The crimson faded from my fledgling's cheek and he subsided into rosy sleep. There was a cessation in the hostile shouts and banging on walls from neighbours. I sat over him and stroked his little fluff of hair and his cheek that was like the inside of a flower and then I must have fallen asleep for I dreamed I was being ripped apart by slash hooks but I woke up and it was his barking cries slicing through the fibres of my nerves.

Vera beamed like a rose as I wheeled him back to the supermarket. Daylight lapped around me like a great, dangerous, glittering sea. After twenty-four hours of torture I had entered a twilight zone and was both light-headed and depressed so that tears slid down my face as I exulted at the endurance of the tiny creature in my custody, the dazzling scope of his language of demand which ranged from heart-rending mews to the kind of frenzied sawing sounds which might have emanated from the corpse stores of Dr Frankenstein, from strangled croaks to the foundation-rattling bellows of a Gargantua. He had broken me. My nerve was gone and even my bones felt loose. I had to concentrate, in the way a drunk does, on setting my feet one in front of the other. I parked him carefully outside the supermarket and even did some shopping, snivelling a bit as I tucked away a little tin of white crab meat for comfort. Then I was free. I urged my trembling limbs to haste. 'You've forgotten your baby!' a woman cried out. My boneless feet tried an ineffectual scarper and the wheels of the push-car squealed in their pursuant haste. Upset by the crisis, the baby began to yell.

There are women who abandon babies in phone booths and lavatories and on the steps of churches, but these are stealthy babies, silently complicit in their own desertion. Vera was like a burglar alarm in reverse. Wherever I set him down, he went off. I tried cafés, cinemas, police stations. Once, I placed him in a wastepaper basket and he seemed to like that, for there wasn't a peep, but then when I was scurrying off down the street, I remembered that vandals sometimes set fire to refuse bins, so I ran back and fished him out. At the end of the day we went home and watched the news in tears. There was no report of a baby missing. Vera's cries seemed to have been slung like paint around the walls so that even in his rare sleeping moments they remained violent and vivid and neighbours still hammered on the walls. Everyone blamed me. It was like being harnessed to a madman. It reminded me of something I had read, how in Victorian almshouses, sane paupers were frequently chained to the bed with dangerous lunatics.

By the third day I could think of nothing but rest. Sleep became a lust, an addiction. I was weeping and twitching and creeping on hands and knees. I wanted to lie down somewhere dark and peaceful where the glaring cave of my baby's mouth could no more pierce me with its proclamations. Then, with relief, I remembered the river-bed. No one would find me there. Feverishly I dressed the child and wheeled him to the bridge. We made our farewells and I was about to hop into oblivion when I noticed a glove, left on one of the spikes that ornament the metalwork, so that whoever had lost it would spot it right away. It was an inspiration, a sign from God. I lifted Vera on to the broad ledge of the bridge, hooked his little jumper on to a spike, and left him there, peering quite serenely into the water.

At the end of the bridge I turned and looked back. The baby had disappeared. Someone had taken him. It seemed eerily quiet without that little soul to puncture the ozone with his lungs. Then I realized just why it was so quiet. There wasn't a someone. There hadn't been anyone since I left him there.

I raced back. 'Vera!' There was no sound, and when I gazed into the water it offered back an ugly portrait of the sky.

'Vera!' I wailed.

After a few seconds the baby surfaced. At first he bounced into view and bobbed in the water, waiting to get waterlogged and go down again. Then he reached out an arm as if there was an object in the murky tide he wanted. He didn't seem frightened. There was something leisurely about that outstretched hand, the fingers slightly curled, like a woman reaching for a cake. He began to show signs of excitement. His little legs started to kick. Out went another arm towards an unseen goal. 'What are you doing?' I peered down into the filthy water in which no other living thing was. Up came the arm again, grabbed the water and withdrew. His feet kicked in delight. The baby's whole body looked delighted. I moved along the wall, following his progress, trying to see what he saw, that made him rejoice. Then I realized; he was swimming. The day was still and there was very little current. He gained confidence with every stroke. 'Wait!' I kept pace along the wall. The baby took no notice. He had commenced his new life as a fish. 'Wait!' I cried. For me, I meant. I wanted to tell him he was wonderful, that I would forgive him all his smells and yowling for in that well-defended casement was a creature capable of new beginnings. He did not strike out at the water as adults do but used his curled hands as scoops, his rounded body as a floating ball. He was merely walking on the water like Jesus, or crawling since he had not yet learned to walk. 'Wait!' I begged as he bobbed past once again. I threw off my raincoat and jumped into the water. As I stretched out to reach the little curving fingers, he began to snarl.

I would like to report a happy ending, but then too I have always hankered for a sighting of a hog upon the wing. It took five more days to locate the mother. She told the police she had had a lovely little holiday by the sea and thought their Clint was being safely looked after by a friend, who, like everyone else in her life, had let her down. As it transpired, I knew the mother and she knew me, although we did not refresh our acquaintance. It was the pinched little woman with all the kids who had watched me wheel her child away. She said their Clint was a bawler, she hadn't had a wink of sleep since the day he was born, but she would take him back if someone gave her a Walkman to shut out the noise. Nobody bothered about me, the heroine of the hour – a woman who had risked her life to save a drowning child. It was the mother who drew the limelight. She became a sort of cult figure for a while and mothers could be spotted everywhere smiling under earphones, just as they used to waddle about in tracksuits a year or two ago. It was left to us, the childless, to suffer the curdling howls of the nation's unattended innocents.

Some women don't deserve to have children.

ANDREW DAVIES

The New Baboon

Andrew Davies (1936–) was born in Cardiff, lives in Warwickshire, and has taught at the University of Warwick. One of the most noted of contemporary British television playwrights, he is the author of *A Very Peculiar Practice*, a TV campus comedy, as well as of such powerful and acclaimed adaptations as *House of Cards*, *Anglo-Saxon Attitudes* and *Middlemarch*. He has also written stage plays, including *Prin* and *Rose*, two novels, *Getting Hurt* (1989) and *B. Monkey* (1992), and a highly comic – indeed black comic – collection of short stories and sketches, *Dirty Faxes* (1990).

'The New Baboon', from *Dirty Faxes*, is a wildly comic and cleverly managed story in which a learned, linguistically adept and extremely self-conscious baboon appears as the main narrator. Like most of Davies's characters –human as well as otherwise – he finds himself in a web of sexual difficulties, when his patriarchal rights and tribal authority are challenged. His solution to his emotional problems is unusual, to say the least, and leads the tale to its outlandish ending. But then, as the story advises us, 'True love is always strange . . .' Crossing the code and the category is a basic comic device. And, after all, we are all supposed to be descended from monkeys, and so from monkey love, which is presumably the unsettling point of the whole story.

The trouble was, that if I kept the females all together in one place they quarrelled with each other and got on my nerves – or, worse than that, ganged up on me and refused to groom me properly, and sat around criticizing my jumping and swinging style and the size of the coconuts I brought home.

But if I kept them all in separate trees and caves it was difficult to see what they were getting up to. Some of my older sons, Ong and Grd in particular, were becoming increasingly ambitious to perform *upoopoo* with my females, and some of the younger females seemed to me to be encouraging Ong and Grd in these efforts to subvert my domination. It became necessary for me to rise very early in the morning, and be the last baboon to retire for sleep at night. And it was increasingly wearisome for me to have to call and display and make *grawgraw* at the young males every single day, and even, on occasion, give heavy *bangbang* to one or another of them.

They were too stupid, or too contentious one against the other, to join forces against me: if I was forced to give *bangbang* to Ong, for example, Grd would watch in a state of excitement and delight, leaping up and down and chittering and pulling on his dogo. But if they were too stupid for that, they were too stupid also to see that their *awa* was to leave the pack, and wander alone until they could find their own females and become senior baboons in their turn.

It was my duty, my *awa* too, to keep my sons from my females. This was so that my offspring would be big and strong like me. And – yes, you are no doubt there before me – grow up into uppity bonkers like Ong and Grd and make their father's life a misery in their turn.

The life of a baboon is full of cruel ironies.

Besides my females and my uppity sons, I also had to worry about the loneboys; fully-grown males who had left their pack or been driven from it in their first maturity, and now travelled the coastline where the jungle reaches down to the silver beach, looking for a pack to conquer and make their own.

I had once been a loneboy, and had won my females from a terrible old bangerboy called Walt in a fight that had frightened all the baboons within ten daynights' walking of the Blue Rock hollow. And since then I had made twenty-seven successful defences of my territory against wandering loneboys. Sometimes it had been enough merely to display and make *grawgraw* and show them my dogo. More often it was necessary to give them heavy *bangbang*. Sometimes tear them with my main teeth, even. Only once did I have to kill a loneboy, and he was a crazy ape, crazy from drinking bad juice. We are not like the human men. A beaten baboon knows when he is beaten and he will ask to go away, and a strong baboon will let him go. Maybe the human men drink bad juice.

That was my life, a hard life, and full of little irritations and big worries too. And then one day the new baboon came along the shore from the West, and that was when my troubles really started.

I woke to hear my females chattering, and for once they had gathered closely round me, each one wanting to touch and snog and groom me. I looked around, and then I saw what they were chattering about. Only fifty jumps away, down by the sea, a new baboon, a big hungry loneboy, sitting on his gopa and displaying his dogo to my females. I felt a great weariness and irritation at having to prepare for another defence. No fear. This new baboon was big and hungry, yes, but nothing to me. One good *bangbang* on his head and he would understand that.

I shook my females off and stood up in all my bigness. He did not move. I blew my face up and gave him *stiffhair* and *hardeye*. He showed me his main teeth. I kept my *hardeye* on him and I walked right down on to the beach, towards him, no back and forth, no shouting, no *grawgraw*; I was very meanbusiness and believe me I was doing bigboy walking. I wanted to get this thing over fast and get some peace and quiet. When I am two jumps from him I stop so that he can see all my meat. And I show him my main teeth and I let him hear my big noise and smell my fierce, fighty smell. All right then, loneboy. I come at him like a big wave – and he's not there! I am going *bangbang* on bare sand!

I heard my females chattering and I turned around. The loneboy was running and wriggling among my females and they were going *chattersqueak looklook*, and then I saw he had captured one – he had captured Lpipi, a young, justready one . . . and I made big noise and went fast like a wind to catch him, but he was much too fast to catch, and he was carrying and pulling Lpipi up a high tree; and though she was going *chattersqueak* she was not fighting him, but holding round his back and helping him to climb; and I gave a big, fighty growl and I went up that tree after him, I was ready to fight him out of that tree and throw him on his head and break him, but he was such a climber that he was a long way ahead of me, and reached the top of the tree when I was only halfway up. And to my terrible shame and anger, when I looked at him, he was doing *upoopoo* with her, onetwothree, so fast that he had finished when I was still five jumps away, and he left her for me, and jumped himself to another tree, and so down to the beach, and away.

*

And so the days of my misery started. Every day, and sometimes in the night, the new baboon would come; and every time he ran away when I went to fight him; and every time he was too fast for me to catch him; and every time he managed to steal Lpipi or one of the other young females; and every time he would perform *upoopoo* with one of them, sometimes two of them. After a time, I saw that there was little that I could do, for he would not behave like a true baboon and understand that he was not strong enough to take my females from me. I stopped trying to chase him, and instead I kept my females with me all the time, so that he could not get at them. He would come to the beach, as he had done the first day, and sit on his gopa displaying his dogo, and all the females would go *chatterchatter looklook*, but I would not move, and he waited for Lpipi and the other justreadies in vain.

But in time I came to see that that was a failure too: kept all day and night together in a big huddle, the females quarrelled with each other and got on my nerves, or ganged up on me and refused to groom me properly, and talked about me without respect. I was unable to venture far to gather food, because of the loneboy. I never knew how far or how near he was hiding. Sometimes I only had to move ten jumps from my females, and I would turn to find him doing *upoopoo* with Lpipi or another one.

Worse still. Sometimes Lpipi and two or three of the other justreadies would steal away when I was dozing, would steal away on purpose to be with the loneboy, the new baboon, and do *upoopoo* with him, because they liked the way he did *upoopoo*. And after that a strange thing happened. I found that I did not want to do *upoopoo* as often as I had been used to doing it. When the new baboon had first come, I had wanted to do *upoopoo* more often than usual, perform it with every female every day, sometimes as much as ten times a day with some of them. But when he had been coming for many days I was weary with the worry of it all and I felt a sadness even in my dogo, and my head had a pain in it every day, even though no one had given it *bangbang*, and I could smell a sad smell, and I knew that it was mine. And after that, I could not do *upoopoo* at all.

One day I awoke and I felt different. The pain in my head had gone. My dogo was still hiding his head and I was still not able to do *upoopoo* but I did not care any more. And I did not want to take care of anyone except myself any more. I wanted to be alone. I was not ashamed of this. I understood it was my *awa* to leave the pack and go away by myself.

And that was what I did.

*

I travelled east, many daynights' walking. I kept to the shoreline, only going into the jungle to get food. It was hard to get food, because there were other packs, and they drove me away from the food, as I had driven other wandering, lonely baboons away from my food. I could have fought for the food, but I did not want to fight any more, I was tired of it. These packs were strange packs, I could not tell who was the leader; it seemed to me that the days of the senior baboon were over. I began to be sad again. I could not change from what I was. I did not want to become a baboon who won his food and his females by tricks and fast climbing, and I was tired of fighting. I did not want *upoopoo* any more. I took the nearest food from the lowest branches and I ate it without happiness. Sometimes I drank bad juice. And I smelled the sad smell again, and I knew that it was my smell.

One day I wanted to walk into the sea. This was a strange want. Baboons live near the sea but they do not go in it. We are not good swimmers and we don't eat fish. But I wanted to go in. I thought it might wash away my sad smell. And I walked into the sea a short way, until the water was as high as my dogo, and it seemed to me that my sad smell was not so strong. So I walked in further, but then a big wave came and I fell into the wet darkness and it felt like a huge leg had been thrust down my throat and I wanted to sleep in the middle of the pain, but then I wanted to fight the water until I could ask it to let me go, and it fought me and gave me heavy *bangbang*, and in the end tumbled me back on to the beach, nearly broken.

And it was there, on that beach, half drowned, choking, exhausted, near to death, that I met my future wife. My dear one. Her name is Leonora, and she will tell you herself how it came about.

*

My heart is too full for many words. Yes, I am engaged to be married. I am the happiest woman in the world, and I pity those who mock at me and shun me: I think they will never know the happiness I know.

One Sunday morning – it was the third of January last – I went with Mrs Pittenden to take the waters and indulge in a sea bath in the warm currents of the Indian Ocean, which has been our daily habit since we came to these shores. The beach is a very secluded one, and we had come to expect that we could enjoy our thalassic romps in the total confidence that not another living soul would be present to witness them. Imagine then our astonishment when, on emerging from the waters in a state of nature, we saw crawling towards us along the strand a poor bedraggled creature, near to death and stretching out an arm towards us in most piteous supplication.

Mrs Pittenden screamed and ran to fetch the servants; but I had seen the poor creature's piteous eyes, and I was not afraid. At first I did not know whether it was a man or a beast, and to tell the truth I did not care; never had I seen such sadness in a face, never such supplication, never had I known such confidence within my own heart that God had put me on that beach to relieve that creature's sadness. And he knew too; even then he knew that we have travelled far, for a meeting that would change the lives of both of us for ever.

How my Albert – for that is what I call him, and is the name he loves to answer to – how Albert recovered his strength with my aid, how he became first my pet baboon, then – as he learned apace – my servant, next my friend, and finally my lover and fiancé: all this must await a more leisured occasion, for I sometimes think that there are enough amusing, instructive and sentimental anecdotes relating to our meeting, our mutual instruction, and our strong and burgeoning love to fill a tidy volume which would well repay the perusal of many a curious young lady. For now, all that is needful for me to say is that I am the happiest girl in the world, and likely to be the happiest married woman.

*

True love is always strange, though, isn't it? Leonora, of course, is exceptional, even amongst those bold and unconventional travellers and wanderers of her time. She even looks exceptional – her face a perfect oval, her brow high and noble, a classic beauty except for her eyebrows, which meet in a single, dark, emphatic line above her nose, quite bushy, and rich with her unique spicy scent.

Albert loves her eyebrows. When they lie together he loves to trace their length with the pink tip of a long prehensile finger, or the pink tip of a long prehensile toe, or with the tip of his long pink tongue. He never thinks about his past life; he is content to have relinquished his status as a senior baboon. He knows he is not Leonora's toy. He does not yearn for Lpipi and the other females. Leonora is fearless and adventurous, and he is teaching her to make love while rocking in the branches of tall trees; she is showing a considerable aptitude. Last night, when they were lying peacefully together, his deep hairy chest to her smooth back, his long clever arms wound round and round her slender waist, her round warm bottom pressed into his lower belly sending its messages of love and healing, the tip of his soft hairy tail nestling gently in her ear, he touched the underside of her soft little toes with his hard hairy toes, and she curled her toes and held his with a strength not far short of the strength of a young female baboon. And she whispered to him that in an earlier life she too had been a monkey and known monkey life and made monkey love. And who is there to say that that was not the truth?

SUZANNAH DUNN

An Outer London Childhood

Suzannah Dunn (1963–) is a young writer living in Brighton. In 1990 Serpent's Tail chose her collection of short stories *Darker Days Than Usual* to launch their 'Nineties Collection' and the book was much admired. Her first novel *Quite Contrary* appeared in 1991, and another is forthcoming.

'An Outer London Childhood', from *Darker Days Than Usual*, shows the wry, dissective approach of her fiction. Much of it deals with the quiet hell of family life, and the uneasy guilts, tensions and disappointments that lie behind ordinary suburban backgrounds. Dunn is a stylist, and discloses the point of her stories – many of them told in the first person by a very observant narrator – only indirectly. Here, in the return to a highly familiar social occasion – a mother's fiftieth birthday party – around which the story is set, we sense, behind the well-done social chatter, the array of conflicts, wrongs and disappointments that go to make up the lives of those present.

'You think you're above the law, don't you,' my mother would say. 'Not above the law,' I'd taunt in reply, 'but below it; below it and waiting for it to swoop.'

Then she would sigh and purse her lips and say it was my age and that she had never brought me up to be like this. It was something she said whenever I skipped school or cheated fares or bought clothes from Marks & Spencer's to wear before returning them for a refund. But she never objected to my great-grandmother leaving restaurants without paying the bill. On these occasions my great-grandmother chose a table by the door to enable a quick getaway. My mother thought it hilarious.

My mother had invited me to her fiftieth birthday party; for family and friends, she said, although she usually claimed to have neither. So I had travelled from Clapham, where I had lived for the past four years, to spend the afternoon at my parents' home in Essex. I had travelled from Liverpool Street Station by train, and paid the full fare. My mother hates me to cheat the fare: 'Don't evade the fare,' she would beg, impressed by posters of fare dodgers losing their jobs as bank managers. Throughout the journey Essex appeared to have been above water but appearances were deceptive: I stepped from the train and sank into mud. There was a cold wind and I regretted having chosen to wear a skirt. The platform was deserted, so after the train had departed I left the platform without relinquishing my ticket and crossed the tracks towards the house.

When I entered the house my mother was at the table eating vol au vents, circled by people holding paper plates and telling her how well she looked.

'Fat, you mean,' she replied to each. She picked the prawn from the top of each vol au vent and ate it. When I was a child she had licked her plate at the end of each meal; my father had objected.

'Waste not want not,' she had giggled in reply.

I had been terrified that she would do it when my friends came to tea; or, worse, that she would sit naked in the garden. She used to like to sit naked in the sun while shaving her legs and telling me how she belonged in the jungle with a bone through her nose. She used to cry whenever it rained and in the summer she wore miniskirts in colours of cough mixture and penicillin syrup. Every evening in the living room she danced on her own to Jackson Five records, and she bought an afro wig to wear at parties.

But now she was fifty; she no longer wore miniskirts and she had never worn the afro wig which had been claimed by us for the dressing-up basket. For the party she wore a dress chosen for her by my father. She caught sight of me and called to me across the room.

'Vegetarian,' she shouted, lifting a plate of prawnless vol au vents.

She turned to the guests who had gathered around her. 'Vegetarian,' she confided to them, 'my daughter is a vegetarian.'

They murmured appreciatively and said to each other that they didn't eat much red meat themselves these days.

My mother joined their conversation with enthusiasm. 'We never did eat much red meat,' she claimed triumphantly, 'because we couldn't afford it.'

But I remembered roast on Sundays and mince on Monday. I sidled close to her and whispered in her ear: 'Boiled bacon.'

She turned to face me. 'Don't start,' she hissed, 'don't start: we had boiled bacon once in a blue moon and you know it.'

'Pease pudding?'

There was silence, and she smiled briefly at her guests before turning again to me. 'You're being unfair,' she protested to me, 'and now you're going to say that I brought you up all wrong.'

But I remembered that I had been brought up well: I had been given tea, toast and cereal for breakfast each morning; and there had been two slices of toast, one with Marmite and one with honey. I had been given the Marmite first and then the honey – savoury things first, then sweet – but had often been unhappy about this. 'Why not the honey first?' I had protested.

My mother had sighed on these occasions and turned to me with her lips pursed and said, 'Just do as I say.'

I moved with my mother from the table to the window. We watched my sister Catherine arrive.

'Larger than life,' my mother remarked to me.

We watched Catherine hurl the car door shut, bracelets and bangles colliding on her arm. We watched as she glanced at her watch and tugged at her blouse and advanced towards the house; her stilettos rapping the pavement; a fiancé behind her. The fiancé carried parcels wrapped in coloured foil and topped with rosettes. We listened as someone opened the front door. Catherine loomed by the window and we overheard the greetings. Within seconds she was in the living room, trotting among grandmothers and aunties and smearing them with kisses.

My mother turned to me. 'Look at her posture,' she whispered, 'she'll have trouble when it comes to childbearing.'

Catherine was swathed in crêpe de Chine, tucked and seamed: Catalogue Classic. Headlines insisted at the start of the summer that shorter skirts would be fashionable; but Catherine, unfortunately, has square knees.

My mother moved behind me. 'You ought to say hello to her,' she said.

I protested: 'She's horrible.'

'Yes, but she's your sister.' My mother stood firm. 'You ought to make an effort.'

Catherine, however, had already seen us. She stopped in the middle of the room, flanked by aunties. 'Hello mum,' she said, her teeth shiny, 'you're looking well.'

'So are you,' replied my mother hastily, 'so are you.'

The aunties gathered around Catherine and asked her about her job, flat, car, and fiancé. They asked me what I was up to, and what I was doing with myself.

'This and that,' I told them.

'Still painting?'

Swimming, mostly: I wondered whether they had noticed that I smelled of chlorine. I had a blue plastic leisure pass: for the unemployed, permitting me to swim at reduced charge during off-peak hours. I swam twenty or thirty lengths every day. I had always liked swimming. I had lessons, weekly, when I was a child: I had taken tests – bronze, silver and gold Personal Survival Awards – treading water wearing old pyjamas. I had had riding lessons too; and ballet, and tap. The dance classes had taken place on Saturday mornings at the Jean Wilson School of Ballet in the High Street. There had been a show every Christmas with printed programmes sponsored by the florist and the butcher. I had passed the exams – Royal School of Ballet, preliminary and elementary, grade one and grade two – with pink silk ribbon wound around my ankles. I had hated school sports; I had hated navy blue knickers and mid-winter hockey games.

'You're not sporty,' my mother had explained, 'because you're academic.'

'But Catherine's neither.'

My brother was considered artistic by my mother because of his asthma.

My mother had wanted lots of children: she had wanted to sit in a rocking chair on a verandah with grandchildren at her feet. She had wanted five children but she has four and I am the eldest. I had been born when she was twenty-five. My parents had been saving for a home of their own and living in the meantime in my grandmother's attic.

'The attic,' my brother would remind us during the rows around the kitchen table on Sunday lunchtimes, 'with no water and no heating.'

'The attic,' my mother would interject, 'which smelled of cabbage. The attic for which I paid rent.' At this point she would lean across the table and jab at him with her fork. 'And I paid my mother for my Sunday lunch too.'

He would then push his plate close to the cruet to display to us his portion of Yorkshire pudding: a lump of sweet-smelling fat crusted upon his gravy.

'I bet your portions were bigger than mine.'

My mother would purse her lips before replying: 'They weren't, as a matter of fact.'

I had been born when my parents were twenty-five: they had bought a home of their own and my mother had commuted to work for six months, retching during each journey with morning sickness. She left work when I was born. The births of Catherine, Luke and Clare followed at four-yearly intervals. She considered naming her last baby Gloria but decided against it on the grounds that it was a barmaid's name. She once told my brother that she had thought of naming him Zebedee; and he replied with disgust that he would have left home. She laughed at him and told us that it was the only mistake she had ever made.

Clare had been born when I was twelve. By that time I had endured a year of Mr Newman's biology classes and learned that when a man and woman love each other the penis becomes erect. No one else in my class had a pregnant mother. No one else had a mother who was a pacifist and an atheist. Our history teacher, Miss Tribe, asked us to discover what our parents thought of Winston Churchill and my mother told me that he was a silly old git. She said the same of the vicar despite the allegations that he had said unorthodox things in confirmation classes. She claimed that I attended a Church of England school because of the good teacher–pupil ratio. She had been obsessively interested in my education and had continued to write to my French penfriends long after I had stopped. She had read all the historical fiction in the local library, and it was she who told me that Anne of Cleves had smelled.

My father cannot believe that I am not a stockbroker. During the Sunday lunchtime rows, whilst splattering trifle into his bowl, he would tell me how he wished that he'd had half the opportunities I had.

'You should work your way up,' he would conclude.

'Up what?' I'd ask.

'Or you should travel.'

I pointed out to him on these occasions that travel necessitates return. When I left home he told me that a girl could do worse than learn to type. My mother agreed: 'It stands you in good stead.' At school she had passed the eleven plus whereas he had failed it. Then she had passed five O levels and left school for a job in an office because her mother had needed her wages. She had wanted me to study hard and find a good job, but I studied too hard and ended up at university. And students, according to my parents, took drugs.

'Drugs,' I'd say, reaching across the table for the milk, 'like tea or coffee perhaps?'

They told me on these occasions not to be clever. My mother's cousin had been clever: he had been a student, and had visited us one Sunday afternoon with his father and been rude throughout *Bridge Over the River*

Kwai. My mother remarked to me after they had left that she didn't like war films either but that his rudeness had been quite unnecessary.

My father disapproved of sex before marriage, and once he told me so while sitting at the kitchen table reading the newspaper. Catherine and Luke had left for work and my mother was accompanying Clare to school.

'I'll never marry,' I told him.

He turned a page. 'All normal people marry,' he said.

'Nowadays they usually marry twice,' I said.

He glanced at me.

'Which must create problems,' I continued, spooning jam on to my toast, 'at Hallowe'en, when a young girl is supposed to light a candle and stand at a mirror to catch a glimpse of her future husband. What do you suppose she sees these days? Two of them, vying for position, pushing and shoving in the background?'

His mouth had dried into a line. He closed the newspaper, placed it on the table, and rose.

'Don't push me, child,' he said, 'because I'm nasty when I'm angry.'

The following day he informed Catherine of his beliefs.

'Crap,' she said slicing bread for sandwiches, 'because you and Mum went on holiday together before you were married, and I know because I've seen the photos, and you can't tell me you had single beds.'

It had been my parents' first holiday together: they have photographs of each other at Lands End, smiling and pointing out at sea.

'It's true,' my mother said. She was kneeling at the fridge, searching each shelf for cheese. She told us that whilst he made the booking she had stayed in the car. I remembered my parents' first car from the photographs: large and black and shiny like something in an Ealing comedy.

'He booked single rooms,' she told us, 'and I cried when he told me.'

She found the lump of cheese and took it from the fridge. She closed the door and turned towards my father.

'You're a hypocrite,' she said, unwrapping the cheese, 'because you don't believe in sex before marriage for your daughters, but for Luke things are different.'

'Luke's a boy,' my father replied.

'I suspected as much,' she said, 'from the pin-ups on his wall and the pornography under his bed; I suspected something was wrong.'

Luke had been fourteen when his ex-girlfriend had called at our house claiming to be pregnant. I had not been at home at the time and I was told about it later. My mother related with sympathy that the girl had been carrying a cushion under her jumper. Clare confirmed that the cushion had been square and edged with tassels.

My mother's story of the cushion was a favourite of mine; and another was how she had been conceived before her parents' wedding. She had discovered that she had been born a healthy baby six months after the wedding.

'It can't be true!' I'd protest, delighted.

'It's true,' she'd confirm with a smile.

But surely it could not be true of my mother's mother: not Grandma, who wore a pinny and collected blue and white china and played *Come Back to Sorrento* on the piano; not Grandma, with her milky puddings and the touch of cold cream around her eyes before bedtime; not Grandma, surely? During the war my grandmother had stayed in London when my mother was evacuated to relatives who dressed her in a liberty bodice and forbade games on Sundays. My grandmother joined her one Christmas with a new baby born deaf and blind and dying. My mother returned after the war, crawling under the dining table and staying there for days, her father a stranger across the parlour telling her stories.

The stories of my mother's London childhood are of attics and cellars and lodgers, of London schools with stone playgrounds and steep staircases and high windows, and of peasoupers and trams. My own memories of London are, however, of the Science Museum: of the simulated rocket launches and of the ice-cream vans that lined the roads outside. The ice-cream was squirted into cones and laced with red sauce.

'No 99s,' my mother decreed whenever she bought me a cone, 'because they're expensive and the flake is unnecessary.'

I have memories of other day trips: I remember the Ideal Home Exhibition, the journey on the train from Cockfosters (cheap day returns, one and a half), and the gadgets and samples, the new type of cheese grater or the wind chimes for my bedroom or the bag full of leaflets about formica kitchens.

When I was a child there was a box of my mother's things in the loft: ballet shoes and a school scarf; ice skating boots and a vanity case. On wintry Sundays I climbed into the loft and sat beside it, close to the water tank, and explored the folds of tissue paper. There were exercise books with royal blue covers, feint ruled, containing English and French, biology and geography; and sketchbooks, four of them, full of sketches. There was a photograph, too, of my mother with two friends in a park: young women in skimpy cardigans, laughing, their arms around one another's shoulders. She worked at that time in an office in the city; the women were workmates. Then she met my father: he worked in the basement as an apprentice among the printing presses. They met every evening after dark on the steps of St Paul's, sheltering under my mother's umbrella and telling each other the stories of their future. She once wore fake tan but it ran in streaks down her legs in the rain.

It rained at their wedding, and the photographs are of bride and groom sheltering in the church porch. My father had wanted a church wedding so they married at a church in his home town: High Anglican, in the High Street. He lived in the countryside, twenty miles from London, and this had impressed my mother. She had wanted to leave London ever since her return after the war; so after saving the earnings from their weekday jobs, their evening jobs and jobs at weekends, they packed their things in boxes lined with tissue paper and left the attic for a home of their own in Essex. They ceased commuting when I was born: my father rented space in a prefab office behind the railway station and my mother did the bookwork on the kitchen table at home.

My mother visited the doctor when I was two years old: she was afraid of gaining weight. He swivelled in his chair, the stethoscope dangling around his neck, and told her that she was not fat.

'No,' she told me later, 'but *he* was.'

He had a drink problem, and his patients knew about it: his wife had retired as Brown Owl because of family problems. His patients blamed him for their illnesses and for the deaths of their relatives. No one ever chose to consult him and the receptionist had to claim that there were no other doctors available. He was right, of course, about my mother not being fat: she was by that time emaciated. She was afraid not only of fatness but of germs and planes. Whenever she heard planes she ran indoors and hid under the table. The doctor's advice to her was that she should ask someone to slap her around the face with a wet fish, and that she should have another baby.

Her second pregnancy was difficult, her blood pressure rose, and she was admitted to hospital for a rest. After a month in hospital she took a lift to the fourth floor hairdressing salon and threatened to jump. She was then allowed home to rest. Catherine was a difficult baby: despite the bows in her hair she was burly and aggressive; she was too fat to crawl but dragged herself screaming to her feet and gripped and shook the bars of her play-pen. When she was six months old my parents went abroad alone for a fortnight, driving across Spain in the family car and sending us postcards of dancers with frilly dresses. Catherine and I stayed at home with grandma, who made for my packed lunch each day a round of sandwiches: white bread spread with lemon curd or honey, folded, wrapped, and laid in a tupperware box. My mother had insisted that I have three rounds: one of meat and two of cheese (one with pickle and one without), along with a yoghurt, a banana, and a chocolate biscuit. When I returned home from school each day grandma was sitting at the kitchen table in a housecoat of light blue cotton and polyester, or pink perhaps, or gingham, with the sleeves rolled up; her elbow on the table, her chin resting in her hand. She read magazines, flicking through pages of knit-one-purl-one Stylish Summer Tops, or of Summer Fayre fruit fool and cheesecakes and date bars with a crunchy nut topping.

Luke had been a lovely baby, my mother claimed, although she had not wanted a boy.

'A boy at last,' the consultant had said to her during the ward round: so she spat at him. She waited four years after the birth of Luke until deciding to have a fourth child. I had wanted a pony. My father insisted that we could have one or the other but not both. My mother won; but then the doctor wanted to know why she had not been happy with three children, and told her that the current population explosion was a serious threat to mankind; and other people wanted to know if the pregnancy had been a mistake, because after all she was nearly forty. She replied on each occasion that the baby had been planned. My father, when he said anything about it at all, claimed otherwise; and then my mother would cross her hands over her stomach and raise her eyes to the ceiling and exclaim that it took two to tango. She gained weight and laughed and patted her stomach, wondering aloud about the possibility of twins. But every night I heard her in the hallway upstairs at the airing cupboard folding towels and crying.

Family photographs have always been taken by my father. At my mother's fiftieth birthday party he waved at me from across the room. 'Out of the way!' he shouted, aiming the camera at my mother. Then he turned his attention to the guests.

'Smile, please, ladies,' he requested, flourishing the camera. He shouted at his grandmother to smile but she did not hear him and continued to nod instead at those whom she considered to be admiring her hat. She had admitted to my mother that it had been stolen from Selfridges. The guests were gathering around the table to admire my mother's presents. I remembered birthdays and Christmases, the wrapping paper rustling in my mother's room each night; the lamplight dimmed behind her door. The guests had begun to call for her to cut the cake.

Birthday girl, they called her.

She turned towards me, the curtain catching on a link in her watchstrap.

'I can't,' she whispered, 'I can't; I don't want to. To tell you the truth, I don't want to do much these days. Is it my age?'

I reached for her wrist and disengaged it from the curtain.

'No,' I said, 'I don't think so.'

There is a photograph in the album in which she is not yet disengaged from the curtain, and her lips are parted but silent; but this is not how I remember her. Before leaving the party I made my excuses to the aunties and then spoke with her again. She had been eating the last of the vol au vents.

'A shame to waste them,' she explained as I approached her.

'Mother,' I said, 'I have a place at art college.'

She licked her forefinger and ran it around the empty plate before licking it again. 'Art college,' she mused. 'How nice.'

'But three more years of study,' I reminded her.

She reached across the table to stack plates.

'So I don't know what to do,' I said.

She shrugged. I handed her an empty plate.

'So what shall I do?' I asked. I reached for her and laid my hand over hers. She laid the pile of plates on the table and turned towards me with a frown.

She sighed. 'Well I wouldn't give it up,' she said with a shrug. 'Not now,' she said, more definitely, 'not if I were you.'

JONATHAN WILSON

Schoom

Jonathan Wilson (1950–) was educated at the Universities of Essex and Oxford and at the Hebrew University of Jerusalem. He now lives and works in America. *Schoom*, a collection of short stories, is his first work of fiction and was published in 1993. He is at work on his first novel and also contributes to the *New Yorker* magazine.

'Schoom', from the volume of that title, is a story of unfolding surprises. It is set in a vividly presented contemporary Israel, a land of new entrepreneurs, psychoanalysis, archaeological digs, and a spirit of 'to hell with the past'. The story-teller, like other of Wilson's narrators, is a smart and amoral young man who is something of a sexual and economic adventurer. He is also, it turns out, an innocent who is unable to fathom what lies underneath the surfaces, and is subject to emotional complications and manipulations much greater than he can possibly imagine. Wilson's gift for dialogue and passing social observation is part of the comic pleasure of his writing, but the other half lies in the unexpected indirectness and hidden implications of the story. Wilson's comic note has been compared to those of Clive Sinclair and Howard Jacobson in its portrayal of contemporary Jewish life in the yuppie age. But he has a voice, and a trick of restraint in his story-telling, that is all his own.

A few months ago I was taken by a friend to the archaeological dig in the Beit She'an Valley. It was a warm summer morning. I had emerged unusually depressed from my therapy session with Dr Schoom, but the anticipation of seeing the excavated city-fortress of Yodfat cheered me up. For two weeks only, the ruins of two-thousand-year-old streets and buildings were to be open to a variety of foreign specialists, but not to the public (the fear of damage was too great); after this, the site would be covered and closed.

My companion, Avital Lorch, had been working on the dig for about eighteen months, and sleeping with me for about half that time. Lately, things hadn't been going too well in our relationship, on account of my philandering. I hadn't *cheated* – we weren't married – and as I explained to Avital, she was away a lot at the dig. But neither she nor Dr Schoom was impressed by my lame excuses. Schoom, of course, wanted to get to the bottom of my inconsistency. Avital didn't care why I had gone to bed with the waitress from The Little Souperie, or the art student, or the daughter of the cleaning woman (who had substituted for her mother one happy, fateful day), but she did think enough was enough. 'Don't be a fool,' she said. 'Don't blow a good thing. Control yourself.'

I might have mastered my desires better if Schoom hadn't kept falling asleep. I would be halfway through a session when he would start to nod off. It didn't matter that I was describing intense or dramatic moments – my father keeling over at my feet when I was nine, or Susan Cranston, my sister's best friend, slowly unzipping my fly and reaching into my pants when I was thirteen – his eyes would begin to glaze over, he would stifle a yawn, and soon enough, head thrown back and breathing deeply, he was gone. I would wait a few moments and then cough, or call 'Dr Schoom, Dr Schoom.' He would come to with a start. 'Are you all right?' I would ask. He would inevitably reply, 'What are you talking about?' and pretend that he hadn't missed a beat.

So I started to think that I was having affairs in order to keep Schoom awake: to give him something juicy to look forward to in my sessions. I told him as much. 'I don't want to bore you,' I said, 'so I'm trying to lead an interesting life.'

'Ah yes,' he replied, 'the middle child desperate for his parents' attention, afraid that it is somewhere else.'

'Well,' I said, 'you have seemed *distracted* recently.'

'Not at all,' he responded, 'although your little joke with me may not be so far off the mark. What *do* all these love affairs have to do with me? Why can't you seem to spend a single night alone? And why do you feel so strongly the need to entertain me?'

'You tell me,' I said.

'No,' he replied, '*you* tell *me*.'

I tried another tack. 'Could it be,' I conjectured, 'that I'm very attracted to women?'

Schoom tilted his ancient head, with its monk-like fringe of white hair, so that he was now viewing me almost sideways. 'Do you really believe that?' he asked. Time was up.

One morning I arrived ten minutes early for my appointment. Oddly, the door to Schoom's office was minutely ajar. I heard a young woman's voice say, 'And what's more, it's like a dungeon in here,' and then she emerged, walking past me, where I sat in a canvas butterfly chair, without glancing my way. But I saw her: short brown hair, green eyes, ever so pretty, but hard too, with a purposeful stride, and a tuned-up body. 'Bet he doesn't fall asleep with her,' I thought.

So I had the Schoom problem and the fidelity problem, and somehow I was to understand they were linked. Never mind that on this morning's drive out of Jerusalem I was transported, as was so often the case, by the dusty blue light over the hills, the warm breeze, and some dizzying, mingled scent – petroleum and almond. 'Let's stop in on my cousin,' I said to Avital. 'We need coffee.'

My cousin Ruthie lived on Kibbutz Hakarosh, which had been founded in the mid-sixties by young immigrants from the Upper West Side – Jewish Left. These intellectual hippies were now fully-fledged, ideologically strict kibbutzniks. No member of Hakarosh was allowed a VCR in their home; and when Ruthie's daughter, Noa, wanted to get contact lenses because she thought glasses made her look ugly, the kibbutz held a meeting and voted not to let her. Ruthie was a lover of socialist constraint, but even she had hoped that her daughter would prevail.

Avital turned off at the Sha'ar Hagai junction and we were soon sitting on the verandah of Ruthie's little bungalow sipping *botz* (which is coffee named after mud) with one of Ruthie's neighbours. When my cousin finally showed up she was dressed in Bedouin clothes and accompanied by an old man, also in Bedouin outfit.

'Hello,' I said. 'Purim was two months ago, what's with the get-up?'

'Oh no,' she said, 'my luck. You.'

Ruth was not a frivolous person, and she thought I was. Nevertheless she patiently offered me an explanation. The kibbutz grew olives but the pressing was done on the West Bank. She always went and oversaw the process, but now it was unsafe for her to go *as herself*. Her Bedouin partners, with whom the kibbutz split the profits, had arranged for her to be accompanied to the Arab town of Ramallah, but in disguise. 'Look,' she said, 'Arafat was once smuggled out of Jordan as a woman, and nobody spotted him; I can certainly make it.'

This deception reminded me of my second Schoom problem. My therapist wanted me to steal something for him, and that was why I had been particularly done in after the morning session. I told him where I was going and with whom, and he woke right up. 'Listen,' he said, 'can you bring something back for me? You know I am a collector.' I did know. His office was filled with artefacts: pottery shards, ancient utensils, slivers of Roman glass.

'I'm an American economist,' I said, 'not a thief. I came here two years ago to advise the Israeli Government, not to steal from it.'

'Don't be ridiculous,' he said. 'You are a reactive depressive with an overdeveloped libido.' In eighteen months this was the first diagnosis he had offered me.

He was very agitated. 'Look,' he said, relenting a little. 'I'm not asking you to plunder the graves of the pharaohs; a memento is all I request. You know very well that the site is to be closed. Bring something from the ground. What will it matter? The Government, quite rightly, is going to let the city lie dormant for eternity. All we laymen shall have then is our photographs. *You* have been offered a great gift. You are going to be in *the place*. If you could return to me just a fraction of that gift, in the form of an earthenware fragment. Really, is that such a big deal?'

I didn't make Schoom any promises. I thought I'd see how things panned out. At Ruthie's place, where the veranda roof had been constructed out of old orange crates and there was absolutely nothing worth swiping, we lingered a while over our coffee. Ruth told me that when we were kids she hated coming to my house because my parents always made her take her shoes off so that our rugs wouldn't get damaged. Then she told me that I used to sweat out of the pores at the sides of my nostrils every time I ate a certain type of candy. Who needed to hear this stuff? Why dredge up the details? What did it lead to? Who did it help? In the distance, a tractor laboriously made its way up the side of a steep hill, pulling a heavy load. 'There goes David with the cow fodder,' said Ruth.

Meanwhile, Avital had been describing the Beit She'an excavations to Dorit, the neighbour, and Farhad, the Bedouin. They had uncovered, she said, along with the usual arrowheads and coins, the remains of a pottery! The prized discovery was a set of intact oil lamps made from moulds in the Middle Roman period. Almost two thousand years ago, for the first time, because of a new technique, ancient Palestinian potters had been able to depict a variety of raised designs on the upper surface of the lamps. The results were stunning. There were representations of Torah shrines, an amphora within an arch, decorative grape patterns, and, most unusually, what looked like a reclining figure (although it couldn't be) with its head resting on the pinched spout set for a wick. Dorit wanted to know more; Farhad gazed around as if nothing that was being said could possibly have anything to do with him.

Two men in blue work shirts began to approach us down the winding dirt path that led to Ruthie's house. 'OK,' I said to Avital. 'Time to go.'

'Excuse me, Daniel, but I'm in the middle of a conversation.' I always got a little nervous on the kibbutz. I had this feeling that if you stayed too long someone would come and get you to work. One minute you could be relaxing with a relative, the next minute it was *you* dragging the cow food up the hill. Avital talked a while longer while I watched the work-shirt men until they were safely out of sight.

After a while, we got up and walked across a cracked-cement basketball court to our car. Avital turned the key in the ignition and waved goodbye to Ruthie. 'Hold up,' I said. I was a little worried about my cousin, and decided to tell her so. I leaned out of the window. 'You're all I've got in this country,' I said. 'I don't think you should play dress-up in the Occupied Territories.'

Ruthie raised the long, richly embroidered sleeve of her Bedouin dress, and gave me the finger. 'Drive on,' I said to Avital.

The sun was high and strong as we crossed the valley toward the site. I looked at Avital dexterously manoeuvring the car around tight curves and down narrow lanes. When she turned her head the three stud earrings that she wore in her right ear caught the sun and sparkled. What a smart, beautiful woman she was. So why the need for the others? The truth was, I knew the answer. I wanted to be enlightened. I slept with other women because I was fascinated by their stories. Don't get me wrong, the sex mattered – sometimes it was great and sometimes it wasn't – but what I especially cherished were certain moments of intimacy, lying in bed afterward, listening. It always amazed me how people who were strangers a week, a day, or even a couple of hours earlier, would reveal their most secret thoughts after making love. For me, living in Jerusalem had become like the Arabian Nights. Every woman I met had a story, and every story was an education. I wanted to stay in school.

The dig, for a layman like myself, turned out to be a bust. A grid had been set out over the site with steel rods. Layer after layer of soil had been painstakingly removed to reveal – what? A few crumbling walls, and something Avital told me was once a hearth. I tried to conceal my disappointment. I didn't want to act like an ignoramus, but I guess I tend to do better with what is here, rather than with what you have to imagine out of the past.

Avital led me past a few small trenches, left over from the trial digging, toward a deep pit. 'The pottery!' she proclaimed with genuine enthusiasm. We descended a wooden ladder and joined a huddle of people carrying pointing trowels, shovels, and buckets. When Avital arrived she gave some directions in Hebrew and the helpers dispersed to begin their careful scraping of the layers of the past.

'Well!' I said. 'Some place! Remarkable! Truly remarkable.'

'We've found more than four thousand fragments here,' Avital announced.

'That's impressive,' I replied. '*Four* thousand.' As soon as I spoke I knew that I had put the emphasis on the wrong word. But Avital's first language wasn't English, so perhaps she didn't notice.

I hadn't forgotten about Schoom. In fact, I found myself casing the place, like the burglar he wanted me to be. Now that I was here, stealing something really didn't seem such a big deal. What was one shard give or take four thousand? Let the old guy have his pleasures. He had to listen to me going on about my extraordinary conquests day in and day out. That must have been a trial. True, my sex life was getting me into all kinds of trouble. But the fact remained that I was young and he was old. I was fucking frequently and he, by the looks of him, was in deep misery. If he wanted to caress a two-thousand-year-old pot – then let him.

Am I saying I stole because I felt sorry for Schoom? Maybe. But there was something else: the girl from the waiting room. I had this weird fantasy that bringing home the Schoom-shard would give me a conversation opener with the gorgeous patient who preceded me. 'Hey – I stole for him,' or 'Excuse me a moment but I wonder if we could have coffee after my session. There's something urgent I need to discuss with you about Dr Schoom.' Whatever the reasons, as we were about to make our way out of the pottery I knelt down, ostensibly to tie my sneaker. Avital was halfway up the ladder. I had chosen to stop close to a worker who had collected several fragments on a tray next to him. As he concentrated on his scraping, I stretched out my hand and covered the largest piece of pottery I could see. I stood up and in one smooth gesture pocketed the prize. I walked around slowly until my heart had returned to normal speed, then I headed toward the ladder. When I reached the top, Avital was nowhere to be seen.

One of the archaeologists had noticed her talking with the head of the dig, Avram Fleischer. A telephonist at the site office thought that she had glimpsed her running past the window. The guard in the parking lot told me that he had seen her getting into her car. She had shouted, 'Tell him I couldn't wait any more.'

'Was it an emergency?' I asked, somewhat baffled.

'Maybe,' he said. 'She seemed in a huge hurry.'

There was nothing for it but to make my own way back to Jerusalem. It was Friday. The workers from the dig were all leaving early to get home before the Sabbath. I picked up a ride to a bus stop on the highway. A blur of traffic was speeding in both directions but there was no sign of a bus. I stood in the shade of a eucalyptus tree and took the shard out of my pocket. It hadn't been properly cleaned yet. It looked like, well, a bit of a pot.

339

Maybe, I thought, it's a part of one of those lamps Avital was talking about. Two thousand years ago someone made a little halo of light around himself with what I was holding. And what did he see? The body of the woman beside him. Yes, it was a bedside lamp. I was convinced.

By the time I got to Jerusalem it was dusk. I called Avital from the Egged station but there was no answer. I began to walk home. Then, suddenly, I changed direction. I would drop off the booty at Schoom's place. It was best to get rid of the evidence before catching up with Avital.

The road to Schoom's took me through the orthodox neighbourhood of Me'a She'arim. Its narrow streets were clogged with Hasidim on their way to prayers. Buzzing blackflies. I made my way through courtyards flickering with candlelight, past empty yeshivas, shuttered store-fronts, kerchiefed mothers dragging their last recalcitrant children from cobble-stone to hearth. At some point I lost my way and found myself in a cul-de-sac. Two poorly inscribed signs had been hammered above a wooden doorway. The top one gave the name Yeshiva Tarfon; the second read, 'You are not required to complete the task, yet you are not free to withdraw from it.' Was this profound? I wasn't sure.

On Ha'bashim Street, I paused outside Schoom's gate. There was a sweet, almost sickly scent of honeysuckle in the air. The street was deserted. The pink dome of the Ethiopian church loomed over Schoom's little house, like a nipple above the obsessions of his patients. I descended the concrete steps at the far end of the analyst's flower-filled yard, and entered the waiting room.

Schoom, of course, was not a religious man. He held sessions until late in the day on Fridays. When I arrived someone was in his office. Again, my absent-minded shrink, my *sleepy* shrink, had failed to close his door properly. Again, I heard voices. Schoom was talking, very directly. It must have been the end of the session, that point when, after all the silences and sighs, Schoom would finally, almost reluctantly, summarize some of *his* thoughts. 'You cannot possibly go,' he was saying. 'You have already told me that you believe this is not something your mother would have wished you to do. I understand that you do not want to be controlled from beyond the grave. But there are other considerations. Do you think that I will be here when you return? I assure you that it is most unlikely.'

(Ah yes, I thought, the old 'interrupt-the-therapy-and-you'll-never-get-back-on-track' routine.)

'And this man,' Schoom continued, 'this Yacki. Do you really believe that you will lead a productive life in San Diego with a jeweller-hippie? You, who spent four years at the Rubin Academy of Music. And what did your dream tell you? Your frightening dream that you have just recounted. According to your own words, it meant that someone was about to make a terrible mistake.'

There was silence. Someone, patient or analyst, about to make a terrible mistake or not, shifted in their chair. I sat in the advancing purple darkness of Schoom's waiting room. Then she emerged, and, braver than any patient that I had ever imagined, she turned and yelled through the door, 'I can't bear it any more. I want to be free.' In a blur of black mini-skirt and black T-shirt she was gone.

I knocked lightly and put my head around the door. Schoom was seated in shadow behind his desk, his face in his hands. I entered the room tentatively. 'Dr Schoom.' He looked up but did not appear to register my presence. 'I brought you what you wanted.'

Schoom gave me a long look. When I finally came into focus he seemed to make a sudden decision. 'You,' he said (just as my cousin Ruthie had said it). 'Of course. Go after her. You, who claim to know so much about women. Go after her. Tell her, please, what a fool she is being. Go. Go!'

'But I have your antiquity.' I began to search around in my pockets.

'Never mind. I can't listen to you now. Do as I say, please. Go after her.'

I went. I sprinted down Ha'bashim Street, lifting my knees high toward my chest, as I had been taught to do in high school. I pumped my arms and puffed like a steam train. But to where? I chose the unorthodox direction, Jaffa Road. And yes, there she was, not too far off, turning down an alleyway next to a falafel and schwarma stand where the bright pink torso of a lamb was turning on a spit. I ran, dodging in and out of late shoppers on their way home loaded down with vegetables and bunches of flowers. Schoom had ordered me to the chase. He had authorized my desires. What luck!

I caught up with her outside a shoe store called Sandalaria where she had stopped to check out the window display. 'Excuse me,' I said, catching my breath. 'I've come from Dr Schoom. He sent me. I mean, I wanted to come anyway. But he asked me. In any case I was going to ask you.'

'What do you want? Who are you?' Her voice was full of irritation, but no surprise – she had been hit on before.

I couldn't very well, at this point, tell her not to go to San Diego with Yacki (what was all that about anyway? The crack in the door had opened into a wide fissure of broken confidentiality), so I said, 'It's a long story and it concerns Dr Schoom. I wonder if we could sit somewhere for a while?'

'You're one of Hillel's patients, aren't you?' she replied. 'I've seen you in the waiting room.'

'Yes,' I said, pleased to acknowledge that we had therapy in common, but disturbed at the same time by her easy use of Schoom's first name. With me it was always *Mr* Winaker and *Dr* Schoom.

We walked up the street and sat in the Ta'amon Café between two tables occupied by chess players. The place was closing. The wizened old waitress was bustling around looking like she didn't want to take another order. I felt pressured and I didn't quite know where to begin. Every time I looked into those green eyes I got unhinged. I mumbled some stuff about being an economist (she looked bored), mouthed a few platitudes about Israel, and then plucked out of the air, 'How long have you been in therapy with Dr Schoom?'

She started to laugh. 'Therapy?' she replied. 'All my life. He's my father.'

OK, OK. If you're thinking I was turned on by this information, you're right. I experienced a brief moment of decline, a perceptible sliding down on the parabola of my desire when the incest taboo first kicked in, but this was quickly reversed. Schoom's daughter! The possibilities (the incestuous possibilities) were endless. There was also a feeling of larceny. He had made me steal, and in doing so he had stolen something from me. Now, I would take from him.

So I launched into my seductive rap – and I could be quite charming. ('You turn your aggression into charm' – Dr Hillel Schoom.) After all, seduction was almost an occupation with me and I worked hard at it. 'What are you on?' Avital had asked in one of our bitter moments. 'A sexual crusade?'

Aviva (that was her name) heard me out while I name-dropped, sprinkled a couple of witticisms, and described my must-see Jerusalem apartment ('set in a walled garden, the scent of oleanders, olive tree overhanging the balcony, once owned by an artist, eccentric landlady former mistress of Moshe Dayan, stars beautiful from the *mirpesset*, blah blah blah'), then she paused, just like her father, before speaking. 'Look,' she said. 'You seem like an intelligent man, but I can tell you right now that I'm not attracted to you sexually.'

The waitress had appeared at my shoulder. 'Bruised ego, please,' I said, 'and could you put a little crushed testicle into the coffee?'

'Same for you, sweetheart?' she asked Aviva. Aviva declined.

My drink and check arrived simultaneously. I realized that, in the general sense of rush, I had failed to do Schoom's bidding. Aviva must be wondering why her father had sent me after her. But what could I say – 'Don't go to San Diego with Yacki. Come home with me instead'? It was ridiculous.

'Listen,' Aviva was saying. 'I really have to go. So if you could give me my father's message.' I loved her rolled r's and singsong Israeli accent, so different from her father's Euro-snob sibilated utterances.

I stared at her. Around her neck she wore a bright cobalt-blue enamelled Star of David, no doubt one of Yacki's creations. 'Your father,' I stuttered, 'wanted me' (long pause) 'to give you this!' Triumphantly, I produced the shard from my pocket. Then I improvised: 'He didn't have time to take it. He was preoccupied with an emergency – a phone call. He asked me to give it to you. He wants you to hold it for him, then return it to him. As soon as possible.' She took the piece of pottery in her hand, stood up and dropped it in her leather bag. 'OK,' she said. 'No problem.'

'Any chance we could go out one night this week?' I begged pathetically.

'How old are you?' she asked.

'Thirty-eight.'

'You need to be younger.'

I smiled virtuously, as if I would make every effort to do as she wished. Then I put my hand to my head and looked down despairingly. Her tanned legs, strapped up calf-high with the long lavender ribbons of her espadrilles, disappeared through the café door.

When I got home there was a message on my answering machine. It was Avital. She spoke in a trembling voice that said, 'If you do not return what you stole I will report you to the police.' Shame and disgrace! I dialled her number in a panic. I had no idea what I would say to her. How had she found out anyway? Some shifty-eyed digger must have seen me. I let the phone ring ten, twenty times. No answer. I was sweating so much my feet felt as if they were swimming in my sandals. There was nothing for it but to return to Schoom's. But I had to take a shower first. I stood under the weak drizzle that was the best I could ever get in Jerusalem, and tried to scrub away my guilt. Dressing, I chose a white shirt and cream-coloured pants. How could a person as clean as me go to jail?

I left my apartment and ran around the back of the Hamashbir department store to Ben Yehuda Street. The cafés had all pulled in their tables and chairs; the centre of town was deserted. There was this overwhelming Sabbath atmosphere that gets me every time, even though I am a person who believes we are lucky there is no God. Anyway, the atmosphere, whatever it was – a violet-stained tranquil path, dust and blessings – slowed me to a walk. I crossed Zion Square and headed up the hill to Schoom's street. I felt momentarily pulled up from my troubles. As usual, this elevation was accomplished by the surface of things: the pink stone of the houses under starlight, the scent of jasmine, the distant cry of the muezzin – all the heady stuff that the city had to offer. But what lay under the sights, smells, and sounds? Something about the place that I didn't want to know? Something about myself?

Schoom's office was locked, so I had to go to the front of the house. I noticed immediately a brightly coloured, oversized mezuzah on the portal of his door. 'Former owners,' I thought, but no, a matching ceramic nameplate – DR HILLEL SCHOOM, entwined with painted flowers – had been nailed above the knocker.

Schoom came to the door. His shirt was uncharacteristically open, there were patches of sweat under his arms, and his face looked drawn and tired. 'Well,' he said, 'did you convince her?'

I wanted to say, 'You're out of your mind,' but it seemed unnecessary. I think he knew. I let him lead me into his sitting room – leather chairs, kilims, subtle abstracts on the walls (originals by local artists). Shrinks, I thought, always tasteful. It was part of the whole quiet, restrained, unobtrusive thing.

Schoom looked like he might shake me if I didn't speak, so I said, 'I'm in bigger trouble than your daughter.' I told him the story. I expected him to take the blame, or at least part of the blame, and then walk over to the phone and call Aviva. Instead, he gave a short, sharp, unhappy laugh.

'Well,' he said, 'now, at last, you have a real problem.'

'What's that supposed to mean?'

'Oh,' he waved his hand at me, 'surely you must be aware of your own silliness. This business with women. Your ceaseless talk about this one and that one. Your ridiculous daily conquests. You are obsessed with the quotidian. Do you know that in your year-and-a-half of therapy you have not once taken the opportunity to present me with a dream?'

'That's not true. What about the hallah that fought my father's prayer shawl, and had the number seven cut into one of its braids?'

Schoom looked at me with contempt. How, I wondered, could he disdain a dream? I thought they were value-free. 'You want to alter your behaviour,' Schoom continued, 'or at least you say you do. But you can't change the present without coming to terms with the past. I have tried, you know, to direct you back, but you resist. All you want to do is tell me stories about bed. I *know* the bed.'

'What about when my father collapsed? You fell asleep.'

'Nonsense, nonsense. I was waiting for the memory to lead you somewhere, to a *reflection*. But no, your father collapses in your memory and you can go no further. The next minute you are again plotting a seduction. Perhaps there is a connection between the two thoughts, but how could you possibly find it? Every time you have a piece of the past in your hands you throw it away.'

It was a piece of the past that had got me into all this trouble. But what was the use of arguing with Schoom? He had nastily transformed from therapist to antagonist. And the realization had slowly dawned on me (the 'resistance' was great) that Schoom *didn't like me*.

'Look,' I said, 'I didn't come here to be scolded. I have to retrieve the shard. Please call your daughter, or else give me her number or address.'

'My daughter, your saviour, has doubtless already passed on what you gave her to her feckless boyfriend. He, the marvellous Yacki, who knows even less than you about the world he wanders through, is probably stringing the shard for a pendant at this very moment.'

Oh, give them a break, I thought, a break from all this knowledge and history. Let them wander in the San Diego desert and smoke dope. Where was it written that everyone has to be weighed down by the stones of Jerusalem? Let them float on their backs in the Pacific wearing nothing but their pendants and earrings. To hell with the past.

Schoom sat down heavily in one of his swivel armchairs. 'You will not find them,' he said. 'They are leaving tonight for California. This, I see, my daughter did not tell you. They are probably at the airport right now.'

Ben Gurion was forty minutes from Jerusalem. It was never easy to find a taxi on a Friday night. I had no money in my pockets. Schoom had no idea what airline they were using. My situation was hopeless.

Outside, a summer thundershower was sending fat drops of rain on to the dusty sidewalk. A police car followed me down the street (they know already!) and then turned off up a hill toward the Old City. There was nothing for it but to plead with Avital to be merciful. The rain blew in sheets across Jaffa Road staining the low buildings apple-grey. My shirt was soaked through, transparent. I walked to a phone booth, but didn't have a token. I had to call collect. I heard the operator say my name. There was a short wait and then Avital, sounding extremely angry, said, 'Have you got it?'

It had been a long day. There was water dripping off my head on to my glasses. I started to go through the whole thing. I think I began by saying, 'I was sitting outside Schoom's office . . .' but Avital interrupted me.

'What you stole was valuable. It came from the most productive layer of the site. How could you do that? Do you even know what you stole? You took the intact handle of a two-thousand-year-old oil lamp!'

I was about to say, 'I thought it might be something like that,' but being pleased with myself for guessing right was not an appropriate response. 'Well, it's gone,' I said. 'It's on its way to California.' Avital started to speak very fast. I put the phone back on its hook.

Where to go? The rain had eased up a little, but miniature flash floods were rolling through the gutters. Only one person could get me out of this mess: Schoom. But I had nothing left to say to him. And he was clearly finished with me. Nevertheless I found myself returning once again to Ha'bashim Street, and once again I stood outside his door. There were no lights at the front of the house and no one answered when I knocked. I squeezed around a side alley, scratching my arms on the bushes that overhung Schoom's neighbour's wall. A diffuse, fuzzy light filled a square of window halfway down the side of the house. An upturned tin bucket that was lying in the alley gave me the pedestal I needed. Two candles were burning on a desk. Otherwise, the room was in darkness. Schoom was bent low over his work. Carefully, with meticulous, guarded movements of his hands, Schoom was cleaning the shard.

MARTIN AMIS

Career Move

Martin Amis (1949–) was born in Oxford, the son of Kingsley Amis. He published his first book, the strong and disturbing *The Rachel Papers*, in 1973, at the age of 24, and was recognized as the voice of a new writing generation. Since then a sequence of greatly admired novels – *Dead Babies* (1975), *Success* (1978), *Money* (1984), *London Fields* (1989) and *Time's Arrow* (1992) – established him as one of the most powerful and striking writers of the last two decades, during which, earlier, like his father he became the sharp, ironic chronicler of his age. He has also published important stories and social and literary criticism – including the volume *Einstein's Monsters: Five Stories* (1989), reflections on living in apocalyptic and corrupted times. A writer of wide interests and influences, he has also written in Hollywood for the movies.

'Career Move', a short story first published in the *New Yorker*, comes out of this experience. Amis's work generally has an edge of biting satire and wit, and it also plays wonderfully with the refraction of images between both sides of the Atlantic that has become part of the Frequent Flyer age. The humour is generally expressed through the permutations of a smart, transatlantic voice, and contains a note of angry, or sometimes resigned, late modern bitterness. 'Career Move' turns on a wonderfully funny conceit: suppose highly-paid screenwriters were treated as poets are, admired for their solemn art, and poets like screenwriters, over-paid but forced to pitch their work to studios. Amis captures the ambiguities of art as promotion and commerce, and the tired public language of our media age, and his well-tuned literary skill is apparent in the way the situation is splendidly resolved.

When Alistair finished his new screenplay, *Offensive from Quasar 13*, he submitted it to the *LM*, and waited. Over the past year, he had had more than a dozen screenplays rejected by the *Little Magazine*. On the other hand, his most recent submission, a batch of five, had been returned not with the standard rejection slip but with a handwritten note from the screenplay editor, Hugh Sixsmith. The note said:

> I was really rather taken with two or three of these, and seriously tempted by *Hotwire*, which I thought close to being fully achieved. Do please go on sending me your stuff.

Hugh Sixsmith was himself a screenplay writer of considerable, though uncertain, reputation. His note of encouragement *was* encouraging. It made Alistair brave.

Boldly he prepared *Offensive from Quasar 13* for submission. He justified the pages of the typescript with fondly lingering fingertips. Alistair did not address the envelope to the Screenplay Editor. No. He addressed it to Mr Hugh Sixsmith. Nor, for once, did he enclose his curriculum vitae, which he now contemplated with some discomfort. It told, in a pitiless staccato, of the screenplays he had published in various laptop broadsheets and comically obscure pamphlets; it even told of screenplays published in his university magazine. The truly disgraceful bit came at the end, where it said 'Rights Offered: First British Serial *only*'.

Alistair spent a long time on the covering note to Sixsmith – almost as long as he had spent on *Offensive from Quasar 13*. The note got shorter and shorter the more he worked on it. At last he was satisfied. There in the dawn he grasped the envelope and ran his tongue across its darkly luminous cuff.

That Friday, on his way to work, and suddenly feeling completely hopeless, Alistair surrendered his parcel to the sub post office in Calchalk Street, off the Euston Road. Deliberately – very deliberately – he had enclosed no stamped, addressed envelope. The accompanying letter, in its entirety, read as follows: 'Any use? If not – w.p.b.'

'W.p.b.' stood, of course, for 'waste-paper basket' – a receptacle that loomed forbiddingly large in the life of a practising screenplay writer. With a hand on his brow, Alistair sidled his way out of there – past the birthday cards, the tensed pensioners, the envelopes, and the balls of string.

When Luke finished the new poem – entitled, simply, 'Sonnet' – he xeroxed the printout and faxed it to his agent. Ninety minutes later he returned from the gym downstairs and prepared his special fruit juice while the answering machine told him, among many other things, to get back to Mike. Reaching for another lime, Luke touched the preselect for Talent International.

'Ah. Luke,' said Mike. 'It's moving. We've already had a response.'

'Yeah, how come? It's four in the morning where he is.'

'No, it's eight in the evening where he is. He's in Australia. Developing a poem with Peter Barry.'

Luke didn't want to hear about Peter Barry. He bent, and tugged off his tank top. Walls and windows maintained a respectful distance – the room was a broad seam of sun haze and river light. Luke sipped his juice: its extreme astringency caused him to lift both elbows and give a single, embittered nod. He said, 'What did he think?'

'Joe? He did backflips. It's "Tell Luke I'm blown away by the new poem. I just know that 'Sonnet' is really going to happen."''

Luke took this coolly. He wasn't at all old but he had been in poetry long enough to take these things coolly. He turned. Suki, who had been shopping, was now letting herself into the apartment, not without difficulty. She was indeed cruelly encumbered. Luke said, 'You haven't talked numbers yet. I mean like a ballpark figure.'

Mike said, 'We understand each other. Joe knows about Monad's interest. And Tim at TCT.'

'Good,' said Luke. Suki was wandering slenderly towards him, shedding various purchases as she approached – creels and caskets, shining satchels.

'They'll want you to go out there at least twice,' said Mike. 'Initially to discuss . . . They can't get over it that you don't live there.'

Luke could tell that Suki had spent much more than she intended. He could tell by the quality of patience in her sigh as she began to lick the sweat from his shoulderblades. He said, 'Come on, Mike. They know I hate all that L. A. crap.'

On his way to work that Monday Alistair sat slumped in his bus seat, limp with ambition and neglect. One fantasy was proving especially obdurate: as he entered his office, the telephone on his desk would actually be *bouncing* on its console – Hugh Sixsmith, from the *Little Magazine*, his voice urgent but grave, with the news that he was going to rush Alistair's screenplay into the very next issue. (To be frank, Alistair had had the same fantasy the previous Friday, at which time, presumably, *Offensive from Quasar 13* was still being booted round the floor of the sub post office.) His girlfriend, Hazel, had come down from Leeds for the weekend. They were so small, he and Hazel, that they could share his single bed quite comfortably – could sprawl and stretch without constraint. On the Saturday evening, they attended a screenplay reading at a bookshop on Camden High Street. Alistair hoped to impress Hazel with his growing ease in this milieu (and managed to exchange wary leers with a few shambling, half-familiar figures – fellow screenplay writers, seekers, knowers). But these days

Hazel seemed sufficiently impressed by him anyway, whatever he did. Alistair lay there the next morning (her turn to make tea), wondering about this business of being impressed. Hazel had impressed him mightily, seven years ago, in bed: by not getting out of it when he got into it. The office telephone rang many times that Monday, but none of the callers had anything to say about *Offensive from Quasar 13*. Alistair sold advertising space for an agricultural newsletter, so his callers wanted to talk about creosote admixes and offal reprocessors.

He heard nothing for four months. This would normally have been a fairly good sign. It meant, or it might mean, that your screenplay was receiving serious, even agonized, consideration. It was better than having your screenplay flopping back on the mat by return post. On the other hand, Hugh Sixsmith might have responded to the spirit and the letter of Alistair's accompanying note and dropped *Offensive from Quasar 13* into his waste-paper basket within minutes of its arrival: four months ago. Rereading his fading carbon of the screenplay, Alistair now cursed his own (highly calibrated) insouciance. He shouldn't have said. 'Any use? If not – w.p.b.' He should have said, 'Any use? If not – s.a.e.'! Every morning he went down the three flights of stairs – the mail was there to be shuffled and dealt. And every fourth Friday, or thereabouts, he still wrenched open his *LM*, in case Sixsmith had run the screenplay without letting him know. As a surprise.

'Dear Mr Sixsmith,' thought Alistair as he rode the train to Leeds. 'I am thinking of placing the screenplay I sent you elsewhere. I trust that . . . I thought it only fair to . . .' Alistair retracted his feet to accommodate another passenger. 'My dear Mr Sixsmith: In response to an inquiry from . . . In response to a most generous inquiry, I am putting together a selection of my screenplays for . . .' Alistair tipped his head back and stared at the smeared window. 'For Mudlark Books. It seems that the Ostler Press is also interested. This involves me in some paperwork, which, however tedious . . . For the record . . . Matters would be considerably eased . . . Of course if you . . .'

Luke sat on a Bauhaus love seat in Club World at Heathrow, drinking Evian and availing himself of a complimentary fax machine – clearing up the initial paperwork on the poem with Mike.

Everyone in Club World looked hushed and grateful to be there, but not Luke, who looked exhaustively displeased. He was flying first class to LAX, where he would be met by a uniformed chauffeur who would convey him by limousine or courtesy car to the Pinnacle Trumont on the Avenue of the Stars. First class was no big thing. In poetry, first class was something you didn't need to think about. It wasn't discussed. It was statutory.

Luke was tense: under pressure. A lot – maybe too much – was riding on 'Sonnet'. If 'Sonnet' didn't happen, he would soon be able to afford neither his apartment nor his girlfriend. He would recover from Suki before very long. But he would never recover from not being able to afford her, or his apartment. If you wanted the truth, his deal on 'Sonnet' was not that great. Luke was furious with Mike except about the new merchandizing clause (potential accessories on the poem – like toys or T-shirts) and the improved cut he got on tertiaries and sequels. Then there was Joe.

Joe calls, and he's like 'We really think "Sonnet" 's going to work, Luke. Jeff thinks so, too. Jeff's just come in. Jeff? It's Luke. Do you want to say something to him? Luke. Luke, Jeff's coming over. He wants to say something about "Sonnet".'

'Luke?' said Jeff. 'Jeff. Luke? You're a very talented writer. It's great to be working on "Sonnet" with you. Here's Joe.'

'That was Jeff,' said Joe. 'He's crazy about "Sonnet".'

'So what are we going to be talking about?' said Luke. 'Roughly.'

'On "Sonnet"? Well, the only thing we have a problem on "Sonnet" with, Luke, so far as I can see, anyway, and I know Jeff agrees with me on this – right, Jeff? – and so does Jim, incidentally, Luke,' said Joe, 'is the form.'

Luke hesitated. Then he said, 'You mean the form "Sonnet" 's written in?'

'Yes, that's right, Luke. The sonnet form.'

Luke waited for the last last call and was then guided, with much unreturned civility, into the plane's nose.

'Dear Mr Sixsmith,' wrote Alistair,

> Going through my files the other day, I vaguely remembered sending you a little effort called *Offensive from Quasar 13* – just over seven months ago, it must have been. Am I right in assuming that you have no use for it? I might bother you with another one (or two!) that I have completed since then. I hope you are well. Thank you so much for your encouragement in the past.
>
> Need I say how much I admire your own work? The austerity, the depth. When, may I ask, can we expect another 'slim vol.'?

He sadly posted this letter on a wet Sunday afternoon in Leeds. He hoped that the postmark might testify to his mobility and grit.

Yet, really, he felt much steadier now. There had been a recent period of about five weeks during which, Alistair came to realize, he had gone clinically insane. That letter to Sixsmith was but one of the many dozens he had penned. He had also taken to haunting the Holborn offices of the *Little Magazine*: for hours he sat crouched in the coffee bars and sandwich nooks opposite, with the unsettled intention of springing out at Sixsmith – if he ever saw him, which he never did. Alistair began to wonder whether Sixsmith actually existed. Was he, perhaps, an actor, a ghost, a shrewd fiction? Alistair telephoned the *LM* from selected phone booths. Various people answered, and no one knew where anyone was, and only three or four times was Alistair successfully connected to the apparently permanent coughing fit that crackled away at the other end of Sixsmith's extension. Then he hung up. He couldn't sleep, or he thought he couldn't, for Hazel said that all night long he whimpered and gnashed.

Alistair waited for nearly two months. Then he sent in three more screenplays. One was about a Machine hit man who emerges from early retirement when his wife is slain by a serial murderer. Another dealt with the infiltration by the three Gorgons of an escort agency in present-day New York. The third was a heavy-metal musical set on the Isle of Skye. He enclosed a stamped, addressed envelope the size of a small knapsack.

Winter was unusually mild.

'May I get you something to drink before your meal? A cappuccino? A mineral water? A glass of sauvignon blanc?'

'Double decaf espresso,' said Luke. 'Thanks.'

'You're more than welcome.'

'Hey,' said Luke when everyone had ordered. 'I'm not just welcome any more. I'm more than welcome.'

The others smiled patiently. Such remarks were the downside of the classy fact that Luke, despite his appearance and his accent, was English. There they all sat on the terrace at Bubo's: Joe, Jeff, Jim.

Luke said, 'How did "Eclogue by a Five-Barred Gate" do?'

Joe said, 'Domestically?' He looked at Jim, at Jeff. 'Like – *fifteen*?'

Luke said, 'And worldwide?'

'It isn't *going* worldwide.'

'How about "Black Rook in Rainy Weather"?' asked Luke.

Joe shook his head. 'It didn't even do what "Sheep in Fog" did.'

'It's all remakes,' said Jim. 'Period shit.'

'How about "Bog Oak"?'

' "Bog Oak"?' Ooh, maybe twenty-five?'

Luke said sourly, 'I hear nice things about "The Old Botanical Gardens".'

They talked about other Christmas flops and bombs, delaying for as long as they could any mention of TCT's "tis he whose yester-evening's high disdain', which had cost practically nothing to make and had already done a hundred and twenty million in its first three weeks.

'What happened?' Luke eventually asked. 'Jesus, what was the publicity budget?'

'On' ' "Tis?" ' said Joe. 'Nothing. Two, three.'

They all shook their heads. Jim was philosophical. 'That's poetry,' he said.

'There aren't any other sonnets being made, are there?' said Luke.

Jeff said, 'Binary is in post-production with a sonnet. "Composed at — Castle". *More* period shit.'

Their soups and salads arrived. Luke thought that it was probably a mistake, at this stage, to go on about sonnets. After a while he said, 'How did "For Sophonisba Anguisciola" do?'

Joe said, '"For Sophonisba Anguisciola"? Don't talk to me about "For Sophonisba Anguisciola".'

It was late at night and Alistair was in his room working on a screenplay about a high-IQ homeless black man who is transformed into a white female junk-bond dealer by a South Moluccan terrorist witch doctor. Suddenly he shoved this aside with a groan, snatched up a clean sheet of paper, and wrote:

Dear Mr Sixsmith,

It is now well over a year since I sent you *Offensive from Quasar 13*. Not content with that dereliction, you have allowed five months to pass without responding to three more recent submissions. A prompt reply I would have deemed common decency, you being a fellow-screenplay writer, though I must say I have never cared for your work, finding it, at once, both florid and superficial. (I read Matthew Sura's piece last month and I thought he got you *bang to rights*.) Please return the more recent screenplays, namely *Decimator, Medusa Takes Manhattan* and *Valley of the Stratocasters*, immediately.

He signed it and sealed it. He stalked out and posted it. On his return he haughtily threw off his drenched clothes. The single bed felt enormous, like an orgiast's fourposter. He curled up tight and slept better than he had done all year.

So it was a quietly defiant Alistair who the next morning came plodding down the stairs and glanced at the splayed mail on the shelf as he headed for the door. He recognized the envelope as a lover would. He bent low as he opened it.

Do please forgive this very tardy reply. Profound apologies. But allow me to move straight on to a verdict on your work. I won't bore you with all my personal and professional distractions.

Bore me? thought Alistair, as his hand sought his heart.

I think I can at once give the assurance that your screenplays are unusually promising. No: that promise has already been honoured. They have both feeling and burnish.

I will content myself, for now, by taking *Offensive from Quasar 13*. (Allow me to muse a little longer on *Decimator*.) I have one or two very minor emendations to suggest. Why not telephone me here to arrange a chat?

Thank you for your generous remarks about my own work. Increasingly I find that this kind of exchange – this candour, this reciprocity – is one of the things that keep me trundling along. Your words helped sustain my defenses in the aftermath of Matthew Sura's vicious and slovenly attack, from which, I fear, I am still rather reeling. Take excellent care.

'Go with the lyric,' said Jim.

'Or how about a ballad?' said Jeff.

Jack was swayable. 'Ballads are big,' he allowed.

It seemed to Luke, towards the end of the second day, that he was winning the sonnet battle. The clue lay in the flavour of Joe's taciturnity: torpid but unmorose.

'Let's face it,' said Jeff. 'Sonnets are essentially hieratic. They're strictly period. They answer to a formalized consciousness. Today, we're talking consciousnesses that are in *search* of form.'

'Plus,' said Jack, 'the lyric has always been the natural medium for the untrammelled expression of feeling.'

'Yeah,' said Jeff. 'With the sonnet you're stuck in this thesis-antithesis-synthesis routine.'

Joan said, 'I mean what are we doing here? Reflecting the world or illuminating it?'

It was time for Joe to speak. 'Please,' he said. 'Are we forgetting that '"Tis" was a sonnet, before the rewrites? Were we on coke when we said, in the summer, that we were going to go for the *sonnet*?'

The answer to Joe's last question, incidentally, was yes; but Luke looked carefully round the room. The Chinese lunch they'd had the secretary phone out for lay on the coffee table like a child's experiments with putty and paint and designer ooze. It was four o'clock and Luke wanted to get away soon. To swim and lie in the sun. To make himself especially lean and bronzed for his meeting with the young actress Henna Mickiewicz. He faked a yawn.

'Luke's lagged,' said Joe. 'Tomorrow we'll talk some more, but I'm pretty sure I'm recommitted to the sonnet.'

'Sorry,' said Alistair. 'Me yet again. Sorry.'

'Oh yes,' said the woman's voice. 'He *was* here a minute ago . . . No, he's there. He's there. Just a second.'

Alistair jerked the receiver away from his ear and stared at it. He started listening again. It seemed as if the phone itself were in paroxysm, all squawk and splat like a cabby's radio. Then the fit passed, or paused, and a voice said tightly but proudly, 'Hugh Sixsmith?'

It took Alistair a little while to explain who he was. Sixsmith sounded

surprised but, on the whole, rather intrigued to hear from him. They
moved on smoothly enough to arrange a meeting (after work, the following
Monday), before Alistair contrived to put in: 'Mr Sixsmith, there's just
one thing. This is very embarrassing, but last night I got into a bit of a state
about not hearing from you for so long and I'm afraid I sent you a
completely mad letter which I . . .' Alistair waited. 'Oh, you know how it
is. For these screenplays, you know, you reach into yourself, and then time
goes by and . . .'

'My dear boy, don't say another word. I'll ignore it. I'll throw it away.
After a line or two I shall simply avert my unpained eye,' said Sixsmith,
and started coughing again.

Hazel did not come down to London for the weekend. Alistair did not go
up to Leeds for the weekend. He spent the time thinking about that place in
Earls Court Square where screenplay writers read from their screenplays
and drank biting Spanish red wine and got stared at by tousled girls who
wore thick overcoats and no make-up and blinked incessantly or not at all.

Luke parked his Chevrolet Celebrity on the fifth floor of the studio car park
and rode down in the elevator with two minor executives in tracksuits who
were discussing the latest records broken by ''Tis he whose yester-
evening's high disdain'. He put on his dark glasses as he crossed the other
car park, the one reserved for major executives. Each bay had a name on it.
It reassured Luke to see Joe's name there, partly obscured by his Range
Rover. Poets, of course, seldom had that kind of clout. Or any clout at all.
He was glad that Henna Mickiewicz didn't seem to realize this.

Joe's office: Jim, Jack, Joan, but no Jeff. Two new guys were there. Luke
was introduced to the two new guys. Ron said he spoke for Don when he
told Luke that he was a great admirer of his material. Huddled over the
coffee percolator with Joe, Luke asked after Jeff, and Joe said, 'Jeff's off the
poem,' and Luke just nodded.

They settled in their low armchairs.

Luke said, 'What's "A Welshman to Any Tourist" doing?'

Don said, 'It's doing good but not great.'

Ron said, 'It won't do what "The Gap in the Hedge" did.'

Jim said, 'What did "Hedge" do?'

They talked about what 'Hedge' did. Then Joe said, 'OK. We're going
with the sonnet. Now. Don has a problem with the octet's first quatrain,
Ron has a problem with the second quatrain, Jack and Jim have a problem
with the first quatrain of the sestet, and I think we *all* have a problem with
the final couplet.'

Alistair presented himself at the offices of the *LM* in an unblinking trance
of punctuality. He had been in the area for hours, and had spent about

fifteen quid on teas and coffees. There wasn't much welcome to overstay in the various snack bars where he lingered (and where he moreover imagined himself unfavourably recollected from his previous *LM* vigils), holding with both hands the creaky foam container, and watching the light pour past the office windows.

As Big Ben struck two, Alistair mounted the stairs. He took a breath so deep that he almost fell over backwards – and then knocked. An elderly office boy wordlessly showed him into a narrow, rubbish-heaped office that contained, with difficulty, seven people. At first Alistair took them for other screenplay writers and wedged himself behind the door, at the back of the queue. But they didn't look like screenplay writers. Not much was said over the next four hours, and the identities of Sixsmith's supplicants emerged only partially and piecemeal. One or two, like his solicitor and his second wife's psychiatrist, took their leave after no more than ninety minutes. Others, like the VAT man and the probation officer, stayed almost as long as Alistair. But by six forty-five he was alone.

He approached the impossible haystack of Sixsmith's desk. Very hurriedly, he started searching through the unopened mail. It was in Alistair's mind that he might locate and intercept his own letter. But all the envelopes, of which there were a great many, proved to be brown, windowed, and registered. Turning to leave, he saw a Jiffy bag of formidable bulk addressed to himself in Sixsmith's tremulous hand. There seemed no reason not to take it. The old office boy, Alistair soon saw, was curled up in a sleeping-bag under a worktable in the outer room.

On the street he unseamed his package in a ferment of grey fluff. It contained two of his screenplays, *Valley of the Stratocasters* and, confusingly, *Decimator*. There was also a note:

I have been called away, as they say. Personal ups and downs. I shall ring you this week and we'll have – what? Lunch?

Enclosed, too, was Alistair's aggrieved letter – unopened. He moved on. The traffic, human and mechanical, lurched past his quickened face. He felt his eyes widen to an obvious and solving truth: Hugh Sixsmith was a screenplay writer. He understood.

After an inconclusive day spent discussing the caesura of 'Sonnet''s opening line, Luke and his colleagues went for cocktails at Strabismus. They were given the big round table near the piano.
Jane said, 'TCT is doing a sequel to " 'Tis".'
Joan said, 'Actually it's a prequel.'
'Title?' said Joe.
'Undecided. At TCT they're calling it " 'Twas".'
'My son,' said Joe thoughtfully, after the waiter had delivered their

drinks, 'called me an asshole this morning. For the first time.'

'That's incredible,' said Bo. '*My* son called me an asshole this morning. For the first time.'

'So?' said Mo.

Joe said, 'He's six years old, for Christ's sake.'

Phil said, 'My son called me an asshole when he was five.'

'My son hasn't called me an asshole yet,' said Jim. 'And he's nine.'

Luke sipped his Bloody Mary. Its hue and texture made him wonder whether he could risk blowing his nose without making yet another visit to the bathroom. He hadn't called Suki for three days. Things were getting compellingly out of hand with Henna Mickiewicz. He hadn't actually promised her a part in the poem, not on paper. Henna was great, except you kept thinking she was going to suddenly sue you anyway.

Mo was saying that each child progresses at his own rate, and that later lulls regularly offset the apparent advances of the early years.

Mo said, 'My son's three. And he calls me an asshole all the time.'

Everybody looked suitably impressed.

The trees were in leaf, and the rumps of the tourist buses were thick and fat in the traffic, and all the farmers wanted fertilizer admixes rather than storehouse insulation when Sixsmith finally made his call. In the interim, Alistair had convinced himself of the following: before returning his aggrieved letter, Sixsmith had *steamed it open and then resealed it.* During this period, also, Alistair had grimly got engaged to Hazel. But the call came.

He was pretty sure he had come to the right restaurant. Except that it wasn't a restaurant, not quite. The place took no bookings, and knew of no Mr Sixsmith, and was serving many midday breakfasts to swearing persons whose eyes bulged over mugs of flesh-coloured tea. On the other hand, there was alcohol. All kinds of people were drinking it. Fine, thought Alistair. Fine. What better place, really, for a couple of screenplay writers to . . .

'Alistair?'

Confidently, Sixsmith bent his long body into the booth. As he settled, he looked well pleased with the manoeuvre. He contemplated Alistair with peculiar neutrality, but there was then something boyish, something consciously remiss, in the face he turned to the waiter. As Sixsmith ordered a gin-and-tonic, and as he amusingly expatiated on his weakness for prawn cocktails, Alistair found himself wryly but powerfully drawn to this man, to this rumpled screenplay writer with his dreamy gaze, the curious elisions of his somewhat slurred voice, and the great dents and bone shadows of his face, all the faulty fontanels of vocational care. He knew how old Sixsmith was. But maybe time moved strangely for screenplay writers, whose flames burnt so bright . . .

'And as for my fellow artisan in the scrivener's trade, Alistair. What will *you* have?'

At once Sixsmith showed himself to be a person of some candour. Or it might have been that he saw in the younger screenplay writer someone before whom all false reticence could be cast aside. Sixsmith's estranged second wife, it emerged, herself the daughter of two alcoholics, was an alcoholic. Her current lover (ah, how these lovers came and went!) was an alcoholic. To complicate matters, Sixsmith explained as he rattled his glass at the waiter, his daughter, the product of his first marriage, was an alcoholic. How did Sixsmith keep going? Despite his years, he had, thank God, found love, in the arms of a woman young enough (and, by the sound of it, alcoholic enough) to be his daughter. Their prawn cocktails arrived, together with a carafe of hearty red wine. Sixsmith lit a cigarette and held up his palm towards Alistair for the duration of a coughing fit that turned every head in the room. Then, for a moment, understandably disoriented, he stared at Alistair as if uncertain of his intentions, or even his identity. But their bond quickly re-established itself. Soon they were talking away like hardened equals – of Trumbo, of Chayevsky, of Towne, of Eszterhas.

Around two thirty, when, after several attempts, the waiter succeeded in removing Sixsmith's untouched prawn cocktail, and now prepared to serve them their braised chops with a third carafe, the two men were arguing loudly about early Puzo.

Joe yawned and shrugged and said languidly, 'You know something? I was never that crazy about the Petrarchan rhyme scheme anyway.'

Jan said, ' "Composed at — Castle" is ABBA ABBA.'

Jen said, 'So was " 'Tis". Right up until the final polish.'

Jon said, 'Here's some news. They say "Composed at — Castle" is in turnaround.'

'You're not serious,' said Bo. 'It's released this month. I heard they were getting great preview reaction.'

Joe looked doubtful. ' " 'Tis" has made the suits kind of antsy about sonnets. They figure lightning can't strike twice.'

'ABBA ABBA,' said Bo with distaste.

'Or,' said Joe. '*Or . . . or* we go unrhymed.'

'*Un*rhymed?' said Phil.

'We go blank,' said Joe.

There was a silence. Bill looked at Gil, who looked at Will.

'What do you think, Luke?' said Jim. 'You're the poet.'

Luke had never felt very protective about 'Sonnet'. Even its original version he had regarded as no more than a bargaining chip. Nowadays he rewrote 'Sonnet' every night at the Pinnacle Trumont before Henna arrived and they called room service. 'Blank,' said Luke. 'Blank. I don't know, Joe. I could go ABAB ABAB or even ABAB CDCD. Christ, I'd go AABB if I didn't think it'd tank the final couplet. But blank. I never thought I'd go *blank*.'

'Well, it needs something,' said Joe.

'Maybe it's the pentameter,' said Luke. 'Maybe it's the iamb. Hey, here's one from left field. How about syllabics?'

At five forty-five Hugh Sixsmith ordered a gin-and-tonic and said, 'We've talked. We've broken bread. Wine. Truth. Screenplay-writing. I want to talk about your work, Alistair. Yes, I do. I want to talk about *Offensive from Quasar 13.*'

Alistair blushed.

'It's not often that . . . But one always knows. That sense of pregnant arrest. Of felt life in its full . . . Thank you, Alistair. Thank you. I have to say that it rather reminded me of my own early work.'

Alistair nodded.

Having talked for quite some time about his own maturation as a screenplay writer, Sixsmith said, 'Now. Just tell me to shut up any time you like. And I'm going to print it anyway. But I want to make one *tiny* suggestion about *Offensive from Quasar 13.*'

Alistair waved a hand in the air.

'Now,' said Sixsmith. He broke off and ordered a prawn cocktail. The waiter looked at him defeatedly. 'Now,' said Sixsmith. 'When Brad escapes from the Nebulan experiment lab and sets off with Cord and Tara to immobilize the directed-energy scythe on the Xerxian attack ship – where's Chelsi?'

Alistair frowned.

'Where's Chelsi? She's still in the lab with the Nebulans. On the point of being injected with a Phobian viper venom, moreover. What of the happy ending? What of Brad's heroic centrality? What of his avowed love for Chelsi? Or am I just being a bore?'

The secretary, Victoria, stuck her head into the room and said, 'He's coming down.'

Luke listened to the sound of twenty-three pairs of legs uncrossing and recrossing. Meanwhile he readied himself for a sixteen-tooth smile. He glanced at Joe, who said, 'He's fine. He's just coming down to say hi.'

And down he came: Jake Endo, exquisitely Westernized and gorgeously tricked out and perhaps thirty-five. Of the luxury items that pargeted his slender form, none was as breathtaking as his hair, with its layers of pampered light.

Jake Endo shook Luke's hand and said, 'It's a great pleasure to meet you. I haven't read the basic material on the poem, but I'm familiar with the background.'

Luke surmised that Jake Endo had had his voice fixed. He could do the bits of the words that Japanese people were supposed to find difficult.

'I understand it's a love poem,' he continued. 'Addressed to your girlfriend. Is she here with you in L.A.?'

'No. She's in London.' Luke found he was staring at Jake Endo's sandals, wondering how much they could possibly have cost.

A silence began its crescendo. This silence had long been intolerable when Jim broke it, saying to Jake Endo, 'Oh, how did "Lines Left Upon a Seat in a Yew-Tree, Which Stands Near the Lake of Easthwaite, on a Desolate Part of the Shore, Commanding a Beautiful Prospect" do?'

' "Lines"?' said Jake Endo. 'Rather well.'

'I was thinking about "Composed at — Castle",' said Jim weakly.

The silence began again. As it neared its climax Joe was suddenly reminded of all this energy he was supposed to have. He got to his feet saying, 'Jake? I guess we're nearing our tiredness peak. You've caught us at kind of a low point. We can't agree on the first line. First line? We can't see our way to the end of the first *foot*.'

Jake Endo was undismayed. 'There always are these low points. I'm sure you'll get there, with so much talent in the room. Upstairs we're very confident. We think it's going to be a big summer poem.'

'No, we're very confident, too,' said Joe. 'There's a lot of belief here. A lot of belief. We're behind "Sonnet" all the way.'

'Sonnet?' said Jake Endo.

'Yeah, sonnet. "Sonnet".'

' "Sonnet"?' said Jake Endo.

'It's a sonnet. It's called "Sonnet".'

In waves the West fell away from Jake Endo's face. After a few seconds he looked like a dark-age warlord in mid-campaign, taking a glazed breather before moving on to the women and the children.

'Nobody told me,' he said as he went towards the telephone, 'about any *sonnet*.'

The place was closing. Its tea trade and its after-office trade had come and gone. Outside, the streets glimmered morbidly. Members of the staff were donning macs and overcoats. An important light went out. A fridge door slammed.

'Hardly the most resounding felicity, is it?' said Sixsmith.

Absent or unavailable for over an hour, the gift of speech had been restored to Alistair – speech, that prince of all the faculties. 'Or what if . . .' he said. 'What if Chelsi just leaves the experiment lab earlier?'

'Not hugely dramatic,' said Sixsmith. He ordered a carafe of wine and inquired as to the whereabouts of his braised chop.

'Or what if she just gets wounded? During the escape. In the leg.'

'So long as one could avoid the wretched cliché: girl impeded, hero dangerously tarrying. Also, she's supernumerary to the raid on the Xerxian attack ship. We really want her out of the way for that.'

Alistair said, 'Then let's kill her.'

'Very well. Slight pall over the happy ending. No, no.'

A waiter stood over them, sadly staring at the bill in its saucer.

'All right,' said Sixsmith. 'Chelsi gets wounded. Quite badly. In the arm. *Now* what does Brad do with her?'

'Drops her off at the hospital.'

'Mm. Rather hollow modulation.'

The waiter was joined by another waiter, equally stoic; their faces were grained by evening shadow. Now Sixsmith was gently frisking himself with a deepening frown.

'What if,' said Alistair, 'what if there's somebody passing who can take her to the hospital?'

'Possibly,' said Sixsmith, who was half standing, with one hand awkwardly dipped into his inside pocket.

'Or what if,' said Alistair, 'or what if Brad just gives her *directions* to the hospital?'

Back in London the next day, Luke met with Mike to straighten this shit out. Actually it looked OK. Mike called Mal at Monad, who had a thing about Tim at TCT. As a potential finesse on Mal, Mike also called Bob at Binary with a view to repossessing the option on 'Sonnet', plus development money at rolling compound, and redeveloping it somewhere else entirely – say, at Red Giant, where Rodge was known to be very interested. 'They'll want you to go out there,' said Mike. 'To kick it around.'

'I can't believe Joe,' said Luke. 'I can't believe I knocked myself out for that flake.'

'Happens. Joe forgot about Jake Endo and sonnets. Endo's first big poem was a sonnet. Before your time. "Bright star, would I were steadfast as thou art." It opened for like one day. It practically bankrupted Japan.'

'I feel used, Mike. My sense of trust. I've got to get wised up around here.'

'A lot will depend on how "Composed at — Castle" does and what the feeling is on the " 'Tis" prequel.'

'I'm going to go away with Suki for a while. Do you know anywhere where there aren't any shops? Jesus, I need a holiday. Mike, this is all bullshit. You know what I *really* want to do, don't you?'

'Of course I do.'

Luke looked at Mike until he said, 'You want to direct.'

When Alistair had convalesced from the lunch, he revised *Offensive from Quasar 13* in rough accordance with Sixsmith's suggestions. He solved the

362

Chelsi problem by having her noisily eaten by a Stygian panther in the lab menagerie. The charge of gratuitousness was, in Alistair's view, safely anticipated by Brad's valediction to her remains, in which sanguinary revenge on the Nebulans was both prefigured and legitimized. He also took out the bit where Brad declared his love for Chelsi, and put in a bit where Brad declared his love for Tara.

He sent in the new pages, which three months later Sixsmith acknowledged and applauded in a hand quite incompatible with that of his earlier communications. Nor did he reimburse Alistair for the lunch. His wallet, he had explained, had been emptied that morning – by which alcoholic, Sixsmith never established. Alistair kept the bill as a memento. This startling document showed that during the course of the meal Sixsmith had smoked, or at any rate bought, nearly a carton of cigarettes.

Three months later he was sent a proof of *Offensive from Quasar 13*. Three months after that, the screenplay appeared in the *LM*. Three months after that, Alistair received a cheque for £12.50, which bounced.

Curiously, although the proof had incorporated Alistair's corrections, the published version reverted to the typescript, in which Brad escaped from the Nebulan lab seemingly without concern for a Chelsi last glimpsed on an operating table with a syringe full of Phobian viper venom being eased into her neck. Later that month, Alistair went along to a reading at the Screenplay Society in Earls Court. There he got talking to a gaunt girl in an ash-stained black smock who claimed to have read his screenplay and who, over glasses of red wine and, later, in the terrible pub, told him he was a weakling and a hypocrite with no notion of the ways of men and women. Alistair had not been a published screenplay writer long enough to respond to, or even recognize, this graphic proposition (though he did keep the telephone number she threw at his feet). It is anyway doubtful whether he would have dared to take things further. He was marrying Hazel the following weekend.

In the new year he sent Sixsmith a series – one might almost say a sequence – of screenplays on group-jeopardy themes. His follow-up letter in the summer was answered by a brief note stating that Sixsmith was no longer employed by the *LM*. Alistair telephoned. He then discussed the matter with Hazel and decided to take the next day off work.

It was a September morning. The hospice in Cricklewood was of recent design and construction; from the road it resembled a clutch of igloos against the sheenless tundra of the sky. When he asked for Hugh Sixsmith at the desk, two men in suits climbed quickly from their chairs. One was a writ-server. One was a cost-adjuster. Alistair waved away their complex requests.

The warm room contained clogged, regretful murmurs, and defiance in the form of bottles and paper cups and cigarette smoke, and the many peeping eyes of female grief. A young woman faced him proudly. Alistair started explaining who he was, a young screenplay writer come to . . . On the bed in the corner the spavined figure of Sixsmith was gawkily arranged. Alistair moved towards it. At first he was sure the eyes were gone, like holes cut out of pumpkin or blood orange. But then the faint brows began to lift, and Alistair thought he saw the light of recognition.

As the tears began, he felt the shiver of approval, of consensus, on his back. He took the old screenplay writer's hand and said, 'Goodbye. And thank you. Thank you. Thank you.'

Opening in four hundred and thirty-seven theatres, the Binary sonnet 'Composed at — Castle' did seventeen million in its first weekend. At this time Luke was living in a two-bedroom apartment on Yokum Drive. Suki was with him. He hoped it wouldn't take her too long to find out about Henna Mickiewicz. When the smoke cleared he would switch to the more mature Anita, who produced.

He had taken his sonnet to Rodge at Red Giant and turned it into an ode. When that didn't work out he went to Mal at Monad, where they'd gone for the villanelle. The villanelle had become a triolet, briefly, with Tim at TCT, before Bob at Binary had him rethink it as a rondeau. When the rondeau didn't take, Luke lyricized it and got Mike to send it to Joe. Everyone, including Jake Endo, thought that now was surely the time to turn it back into a sonnet.

Luke had dinner at Rales with Joe and Mike.

'I always thought of "Sonnet" as an art poem,' said Joe. 'But things are so hot now, I've started thinking more commercially.'

Mike said, 'TCT is doing a sequel *and* a prequel to " 'Tis" and bringing them out at the same time.'

'A sequel?' said Joe.

'Yeah. They're calling it " 'Twill".'

Mike was a little fucked up. So was Joe. Luke was a little fucked up, too. They'd done some lines at the office. Then drinks here at the bar. They'd meant to get a little fucked up. It was OK. It was good, once in a while, to get a little fucked up. The thing was not to get fucked up too often. The thing was not to get fucked up to excess.

'I mean it, Luke,' said Joe. He glittered potently. 'I think "Sonnet" could be as big as "—".'

'You think?' said Luke.

'I mean it. I think "Sonnet" could be another "—".'

' "—"?'

' "—".'

Luke thought for a moment, taking this in. ' "—" . . .' he repeated wonderingly.

WILL SELF

A Short History of the English Novel

Will Self (1961–), who was born in London, worked for a time as a cartoonist before he began writing fiction. Unusually he established himself as a significant new writer of the nineties with a short story collection, *The Quantity Theory of Insanity* (1991). Then came the two linked novellas *Cock & Bull* (1992), about the disordered world of contemporary gender relations, and he has published a first novel, *My Idea of Fun* (1993).

'A Short History of the English Novel', which was first published in *The Time Out Book of London Short Stories* (1993), shows Self's original talent, his strongly literary preoccupations, his witty, topical, streetwise vision, and the touch of darkness about personal relations and urban life which seems to mark so much fiction in the nineties. Less macabre than some of Will Self's other tales, it shows, as Doris Lessing has said, that his work has 'the unmistakable sign of the genuine comic writer'.

'The sun shone down on nothing new' – Beckett

'**A**ll crap,' said Gerard through a mouthful of hamburger, 'utter shite – and the worst thing is that we're aware of it, we know what's going on. Really, I think, it's the cultural complement to the decline of the economy in the seventies coming lolloping along behind.'

We were sitting in Joe Allen's and Gerard was holding forth on the sad state of the English novel. This was all I had to pay for our monthly lunch together: listening to Gerard sound off.

I came back at him. 'I'm not sure I agree with you on this one, Gerard. Isn't that a perennial gripe, something that comes up time and again? Surely we won't be able to judge the literature of this decade for another thirty or forty years?'

'You're bound to say that, being a woman.'

'I'm sorry?'

'Well, in so much as the novel was very much a feminine form in the first place and now that our literary culture has begun to fragment, the partisan concerns of minorities are again taking precedence. There isn't really an "English novel" now, there are just women's novels, black novels, gay novels.'

I tuned him out. He was too annoying to listen to. Round about us the lunchtime crowd was thinning. A few advertising and city types sipped their wine and Perrier, nodding over each other's shoulders at the autographed photos that studded the restaurant's walls, as if they were saluting dear old friends.

Gerard and I had been doing these monthly lunches at Joe Allen's for about a year. Ours was an odd friendship. For a while he'd been married to a friend of mine but it had been a duff exercise in emotional surgery, both hearts rejecting the other. They hadn't had any children. Some of our mutual acquaintances suspected they were gay, and that the marriage was one of convenience, a coming-together to avoid coming out.

Gerard was also a plump, good-looking man, who despite his stress-filled urban existence, still retained the burnish of a country childhood in the pink glow of his cheeks and the chestnut hanks of his thick fringe.

Gerard did something in publishing. That was what accounted for his willingness to pronounce on the current state of English fiction. It wasn't anything editorial or high-profile. Rather, when he talked to me of his work – which he did only infrequently – it was of books as so many units, trafficked hither and thither with as little sentiment as if they were boxes of washing-powder. And when he spoke of authors, he managed somehow to reduce them to the status of assembly-line workers, trampish little automata who were merely bolting the next lump of text on to an endlessly unrolling narrative product.

'. . . Spry old women's sex novels, Welsh novels, the Glasgow Hard

367

Man School, the ex-colonial guilt novel – both perpetrator and victim version . . .' He was still droning on.

'What are you driving at, Gerard?'

'Oh, come on, you're not going to play devil's advocate on this one, are you? You don't believe in the centrality of the literary tradition in this country any more than I do, now do you?'

'S'pose not.'

'You probably buy two or three of the big prize-winning novels every year and then possibly, just possibly, get round to reading one of them a year or so later. As for anything else, you might skim some thrillers that have been made into TV dramas – or vice versa, or scan something issue-based, or nibble at a plot that hinges on an unusual sexual position, the blurb for which happens to have caught your eye . . .'

'. . . But Gerard,' despite myself I was rising to it, 'just because we don't read that much, aren't absorbed in it, it doesn't mean that important literary production isn't going on . . .'

'Not that old chestnut!' he snorted. 'I suppose you're going to tell me next that there may be thousands of unbelievably good manuscripts rotting away in attic rooms, only missing out on publication because of the diffidence of their authors, or the formulaic, sales-driven narrow-mindedness of publishers, eh?'

'No, Gerard, I wasn't going to argue that . . .'

'. . . It's like the old joke about L.A., that there aren't any waiters in the whole town, just movie stars "resting". I suppose all these busboys and girls,' he flicked a hand towards the epicene character who had been ministering to us our meal, 'are great novelists hanging out to get more material.'

'No, that's not what I meant.'

'Excuse me?' It was the waiter, a lanky blond who had been dangling in mid-distance. 'Did you want anything else?'

'No, no,' Gerard started shaking his head – but then broke off, 'actually, now that you're here would you mind if I asked you a question?'

'Oh Gerard,' I groaned, 'leave the poor boy alone.'

'No, not at all, anything to be of service,' he was bending down towards us, service inscribed all over his soft-skinned face.

'Tell me then, are you happy working here or do you harbour any other ambition?' Gerard put the question as straight as he could but his plump mouth was twisted with irony.

The waiter thought for a while. I observed his flat fingers, nails bitten to the quick and his thin nose coped with blue veins at the nostrils' flare. His hair was tied back in a ponytail and fastened with a thick rubber band.

'Do you mind?' he said at length, pulling half-out one of the free chairs.

'No, no,' I replied, 'of course not.' He sat down and instantly we all became intimates, our three brows forming a tight triangle over the cruets. The waiter put up his hands vertically, holding them like parentheses into which he would insert qualifying words.

'Well,' a self-deprecatory cough, 'it's not that I mind working here – because I don't, but I write a little and I suppose I would like to be published some day.'

I wanted to hoot, to crow, to snort derision, but contented myself with a 'Ha!'

'Now come on, wait a minute,' Gerard was adding his bracketing hands to the manual quorum, 'OK, this guy is a writer but who's to say what he's doing is good, or original?'

'Gerard! You're being rude . . .'

'. . . No, really, it doesn't matter, I don't mind. He's got a point,' his secret out, the waiter was more self-possessed, 'I write – that's true. I think the ideas are good. I think the prose is good. But I can't tell if it hangs together.'

'Well, tell us a bit about it. If you can, quote some from memory.' I lit a cigarette and tilted back in my chair.

'It's complex. We know that Eric Gill was something more than an ordinary sexual experimenter. According to his own journal he even had sex with his dog. I'm writing a narrative from the point of view of Gill's dog. The book is called *Fanny Gill*, or *I was Eric Gill's Canine Lover*.' Gerard and I were giggling before he'd finished; and the waiter smiled with us.

'That's very funny,' I said, 'I especially like the play on . . .'

'. . . *Fanny Hill*, yeah. Well, I've tried to style it like an eighteenth-century picaresque narrative. You know, with the dog growing up in the country, being introduced to the Gill household by a canine pander. Her loss of virginity and so on.'

'Can you give us a little gobbet then?' asked Gerard. He was still smiling but no longer ironically. The waiter sat back and struck a pose. With his scraped-back hair and long face, he reminded me of some Regency actor–manager.

Then one night, as I turned and tossed in my basket, the yeasty smell of biscuit and the matted ordure in my coat blanketing my prone form, I became aware of a draught of turpentine, mixed with the lavender of the night air.

My master, the artist and stone-carver, stood over me.

'Come Fanny,' he called, slapping his square-cut hands against his smock, 'there's a good little doggie.' I trotted after him, out into the darkness. He strode ahead, whilst I meandered in his wake, twisting in the smelly skeins betwixt owl pellet and fox stool. 'Come on now!' He was sharp and imperious. A tunnel of light opened up in the darkness.

369

'Come in!' he snapped again, and I obeyed – poor beast – unaware that I had just taken my last stroll as an innocent dog.

Later, when Gerard had paid the bill and we were walking up Bow Street towards Long Acre, for no reason that I could think of I took Gerard's arm. I'd never touched him before. His body was surprisingly firm, but tinged with dampness like a thick carpet in an old house. I said, trying to purge the triumph from my tone, 'That was really rather good – now wasn't it?'

'Humph! S'pose so, but it was a "gay" novel, not in the mainstream of any literary tradition.'

'How can you say that?' I was incredulous. 'There was nothing obviously gay about it!'

'Really, Geraldine. The idea of using the dog as a sexual object was an allegory for the love that dare not speak its name, only whuffle. Anyway, he himself – the waiter, that is – was an obvious poof.'

We walked on in silence for a while. It was one of those flat, cold London days. The steely air wavered over the bonnets of cars, as if they were some kind of automotive mirage, ready to dissolve into a tarmac desert.

We normally parted at the mouth of the short road that leads to Covent Garden Piazza. I would stand, watching Gerard's retreating overcoat as he moved past the fire-eaters, the jugglers, the stand-up comedians; and on across the parade-ground of flagstones with its manœuvring battalions of Benelux au pair girls. But on this occasion I wouldn't let him go.

'Do you have to get back to the office? Is there actually anything pressing for you to do?' He seemed startled and turning to present the oblong sincerity of his face to me, he almost wrenched my arm.

'Erm . . . well, no. S'pose not.'

'How about a coffee then?'

'Oh, all right.'

I was sure he had meant this admission to sound cool, unconcerned, but it had come out as pathetic. Despite all his confident, wordy pronouncements, I was beginning to suspect that Gerard's work might be as meaningless as my own.

As we strolled still coupled down Long Acre, the commercial day was pushing towards its postprandial lack of swing. The opulent stores with their displays of flash goods, belied what was really going on.

'The recession's really starting to bite,' Gerard remarked, handing a ten-pence piece to a dosser who sat scrunched up behind a baffler of milk crates, as if he were a photographer of feelings at life's event.

'Tell me about it, mate.' The words leaked from the gaps in the dosser's teeth, trickled through the stubble of his chin and flowed across the pavement carrying their barge-load of hopelessness.

The two of us paused again in front of the Hippodrome.

'Well,' said Gerard, 'where shall we have our coffee, then? Do you want to go to my club?'

'God no! Come on, let's go somewhere a little youthful.'

'You lead – I'll follow.'

We passed the Crystal Rooms, where tense loss adjusters rocked on the saddles of the stranded motor-cycles, which they powered on through virtual curve after virtual curve.

At the mouth of Gerrard Street, we passed under the triumphal arch with its coiled and burnished dragons. Around us the Chinese skipped and altercated, as scrutable as ever. Set beside their scooterish bodies, adolescent and wind-cheating, Gerard appeared more than ever to be some Scobie or Brown, lost for ever in the grimy Greeneland of inner London.

Outside the Bar Italia a circle of pari-cropped heads were deliberating over glasses of *caffè e latte* held at hammy angles.

'Oh,' said Gerard, 'the Bar Italia. I haven't been here in ages, what fun.' He pushed ahead of me into the tiled burrow of the café. Behind the grunting Gaggia a dumpy woman with a hennaed brow puffed and pulled. '*Due espressi!*' Gerard trilled in cod-Italian tones, '*Doppi!*'

'I didn't know you spoke Italian,' I said as we scraped back two stools from underneath the giant video screen swathing the back of the café.

'Oh well, you know . . .' He trailed off and gazed up as the flat tummy filling the hissing screen rotated in a figure-eight of oozing congress. A special-effect lipoma swelled in its navel and then inflated into the face of a warbling androgyne.

A swarthy young woman, with a prominent mole on her upper lip, came over and banged two espressos down on the ledge we were sitting against.

'Oh really!' Gerard exclaimed: coffee now spotted his shirt-front like a dalmatian's belly. 'Can't you take a little more care?' The waitress looked at him hard, jaw and brow shaking with anger, as if some prisoners of consciousness were attempting to jack-hammer their escape from her skull. She hiccuped despair, then ran the length of the café and out into the street, sobbing loudly.

'What did I say?' Gerard appealed to the café at large. The group of flat-capped Italian men by the cake display had left off haggling over their pools coupons to stare. The hennaed woman squeezed out from behind the Gaggia and clumped down to where we sat. She started to paw at Gerard's chest with a filthy wodge of J-Cloths.

'I so sorry sir, so sorry . . .'

'. . . Whoa! Hold on – you're making it worse!'

'Iss not her fault you know, she's a good girl, ve-ery good girl. She have a big sadness this days . . .'

'Man-trouble I'll be bound.' Gerard smirked. It looked like he was enjoying his grubby embrocation.

'No iss not that . . . iss, 'ow you say, a re-jection?'

I sat up straighter. 'A rejection? What sort of rejection?' The woman left off rubbing Gerard and turned to me. 'She give this thing, this book to some peoples, they no like . . .'

'Ha, ha! You don't say. My dear Gerard,' I punched him on the upper arm, 'it looks like we have another scrivenous servitor on our hands.'

'This is absurd.' He wasn't amused.

'My friend here is a publisher, he might be able to help your girl, why don't you ask her to join us?'

'Oh really, Geraldine, can't you let this lie. We don't know anything about this girl's book. Madam . . .'

But she was already gone, stomping back down the mirrored alley and out the door into the street, where I saw her place a soft arm round the heaving shoulders of our former waitress.

Gerard and I sat in silence. I scrutinized him again. In this surrounding he appeared fogeyish. He seemed aware of it too, his eyes flicking nervously from the carnal cubs swimming on the ethereal video screen, to their kittenish domesticated cousins, the jail-bait who picked their nails and split their ends all along the coffee bar's counter.

The waitress came back down towards us. She was a striking young woman. Dark but not Neapolitan, with a low brow, short bobbed hair and deep-set, rather steely eyes that skated away from mine when I tried to meet them.

'Yes? The boss said you wanted to talk to me – look, I'm sorry about the spillage, OK?' She didn't sound sorry. Her anger had evaporated, leaving behind a tidal mark of saline bitterness.

'No, no, it's not that. Here, sit down with us for a minute.' I proffered my pack of cigarettes; she refused with a coltish head jerk. 'Apparently you're a writer of sorts?'

'Not "of sorts". I'm a writer, full stop.'

'Well then,' Gerard chipped in, 'what's the problem with selling your book? Is it a novel?'

'Ye-es. Someone accepted it provisionally, but they want to make all sorts of stupid cuts. I won't stand for it, so now they want to break the contract.'

'Is it your first novel?' asked Gerard.

'The first I've tried to sell – or should I say "sell out" – not the first I've written.'

'And what's the novel about, can you tell us?'

'Look,' she was emphatic, eyes at last meeting mine. 'I've been working here for over a year, doing long hours of mindless skivvying so that I have the mental energy left over for my writing. I don't need some pair of smoothies to come along and patronize me.'

'OK, OK.' For some reason Gerard had turned emollient, placatory. 'If you don't want to talk about it, don't, but we are genuinely interested.' This seemed to work: she took a deep breath, accepted one of my cigarettes and lit it with a *fatale*'s flourish.

'All right, I'll tell you. It's set in the future. An old hospital administrator is looking over her life. In her youth she worked for one of a series of hospitals that were set around the ring road of an English provincial town. These had grown up over the years from being small cottage hospitals serving local areas, to become the huge separate departments – psychiatry, oncology, obstetrics – of one great regional facility.

'One day a meeting is held of all the region's administrators, at which it is realized that the town is almost completely encircled by a giant doughnut of health facilities. At my heroine's instigation policies are fomented for using this reified cordon sanitaire as a means of filtering out undesirables who want to enter the town and controlling those who already live in it. Periods of enforced hospitalization are introduced; trouble-makers are subjected to "mandatory injury". Gradually the administrators carry out a slow but silent *coup* against central as well as local government.

'In her description of all these events and the part she has played in them, my heroine surveys the whole panorama of such a herstory. From the shifting meaning of hygiene as an ideology – not just a taboo, to the changing gender-roles in this bizarre oligopoly . . .'

'. . . That's brilliant!' I couldn't help breaking in, 'that's one of the most succinct and clearly realized satirical ideas I've heard in a long time.'

'This is not a satire!' she screamed at me. 'That's what these stupid publishers think. I have written this book in the grand tradition of the nineteenth-century English novel. I aim to unite dramatically the formation of individual character to the process of social change. Just because I've cast the plot in the form of an allegory and set it in the future, it has to be regarded as a satire!'

'Sticky bitch.' This from Gerard, some time later as we stood on the corner of Old Compton Street. Across the road in the window of the catering supplier's, dummy waiters stood, their arms rigidly crooked, their plastic features permanently distorted into an attitude of receptivity, prepared-ness to receive orders for second helpings of inertia.

'Come off it, Gerard. The plot sounded good – more than good, great even. And what could be more central to the English literary tradition? She said so herself.'

373

'Oh yeah, I have nothing but sympathy for her sometime publishers, I know just what her type of author is like to deal with. Full of themselves, of their bloody idealism, of their fernickety obsession with detail, in a word: precious. No, two words: precious and pretentious.

'Anyway I must get . . .' but he bit off his get-out clause; someone sitting in the window of Wheeler's – diagonally across the street from us – had caught his eye. '. . . Oh shit! There's Andersen. The MD. Trust him to be having a bloody late lunch. I'll have to say hello to him, or else he'll think that I feel guilty about not being at the office.'

'Oh I see, negative paranoia.'

'Nothing of the sort. Anyway, I'll give you a ring, old girl . . .'

'Not so fast, Gerard, I'll come and wait for you. I want to say goodbye properly.'

'Please yourself.' He shrugged in the copula of our linked arms.

I stood just inside the entrance while Gerard went and fawned over his boss. I was losing my respect for him by the second. Andersen was a middle-aged stuffed suit with a purple balloon of a head. His companion was similar. Gerard adopted the half-crouch posture of an inferior who hasn't been asked to join a table. I couldn't hear what he was saying. Andersen's companion gestured for the bill, using that universal hand signal of squiggling with an imaginary pen on the sheet of the air.

The waiter, a saturnine type who had been lingering by a half-open serving hatch in the oaken mid-ground of the restaurant, came hustling over to the table, almost running. Before he reached the table he was already shouting:

'What are trying to do? Take the piss!'

'I just want the bill,' said Andersen's companion, 'what on earth's the matter with you?'

'You're taking the piss!' the waiter went on. He was thin and nervy, more like a semiologist than a servant. 'You know that I'm really a writer, not a waiter at all. That's why you did that writing gesture in the air. You heard me talking, talking frankly and honestly to some of the other customers, so you decided to make fun of me, to deride me, to put me down!' He turned to address the whole room. The fuddled faces of a few lingering lunchers swung lazily round, their slack mouths O-ing.

'I know who you are!' the waiter's rapier finger pointed at Andersen's companion, 'Mister bloody Hargreaves. Mister big fat fucking publisher! I know you as well, Andersen! You're just two amongst a whole school of ignorami, of basking dugongs who think they know what makes a jolly fucking good read. Ha!' Gerard was backing away from the epicentre of this breakdown in restraint, backing towards me, trying to make himself small and insignificant. 'Let's get the hell out of here,' he said over his shoulder. The waiter had found some uneaten seafood on a plate and was starting to chuck it around, *flotch*! A bivalve slapped against the flock wallpaper, *gletch*! A squiggle of calamari wrapped around a lamp-bracket.

'I'll give you notes from underwater! I'll give you a bloody lobster quadrille . . .' he was doing something unspeakable with the remains of a sea bream, '. . . this is the *fin* of your fucking *siècle*!' He was still ranting as we backed out into the street.

'Jesus Christ.' Gerard had turned pale; he seemed winded. He leaned up against the dirty frontage of a porn vendor. 'That was awful, awful.' He shook his head.

'I don't know, I thought there was real vigour there. Reminded me of Henry Miller or the young Donleavy.' Gerard didn't seem to hear me.

'Well, I can't go back to the office now, not after that.'

'Why not?'

'I should have done something, I should have intervened. That man was insane.'

'Gerard, he was just another frustrated writer. It seems the town is full of them.'

'I don't want to go back, I feel jinxed. Tell you what, let's go to my club and have a snifter, would you mind?' I glanced at my watch: it was almost four thirty.

'No, that's OK, I don't have to clock on for another hour.'

As we walked down Shaftesbury Avenue and turned into Haymarket the afternoon air began to thicken about us, condensing into an almost palpable miasma that blanked out the upper storeys of the buildings. The rush-hour traffic was building up around us, Homo Sierra, Homo Astra, Homo Daihatsu, and all the other doomsday subspecies, locking the city into their devolutionary steel chain. Tenebrous people thronged the pavements, pacing out their stay in this pedestrian purgatory.

By the time we reached the imposing neoclassical edifice of Gerard's club in Pall Mall, I was ready for more than a snifter.

In the club's great glass-roofed atrium, ancient bishops scuttled to and fro like land crabs. Along the wall, free-standing notice-boards covered in green baize were hung with thick curling ribbons of teletext news. Here and there a bishop stood, arthritic claw firmly clamped to the test score.

I had to lead Gerard up the broad red-carpeted stairs and drop him into a leather armchair, he was still so sunk in shock. I went off to find a steward. A voice came from behind a tall door that stood ajar at the end of the gallery. Before I could hear anything I caught sight of a strip of nylon jacket, black trouser-leg and sandy hair. It was the steward and he was saying, '. . . of course *Poor Fellow My Country* is the longest novel in the English language, and a damn good novel it is too, right?' The meaningless interrogative swoop in pitch, an Australian: 'I'm not trying to do what Xavier Herbert did. What I'm trying to do is invigorate this whole tired tradition, yank it up by the ears. On the surface this is just another vast *Bildungsroman* about a Perth boy who comes to find fame and fortune in London, but underneath that . . .'

I didn't wait for more. I footed quietly back along the carpet to where Gerard sat and began to pull him to his feet.

'Whoa! What're you doing?'

'Come on, Gerard, we don't want to stay here . . .'

'Why?'

'I'll explain later – now come on.'

As we paced up St James's Street I told him about the steward.

'You're having me on, it just isn't possible.'

'Believe me, Gerard, you were about to meet yet another attendant author. This one was a bit of a dead end, so I thought you could give him a miss.'

'So the gag isn't a gag?' He shook his big head and his thick fringe swished like a heavy drape against his brow.

'No, it isn't a gag, Gerard. Now let's stroll for a while, until it's time for me to go to work.'

We recrossed Piccadilly and plunged into fine-art land. We wandered about for a bit, staring through window after window at gallery girl after gallery girl, each one more of a hot-house flower than the last.

Eventually we turned the corner of Hay Hill and there we were, on Dover Street, almost opposite the jobcentre that specializes in catering staff. What a coincidence. Gerard was oblivious as we moved towards the knot of dispirited men and women who stood in front. These were the dregs of the profession, the casual waiters who pick up a shift here and a shift there on a daily basis. This particular bunch were the failures' failures. The ones who hadn't got an evening shift and were now kicking their heels, having a communal complain before bussing off to the 'burbs.

Stupid Gerard, he knocked against one shoulder, caromed off another.

'Oi! Watch your step, mate, can't you look out where you're going?'

'I'm awfully sorry.'

' "Aim offly sorry",' they cruelly parodied his posh accent. I freed my arm from his and walked on, letting him fall away from me like the first stage of a rocket. He dropped into an ocean of Babel.

Terrified Gerard, looking from face to face. Old, young, black, white. Their uniform lapels poking out from their overcoat collars; their aprons dangling from beneath the hems of their macs. They sized him up, assessed him. Would he make good copy?

One of them, young and lean, grabbed him by the arm, detaining him. 'Think we're of no account, eh? Just a bunch of waiters – is that what you think?' Gerard tried to speak but couldn't. His lips were tightly compressed, a red line cancelling out his expression. 'Perhaps you think we should be proud of our work. Well, we are, matey, we fucking are. We've been watching your kind, noting it all down, putting it in our order pads while you snort in your trough. It may be fragmentary, it may not be prettified, it may not be in the Grand Tradition, but let me tell you,' and with this the young man hit Gerard, quite lightly but in the face, 'it's ours, and we're about ready to publish!'

Then they all waded in.

I was late for work. Marcel, the maître d', tut-tutted as I swung open the door of the staff entrance. 'That's the third time late this week, Geraldine. Hurry up now and change – we need to lay up.' He minced off down the corridor. I did as he said without rancour. Le Caprice may no longer be the best restaurant in London to eat at, but it's a great place to work. If you're a waiter, that is.

BIBLIOGRAPHY

There is a vast variety of work on comedy, but the following is a selection of some of the most useful items for anyone interested in pursuing the ever-interesting topic.

ITALO CALVINO, *The Literature Machine*, trans. Patrick Creagh (London: Secker and Warburg, 1987).

SARAH BLACHER COHEN (ed.), *Comic Relief: Humor in Contemporary American Literature* (Urbana, Chicago/London: University of Illinois Press, 1978).

J. J. ENCK, E. T. FORTER AND A. WHITLEY (eds) *The Comic in Theory and Practice* (New York: Appleton-Century-Crofts, 1960).

BRUCE JAY FRIEDMAN (ed.), *Black Humor* (New York: Bantam, 1965).

KARL S. GUTHKE, *Modern Tragicomedy: An Investigation Into the Nature of the Genre* (New York: Random House, 1966).

RICHARD B. HAUCK, *A Cheerful Nihilism: Confidence and the Absurd in American Humorous Fiction* (Bloomington: Indiana University Press, 1971).

HARRY LEVIN (ed.), *Veins of Humor* (Cambridge, Mass: Harvard University Press [Harvard English Studies 3], 1972).

DWIGHT MACDONALD (ed.), *Parodies: An Anthology from Chaucer to Beerbohm and After* (London: Faber, 1960).

VIVIEN MERCIER, *The Irish Comic Tradition* (Oxford: Oxford University Press, 1969).

JOHN MORREAL, *The Philosophy of Laughter and Humor* (New York: State University of New York Press, 1987).

T. G. A. NELSON, *Comedy: The Theory of Comedy in Literature, Drama, and Cinema* (Oxford and New York: Oxford University Press, 1990).

SANFORD PINSKER, *The Schlemiel as Metaphor: Studies in the Yiddish and American Jewish Novel* (Carbondale: Southern Illinois University Press, 1971).

MARGARET A. ROSE, *Parody/Meta-Fiction* (London: Croom Helm, 1979).

CONSTANCE ROURKE, *American Humor: A Study of the National Character* (New York: Harcourt Brace, 1931).